D0521833

THE ENCYCLOPEDIA OF
DO-IT-YOURSELF &
HOME IMPROVEMENT

BLACK CAT

CONTENTS

Acknowledgements
Photography by Jon Bouchier, Simon Butcher, Paul Forrester, Jem Grischotti, Oliver Hatch, Keith Morris, Karen Norquay, Merle Nygate, Ian O'Leary, Thorn EMI lighting, Roger Tuff and Zefa. Illustrations by Drury Lane Studios, Nick Farmer, Tony Hannaford, Val Hill, Trevor Lawrence, Linden Artists, David Pope, Mike Saunders, Ian Stephen, Craig Warwick and Brian Watson

© Copyright Orbis Publishing Limited 1986
© Copyright Macdonald & Co (Publishers) Ltd 1988

First published in 1986 in Great Britain by Orbis Publishing Limited

Reprinted 1988 under Popular Press imprint.
Reprinted 1990 by Macdonald & Co (Publishers) Ltd under Black Cat imprint.

A member of Maxwell Macmillan Pergamon Publishing Corporation

ISBN 0-7481-0304-X

Printed and bound in Hungary

Macdonald & Co (Publishers) Ltd
Orbit House
1 New Fetter Lane
London EC4R 1AR

PART 1

PAINTING & DECORATING

STRIPPING WOOD

Wood has a natural beauty, but it's often a beauty concealed by layers and layers of paint. Doors, window frames, even skirting boards and architraves can all become attractive features in themselves when stripped back to reveal the wood. Even if you prefer to repaint, using the right techniques to strip off the old will give the best possible surface on which to work.

Stripping wood of old paint or layers of ancient varnish isn't the easiest of jobs. It's usually only done because you're after a natural finish, or because the painted surface has degenerated to such an extent that further coats of paint simply can't produce a smooth finish. Either way, once wood has been stripped back to its natural state, it then has to be sealed again – to protect it from moisture which can cause cracking, warping and ultimately decay. Both varnishes and paints act as sealants, giving a durable finish. But which one you choose might depend on the wood itself – and you won't know what that's like until you've stripped it. If you're unsure of its quality, it's advisable to strip a test area first.

Some of the timber used in houses is of a grade that was never intended for a clear finish – large ugly knots, cracks, splits or even an unattractive grain are some of the signs. In cases like this it is probably better to treat the problems (eg, applying 'knotting' – a special liquid sealer – to make the knots tight and prevent them 'bleeding', filling cracks and splits to give a flush surface) and then paint to seal.

If you are set on having the wood on show and don't want to paint it – because it wouldn't fit in with a colour scheme or make the feature you want – you can give it a better appearance and extra protection with stain or coloured varnish.

Stripping with abrasives

For dry stripping there are several different kinds of powered sanders available, all of which use abrasive papers of some kind to strip the surface off wood. On large areas such as floors it is best to use a purpose-made power sander which you can hire. A drill with a sanding attachment, however, is useful for getting small areas smooth after paint has been removed by other methods.

One such attachment is a 'disc sander' and is quite tricky to use effectively without scoring the wood surface. Hold it at a slight angle to the wood and present only half the disc to the surface. Work in short bursts and keep the disc moving over the surface – if it stays too long in one place it can damage the wood.

A 'drum sander' attachment has a belt of abrasive paper stuck round the edge of a cylinder of foam, and if used along the grain only is rather easier to handle than a disc

USING SCRAPERS

1 A triangular shavehook needs two hands when paint is thick. Hold the blade at an angle to the wood so it doesn't cause gouges.

2 A combination shavehook has round, straight and pointed edges to help remove paint and varnish from mouldings round windows and doors.

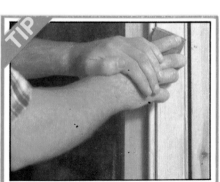

3 A special hook scraper has a sharp replaceable blade suitable both for scraping paint off flat surfaces and for getting into awkward crevices.

sander. Whichever type is chosen, a fine grade abrasive should be used for finishing stripped wood.

Orbital sanders (which are also known as finishing sanders) usually come as self-powered tools – although attachments are available for some drills. These have a much milder action and as long as the spread of wood isn't interrupted by mouldings they smooth well and are useful for rubbing down between coats. These sanders are rectangular and should be moved over the surface in line with the grain. Make sure you choose the right type of sander, depending on the work in hand.

For sanding by hand – hard work, but much better for finishing – there are many grades of glasspaper from the coarse to the very fine. On flat surfaces it's best to wrap the paper round a small block of wood. As an alternative to glasspaper, there's also steel wool, which is most useful when you're trying to smooth down an intricate moulding. Always sand backwards and forwards *with the grain of the wood,* not across it. Scratches across the grain will always be highlighted by a clear finish. To remove remaining bits of paint use medium grade glasspaper; for finishing, a fine grade is better. Renew the glasspaper frequently as the paint will clog the surface,

although a useful tip is to try cleaning clogged paper with a wire brush. It'll work once or twice, but after that the abrasive surface is usually lost. Alternatively pull the sheet backwards and forwards, abrasive side uppermost, over a table edge to dislodge paint particles.

A useful tool for cleaning paint from corners and mouldings is a hand scraper with replaceable blades. These 'hook' scrapers are also used for 'smoothing' and often need two-hands – they slightly raise the surface of a clear run of wood, giving an attractive finish under a clear seal. Use with the grain.

Heat stripping

Heat stripping is the quickest way to remove paint or varnish, but it needs a lot of expertise if you are to avoid charring the wood. So it is best reserved for stripping out of doors where a less-than-perfect surface will be less noticeable. A gas blow-torch is used along with metal scrapers to lift the finish off the wood while it's still warm. Blow-torches with gas canister attachments are light to use and a flame spreader nozzle makes the job easier (it can be bought separately).

Where there's no glass, it's a two-handed operation. Light the blow-torch and hold it a

HEAT STRIPPING

1 *Play the blow-torch onto the paint and when it begins to bubble, start to scrape. Protect floor and sills with a sheet of non-flammable material.*

3 *Working overhead can be tricky if using a blow-torch. Protect your hands with gloves, your eyes with safety goggles and cover surfaces below.*

2 *When stripping paint near windows one hand must hold protection for glass. When paint hardens again, return the flame to the area.*

4 *To strip paint overhead, remove torch (be careful where it points), blow out flames and scrape quickly. As the paint loses heat it hardens.*

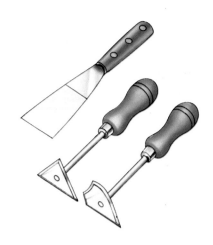

little way from the surface. Move it back and forth, going nearer and withdrawing, till the paint starts to wrinkle and blister. Now begin to scrape – be careful where you point the flame at this stage or you may damage other surfaces. As soon as the paint is hard to move return the flame to the area. Wear gloves to save your hands from being burnt by the falling paint, and cover areas below where you are working with a sheet of non-flammable material to catch the scrapings. In awkward areas, especially overhead, you should wear protective goggles for safety's sake.

Chemical stripping

Chemical strippers are probably the easiest way to strip wood. Available in liquid, gel and paste forms, their methods of application and removal vary, so always remember to read the manufacturer's instructions before you begin. Though all of them will remove paint and varnish, if you are dealing with a large area of wood they can work out to be very expensive – they're also very messy.

Liquid and gel strippers, decanted if necessary into a more convenient-sized container (read the instructions as to whether it can be heavy gauge plastic or should be glass or metal), are stippled onto the surface with a brush and left till the paint bubbles before scraping. Usually these strippers will work through only 1 layer of paint at a time so several applications can be necessary. If stripping a chair or table, stand the legs in old paint cans or jam jars so that any stripper which runs down the legs can be recycled. Artists brushes rather than paint brushes are useful when applying these strippers to mouldings or beading in windows and No 2 steel wool is useful for removing it.

After liquids or gels have been used, the surface must be cleaned down with white spirit or water (it depends on the stripper used) to remove any trace of chemical and must be left till completely dry before any stain or seal is applied.

Pastes are mostly water soluble and manufacturers stress important conditions for using them safely (eg, not in direct sun, in well ventilated rooms, the wearing of protective gloves, etc). Bought in tubs ready-mixed or in powder form to be made up, they are spread in thick (3-6mm) layers over the wood which must then be covered with strips of polythene (good way of using up plastic carrier bags) or a special 'blanket' (supplied with the tub) which adheres – when you press it – to the paste. They have to be left for between 2 and 8 hours after which the paste can be scrubbed off (with a firm brush) or washed down. Frequent changes of water are needed; follow manufacturer's advice about additives (eg, vinegar). Pastes are particularly effective with extraordinarily stubborn paint or varnish in very awkward places (eg, windows, bannisters etc); or where using a scraper might damage old wood. Some pastes are unsuitable for certain types of wood and can stain it – so read instructions carefully. Washing down should not be done, for example, with valuable furniture for this can raise the grain of the wood.

Bleaching

If the wood is discoloured once stripped (either from the stripper used or from some other source) you can try and achieve an overall colour with bleach – the household type, used diluted 1:3 with water to begin with and more concentrated if necessary, or better still a proprietary wood bleach.

Clean the surface of the stripped wood with paint thinner and steel wool and leave for 15 minutes to dry. Cover areas you don't want bleached with polythene, then brush bleach on generously. Work it into the wood *with the grain* using medium steel wool.

Leave for 2-4 minutes, then wipe off with rags. Leave to dry (up to 5 hours) before sanding after which you can finish the surface as desired.

CHEMICAL STRIPPING

1 *Liquid strippers are stippled onto wood with a brush. First pour the liquid into a smaller container — but remember it will dissolve light plastic.*

2 *When paint is bubbling use a scraper to remove it. Work upwards and be careful not to gouge the wood with the blade.*

3 *Several applications of liquid may be needed as chemicals often only eat through one layer at a time. Use gloves to protect your hands.*

4 *After all paint has been stripped off, wipe the wood down with white spirit or water so that the chemicals are neutralised.*

5 *A good way to deal with mouldings is to apply a thick layer of stripping paste. This needs to be covered while it works, but is very effective.*

6 *After leaving for the specified time (can be several hours) wash the paste off with sponge or a scrubbing brush, changing the water often.*

PAINT BRUSHES, ROLLERS AND PADS

You can put paint onto the many surfaces of your home in several different ways, using brushes, rollers, pads or even spraying equipment. Choosing the right tool is a major step on the route to success.

It's unlikely you will not at some time or another have wielded a paint brush, but you may not be aware of the range available.

Types of brushes
Brushes are the most versatile paint applicators; a good set will cope with almost every painting requirement and if looked after properly will last a lifetime. Different types include:

Flat paint brushes: also known as varnish brushes, these are used to apply solvent-based paints and varnishes where a high quality finish is required. They are made from natural or synthetic bristles, or a mixture of the two, fixed to a wooden or plastic handle with a ferrule, usually made of steel. The most commonly available sizes are: 12mm (½in), 25mm (1in), 38mm (1½in), 50mm (2in), 62mm (2½in), 75mm (3in) and 100mm (4in) wide but 6mm (¼in), 16mm (⅝in) and 19mm (¾in) versions are also to be found. The bristles are tapered so that when they are loaded they give the brush a sharp 'cutting edge'.

Cutting-in brushes: sometimes called window brushes, these are flat paint brushes that have the ends of the bristles angled to make it easier to 'cut in' accurately when painting to a line on window frames or other areas.

Radiator brushes: are used for painting awkward areas such as behind radiators. They have a flat paint brush head between 25 and 50mm (1 and 2in) wide, with a long, bendable wire handle emerging at right angles from the side. A short wooden handle is fixed to the end of this so the brush can be easily held.

Angle brushes: have a solid handle about 300mm (12in) long from which the head emerges at an angle of between 30° and 45°. Some have a flat head about 38mm (1½in) wide; others have a round head between 6mm (¼in) and 19mm (¾in) wide. They are also used for painting awkward corners but are less versatile than radiator brushes.

Stencil brushes: are designed for the stippling action needed to produce a crisp outline when painting through a stencil. They have a short, round wooden handle and short, stiff bristles tightly bunched to give a round head between 6mm (¼in) and 60mm (2⅜in) in diameter.

Sash brushes: are specially shaped for painting window frames but a standard 12-25mm (½-1in) wide flat brush will do equally well.

Wall brushes: these are for painting walls with emulsion paint and are often called emulsion brushes. They are extra large, flat paint brushes, normally 100, 125, 150 or even 175mm (4, 5, 6 or 7in) wide, but the bristles tend to be coarser and do not have the same degree of tapering; and the handles are usually stronger and more crudely shaped. Though many have steel ferrules, better-quality brushes have ferrules made from copper so they don't rust when used with water-based paint.

Choosing brushes
To meet all your painting requirements you'll have to get several brushes. A set of flat paint brushes is a must for gloss work; you'll need a 25mm (1in) wide brush, a 50mm (2in) wide brush and also one which is 75mm (3in) wide. These should enable you to cope with most situations, but if you intend doing lots of fiddly, very precise work, get a 12mm (½in) brush as well. A radiator brush will be useful too; it takes time getting used to but saves you the trouble of removing the radiators when you want to paint the walls.

If you don't intend to do a great deal of painting you can make do without a cutting-in brush. Given care and patience, you can achieve the same results using a 25mm (1in) flat brush. But to complete the set, buy a wall brush, though you must make sure it's not too big. While it may seem that the larger the brush, the faster you will get the job finished, in practice, brushes larger than 100 or 125mm (4 or 5in) wide are too tiring on the wrist to use for any length of time.

Regarding quality, unless you're going to do a great deal of painting it's not worth investing in really top-quality brushes.

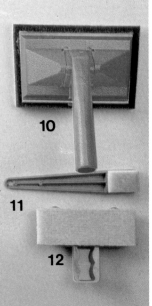

Types of brushes
1 emulsion brush

Flat brushes of various sizes
2 75mm (3in) brush
3 50mm (2in) brush
4 25mm (1in) brush
5 15mm (½in) brush

6 sash brush
7 cutting-in brush
8 angle brush
9 stencil brush

Paint pads
10 standard pad
11 small (wand) pad
12 edge pad

Professional quality brushes in mint condition may not, in fact, be suitable; for example, a flat paint brush of this quality has very long bristles so the brush can hold a lot of paint, increasing the time during which you can work before it needs to be reloaded. But a professional decorator would not normally use a brush like this for finished glossy work; instead he would break the brush in (ie, wear down the bristles slightly) by using it to apply undercoats before using it for gloss paint. For the occasional decorator, therefore, a brush with a shorter, cheaper bristle is preferable. However, don't make the mistake of buying too cheap a brush, unless you intend to throw it away when you have finished.

Check that the brush you buy has a reasonable thickness of bristles in the head. (If you open up the bristles, you'll often find a wooden wedge bulking out the head but this is not necessarily a bad thing unless the wedge is very large.) Purely synthetic bristles are all right for wall brushes but they tend not to make a very good brush for gloss work. Finally, make sure the bristles are secure and that the brush has a firmly fixed ferrule. A few loose bristles are inevitable, even in a good brush, but a poor brush will moult at an alarming rate when you run your fingers through it. Many top-quality brushes will have the bristles bonded securely into the ferrule with two-part adhesive, which forms a solid block and minimises bristle loss.

Types of paint rollers

Paint rollers are less accurate than brushes and you will have to use brushes along with them for any precise work. But they cover surfaces much faster and are ideal for painting large, uncomplicated areas.

A roller consists of a metal frame containing the roller mechanism with a handle fitted to one end and a roller sleeve on the other. They come with a special tray in which you load the sleeve with paint. Most rollers are 175mm (7in) wide, though larger and smaller versions are available.

The cheapest type of sleeve is made from foam. There are sleeves made from other materials: mohair sleeves which have a fine, short pile; sheepskin or synthetic fibre sleeves with a longer pile; and embossed rollers for use with textured paints.

There are also special paint rollers with a very slim sleeve for painting behind radiators and ones with two or more narrow rollers fitted on a flexible axle for painting pipes. For painting ceilings and high walls you can buy an extension pole which screws into the end of the roller handle, but it's cheaper to improvise an extension by fitting a broom handle or a length of 25mm (1in) thick dowel.

Choosing roller sleeves

When buying a roller, watch out for a cheap flimsy frame which won't last long or too large a frame which can be tiring to use. Choosing the sleeve for a roller is, however, the most crucial factor.

● *Before using a brush, especially a new one, 'flirt' the bristles through your fingers and 'strop' the brush head in the palm of your hand, to remove any dust and loose bristles.*

● *When loading a brush, never dip it into the paint too deeply or it will work up around the base of the bristles, dry, and shorten the brush's useful life. Make sure only the end third (or less) of the bristles enters the paint.*

● *Soak a new fibre roller sleeve in soapy water for a few hours before you use it. Then run the roller (without any paint) over the wall to dry it out. This will make sure you get rid of any loose fibres from the sleeve.*

● *Never overload a paint roller and never work it too briskly across the surface you are painting. If you do, paint will fly off in all directions, spattering you and areas you don't want covered in paint.*

● *Hold a brush round the ferrule rather like a pencil, when using it. This gives more control than if you clench your fist round the handle.*

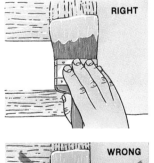

RIGHT

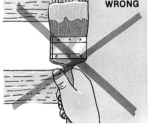

WRONG

Foam sleeves tend not to last long and can be difficult to clean. They can also be splashy in use and paint can drip from the ends if too much pressure is applied or the sleeve is overloaded with paint. That said, they are suitable for use on smooth or slightly textured surfaces. Sheepskin sleeves are expensive but worthwhile where you are dealing with a very rough surface and need a very hardwearing roller. As for the rest, you should aim to get a sleeve with the correct length of pile. When considering coverage, choose short-piled sleeves for smooth surfaces and long-piled sleeves for rough surfaces. But if it's a really good

Rollers

1 short-pile sleeve
2 long-pile sleeve on handle
3 sheepskin sleeve
4 radiator roller
5 extension for handles
6 foam-sleeved roller in tray

finish you're after, short-piled sleeves tend to give better results, though a lot here depends on the type of paint: sleeves made from natural materials work best with solvent-based glosses; synthetic sleeves are best with emulsions.

Paint pads
Paint pads consist of a square or rectangle of short pile fibre (synthetic or mohair), usually backed with foam, attached to a metal or plastic plate and handle. They come in a range of sizes varying from 62mm (2½in) up to 187mm (7½in) wide. You can also buy special edging pads for cutting in between walls and ceilings and at corners; these have small guide wheels which run against the surface you are not painting. And there are very small pads (often with a flexible handle) for precision painting such as in crevices and behind radiator pipes and other hard to get at areas.

For high walls and ceilings, pads are available with a socket to which you can fit a broom handle. By providing you with the extra reach you need, this cuts out the need for ladders.

Pads are sold with special trays (narrower and deeper than a roller tray) for loading them with paint, some trays have a grooved roller for transferring the paint to the pad you are using.

You can use paint pads with all commonly available paints (though thixotropic paints must first be thoroughly stirred to destroy the jelly texture). They are not particularly expensive but many are sold as complete sets which may be inconvenient if you want only one size as a replacement.

Paint sprays
Another way of applying paint is to use a paint spray. Gloss paint is available in aerosol form but, since it is very expensive, it is only worth using on small jobs such as repainting a wicker chair (where it's ideal for all the nooks and crannies) or to spruce up an old domestic appliance. For larger areas you can use a spray gun. This consists of a compressor (usually electric) connected to a paint reservoir and nozzle; you squeeze a trigger to apply the paint. These have the limitation that, for interior use, you would have to spend a great deal of time masking off areas you don't want painted, so it's better to use them for exterior work such as painting the outside walls of the house. Because of their restricted usefulness it's worth hiring a spray gun rather than buying one. When hiring, make sure the paint reservoir is neither so large as to make the gun too heavy, nor so small that you are forever refilling it. Also check that the gun is suitable for use with the type of paint you have in mind. Exterior paints sometimes contain fibre or granular 'filler' and not all guns are able to cope with this kind of solid matter. Usually a special nozzle must be fitted.

Pressurised paint systems
A recently developed product is the pressurised paint system. This consists of a container into which you fit special tubs of paint; an ordinary soda syphon bulb then provides the pressure to force the paint along a flexible tube to the painting head, which may take the form of a flat brush, a paint pad or a roller (these are interchangeable). The paint flow is controlled by a push-button in the head.

This method is a lot less messy than painting with conventional equipment but it's expensive and you can only use the type of paint recommended by the manufacturer of the machine.

Care of equipment
If you want your painting equipment to last you will have to look after it properly, which means you must clean it after use.

Where brushes are concerned, you should work the brush over several sheets of clean newspaper to remove as much paint as possible, then work it up and down in the appropriate solvent (white spirit for most solvent based paints, water for emulsions) changing this frequently to remove the remaining paint. Make sure when you do this that the solvent is worked right up to the point where the bristles are set into the brush.

When you reach the point where no amount of working in solvent appears to remove any more paint, wash the brush out in warm, soapy water (to remove the last vestiges of paint and solvent) and pat dry with a clean cloth. Mould the bristles into their correct shape, then wrap the brush head in paper secured around the ferrule with a rubber band before storing it away. The paper both absorbs residual moisture and helps the bristles keep their shape to prolong their useful life.

Clean roller sleeves in the appropriate solvent, too, but do not leave them to soak in solvent or they may be damaged. Rinse them well and dry them away from direct heat. Paint pads can be cleaned in a similar fashion; again, prolonged immersion in cleaning solvents may cause damage by lifting the pad away from its handle.

Cleaning obviously takes time and if you intend to stop work for only an hour or two and then restart, merely wrapping the brush, pad or roller tightly in polythene will mean it's ready for use when you want it. If, however, you are leaving the paint applicator overnight, it's worth cleaning it out properly. Don't simply leave it standing in solvent until you are ready to re-use it. The solvent in the bristles or fibre will ruin your work when you re-start unless you clean it out.

To store equipment after it's dried out, it's best to hang brushes on nails through holes drilled in the top of the brush handle and store roller sleeves and paint pads securely in polythene bags.

Other paint applicators

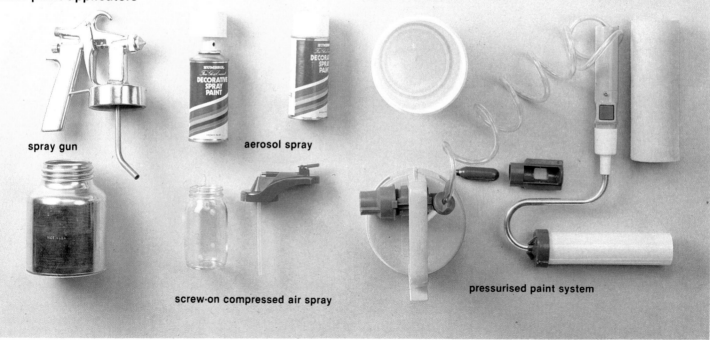

spray gun

aerosol spray

screw-on compressed air spray

pressurised paint system

PRIMERS

For a successful result when painting you will often need to prime the surface first. There are a number of primers available; find out what they are and where they should be used.

A primer performs a vital function in any paint system, sealing the surface to which it is applied (so subsequent coats don't soak in), providing a good key for the next coat to be applied and sticking securely to the bare surface so that the layers of paint don't simply flake off. It's not a permanent protection for the surface it's applied to, and should be covered with undercoat or top coats as soon as possible.

Most primers are solvent-based; the exceptions are some acrylic primers and primer/undercoats, which are water-based and therefore very quick-drying.

The governing factors in deciding whether or not a primer is needed are the surface to be decorated and the type of paint to be used to finish. They also help establish the type of primer required.

Wood surfaces Bare wood should always be primed. Prepare the surface by applying shellac knotting to knots and resinous patches to prevent bleeding. If the wood has been treated with creosote, use an aluminium sealer before applying a standard wood primer.

Metal surfaces Prime all metal surfaces regardless of the finishing paint. Apply the primer as soon as the surface is prepared to prevent the development of rust. Zinc chromate primer is the most versatile type as it can be used on both aluminium and galvanized iron.

Walls and ceilings If the surface is porous, prime with a coat of thinned emulsion paint. This can also be used on interior surfaces like wallpaper which are having an oil-based paint finish; use an oil-based primer on other surfaces. Exterior surfaces like powdery rendering or surfaces to be painted for the first time require a stabilizing primer or masonry sealer.

Painted surfaces Painted surfaces require priming in the odd areas where paint has been removed. If it is chalky or coated with bituminous paint a coat of primer is needed. Scrape or wash off old distemper and apply primer to an interior surface; stabilizing primer to an exterior one. For drains with a thick coat of bituminous paint use an aluminium spirit-based sealer to prevent staining.

Wall and ceiling primers
1, 2: *silicone waterproofing liquid (for waterproofing exterior surfaces;* *make sure the surface is dry first);* 3: *stabilising solution;* 4: *alkali-resisting primer.*

Wood primers
1, 2: *white and brown knotting;* 3: *acrylic primer;* 4: *acrylic primer/* *undercoat;* 5: *aluminium sealer and wood primer;* 6: *standard primer (pink; also comes in white).*

Metal primers
1: *red oxide primer (same uses as red lead primer);* 2: *zinc chromate* *primer;* 3: *calcium plumbate primer;* 5: *red lead primer (danger: poisonous – do not use indoors).*

PAINTING WOOD

Painting is the most popular way of decorating and protecting much of the wood in our homes. As with so many do-it-yourself jobs, getting a good finish depends on your skill. Here's how to paint wood perfectly.

Wood is used extensively in every part of our homes — from roof trusses to skirting boards. Structural timber is usually left rough and unfinished, while joinery — windows, doors, staircases, architraves and so on — is usually decorated in some way. Wood has just one drawback; as a natural material it's prone to deterioration and even decay unless it's protected. Painting wood is one way of combining decoration and protection, and the popularity of paint is a testimony to its effectiveness. Properly applied and well looked after, it gives wood a highly attractive appearance and also provides excellent protection against dampness, dirt, mould, insect attack, and general wear and tear.

Of course, paint isn't the only finish you can choose for wood. If its colour and grain pattern are worth displaying, you can use

PREPARING WOOD FOR PAINT

1 Before you can apply the paint you must fill any cracks or holes with wood filler (applied with a filling knife) and leave to dry.

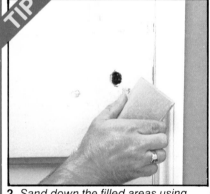

2 Sand down the filled areas using medium-grade glasspaper. Wrap the abrasive around a sanding block or wood offcut so it's easier to use.

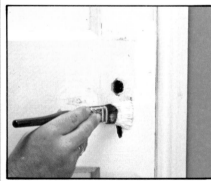

3 Where paint has been chipped off, sand down the area and apply an ordinary wood primer to the bare wood using a small paintbrush.

4 When the surface of the wood is smooth, apply undercoat (as the maker recommends) and leave to dry before you put on the top coat.

PREPARING PAINT

1 *Remove the lid from the paint can using the edge of a knife as a lever – don't use a screwdriver or you'll damage the lip of the lid.*

2 *Stir the paint (if recommended by the maker) using an offcut of wood, with a turning, lifting motion, or use an electric drill attachment.*

3 *Decant some paint into a paint kettle, which you'll find easier to carry than a heavy can. Top up the kettle from the can as you work.*

4 *To load the brush, dip the bristles into the paint to one-third of their length and wipe off excess on a string tied across the kettle rim.*

---

oils, stains or varnishes to enhance the overall effect and protect the surface. But as most of the wood used in our houses is chosen more for performance and price rather than looks, bland and uninteresting softwoods are generally the order of the day for everything from windows and door frames to staircases, skirting boards and door architraves. And painting them offers a number of distinct advantages.

Firstly, paint covers a multitude of sins — knots and other blemishes in the wood surface, poorly-made joints patched up with filler, dents and scratches caused by the rough and tumble of everyday life — and does it in almost every colour of the spectrum. Secondly, paint provides a surface that's hard-wearing and easy to keep clean — an important point for many interior surfaces in the home. And thirdly, paint is easy to apply ... and to keep on applying. In fact, redecorating existing paintwork accounts for the greater part of all paint bought.

What woods can be painted?

In theory you can paint any wood under the sun. In practice, paint (solvent-based or emulsion, see *Ready Reference*), is usually applied only to softwoods — spruce (whitewood), European redwood (deal), pine and the like — and to man-made boards such as plywood, blockboard, hardboard and chipboard. Hardwoods and boards finished with hardwood veneers can be painted, but are usually given a clear or tinted finish to enhance their attractive colour and grain pattern.

Paint systems

If you're decorating new wood, there's more to it than putting on a coat of your chosen paint. It would just soak in where the wood was porous and give a very uneven colour — certainly without the smooth gloss finish expected. It wouldn't stick to the wood very well, nor would it form the continuous surface film needed for full protection. All in all, not very satisfactory. So what is needed is a paint system which consists of built-up layers, each one designed to serve a particular purpose.

The first in the system is a primer (sometimes called a primer/sealer) which stops the paint soaking into porous areas and provides a good key between the bare wood and the paint film. Next, you want another 'layer' — the undercoat — to help build up the paint film and at the same time to obliterate the colour of the primer, so that the top coat which you apply last of all is perfectly smooth and uniform in colour. With some paints — emulsions and non-drip glosses — an undercoat is not always used and instead several coats of primer or two

HOW TO APPLY PAINT

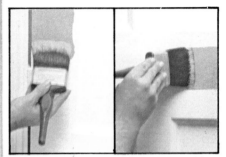

1 *Apply the paint along the grain; with non-drip paint (left) you can apply a thicker coat in one go without further spreading (brushing out).*

4 *Now you must 'lay off' the paint with very light brush strokes along the grain to give a smooth finish that's free from brush marks.*

---

top coats are applied with the same result.

The general rule to obey when choosing primer, undercoat and top coat is to stick with the same base types in one paint system, particularly out of doors and on surfaces subjected to heavy wear and tear (staircases and skirting boards, for example). On other indoor woodwork you can combine primers and top coats of different types.

If the wood you are painting has been treated with a preservative to prevent decay (likely only on exterior woodwork) an ordinary primer won't take well. Instead use an aluminium wood primer — not to be confused with aluminium paint — which is recommended for use on all hardwoods too. Oily woods such as teak must be degreased with white spirit and allowed to dry before the primer is applied.

As far as man-made boards are concerned, chipboard is best primed with a solvent-based wood primer to seal its comparatively porous surface. Hardboard is even more porous, and here a stabilising primer (a product more usually used on absorbent or powdery masonry surfaces) is the best product to use. Plywood and blockboard should be primed as for softwood. There's one other

2 Still working with the grain and without reloading the brush, paint another strip alongside the first one and blend the two together.

3 Reload the brush and apply strokes back and forth across the grain over the area you've just painted to ensure full, even coverage.

5 Paint an area adjoining the first in the same way, blending the two sections together by about 50mm (2in) and laying off as before.

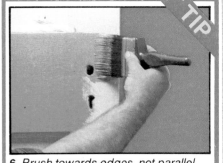

6 Brush towards edges, not parallel with them or onto them, as the paint will be scraped onto the adjacent face, forming a ridge.

WHAT CAN GO WRONG WITH PAINT

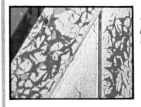

Left: Lifting and flaking occurs if paint is applied over a surface that is damp or powdery.

Right: Crazing is caused when paint is applied over a previous coat that was not completely dry.

Left: Blistering occurs when damp or resin is trapped beneath the paint film and is drawn out by heat.

Right: Cratering results from rain or condensation droplets falling onto the wet paint surface.

Left: Running, sagging or 'curtaining' happens when paint is applied too thickly on vertical surfaces.

Right: Wrinkling or shrivelling can occur on horizontal surfaces if paint is applied too thickly.

thing you need to know. If the wood you want to paint has knots in it you should brush a special sealer called knotting over them to stop the resin oozing up through the paint film and spoiling its looks. If the knots are 'live' — exuding sticky yellowish resin — use a blow-torch to draw out the resin and scrape it off before applying knotting.

Paint on paint

You'll often want to paint wood that has already been painted. How you tackle this depends on the state of the existing paintwork. If it's flaking off and is in generally poor condition, you will have to remove the entire paint system — primer, undercoat and top coat — by burning off with a blow-torch,

applying a chemical paint stripper or rubbing with an abrasive. You then treat the stripped wood as already described for new wood.

Where the paintwork is in good condition, you simply have to clean it and sand it down lightly to provide a key for the new paint and to remove any small bits that got stuck in the surface when it was last painted. Then you can apply fresh top coat over the surface; the paint system is already there. You may, of course, need two top coats if you add a light colour to a dark one to stop the colour beneath from showing through.

If the paintwork is basically sound but needs localised attention, you can scrape or sand these damaged areas back to bare wood and 'spot-treat' them with primer and

undercoat to bring the patch up to the level of the surrounding paintwork, ready for a final top coat over the entire surface.

Painting large areas

Though the same principle applies to wood as it does to any other large surface area — ie, you divide it into manageable sections and complete one before moving on to another — if you're using an oil-based gloss paint you have to make sure that the completed area hasn't dried to such an extent that you cannot blend in the new. On the rare occasion that you might want to paint a whole wall of wood you should make the section no wider than a couple of brush widths and work from ceiling to floor.

With emulsions there isn't the same problem for although they are quick drying the nature of the paint is such that brush marks don't show.

You might think that a wide brush is the best for a large area but the constant flexing action of the wrist in moving the brush up and down will tire you out fast. Holding a brush is an art in itself and aches are the first indication that you're doing it wrongly. A thin brush should be held by the handle like a pencil, while a wider brush should be held with the fingers and thumb gripping the brush just above the bristles.

You'll find a variety of paint brushes on sale — some are designed to be 'throwaway' (good if you only have one or two jobs to do), others will stand you in good stead for years. But remember before using a new brush to brush the bristles back and forth against the palm of your hand — this is called 'flirting' and will dislodge any dust or loose hairs that could spoil your paintwork.

It is wise to decant the paint to save you moving a heavy can from place to place — a paint kettle which resembles a small bucket is made for the purpose. Plastic ones are easier to keep clean than metal ones.

Never be tempted to dip the bristles too far into the paint and always scrape off excess from both sides. Paint has the habit of building up inside the brush and if this happens on overhead work, you risk it running down the handle and onto your arm.

ORDER OF PAINTING

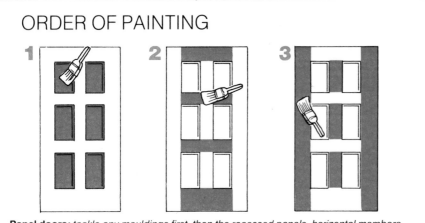

Panel doors: *tackle any mouldings first, then the recessed panels, horizontal members, vertical members and lastly the edges.*

Casement windows: *start with any glazing bars, then paint the opening casement itself (the hinge edge is the only one which should match the inside); lastly paint the frame.*

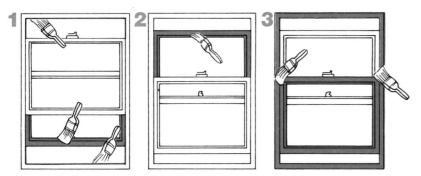

Sash windows: *paint the inside top and bottom and a little way up and down the sides of the frame first. Then paint the bottom of the outer sash. Move the sashes and do the rest of the outer sash, the inner sash and finally the frame.*

Painting small areas

These tend to be the fiddly woodwork on windows, around doors and lengths of stairs or skirting boards — and the hardest bit about all of them is working out how much paint you'll need (see *Ready Reference*).

Special shaped or narrow brushes can make painting these areas easier — for example, they prevent you 'straddling' angles in wood (like you find on mouldings) which damages the bristles in the middle of the brush. With windows and panelled doors you should also follow an order of working to avoid causing overlap marks on the parts you've already painted.

Fiddly or not, they are the jobs you have to do first if you are putting up wallcoverings (if you're painting a room, the walls should be done before the woodwork) so that the drops can be placed against finished edges. If you want to touch up the paint without changing the wallpaper, it's best to use a paint shield.

Getting ready to paint
Ideally, before painting doors and windows you should remove all the 'furniture' — handles, fingerplates, keyholes, hooks etc — so you can move the brush freely without interruption. You should also take time to read the manufacturer's instructions on the can. If, for example, they tell you to stir the paint, then stir it for this is the only way of distributing the particles which have settled.

If you open a can of non-drip paint and find a layer of solvent on the top, you should stir it in, then leave it to become jelly-like again before painting.

All your brushes should be dry — this is something to remember if you are painting over several days and have put them to soak overnight in white spirit or a proprietary brush cleaner. If you don't get rid of all the traces of the liquid it will mess up your paint-

work. They should be rinsed, then brushed on newspaper till the strokes leave no sign.

Cleaning up
When you've finished painting clean your brushes thoroughly, concentrating on the roots where paint accumulates and will harden. They should be hung up, bristles down, till dry, then wrapped in aluminium foil for storage. Don't ever store them damp for they can be ruined by mildew.

If there's only a small amount of paint left, you can either decant it for storage into a dark glass screw-topped jar so you can use it to touch up damaged spots — it's important to choose a suitable sized jar so there's very little air space. Air and dust are both potential paint spoilers and there are two ways to keep them out if you're storing the can. Either put a circle of aluminium foil over the paint surface before putting the lid on securely, or — and this is the best way if the lid is distorted — put on the lid and then invert the can to spread the paint round the inner rim to form an airtight seal. Set it back the right way for storage.

If despite these safeguards a skin forms on the paint (usually over months of storage) you have to cut round the edge of it with a sharp knife and carefully lift it off.

PAINTING WINDOWS

1 Apply masking tape to a window pane to prevent paint getting onto the glass – leave 3mm (1/8in) of glass exposed so the paint forms a seal.

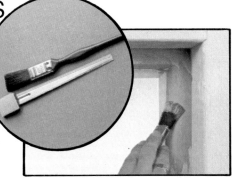

2 Apply paint to the frame and the glazing bars using a small brush, or (inset) a cutting-in brush or a sash paint pad.

3 Apply the paint along the grain; remove the tape when the paint is almost dry – if it dries completely you might peel it off with the tape.

4 An alternative way of keeping paint off the glass is to use a paint shield or offcut of plywood but, again, leave a paint margin on the glass.

PAINTING WALLS AND CEILINGS

The quickest and cheapest way to transform a room is to paint the walls and ceiling. But, for a successful result, you have to prepare the surfaces properly and use the correct painting techniques.

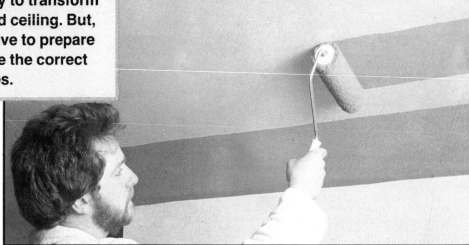

Dulux Russet over Dulux Cameo

Paint is the most popular material used to protect and decorate walls and ceilings in the home. Whereas many people hesitate before hanging wallpaper or sticking more permanent wall and ceiling coverings in place, few would worry about wielding a paint brush for the first time.

One of the chief advantages of painting a room is that it doesn't take much time; large areas can be given two or even three coats of emulsion paint in a day. The paints now available are hardwearing and totally unlike earlier distemper and water paints. They are easy to apply by brush, roller or pad and can be safely washed at frequent intervals to keep them looking fresh.

Any drawbacks are usually caused by faults in the wall or ceiling surface, rather than by the paints. A standard paint alone cannot cover up defects in the same way that some other wallcoverings can, so a surface which is to be painted usually needs more careful preparation than one which is to be papered.

The majority of walls and ceilings are plastered and this type of surface, when in sound condition, is ideal as a base for emulsion and other paints. But it is not the only surface finish you are likely to come across.

Previous occupiers of the house may well have covered the walls with a decorative paper and even painted on top of that. At the very worst there may be several layers of paper and paint, making it very difficult to achieve a smooth paint surface. In this situation it is invariably better to strip the surface completely down to the plaster and to start again from scratch.

This does not mean that no paper should be overpainted. Certain types such as plain white relief wallcoverings and woodchips are intended to be so treated, and actually look 'softer' after one or two redecorations. In short, most wall or ceiling surfaces you are likely to encounter will be paintable. All you have to do is select the right paint for the job and get the surface into as good a condition as possible.

Choosing paints

Vinyl emulsion paints are the most commonly used types of paint for painting walls and ceilings. They are easy to apply and come in a wide range of colours. You will usually have a choice of three finishes: matt, silk, or gloss.

There are also textured paints which are increasing in popularity, particularly for ceiling use. These are vinyl emulsion paints with added 'body' so they can be applied more thickly and then given a decorative textured finish.

Oil-based eggshell paints can be used where a more durable surface is needed or where you want to use the same colour on both walls and woodwork. Resin-based gloss paint is used occasionally also on walls and ceilings, particularly in humid rooms like kitchens and bathrooms.

You should choose paint carefully. The fact that one make is half the price of another may indicate that it has only half the covering power and you would therefore need to apply two coats of the cheaper paint. Also, if you're using white paint, you may find that one brand is noticeably 'whiter' than another.

Tools and equipment

Few specialised tools are needed for wall and ceiling paintwork. If you are content to work with only a brush you will require two sizes: one larger one for the bulk of the work, and a smaller brush for working into corners. It is worth decanting quantities of paint into a paint kettle which is easier to carry around than large heavy cans.

Rollers make the job of painting large areas of wall or ceiling much quicker and also help to achieve a better finish. But you will still need a small brush for working into corners and for dealing with coving, cornices etc.

To prepare a new fibre roller for painting, soak it in soapy water for 2 to 3 hours to get rid of any loose bits of fibre, then roll it out on the wall to dry it off. One point to remember: if you intend using silk vinyl emulsion paint, it's best not to use a roller as this tends to show up as a stippled effect on the silk surface.

Large paint pads will also enable you to cover big expanses of wall or ceiling very quickly. You can use a brush or a small paint pad for work in corners.

Apart from these paint application tools you'll need a variety of other items for preparing the surfaces so they're ready for the paint. The walls must be cleaned, so you'll need washing-down equipment: sponges, cloths, detergent, and a bucket or two of water.

You'll need filler for cracks and a filling knife about 75mm (3in) wide. When any filler is dry it will need to be sanded down, so have some glasspaper ready for wrapping round a cork sanding block. A scraper will also be needed if old wallpaper has to be stripped from the walls.

Finally, because of the height of the walls and ceiling, you'll need access equipment, such as a stepladder, to enable you to reach them safely and comfortably.

Preparing the surface

No painting will be successful until the

PAINTING THE CEILING WITH A ROLLER

1 *Use a brush to paint a strip about 50mm wide round the outside edge of the ceiling; a roller cannot reach right into angles or corners.*

2 *Pour paint into the roller tray; don't put in too much at a time or you risk overloading the roller and splashing paint out of the tray.*

3 *Dip the roller in and pull it back so there is paint at the shallow end of the tray. Push the roller back and forth in the paint at the shallow end.*

4 *Run the roller over the ceiling so there is a band of paint next to the strip of paint you have brushed along the edge of the ceiling.*

5 *Reverse the roller's direction so you join up the two strips of paint into one band. Then finish off by running the roller over the band.*

6 *Now start the next section by running the roller alongside the completed band. Work your way round the ceiling in bands.*

Ready Reference

LINING WALL SURFACES
You can use lining paper to do the same job for paint as it does for wallpapers, covering minor cracks and defects on the wall or ceiling and providing a smooth surface for painting.

TIP: SEAL STRONG COLOURS
Wallcoverings with strong colourings, and particularly those tinted with metallic inks, will almost certainly show through the new paint. To prevent this they should be stripped off, or sealed with special aluminium spirit-based sealer.

FILLING HAIRLINE CRACKS
You may not be able to push enough filler into hairline cracks to ensure a good bond:
● it is often better to open the crack up further with the edge of an old chisel or screwdriver so the filler can penetrate more deeply and key better to both sides of the crack
● when using a textured vinyl paint there is no need to fill hairline cracks, but cracks wider than 1mm ($^{1}/_{32}$in) should be filled.

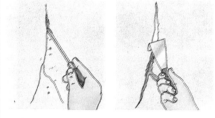

DEALING WITH FITTINGS
Protect electrical fittings so paint or water can't enter them during cleaning and decorating:
● ideally, power to these fittings should be cut off and the fittings removed
● if items cannot be removed, use masking tape to protect them.

SELECTING PAINTS
When choosing paints, remember that:
● emulsion paints are quicker to apply, dry more quickly and lack the smell of resin- or oil-based paints. They are also cheaper and can be easily cleaned off painting equipment with water
● non-drip paints are best for ceilings and cover more thickly than runny ones, cutting down on the number of coats
● a silk or gloss finish will tend to highlight surface irregularities more than a matt finish
● textured paints are suitable for use on surfaces which are in poor condition since they will cover defects which a standard emulsion paint cannot.

PAINTING THE WALL WITH A BRUSH

1 *Use a small brush to cut in at the wall and ceiling join and in corners. With a larger brush paint the wall in bands. First, brush across the wall.*

2 *Move the brush across the wall in the opposite direction. The bands of paint should be about 1m wide and you should be working downwards.*

3 *When you are working at the top of the wall your next strokes should be downwards to complete the area you have covered with crossways strokes.*

4 *At the bottom two-thirds of the wall continue working in crossways strokes, but this time finish off each section by brushing upwards.*

USING PAINT PADS

1 *Thin the paint a little (with water for emulsions, turps for oil-based ones). Cut in with a small brush or pad and use a larger pad to paint in bands.*

2 *For precise work you can use a small pad like this. Ensure that you cover areas you don't want painted with masking tape.*

surface beneath has been properly prepared. Unless wallpaper is of a type intended for painting it is usually better to strip it off, and walls which have been stripped of their previous wallcoverings need a thorough washing to remove all traces of old paste. Make sure the floor is protected against debris by covering it with a dust sheet or sheets of old newspaper. Emulsion-painted walls also need washing to remove surface dirt. In both cases, use warm water with a little household detergent added. Then rinse with clean water.

If you decide to leave the wallpaper on the walls you will have to wash it down before you paint. Take care to avoid overwetting the paper, particularly at joins. When the surface is dry, check the seams; if any have lifted, stick them down with a ready-mixed paste.

Ceilings should be washed in small areas at a time and rinsed thoroughly before you move onto another section systematically.

If the surfaces are left in perfect condition, they can be painted as soon as they are dry.

It's possible that walls or ceilings may have been painted with distemper, which may only become apparent after you have removed the existing wallcovering. Unless it is the washable type, you will have to remove it completely since emulsion paint will not adhere well to it. Use hot water, detergent and a scrubbing brush to soften and get rid of the coating; this is hard work, but you could use a steam stripper to speed up the process.

With all the surface cleaned, the next job is to fill any cracks and repair defects such as indentations caused perhaps by knocks or the blade of a carelessly handled wallpaper scraper (see *Ready Reference*).

Whenever a filler has been used it should be sanded down flush with the wall surface,

once dry, and the resulting dust should be brushed away.

If the plaster is in bad condition and obviously covered in cracks you should consider covering it completely with liningpaper, woodchip or other relief wallcovering before painting it. The paper will provide a good base for redecoration, and will save a great deal of preparation time. However, this can only be done if the plaster itself is still bonded securely to the wall. If it is coming away in chunks or sounds hollow behind the cracks, then the wall should be replastered

Cracks which have developed round door and window frames are best filled with a flexible sealant, which will be unaffected by movement of the frames. Acrylic-based sealants are available for this purpose and they can be easily overpainted.

After all the preparation work has been

PAINTING PROCEDURE

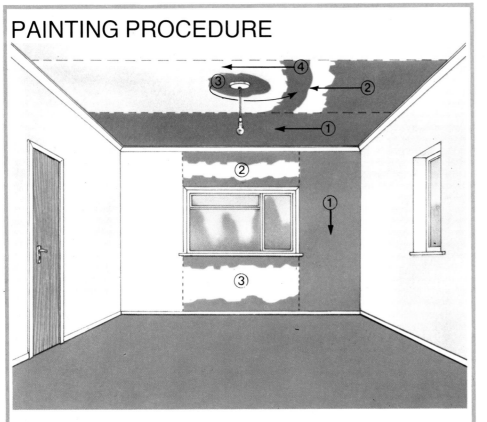

Paint the ceiling first in 1m-wide bands (1 & 2). Paint round a ceiling rose (3), then complete the rest of that band (4). On walls work downwards (1). At a window, paint along the top band (2) and repeat the process at the bottom (3). Work from right to left unless you are left-handed.

Ready Reference

HOW MUCH PAINT?
Coverage per litre depends on the wood's porosity and roughness and the painter's technique but an approximate guide is:
Runny gloss 17 sq m (183 sq ft)
Non-drip gloss 13 sq m (140 sq ft)
Satin gloss (eggshell) 12 sq m (130 sq ft)
Runny matt emulsion 15 sq m (161 sq ft)
Non-drip matt emulsion 12 sq m (130 sq ft)
Silk emulsion 14 sq m (150 sq ft)
Gloss emulsion 14 sq m (150 sq ft)

TIP:PAINTING POLYSTYRENE
Paint polystyrene tiles only with emulsion paint. Don't use a solvent or oil-based paint since this will cause a fire risk.

BRUSH SIZES
If you are using brushes only, you will need:
● a brush about 100mm (4in) wide; brushes wider than this tend to be unwieldy and very tiring to use
● a brush about 25mm (1in) wide for cutting in at edges and in corners.

THE RIGHT ROLLER
For emulsion, use a foam or short-pile synthetic fibre sleeve along with a roller tray. Remember that:
● emulsion paints make natural fibre sleeves go soggy
● a sleeve with long fibres will leave an 'orange peel' effect finish.

PAD SIZE
For painting walls and ceilings, choose a pad measuring around 190 x 100mm (7½ x 4in) for the main area, and a smaller pad (or a paint brush) for touching-in work.

MAKING ACCESS EASIER
Use scaffold boards as well as stepladders so you can work over large areas at a time without having to keep moving the ladders. You can hire scaffold boards or mobile scaffold platforms.

completed, have a good clear-up in the room so that when you begin painting you do not stir up dust and have to work around numerous bits and pieces scattered over the floor space.

Re-lay dust sheets and set up your access equipment before even opening the first can of paint. Make sure your brushes or rollers are clean and ready for use.

Painting sequences
If possible, do all your painting in daylight hours. Artificial light is less easy to work by and can lead to small areas being missed.

Painting is always done from the highest point downwards, so ceilings are the first areas to be tackled. The whole ceiling will be painted in bands across the room no wider than you can easily reach without stretching on your stepladder or platform. This generally means that at any one time you will probably be painting a band no wider than 1m and less than 2m long unless you are using scaffolding boards to support you.

You start at the edges first and then work into the main body of the room.

Linking one section to another is seldom difficult with emulsion paint and is simply a matter of blending the paint from the new section back into the previous one.

Walls are treated similarly, starting at the top and working downwards in sections about 1m wide, cutting in at the ceiling and at return walls.

Painting tips
The number of coats required will depend on the previous colour and condition of the surface and the type of paint. If another coat has to be applied, be sure that the previous one is fully dry first. With modern vinyl emulsion paint it may be that because the paint is water-based it will cause the paper underneath to swell and bubble; however, you shouldn't worry about this because as the water in the paint dries out the paper and paste behind the paint surface will begin to flatten again.

If the paper is badly hung with a lack of adhesive at the edge, seams may lift as the paint dries. They will have to be stuck down in the same way as if they had lifted during washing. Careful preparation would prevent this problem anyway.

PUTTING UP COVING

You can enhance the decorative effect of a room – and hide defects – by adding coving and a complementary centre to the ceiling. Installation is quite straightforward and it should be no trouble to find a variety which suits your room.

When you are planning your decoration scheme, don't forget the ceiling. Often this simply ends up being painted white and without ornament. Sometimes this may be the right solution but at others a more imaginative treatment can enhance the overall appearance of a room.

You can use colour on the ceiling to make a very tall room appear lower; or change the proportions of a box-like room to make the shape seem more interesting; or even increase the apparent size of a small room. Alternatively, you can add some form of ornament to the ceiling surface. In bathrooms and bedrooms where you will be aware of the ceiling much more often than in other rooms – when you are lying in the bath or in bed – it's particularly worth making the view more interesting.

Ornamental ceilings can be created either by using cornices – mouldings fixed in the angle between the wall and the ceiling – or more simple coving which links the two surfaces. (There is a clear distinction architecturally, but here both will be referred to as coving.) Ceiling centres – ornamental mouldings fixed in the middle of the ceiling – will provide an attractive focal point.

In practical terms, a nice, neat coving between wall and ceiling, apart from looking more elegant and 'finished', will hide the joints between ceiling and wall decorations or hide cracks, wires or pipes; sometimes it may be continued to form a pelmet for curtains or blinds, or to conceal strip lighting. Ceiling centres, used to complement coving, will also disguise a poorly plastered ceiling, hide joins, bumps and electrics and are a perfect foil to attractive light fittings like chandeliers.

Types of ceiling ornaments

It is still possible to find a craftsman who will 'sculpt' a decorative coving or ceiling centre for you but this is likely to be prohibitively expensive. It is cheaper to use some form of prepared, preformed coving or ceiling centre.

These come in various materials which break down into four categories: fibrous plaster, plasterboard or gypsum, plastic and wood. Fibrous plaster covings and ceiling centres are available in different styles, mostly traditional. Plasterboard or gypsum covings are streamlined and simple to install. Of the various plastic types there are covings and ceiling centres made from glass fibre and also ones made from cellular plastics such as polyurethane and expanded polystyrene: these are all light and easy to handle. There are also covings and ceiling centres made from a new plastic resin product that looks like genuine plasterwork and can be sawn, drilled and sanded like wood; and, unlike the other plastics, it is fire-resistant.

Wood covings – a final variant – are particularly effective in a room with walls completely or partly covered in wood cladding where they will provide a feature in keeping with the rest of the room.

Types of adhesives

Manufacturers usually recommend a suitable adhesive – always check with their instructions when buying the coving or ceiling centre. Adhesives come ready-mixed or, for fixing plasterboard or gypsum coving, in powder form – you mix the adhesive with water.

As a guideline, fibrous plaster ornaments should be stuck with a wall panel adhesive or a contact adhesive – it will be easier to manage if an application gun is used. Plasterboard or gypsum coving is fixed with plaster – you can use this to fill any gaps as well. Glass fibre is fixed with the same types of adhesive as fibrous plaster. For polyurethane you will need a ready-mixed paste adhesive which again can be used to fill gaps. Polystyrene should be stuck with a special expanded polystyrene adhesive of

PREPARING THE SURFACE

1 Using a length of coving as a guide, mark guidelines on the ceiling and on the wall. Continue the lines so they go right round the room.

2 Score along the guidelines with a handyman's knife or other sharp instrument as a first step to removing the wallpaper from the ceiling and wall.

3 Scrape off wallpaper and flaky paint in the area between the guidelines. Soak paper if necessary, taking care to protect wallpaper lower down the wall.

4 Provide a key so the adhesive grips properly by slightly roughening the surface, gently scoring the area where the coving will be fixed.

the type used to fix ceiling tiles. Plastic resin ornaments are fixed in a similar way to wood. Choose a wood adhesive such as PVA, synthetic resin adhesive, a multi-purpose type, or even a wall panel adhesive in an easy-to-apply gun. For wooden covings you will need a wood adhesive – this is often used in conjunction with nails or screws.

Any adhesive is only really effective if it is applied to a clean, dust-free surface. New plaster should be allowed to dry out before

multi-purpose, wood, or expanded polystyrene adhesives are used, although the plaster/gypsum filler type can be used on damp plaster.

Always follow the manufacturer's instructions carefully when using any type of adhesive. If you are using an adhesive which is likely to 'go off', or harden quickly, work on manageable lengths of coving at a time. With powder adhesives, don't guess how much water to add, follow the instructions.

CUTTING A MITRE

1 When using a mitre box, place the coving so the 'ceiling' edge is at the bottom of the box and use the slots in the box to provide a saw guide.

2 Where a paper template is provided, mark the cutting line using the template as a guide and then carefully saw along the marked line.

Ready Reference

CUTTING MITRES

● Check coving orientation in box before cutting – the 'ceiling' edge should be on the base of the box.
● Lengths with one internal and one external mitre (A) have parallel cuts done in the same box groove; lengths with two external mitres (B) or two internal mitres (C) are cut using both box grooves (one for each end).

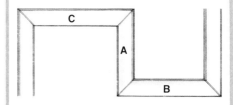

MAKING A MITRE BOX

● Make the box from timber about 450mm (18in) long and 19mm (¾in) to 25m (1in) thick, with internal dimensions chosen so the coving is held exactly at 90° within the box.
● Mark out the 45° angles using a combination square or basic geometry.

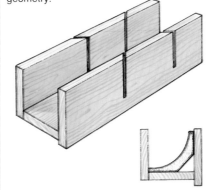

FIRE HAZARDS

Never paint foamed plastic coving or ceiling centres with gloss or other solvent-based paints as you will create a fire hazard – the painted plastic could rapidly spread flames in a fire.

EASY ELECTRICS

So you don't have to remove – and risk damaging – a ceiling centre to get at wiring, remove the existing ceiling rose and rewire to a junction box installed in the ceiling void – access can then be gained from above.

Planning

As with all decorating operations, time and care spent on planning will pay off later, helping you make sure of a successful result. To judge the optimum coving depth before buying, cut a paper template to a likely depth and a length of 1.5 to 1.8m (5 to 6ft) and pin it in the angle between the wall and ceiling where the coving will go. This should be long enough for you to gain an idea of the finished effect. If it seems wrong, (ie, too shallow or too deep), repeat the operation with a template of a different depth until you have the right size.

Having decided on the depth of the coving, the next step is to measure up the ceiling accurately. If it is going to be a difficult shape to deal with – for example, if there is a chimney breast or corners which are out of square – make a scale plan of the ceiling on squared paper. This way you will be able to work out exactly where the joins will come in the lengths of coving and where you will need to cut or mitre the coving for the corners. Use your plan or measurements as a guide for ordering the correct amount of coving.

A ceiling centre is going to be a focal point of interest, and it is essential therefore to choose one which is the right size for the room. They range in size from 150mm (6in) to 685mm (2ft 3in) in diameter; smaller ones suit smaller rooms and larger ones large rooms. To help you decide on the size of the ceiling centre, you can again make a paper template to gain an impression of the finished effect.

Marking up and preparation

You will need to mark guidelines for fixing the coving. You can use a piece of coving to indicate where lines should be drawn at the correct level on wall and ceiling.

The surface must be properly prepared. You will need to make sure all old wallpaper, flaking paint or distemper is removed from between the guidelines. It is also advisable to fill any cracks. Leave the filler to harden and then, if necessary, sand smooth. Bumpily filled cracks could throw the coving out of alignment, making it look distorted. With some types of adhesive you will also have to provide a key, so the adhesive grips properly, by slightly roughening the surface of the wall and ceiling where the coving will be fixed.

For a ceiling centre you can cut a paper or cardboard template round which to draw a guideline before preparing the surface in the same way as preparing for fixing coving. Make the template slightly smaller – by about 6mm (¼in) – than the actual ceiling centre so areas where paper or paint have been removed will not show when the ceiling centre is in place.

Cutting coving

Measure the coving for length. Remember that corners will have to be mitred and that there is a different technique for internal and external angles (see *Ready Reference*). Some preformed coving comes with a special template provided in the pack to make cutting and mitring easier – you place the template on the coving and trace the required mitre shape with a pencil. If you are using coving which does not have such a template provided, you will need to make up a mitre box which you can use to hold the coving while you cut it at the correct angle (see *Ready Reference*). For cutting you will need a fine tooth saw and you should cut from the face of the coving to ensure you get a clean edge.

Fixing coving

A plaster/gypsum adhesive will have to be mixed according to the manufacturer's instructions. If the job is likely to take a while, mix up only part of the adhesive at a time so you don't waste any if it dries out too soon. With some types of adhesive you will need to dampen the surface to be coved with water. If the surface is very porous you will have to seal it with a coat of diluted emulsion or PVA adhesive first.

You can then spread out the adhesive onto the back edges of the coving. Push each length firmly into position and hold it in place until it sticks. If you are using a contact adhesive, spread it on the back of the coving. Press the coving in position, then pull it away immediately and leave for about 10-20 minutes – the honeycomb structure of the adhesive will be on coving, wall and ceiling surfaces. Then fix the coving back in position and adjust its positioning at once as the adhesive will harden quickly and will be firmly bonded within an hour.

Heavier covings may have to be nailed or screwed, as well as stuck, into position. You should use galvanized nails or rustproof screws spaced 500mm (20in) apart, and, so they won't be visible on the finished surface, punch the nails below the surface with a nail punch, or countersink screws and fill the holes you have created with surplus adhesive or with cellulose filler.

Scrape off surplus adhesive which squeezes out from under the coving. (Sometimes this can be used to fill nail holes and gaps. Otherwise you will have to use a cellulose filler).

Fixing ceiling centres

Ceiling centres are fixed in the same way as coving. Heavier types may need extra support from nails or screws: make sure the heads are countersunk or punched home and fill the gaps with adhesive or other filler.

If the ceiling surface is bad and you want

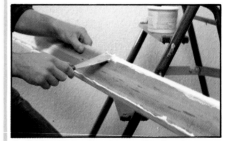

FIXING COVING

1 *Butter the adhesive on the back edges of the coving with a filling knife – try to avoid getting adhesive on the front of the coving.*

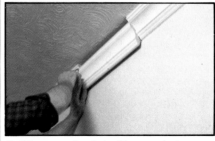

5 *Where coving is to fill a gap between lengths already fixed, hold a piece up so it rests against one fixed length and mark a cutting line on the other end.*

to use a textured paper to help disguise this, it is easier to paper the ceiling first and then cut out the area to be covered with the ornament rather than fixing the ceiling centre and then papering round it.

Where a ceiling centre is to be used to enhance a central light fitting, you will also have to cope with the electrics. As a first step, you will have to remove the existing bulb and lampholder. Where the ceiling centre has a hollow in the middle, it may be possible to leave the existing ceiling rose in place and fit the new ceiling centre over it. Simply pull down the flex through the hole in the middle of the new centrepiece (some already have holes bored; with others you may have to make the hole).

With other types of ceiling centres which are flatter in the middle, you may have to remove the existing rose and replace it with a terminal connector strip which will fit in the space available before fixing the new ornament. Both these solutions have the disadvantage that if at a later date you wish to gain access to the wiring, you will have to remove the ceiling centre. As an alternative you can rewire the light so access can be gained from above (see *Ready Reference* on previous page).

If you have a very heavy chandelier, it may be necessary to have a hook to support it –

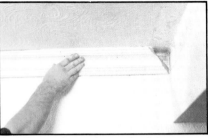

2 Offer up the coving to the fixing area and, when you are sure it is in the right position, press it firmly into place. The adhesive will squeeze out of the edges.

3 To provide support till the adhesive sets, drive nails into the edges of the coving. These can be punched home or removed and the holes filled later.

4 At a corner, place coving so mitred edges meet and fix it in position. You can then use a filling knife to smooth adhesive down for a neat joint.

6 After you have cut the filler piece and applied adhesive, offer it up and install it so it butts against the lengths of coving already fixed.

7 Remove excess adhesive by running a filling knife along the edges of the coving. This can be used to fill in any gaps, joins or nail holes.

8 For final cleaning up, use a sponge which has been soaked in clean water to remove any adhesive from the coving face, the wall and ceiling.

coming through the hole in the middle of the decorative centre – and this will have to be fixed to a beam or joist to take the weight. This may also determine the position of the fitting, since there may not be a conveniently placed central support.

Decoration

If you intend painting the ceiling, emulsion paint, which can be applied without silting up any of the more decorative mouldings, is particularly suitable. A matt or eggshell lustre-finish oil-based paint can also be used, but this is not very suitable for delicate mouldings. Lastly, you can use multi-purpose paint (ie one which can be used on walls, ceilings and woodwork). Gloss and other solvent-based paints should never be used on plastic.

Colour is a matter of personal choice but usually the 'bed' – the flat part of the ceiling – looks best in a colour which can be dark, rich or strong if the room is fairly tall and paler if it is low. The relief decorations can be picked out in white or any other contrasting neutral shade, or in a pale, toning or contrasting colour. Give the ceiling decorations their first coat, then paint the ceiling itself with two coats, taking particular care at the edges and where it meets the ornaments. Apply a final coat to the decorations.

FIXING A CEILING CENTRE

1 Draw round a paper template which is slightly smaller than the ceiling centre. You can then prepare the surface within the marked area.

2 Spread adhesive on the outer rim at the back of the ceiling centre, feed the flex down through the hole in the middle and fix the centre in place.

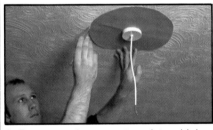

3 Run a filling knife round the edge of the ceiling centre to remove excess adhesive between the centre and ceiling.

4 Use a damp sponge to wipe off traces of adhesive left on the surface of the centre and ceiling.

INTERIOR PAINT FINISHES

Painting walls, ceilings, woodwork and metal is something everyone seems to have tackled at some time. Every year the paint makers sell us millions of tins of paint, in hundreds of colours. Here's what you need to know to pick the right one.

To understand how paint works, you need a little technical background information. All paints consist of three main ingredients – binder, thinner and pigment.

The **binder** makes the paint stick to the surface. As it dries it forms a solid but elastic film that's resistant to water and chemicals and wears well if rubbed or knocked. Binders used to be natural oils or resins such as linseed oil or copal, but now man-made chemicals are usually used. You'll recognise their names from paint tins – words like alkyd, poly-vinyl acetate (PVA), acrylic, polyurethane and Silthane.

The binder is mixed with the **pigment** – usually titanium white, along with other coloured dyes.

The **thinner** makes the binder liquid enough to be applied easily and evenly, and evaporates as the paint dries. Paints are thinned either with water or with a petroleum-derived solvent, usually mineral turpentine (turps or white spirit). Water-based paints are usually called **emulsions**. Most people think of the second category as 'gloss paint' – paint that dries to a shiny finish. But because it's actually the binder that dictates what finish the paint will have, it makes more sense to call these paints **solvent-based.**

Jelly (gel) paints
Traditionally, paints are runny liquids. But nowadays many paints – both emulsions and solvent-based paints – have special additives to give them a jelly-like consistency. They're called 'thixotropic', or non-drip paints, and can be applied in thicker films (and with fewer drips) than runny paints. They should not be stirred in the tin (they go runny, and drip) but, if it is necessary to mix in any clear liquid that may have separated out, the paint will revert to a jelly if left to stand for a couple of hours.

How paint dries
Once the paint is applied it begins to dry. In modern paints with resin binders, the thinner (water or solvent) evaporates and the resin molecules start combining chemically to form a continuous film. Good ventilation, warmth and light help to speed up the drying process; cold and damp slow it down, and can stop the film forming properly.

Different finishes
The finish you get when the paint has dried can be high gloss, a silky sheen or matt (non-reflective). Paints giving a matt finish contain more pigment than ones drying to a high gloss, and the particles are actually larger. As a result, the surface is slightly rough and scatters light falling on it instead of reflecting it like a mirror.

Gloss, satin (or silk) and matt finishes are available in both emulsion and solvent-based paint types. Water-based gloss paints are not as durable as solvent-based ones, lose their gloss more quickly and come in a smaller range of colours. However, they are widely used in countries where high temperatures would make solvent-based paints dry too quickly.

Gloss finishes are commonly used on wood and metal; matt finishes on walls and ceilings. However, there's nothing to stop you using them the other way round (but remember that a gloss finish highlights the imperfections of a rough surface).

Satin-finish paints are widely used on all surfaces nowadays, although solvent-based types perform best on wood and metal. Gloss finishes are generally more durable and easy to clean than satin or matt ones.

Pros and cons
The different properties of emulsions and solvent-based paints will affect your choice of type for a particular job. Here are the advantages and disadvantages of each type.

Ease of application: most people find emulsion paints quicker to apply than solvent-based ones, and also find it easier to get even coverage free from brush marks. Brushes, rollers and paint pads (and even spraying equipment) can be used with

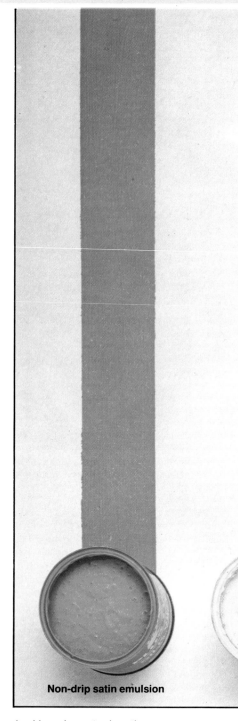

Non-drip satin emulsion

Hints

- *Before you open a can of paint, wipe off any dust from the top so that it doesn't get into the paint.*

- *If you are opening a partly used can, take care not to knock bits of dried paint into the tin as you open it.*

- *Don't use a screwdriver to prise off the tin lid – you will buckle the edge of the lid making it difficult to reseal the tin properly. Use a broad lever, such as the back of a knife, instead.*

- *If there's a small amount of paint left, strain it into a dark glass screw-topped jar for storage. Choose a suitable-sized jar so there's very little air space. Label the jar.*

- *To store a larger amount of paint, strain any left in the paint kettle back into the tin. Wipe any paint from the rim and then put a circle of aluminium foil over the paint surface before putting the lid on. Tap it home securely with a block of wood.*

- *Where a skin has formed on the paint in the can, cut round the edge of it with a sharp knife and lift it out carefully so bits don't break off and fall back into the paint.*

- *Where the lid is distorted, you can instead put on the lid and then invert the can to spread the paint round the inner rim to form an airtight seal, then store the can the right way up.*

| Textured emulsion | Matt (flat) emulsion | Non-drip satin gloss | Solvent-based eggshell | Full gloss (enamel) |

either type, but rollers are seldom used with gloss finishes.

Coverage: solvent-based paints usually cover a bigger area per litre than water-based paints. Runny paints cover 25 to 30 per cent more than the same volume of non-drip paints.

Drying: emulsions dry much more quickly than solvent-based paints, so there's less disruption in the house after you've finished decorating and second coats can be put on more quickly (read the instructions on the tin for precise details about re-coating times). Solvent-based paints have a

distinctive (and some say, an unpleasant) smell, while emulsions have little smell.

Durability: solvent-based paints are generally harder-wearing than emulsion paints. Repeated washing of matt emulsions can give the surface a noticeable sheen.

Priming: emulsions can be used on bare walls and ceilings, acting as their own primer and undercoat. Solvent-based paints need separate primers and undercoats. adding to the time involved in using them – see page 10.

Cleaning equipment: emulsions can be cleaned from painting equipment with water, while solvent-based paints generally need a special cleaner – white spirit, paraffin or else a proprietary brush cleaner; even paint stripper if the paint has hardened. Some solvent-based paints now have special additives that allow you to wash them out with hot soapy water.

Price: when gloss paints for woodwork were oil-based, and walls were painted with distemper, the price of the former was much higher than the latter. Nowadays, with man-made resins

and pigments being used in both types, the price gap has virtually disappeared and cost is unlikely to be a big factor in your choice of paint type.

Paint sizes
Paint is now sold only in metric-sized tins. Common sizes include 500ml ($7/8$ pint), 1 litre ($13/4$ pints), $21/2$ litres ($41/2$ pints) and 5 litres (9 pints). Emulsions are seldom available in tins smaller than 1 litre, while solvent-based gloss may be available in tins as small as 125 ml (about $1/4$ pint) – ideal for touch-up jobs or for picking out contrasting colours on small areas.

MAKING GOOD
walls and ceilings

If you're making a lot of alterations to your house, you'll probably pull out cupboards, partitions, remove fixings and strip off old wallcoverings. Don't worry if you cause some damage, since you can quite easily put it right.

No matter what sort of decorating you intend to do, the surface you're covering must be sound. If you paint, paper or tile over cracks or loose plaster you're wasting your time. The professionals call this preparation 'making good' — and the reason is obvious. Without time spent here the end result will be less attractive, won't last very long, and you won't be getting value for the money you've spent on decorating materials. Making good takes time, but it is never wasted. Here is a guide for the sort of problems you'll face in making good walls and ceilings ready for decorating.

Cracks

There are two types of cracks in walls to watch for. A structural one will be large, deep, and often wider at one end than the other — this has been caused by subsidence and you should seek the advice of a professional before any attempt is made to repair it. The second type is usually just a crack in the surface covering of the wall — the plaster, for instance — and because it's only superficial it can be easily repaired.

For such superficial cracks in plaster, first detach all loose material with the edge of a stripping knife and brush out thoroughly. If more plaster than you bargained for comes away, the plaster must have been weak — in which case, treat as large holes. Fill hairline and small cracks with cellulose filler, bought as powder and mixed with water to a thick

creamy paste (mix only small quantities to avoid waste). Smooth it on with a filling knife and sand it down when dry.

In wood, cracks and opened grain can again be filled with cellulose filler — but it will show up rather than blend. If the wood is going to be painted, this probably won't matter. But if you're going to finish the wood with a clear varnish, plastic wood or stopping should be used to ensure the best possible finish.

Gouges

These are superficial marks caused by a badly-used shavehook or stripping knife (held at the wrong angle or because it slipped) or an electric abrasive tool which during the smoothing created ridges in the surrounding plaster. Fill as in cracks with cellulose filler, making it slightly proud of the surface. Leave it to dry hard and then sand

flush with medium glasspaper. Gouges in wood should be treated in exactly the same way as cracks.

Holes

Small holes are often left when old screws and nails are removed or if wires have been chased in — for these the remedy is simple. Large holes, however caused, can require a lot more attention especially if they're deep as well as wide (eg, if a partition has been removed leaving gaps in walls or ceilings).

It can boil down to a question of cost — cellulose filler bought in the quantity required for a large hole will be more expensive than a small bag of plaster. Plaster, however, has its own problems — it's difficult to mix properly, sets very fast and takes some skill to get it to stick to the wall in the first place. In small areas there are ways around this (see page 29 for *Ready*

STRIPPING WALL COVERINGS

● Brush wallpaper with a solution of warm water and washing-up liquid or a proprietary stripper. Leave for about 5 minutes to allow the water to soak through to the old paste. Ease the stripping knife under the paper at a join and lift the paper off and away. This will prevent gouges in the plaster.

● If the paper clings stubbornly, soak it again but add a handful of wallpaper paste to the water. This will help the water soak in.

● Vinyl wallcoverings are removed simply by lifting the plastic coating at the

bottom edge of the drop, then pulling it upwards and off in a complete sheet. Strip off the thin paper backing if it is damaged by soaking as above.

● Washable or gloss painted heavy wallcoverings will resist water. If you can get a scraper behind the paper at a join or at the top, spray water containing some wallpaper paste in with a pot-plant spray. Leave for a few minutes, then move the scraper backwards and forwards between the wall and the paper. Or you can break down the surface. Use either a wire brush or a serrated scraper.

Reference on plasters and fillers).

Very large holes need to be treated in the same way as plastering a wall — you start with an 'undercoat' plaster (it's much coarser than a 'finishing' plaster) to fill to about 6mm (¼in) from the surface, and this provides a key for two coats of finishing plaster which is applied with a float. As it dries it has to be 'polished' by applying water and smoothing with the float. Because of the speed at which plaster dries, this can be a difficult skill to master and telltale ridges may remain where the plaster has dried before the polishing began. Experience will overcome this problem.

Large or small holes in a plastered wall first have to be thoroughly cleaned out. Chip out all loose material and undercut the edges with a knife, then brush out thoroughly to remove all the dust.

If the wall is block or brick underneath, and the hole is no more than 100mm (4in) in diameter, then use a small trowel and build up the surface with thin layers of filler.

With a wall constructed of laths (thin strips of wood) and plaster, you first have to

expose the laths, removing all loose plaster in the same way as above. But you won't be able to undercut the edges so easily, so you have to make sure that the filling goes between the slats. If the slats are damaged then treat as plasterboard. Otherwise, build up the filler in layers.

Always overfill a large hole, and to get it flush use a batten (long enough to bridge it) in a sawing action to reduce excess or redistribute it till the required level is reached. Finally smooth the finished surface with a filling knife or trowel, and sand down when dry with glasspaper or an orbital sander.

If holes aren't too large but are deep, an alternative method is to press in balls of wet newspaper, then skim a layer of plaster or cellulose filler over the top.

If there's a hole or holes where walls meet to make an external corner, nail a batten vertically along the edge of one wall and fill the hole on the other as described above. When this patch is dry remove the batten and repeat on the other wall. If the damage to an exposed corner is extensive, or if it is particularly vulnerable, greater reinforce-

SURFACE CRACKS

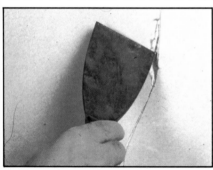

1 *These tiny cracks usually occur in plaster and are superficial. Use the edge of a stripping knife to remove any loose material along its length.*

2 *Brush out the crack thoroughly so there's no dust left. In a small carton mix some cellulose filler to a creamy paste with water.*

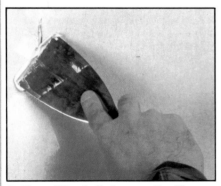

3 *Use a filling knife to press the filler onto the wall surface over the tiny cracks. Leave the filler slightly proud as it will shrink a little.*

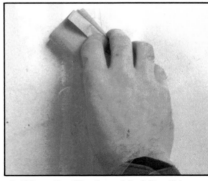

4 *When the filler has dried (it will lose the grey look and turn white) use glasspaper wrapped round a wood block to make the surface flush.*

Ready Reference

WHICH FILLER TO USE

Cellulose filler or ready-mixed filler for
● superficial cracks in plaster and plasterboard
● small holes (up to 50mm/2in) across
● gouge marks in plaster
● joint cracks in plasterboard or coving
● filling dents and cracks in wood to be painted.

Finishing plaster or brush-on skim plaster for
● large holes (over 50mm/2in) across
● deep cracks in plaster
● patches where unsound plaster has been stripped off
● skim coats on plasterboard.

Wood stopper in matching shade for
● wood to be given a natural finish.

Flexible mastic or ready-mixed filler for
● gaps between woodwork and walls (round windows and door frames).

TOOLS FOR MAKING GOOD

● a *filling knife* with a 25-50mm (1-2in) wide blade. This has a more flexible blade than a wallpaper stripping knife, and is useful for small repairs

● a *hawk* for holding plaster close to the work (something you can make yourself from a square of plywood 450 x 450mm with a piece of thick dowelling for the handle)

● a *plasterer's trowel* (also called a steel float) used for applying plaster and polishing the surface

● an *angle trowel* is also useful for making neat right-angled internal corners

HOLES IN PLASTERBOARD

1 With large holes in ceilings or walls use a handyman's knife and straight edge to cut back the plasterboard to the nearest joists or studs on each side.

2 The new piece of plasterboard should fit the hole fairly neatly. Press it in and fix to joists or studs on either side using galvanised plasterboard nails.

3 Use a steel trowel to press finishing plaster well into gaps. Then smooth the whole area keeping the top of the trowel angled away from the wall.

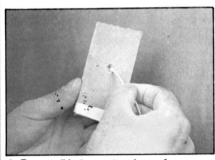

4 For small holes, cut a piece of plasterboard a little larger than the hole (but small enough for you to get it through) and drill a hole in the middle.

TIP
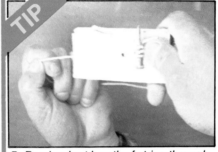

5 Feed a short length of string through the hole, then tie a nail to one end — this will keep the string secure and prevent it being pulled out later.

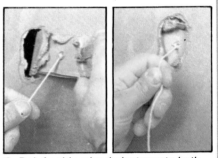

6 Dab freshly mixed plaster onto both ends of the piece of plasterboard, then guide it into the hole. Pull on the string to position it in the hole.

7 Still holding the string, press plaster into the hole then use a trowel to remove the excess so that it's not quite flush with the surface.

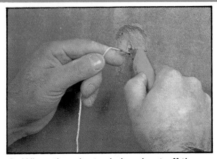

8 When the plaster is hard cut off the length of string with a handymans' knife. After the cut is made there should be no sign of the string.

9 Apply a thin finishing coat of plaster to the surface. Lightly flick water onto the surface as you use the trowel to polish the surface smooth.

ment may be desirable. Cut back the plaster as described under weak plaster (see page 29) to beyond the limit of the damage and square off to neaten edges. Then fix an expanded metal corner-piece to the underlying wall with dabs of plaster and plaster over it using the batten technique. Internal corners are a bit trickier. There are two methods. Either fill one side, smooth with batten, then leave to dry before doing the other. Or fill both and when semi dry, smooth down with an angle trowel.

For small holes in plasterboard use cellulose filler. Edges of larger holes should be cleaned up with a handyman's knife and can be covered with a patch of scrim cloth (available from most builders' merchants and hardware shops) stuck in place with dabs of plaster. Or you can use an offcut of plasterboard (see the photographs above). When secure, gently plaster over using a creamy mixture of filler or finishing plaster and allow to dry. Finally sand smooth.

Large holes in plasterboard must be patched with plasterboard offcuts. To nail in position it will be necessary to cut a hole big enough to expose the nearest wooden supports (in a wall these are called 'studs', in a ceiling 'joists'). On a ceiling, if you can get at it from above, the hole can be cut square and battened along each side, the battens being nailed to the joists. Use 30mm or 40mm galvanised nails to fix the plasterboard in place, then fill in gaps as above.

Holes in wood are best filled with wood, and if the hole is circular, use a piece of

SEALING GAPS

1 *Gaps between woodwork and walls can be filled with a flexible sealer. The nozzle is directed into the space with the help of a special gun.*

2 *For a smooth finish, lightly sprinkle the sealer with water then run down the corner with a flexible bladed knife. It can be painted 24 hours later.*

dowelling glued in place with PVA adhesive. With some holes, you can achieve the same result with a wedge — hammered into place, and then planed off for a flush finish. Alternatively, use plastic wood or stopping and sand the finish down when dry. If knots are loose and very dry, they should be cut out and the hole filled with a small piece of dowelling, glued in place.

Gaps

Where gaps occur between woodwork and walls (eg, near windows, architraves and skirting boards), a flexible sealant will fill them. Bought as 'cartridges', they have a nozzle which can be directed straight into the gap. A 'gun' attachment gives even more control and is especially useful in awkward places. The sealant can be painted 24 hours later. Cellulose filler can also be used for gaps but take care to get it smooth. If the gaps are particularly deep partly fill them with strips of folded newspaper and apply flexible sealer over the top. If they're wide, use thin wood to fill and wood filler to finish, then sand down when dry.

Gaps in plaster cornices (the shaped moulding where walls meet ceilings) occur when a framework (eg, an old cupboard) has been pulled away. Clean up the gap and apply liberal quantities of cellulose filler. When the filler is 'stiff' but not hard take a pro-file comb (you can make this yourself from a piece of card cut to the same 'profile' or shape as the coving) and run it along from the existing coving onto the filler. When the match is perfect allow the filler to dry and then gently smooth with the folded edge of a sheet of glasspaper.

Weak plaster

Old plaster may be loose against its backing and will move when you press it. If this is the case in any more than small areas, then complete replacement may be necessary. Unsound plaster will sound hollow when you tap it gently with your knuckles.

The extent of the weak area should be found by tapping, then lines drawn around it with a pencil. Using a club hammer and a bolster, gently chip out the weak area start-ing at the outside edges of the patch and working inwards (cover the floor below to catch the mess). If you don't start at the edges of the weak areas and work inwards, you may end up removing half the wall. When the patch has been removed you should fill as in holes. With larger areas you may need a professional plasterer. If the weakness was caused by damp the under-lying wall should also be treated with a suitable damp sealant before repairing.

Mould

This may be found in steamy conditions which encourage its growth or where con-densation is a problem (eg, in kitchens and bathrooms). Mould appears as grey, green or black spots or patches, and first should be treated with a fungicidal solution. Alterna-tively you can use a three parts water to one part household bleach solution. The wall should be dry before redecoration. If the problem persists, then you'll have to tackle the underlying cause — which may be damp penetrating the wall from outside or from below, or lack of insulation and ventilation which causes persistent condensation.

Old adhesives

Where ceramic tiles have been removed tile cement may remain fixed to the wall. In some situations — if you're retiling, for instance — this won't matter because as long as the surface is fairly flat any new adhesive will stick perfectly well. In the case of poly-styrene tiles on a ceiling there may be dabs of adhesive left when you remove them and

REPAIRING HOLES

1 Mark straight guide lines slightly beyond the weak area. Use a bolster and club hammer to cut back to the brick, block or laths underneath.

2 Brushing out any dust and then dampening the surface with a little water helps the plaster stick and stops it drying too quickly.

3 Apply a plaster backing coat to the hole — use either a coarse type which sets slowly, one-coat gypsum with an added retarder, or 'brush-on' plaster.

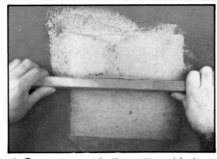

4 To level, use a batten with a side-to-side sawing action. As the plaster hardens, cut it back with a trowel so it's not quite flush with the wall surface.

5 When putting on the finishing coat, scoop plaster from the hawk onto the trowel, then angle the bottom edge of the trowel in to the wall.

6 Keep the trowel moving at all times. Smooth upwards, then from side to side. To 'polish' flick on drops of water, and move the trowel in a circular motion.

CORNERS

1 Repairing corners is a two-stage job. Brush out the damaged area, then fix a batten on one side. To ease removal, don't drive the nails fully home.

2 Use the edge of the trowel to fill in the hole with traditional quick setting gypsum plaster. When it's dry move the batten to the other side.

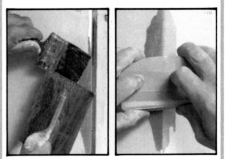

3 Fill in the rest of the hole, damping down with water. Leave to dry, then remove the batten. Gently smooth the new edge to match the old.

---

the surface has to be cleaned off. The only answer to this is an arduous, bit by bit, removal of each dab. (In places, plaster may come away with the tile or adhesive in which case treat as holes in plaster.) Gently ease the adhesive or cement away from the surface using a stripping knife and a mallet. Then sand the area smooth before decorating. If cork tiles have been taken down, any adhesive remaining will have to be sanded off with an orbital sander — another time-consuming but essential job — if you're decorating with paint or wallpaper.

Paint problems

If the paint on plaster, plasterboard or wood has flaked, blistered or bubbled scrape off the damaged area with a scraper or a coarse abrasive until a sound paint edge is reached. Wash down the exposed surface, allow to dry and prime before repainting.

If paint on wood repeatedly blisters or discolours, this could mean that there's a knot there that's giving out resin. Use a blow-torch to burn off the discoloured part then play the flame gently on it to draw the resin out. Scrape this off, sand the surface and wipe off all traces of dust, then apply two coats of 'knotting' sealer (available from most hardware shops) to the patch. It must be dry before painting.

Crazing is another common problem, visible as very fine hair-like cracks in a painted surface. On a plastered wall it's often caused by applying the paint before the plaster is completely dry. On wood it may be because the paint underneath the top coat had not completely dried. The remedy is to scrape off the surface and repaint (see also pages 4-6).

PAPERING WALLS
the basics

No other wall covering can quite so dramatically alter the look and feeling of a room as wallpaper. Correctly hung paper makes the walls sharp and fresh, and to achieve this finish there are important things to know. What do you do if the walls are out of true? Where's the best place to start? How do you prevent bubbles and creases? The answers are here.

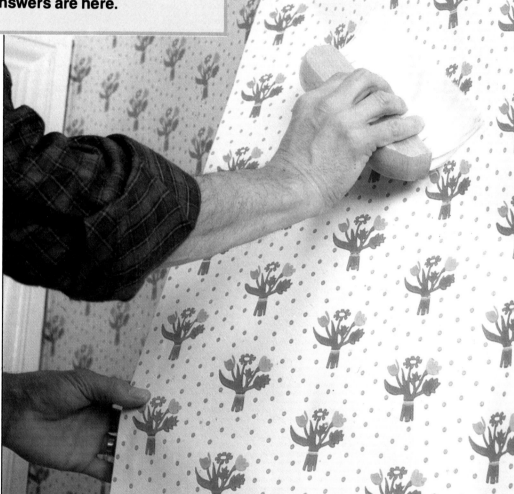

Wallpapering isn't so much an art, it's more a matter of attention to detail. And perhaps the first mistake that's made by many people is expecting too much of their walls. Rarely are walls perfectly flat, perfectly vertical and at right angles to each other. So the first and most crucial part of hanging wallpaper is to prepare the walls properly. Obviously you can't change their basic character − if they're not entirely flat or vertical, you're stuck with them − but you can make sure that the surface is suitably prepared so that the new paper will stick.

This means that any old wallpaper really should come off before you do anything else. Papering on top of old wall coverings won't *always* lead to disaster, but it will quite often simply because the new adhesive will tend to loosen the old. The result will be bubbles at best and peeling at worst.

Adhesives
Always use the correct adhesive for the wallcovering and follow the manufacturers instructions for mixing. Using the wrong paste can result in the paper not sticking, mould growth or discoloration of the paper.

A cellulose-based adhesive is used for all standard wallcoverings. There are two types, ordinary and heavy-duty which relates to the weight of the paper being hung. Heavy-duty pastes are for heavyweight wallcoverings. Certain brands of paste are suitable for all types of wallcoverings − less water being used for mixing when hanging heavy papers.

Since vinyls and washable wallcoverings are impervious, mould could attack the paste unless it contains a fungicide. Fungicidal paste is also needed if the wall has previously been treated against mould or if there is any sign of damp.

Some wallcoverings (like polyethylene foam, some hessians and foils) require a specially thick adhesive which is pasted onto the wall. Follow manufacturers' instructions.

Ready-pasted papers are exactly that and require no extra adhesive − although it's useful to have a tube of latex glue handy for finishing off corners and joints which mightn't have stuck. (The same applies to all washable wallpapers).

Glue *size* (a watered down adhesive) is brushed over the walls before papering to seal them and prevent the paste from soaking in to the wall. It also ensures all-over adhesion and makes sliding the paper into place easier.

Although size can be bought, most wallpaper pastes will make size when mixed with the amount of water stated in the instructions.

If you buy a proprietary size and the wallcovering you are using needs an adhesive containing fungicide, make sure that the size you buy also contains a fungicide. Use an old brush to apply and a damp cloth to clean off any that runs on to paintwork. It can be difficult to remove after it has dried. Sizing can be done several days or an hour before.

Where to begin
The traditional rule is to start next to the window and work away from it, but that is really a hangover from the days when paper was overlapped and shadows showed up joins. Today, papers butt up, so light isn't the problem. But as inaccuracies can occur with slight loss of pattern, you have to be able to make this as inconspicuous as possible. In

Ready Reference

STRIPPING OLD WALLPAPER

Never hang new coverings over existing wallpaper – the old may lift and bring the new with it.

Ordinary wallpaper:
● use hot water with washing-up liquid or proprietary wallpaper stripper to soak the surface
● scrape off old paper in strips with broad-bladed scraper, re-soaking stubborn areas; wash surface down to remove bits

Washable or painted wallpaper:
● always score surface coating with serrated scraper before soaking and scraping
● for large areas a steam stripper (from hire shops) is a real time-saver

Vinyl wallcovering:
● lift corner of vinyl coating at skirting board level and peel away from backing paper by pulling steadily up and away
● then soak and scrape off backing paper

WHERE TO START

Room with a chimney breast: start at its centre and work outward to each end of the chimney wall, then on down the two side walls towards the door. Any loss of pattern will be least noticed in the short lengths hung over the door.

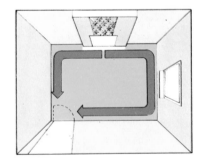

Room without a chimney breast: start at one corner of the room – ideally near the door – and work around continuously until you return to your starting point.

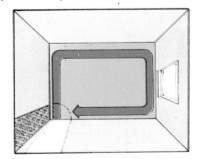

an average room, the corner nearest the door is the best starting point. Any loss of pattern will then end up behind you as you enter the room. In a room with a chimney breast, hang the first drop in the centre and work outwards from both sides of the drop.

Problem areas in a house (recesses, arches, stairwells) are dealt with on pages 36-39.

Measuring and cutting

Measure the height of the wall you want to paper using a steel tape measure and cut a piece of paper from the roll to this length, allowing an extra 50mm (2in) top and bottom for trimming. This allowance is needed for pattern matching, and to ensure a neat finish at skirting board and ceiling.

Lay the first drop — that's the name given to each length of paper — pattern side up on the table and unroll the paper from which the

second drop is to be cut next to it. Move this along until the patterns match, then cut the second drop using the other end of the first as a guide. Subsequent lengths of paper are cut in exactly the same way, with each matching the drop that preceded it.

Remember some wallpapers have patterns that are a straight match across the width, while others have what is called a drop pattern that rises as it extends across the width. With drop match papers the second length will begin half a pattern repeat further along the roll. Length 3 will match length 1, length 4 will match length 2 and so on.

For things to run smoothly, you should establish a work routine when paper hanging. Cut all the wall drops first (so you only have to measure once) and cut bits for papering above windows and doors as you come to them. If you paste say 3 drops, the first will have had its required soaking time

HOW TO CUT AND PASTE

1 Mark the pasting table with lines at 150mm (6in) and 300mm (1ft) intervals. Measure wall drop and use guidelines to cut your first length.

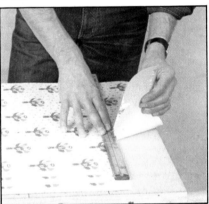

2 Use the first length as a guide for the other drops, matching the pattern carefully. Tear off the waste against a wooden rule.

3 Lay all the drops pattern down, overhanging the far edge of the table. Pull the first drop to the near edge and paste it from centre to edges.

4 Fold pasted end, paste the rest and fold in. Now fold up the whole drop and leave it to soak. The top of the longer fold always goes to the top of the wall.

PAPER HANGING TECHNIQUES

1 Place chosen pattern on ceiling line with waste above. Align side edge with vertical and turn waste onto adjacent wall. Brush up to ceiling first, then corners and edges, and then down. Open out short fold last.

2 Mark cutting line for waste at ceiling and skirting board with a pencil — ends of scissors won't fit creases neatly and can give a thick line which causes you to cut the paper inaccurately and will give an uneven look at ceiling and skirting.

3 To cut waste, pull short length of paper away from wall so pencil line catches the light. Cut using full length of blades — hurried, short cuts can make the edges jagged. Brush paper back on wall so that it is perfectly flat.

4 Reduce waste on adjacent wall to 6mm (¼in) to lessen bulk when paper overlaps from other direction.

5 Continue along wall matching the pattern horizontally. Press drop onto wall so long edges butt.

6 As each drop is hung, brush up first, then to edges and finally down to remove any trapped air.

7 To turn a corner, measure between hung paper and corner at the top, middle and bottom of wall. Add 6mm (¼in) to widest width, then use this measurement to cut the pasted and folded drop into two. Set aside offcut for new wall.

8 Hang drop to complete wall, brushing the waste round the corner. Find the new vertical and mark the line the width of offcut from the corner. Check this measurement at the top, middle and bottom of wall. If the same, hang offcut.

9 If corner is out of true, offcut and wall measurements will differ. To disguise pattern loss, hang the offcut so waste laps onto completed wall. Brush into corner, run pencil down crease line and cut waste.

Ready Reference

HANGING TO A VERTICAL

For perfect results wallcoverings must be hung absolutely vertical. You can't trust the corners of rooms to be perfectly true so you must
● mark a vertical line on the wall against which the first length can be aligned
● mark a similar line on the next wall every time you turn a corner

Mark line on first wall 25mm (1in) less than a roll's width from the corner, using a plumb bob and line
● hold the line at the top of the wall and allow the bob to come to rest just above skirting board level
● mark the string's position at three points on the wall with a pencil
● join up the marks using a long straight timber batten as a ruler

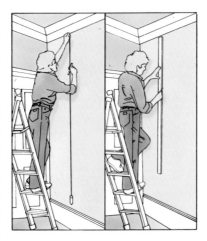

PAPERHANGING TOOLS

Plumb bob and line: for establishing a true vertical. Any small weight attached to a string will do.
Pasting brush: it's thicker than a paint brush and about 150mm (6in) wide. A paint brush will do as a substitute.
Paperhanger's scissors: for trimming on or off the wall. Long-bladed household scissors can be used instead.
Paperhanging brush: for smoothing paper onto walls and into angles. Use a sponge on washable and vinyl papers.
Seam roller: for ensuring good adhesion along seams (not used with embossed papers). A cloth-wrapped finger does almost as well.
Pasting table: for pasting lengths prior to hanging, it's slightly wider than a standard roll width. Any table over about 1.8 metres (6ft) long can be used.

(with medium weight paper) by the time the third is pasted and folded and is ready to be hung. With heavy papers paste, fold and soak 6 drops at a time as extra soaking time is needed.

Avoiding bubbles

The purpose behind soaking time (apart from making paper supple enough to handle) is to give it time to expand to its natural limit. On the width this can be 6mm-12mm (¼in-½in) and the average wall-size drop will gain 24mm (1in) on the length – this explains why you have more to cut as waste than you started with.

If you haven't given paper the time it needs, it will expand on the walls – but its spread will be contained by adjoining drops and so you get bubbles in the central part.

Soak medium weight papers for 3-4 minutes, heavy weights for about 10. Ready-pasted papers don't need too long a soaking, but to ensure they get wet all over, roll drops loosely and press into water till they are completely covered.

Pasting and soaking

Position the paper with its top edge at the right-hand end of the table (or at the other end if you're left handed). Paste it carefully to ensure that all parts, the edges especially, are well covered. Work from the centre outwards in herring-bone style using the width of the brush to cover the drop in sweeps, first to the nearest edge, then the other – excess paste here will go onto second drop, not the table. Cover two-thirds of the drop, then fold the top edge in so paste is to paste. Move the drop along the table and paste the remainder, folding bottom edge in paste to paste. Because the first folded part is longer than the other, this will remind you which is the

top. Fold the drop up and put aside to soak while you paste the others.

This technique will give you a manageable parcel of paper to hang no matter what length the drop – but always remember to make the first fold longer – this is the one offered to the ceiling line. If in doubt mark the top edge lightly with a pencil cross.

Hanging pasted paper

Wallpaper must be hung absolutely vertical if it is to look right, so always work to a vertical line (see *Ready Reference*).

Position your step ladder as close as possible to where you want to work, and climb it with the first length of paper under or over your arm. Open out the long fold and offer the top edge up, placing the pattern as you want it at the ceiling with waste above. Align the side edge of the drop with your vertical guide line, allowing the other side edge to turn onto the adjacent wall if starting at a corner. Smooth the paper onto the wall with the paperhanging brush, using the bristle ends to form a crease between wall and ceiling, and at corners. When brushing paper into place, always work up first then to the join, then to the side edge, then down. This will remove trapped air.

As soon as the paper is holding in place, work down the wall, brushing the rest of the drop in position, opening out the bottom fold when you reach it. Again use the bristle ends to form a good crease where paper meets the skirting board.

The next step is to trim off the waste paper at the top and bottom. Run a lead pencil along the crease between the ceiling or skirting and the wall — the blades or points of scissors wil make a line that's too thick for accurate cutting. Gently peel paper away from the wall and cut carefully along the line with your scissors. Finally brush the paper back in place.

Hanging the second drop is done as the

Estimator

Most wallpaper is sold in rolls 10.05m (11yds) long and 530mm (21in) wide. Calculate rolls needed by measuring perimeter of the room and height from skirting board to ceiling.

WALLS	Distance around the room (doors and windows included)										
Height from skirting	10m 33'	11m 36'	12m 39'	13m 43'	14m 46'	15m 49'	16m 52'	17m 56'	18m 59'	19m 62'	20m 66'
2.15–2.30m (7'–7'6")	5	5	5	6	6	7	7	8	8	9	9
2.30–2.45m (7'6"–8')	5	5	6	6	7	7	8	8	9	9	10
2.45–2.60m (8'–8'6")	5	6	6	7	7	8	9	9	10	10	11

The number of rolls needed can be greatly affected by the frequency of pattern repeat. With a large pattern repeat, buy an extra roll.

first except that you have to butt it up against the edge of the first length, matching the pattern across the two. The secret here is not to try and do it all in one go. Get the paper onto the wall at the right place at the ceiling join but just a little way away from the first length. Now press against the paper with the palms of your hands and slide it into place. Using well-soaked paper on a wall that's been sized makes this easy, but if you're using a thin wallpaper press gently as it could tear. Butt the paper up after pattern matching and brush into place.

When trimming waste from drops other than the first, cut from where the lengths butt to ensure even ceiling and skirting lines.

Hanging ready-pasted wallpaper

With these you won't need pasting table, bucket and pasting brush but you will need a special light plastic trough made for the purpose. Put it below where the first drop is to be hung and fill with water – covering the floor with layers of newspaper will soak up accidental spillages. Don't try to lift the trough; slide it along the floor as the work progresses.

Cut each drop so patterns are matching, then roll the first one loosely from the bottom up with the pattern inside. Place it in the trough and press it down so water can reach all the parts covered with paste. Leave for the required soaking time (check manufacturers' instructions but, it's usually between 30 seconds and 2 minutes), then pick the drop up by the two top corners and take it to the ceiling line. Press onto the wall using an absorbent sponge to mop up and push out air bubbles. Press firmly on the edges with the sponge or a seam roller, then trim waste.

COPING WITH WALL FITTINGS ... AND CREASES

Few walls present a perfectly clear surface for paperhanging. Almost all will contain such small obstacles as light switches and power points, while some may carry wall-mounted fittings such as curtain tracks and adjustable shelving. Small obstacles can be papered round with some careful trimming, but larger obstacles are best taken down from the wall and replaced when you have finished decorating. That way you will get a really professional finish.

Creases can also spoil the look of your work. If they occur, take steps to remove them before the paste dries. Here's how.

1 To cut round light switches, mark centre of plate, insert scissor tips and cut out towards plate corners.

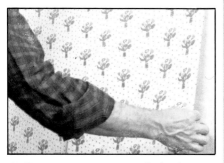

1 Creases are a common fault where the wall is out of true or if you haven't brushed the paper out properly.

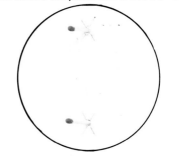

1 Use matchsticks, pushed head out into wall plugs, to show where wall fittings have been taken down.

2 Crease tongues of paper against edges of plate, lift away from wall, trim along line and brush back into place.

2 To remove the crease, peel the paper from the wall to a point above the crease – to the ceiling if necessary.

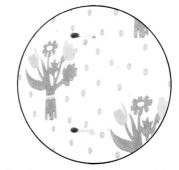

2 Brush paper firmly over match heads so they pierce it. With hanging complete remove matches and replace fittings.

3 With washable and vinyl papers push a strip of rigid plastic against plate edges and trim with a sharp knife.

3 Brush the paper back into position – across towards the butt join, then to the other edge and down to the bottom.

PAPERING AWKWARD AREAS

The techniques for papering round tricky areas like corners and reveals are quite basic. But care and patience is required if you are going to get really professional results from your paperhanging.

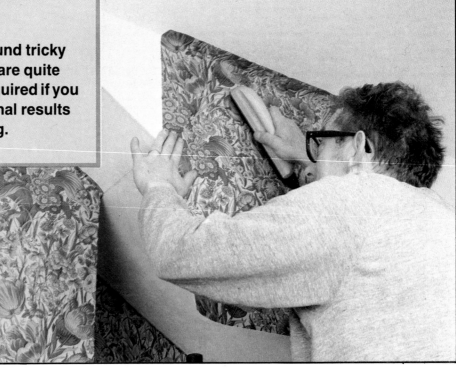

Although the major part of wallpapering, hanging straight lengths is fairly quick and straightforward. The tricky areas – corners, doorways and so on – which call for careful measuring, cutting and pattern matching are the bits that slow the job down. There's no worse eye-sore than a lop-sided pattern at a corner; but if you use the right techniques you can avoid this problem.

You have to accept in advance that the continuity of a pattern will be lost in corners and similar places; even a professional decorator can't avoid this. However, he has the ability to match the pattern as closely as possible so that the discontinuity is not noticeable, and this is what you have to emulate.

Things would, of course, be a lot simpler if all corners were perfectly square, but this is rarely the case. When you wallpaper a room for the first time you are likely to discover that all those angles that appeared to be true are anything but.

You can, however, help to overcome the problem of careful pattern matching at corners by choosing a paper with the right design (see *Ready Reference*). The most difficult of the lot to hang are those with a regular small and simple repeat motif. The loss of pattern continuity will be easy to spot if even slight errors are made. The same is often true of large, repeat designs. With either of these types, a lot more time will be involved and it could well take a couple of hours to hang a few strips around a single window reveal.

Sloping ceiling lines are another problem area and certain patterns will show it up clearly. You can understand the nuisance of a sloping ceiling by imagining a pattern with, say, regular rows of horizontal roses. Although the first length on the wall may be hung correctly to leave a neat row of roses along the ceiling line the trouble is that as subsequent lengths are hung and the pattern is matched, you will see less and less of that top row of roses as the ceiling slopes down. And, conversely, if the ceiling line slopes upwards, you will start to see a new row of roses appearing above. So, despite the fact that each length has been hung

vertically, the sloping ceiling will make the job look thoroughly unsightly.

Internal and external corners
Before you begin papering round a corner, you must hang the last full length before the corner. Your corner measurement will be done from one edge of this length. You can use a steel tape or boxwood rule to measure the gap to the corner (see *Ready Reference*) and then cut the piece required to fill it, plus a margin which is carried round onto the new wall. Since it's likely that the walls will be out of square and that the margin taken round the corner will not be exactly equal all the way down, it's obvious you would have a terrible job hanging the matching offcut strip to give a neat butt join.

For this reason you must hang the matching offcut which goes on the 'new' wall to a true vertical and then brush it over the margin you've turned onto this wall. You should aim to match the pattern at the corner as closely as possible. Since the paper overlaps, the match will not be perfect, but this is unavoidable and will not, in any case be noticeable as the overlap is tucked into or round the corner out of sight (see *Ready Reference*).

Papering round window reveals
Unless you intend to paper just one or two walls in a room you will eventually have to cope with papering round a window. Pattern matching is the problem here, but you should find cutting the paper to fit above and

below a window is not too difficult provided you work in a logical order (see box opposite). But you may have to be prepared for lots of scissor work when you cut out strips of paper for the two sides and top of the reveal to ensure the pattern matches the paper on the facing wall. (It's worth getting into the habit of marking some sort of code on the back of each piece of paper before it's cut up so you will be able to find matching pieces quickly.)

Make sure that you don't end up with a seam on the edge of the reveal, where it will be exposed to knocks and liable to lift. Before you begin work on the window wall, take a roll of wallcovering and estimate how many widths will fit between the window and the nearest corner. If it looks as though you will be left with a join within about 25mm (1in) of the window opening you should alter your starting point slightly so that, when you come to the window, the seam will have moved away from the edge of the reveal.

Where the lengths of paper are positioned on the window wall obviously depends on the position of the window, its size and the width of the wallpaper. But the ideal situation occurs when the last full length before you reach the window leaves a width of wall, plus window reveal, that measures just less than the width of the wallpaper. You can then hang the next length so its upper part goes on the wall above the window, the lower part on the wall below it and (after making two scissor cuts) turn the middle part to cover the side of the window reveal. The edge of

PAPERING ROUND A WINDOW

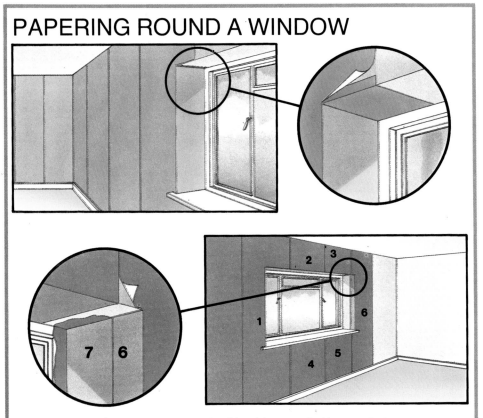

Top: Fill the narrow gap left on the underside of the reveal with a small offcut.
Above: The papering sequence; piece 7 fills the gap left on the reveal by piece 6.

Ready Reference

TIP: CHOOSE PATTERNS CAREFULLY
In rooms full of awkward corners and recesses, pick a paper with a random, busy design which the eye doesn't try to follow. This will help disguise the fact that a corner is out of square, or a ceiling is sloping.

MEASURING AT CORNERS
When you are measuring for the width of paper required to fill a corner gap:
● measure from the last full fixed length to the corner at the top, middle and bottom of the gap
● take the largest measurement; for an internal corner add 12mm (1/2in) and for an external corner add 25mm (1in) to give you the width to cut from the next length
● the offcut left is used on the 'new wall' and overlaps the 12mm (1/2in) or 25mm (1in) strip turned round the corner.

TIP: TURN NARROW STRIPS
Never try to take a lot of paper round a corner. If you do, you will end up with it badly creased into the angle of the corner, and the part that is taken onto the 'new wall' will be completely askew.

AVOID OBVIOUS JOINS
On an external corner the overlap of the edges of the two strips of paper which cover the corner should be positioned where they will be least obvious (eg, on a chimney breast it is better to make the overlap on the side wall rather than have it on the wall facing into the room).

PAPERING ROUND A DOORWAY
Ideally, you'll use the minimum of paper if you centre a full-width strip of paper over the door opening. Where the door is close to a corner, fit a narrow strip above the doorway. Pattern discontinuity will be least noticed in between two full strips.

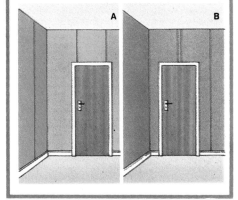

the middle part can then be creased and trimmed so it fits neatly up against the window frame.

Go on to hang short lengths of wallpaper above the window, cutting them so their lower parts can be taken on to the underside of the top window reveal, and again trim them so they fit neatly up against the window frame. When you reach a point where the reveal on the opposite side of the window is less than the width of the wallpaper away from the last edge hung, you should stop and repeat the papering process below the window between the sill and skirting board, trimming as you go.

You can then hang the next full length in the same way as the one you hung on the first side of the window. You should, first, however, hang a plumbline over the pieces in place above the top and bottom of the window then hang the full length to the plumbline, trimming any slight overlap on the new length if necessary. (By doing this, you will ensure that the lengths to be hung on the rest of the wall will be truly vertical.)

Often, however, the position of the last full length at the window will fall so that the paper does not cover the reveal at the side of the window, and in this case you will have to cut matching strips to fill the gap. Similarly, you

will have to cut strips to fill the gaps on the underside of the reveal at the top of the window.

Dormer windows
In attics and loft rooms there will be sloping ceilings and dormer windows with which you will have to contend. If you decide to paper rather than paint the sloping ceiling, then you treat it in the same way as you would a vertical wall; there are no unusual problems involved, other than the peculiar working angle. Remember, too, that if you choose the wrong type of paper the irregular pattern-matching could give unfortunate results.

Paper the wall alongside the window and then round the window itself, moving on to the wall below the other side of the sloping ceiling (see step-by-step photographs). Finally, you can paper the dormer cheeks.

Chimney breasts and fireplace surrounds
Special rules apply to chimney breasts. For a start, since they are a focal point in the room, any pattern must be centralised. The design of the paper will affect where you begin to hang the wallpaper. Where one length of paper contains a complete motif, you can simply measure and mark off the central point of the chimney breast and use a

PAPERING AN INTERNAL CORNER

1 Hang the last full length before the corner. Then measure the gap (see Ready Reference) to determine the width to be cut from the next length.

2 Cut from the next length a piece which will overlap 12mm (¹/₂in) round the corner. Then paste and fix it in position so it fills the corner gap.

3 Measure the width of the matching offcut strip of paper and use a plumbline to mark a guideline on the wall this distance from the corner.

4 Hang the offcut so its cut edge overlaps the matching edge of the first corner piece and its 'good' edge aligns with the vertical guideline.

FLUSH WINDOWS

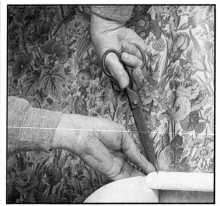

1 Fix the last full length of paper before the window and pull the excess across. Cut round the sill and fix the paper beneath it.

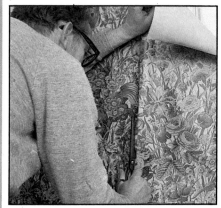

2 You can then trim off the excess paper which runs alongside the window. Now press and brush the pasted paper into position.

3 Work along the wall underneath the window, fixing, creasing and trimming as you go. Afterwards you can fix the paper on the other side of the window.

plumbline at this point to help you draw a vertical line down the centre. You can then begin hanging the wallpaper by aligning the first length with this line.

On the other hand, if it is the type of paper where two lengths, when aligned, form a motif, you will first have to estimate the number of widths which will fit across the chimney breast and then draw a line as a guide for hanging the first length of paper so the combined motif will, in fact, be centralised.

Your order of work should be from the centre (or near centre) outwards and you will then have to turn the paper round the corners at the sides so you form an overlap join with the paper which will be applied to the sides of the chimney breast. Follow the usual techniques for measuring and papering round external corners, remembering in particular not too take too much paper round the corner.

When it comes to fireplace surrounds, there are so many varying kinds of mantelshelfs and surrounds that only general guidance can be given. Usually the technique is to brush the paper down on to the top part of the wall and then cut it to fit along the back edge of the mantelshelf. You can then cut the lower half to fit the contours of the surround. If it's a complicated outline then you'll have to gradually work downwards, using a small pair of sharp scissors, pressing the paper into each shape, withdrawing it to snip along the crease line, then brushing it back into place.

If there is only a small distance between the edge of the mantelshelf and the corner, it's a lot easier if you hang the paper down to the shelf and then make a neat, horizontal cut line in the paper. You can then hang the lower half separately and join the two halves to disguise the cut line.

PAPERING ROUND A DORMER

1 Where the dormer cheek meets the junction of the wall and ceiling, draw a line at right angles to the wall on the ceiling by the dormer cheek.

2 Draw a vertical line at right angles to the first line on the dormer cheek. You can then fix the first length of paper in place on the dormer cheek.

3 Work along towards the window, trimming as you go. Gently tear along the overlap to feather its edge so you won't get a bulky join later.

4 At the window, crease along the side of the frame by running the edge of the scissors along it. You can then carefully trim along the creased line.

5 Return to the small gap which needs to be filled at the narrow end of the dormer cheek; fix this piece in position, crease and trim.

6 Mark a straight line on the sloping ceiling to serve as a guideline for fixing the first length of paper on the underside of the dormer cheek.

7 Cut a piece of paper so it reaches from the point you have marked up to the window and brush it into position ensuring that it covers the feathered edges of the overlap.

8 At the junction of the wall and ceiling you will have to cut round awkward angles. You can then go ahead and brush the paper into its final position.

9 Finally, you can brush the strip of paper which fills the gap between the wall and the underside of the dormer cheek into position to finish off the dormer area neatly.

WALLCOVERINGS

'Wallpapers' – patterns and textures by the roll, as most people think of them – come in a number of different types. Often it's the design that influences your choice, but you should also pick the right type for the job.

True wallpapers – pure paper with a printed design – are probably the wallcoverings with which most people are familiar, but there are wallcoverings made of other materials as well, such as plastics and woven fabrics.

There are wallcoverings which are particularly good at covering up uneven surfaces or at coping in areas where they are likely to be subject to damp conditions. Some are ideal for places round the house where they will have to put up with heavy wear; others are more fragile and are best used purely for decorative effect.

Surface printed papers are among the least expensive wallpapers. They are colourfast, and can be printed in up to 20 colours in any one design. Thinner types need careful hanging to avoid them being overstretched and then tearing. They can usually be lightly wiped when dirty but must not be washed, so don't use them on walls which are subject to wear.

Hand-printed wallpapers are much more expensive. They are sold in a variety of roll widths and lengths and usually the side edges need trimming to match patterns. Cross-lining (see Hints) is also recommended. Don't hang these where there is steam or condensation.

Washable wallpapers come in two types. The first is really just printed wallpaper that has been given a clear protective coating of polyvinyl acetate (PVA). The second is printed with water-resistant inks. Both types come in standard sized rolls and are ideal in rooms where a washable wall surface is required.

Washable wallpapers should not be scrubbed, or rubbed too hard or you'll break through the coating. Coated washable papers can be difficult to remove – you need to score the surface before soaking and stripping.

'Whites' or relief wallpapers are made from thicker paper (Anaglypta and other paper-based types) or from cotton fibres (Supaglypta), and once hung are intended to be painted over with emulsion or resin-based paints. The surface is embossed to give a textured finish ranging from a random linen weave to repeating sculptured reliefs. Because the texture disguises lumps and bumps, they are ideal for use on poor surfaces, on both walls and ceilings. They're all sold in standard-sized rolls.

They are suitable for areas that need regular wiping, but heavily embossed types will be damaged by heavy wear. The decoration can be changed by a new coat of paint. However, once overpainted, this kind of wallcovering can be hard to strip.

Ingrain or woodchip wallpapers are plain papers with a textured oatmeal surface made by impregnating the paper pulp with woodchips and sawdust during manufacture. Roll sizes are

hints

Look for symbols printed on the back of samples in pattern books or on product labels to find out if a wallcovering is ready-pasted, washable, light-fast, strippable or peelable.

∿	spongeable	⌷	ready pasted
≈	washable	→∘	free match
▨	scrubbable	⇥⇤	straight match
☀	good light fastness	⇥⇥	offset match
⌐	strippable	50/25 cm	design repeat distance offset
⌐	peelable	↑↓	reverse alternate lengths

You can provide a better surface by cross-lining the wall – hanging lining paper horizontally on the walls before papering vertically.

● When buying wallcoverings check the batch number to make sure the rolls come from the same printing to avoid a mis-match.

● Flocks and other fabric effects should be gently cleaned with the dusting or upholstery attachment of a vacuum cleaner.

● To clean a non-washable paper make a firm dough of flour and water and a few drops of detergent. Stroke the wall with wide, even movements, turning the dough to expose clean parts as it becomes dirty. Smallish marks can be rubbed off with a slice of white bread.

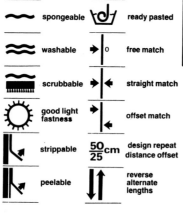

STANDARD ROLL SIZES

Printed wallpapers are sold in rolls 10.05 metres (11 yd) long and 530mm (21in) wide – the standard roll size for most wallcoverings.

usually standard, although double-length (20.1 metres/22yd) rolls are made by some manufacturers. They are painted over like the relief papers previously described, and are ideal for use on walls in reasonable condition.

Flock wallcoverings are made by sticking the pile of silk, wool or synthetic fibres to a paper backing so the pile stands out in relief, forming a pattern. Colours are usually limited to tone-on-tone effects, though sometimes two or three colours are used. Ordinary flock papers can be difficult to hang since care must be taken to avoid getting paste on the front, but with vinyl flocks this is no longer a problem. Rolls of all three types are standard-sized.

Paper flocks should only be used on areas which don't get much wear, condensation or dust but vinyl flocks can be hung almost anywhere as they are tough and washable.

Foil wallcoverings are made by fusing a metallized plastic film onto a paper backing giving a shiny, reflective surface. Rolls are standard-sized.

Because they reflect light they are particularly suitable for use in dark areas or to make small rooms look bigger, but they should not be used on a poor wall surface as they show up every imperfection. Foils stand up to hard wear and are easy to clean, but they must be hung with a fungicidal paste. Because they can conduct electricity, they must not be tucked behind the faceplates of light switches or power points.

Novamura is a unique wallcovering made from foamed polyethylene. It is printed in a wide range of colours, patterns and designs, and comes in standard-sized rolls. Since no paper is used in its manufacture it is very light in weight; it is also easy to hang (by the paste-the-wall method, using a fungicidal paste) and to strip.

Novamura is warm to the touch, so it is particularly suitable for use in bathrooms and kitchens where there is a condensation problem. It's best not to use it on walls which get scuffed easily, since knocks easily damage it.

Vinyl wallcoverings are made by fusing a printed design onto a vinyl layer which is then backed with paper, or occasionally, fabric. This makes a very durable wallcovering, which in most cases can be scrubbed. Rolls are standard-sized, and the range of designs, colours and textures available is very wide.

Vinyls should be hung with a fungicidal paste. Where overlapping is unavoidable, a special adhesive must be used.

Vinyl wallcoverings are easy to strip – they peel away leaving the paper backing on the wall and can be used as a lining paper for subsequent redecoration.

Embossed relief wallcoverings made from vinyl (such as Vynaglypta) are intended for over-painting and are much easier to strip than 'white' wallpapers.

Expanded (blown) vinyl wallcoverings are thicker than ordinary vinyls and are made by using compressed air to form an expanded plastic foam which is coated onto the base paper. They come in standard-sized rolls.

Many surface effects are available, including tile patterns, simulated cork, wood panelling and grasscloths. They are hung like other vinyls, and a firm heavy-duty rubber roller should be used for smoothing them in position, rather than a paperhanger's brush. They can be stripped as easily as other vinyls and are especially suitable for use in bathrooms and kitchens or any room where there is a condensation problem.

PAPERING CEILINGS

One way to cover up a ceiling with cracks or other imperfections is to use lining paper or a textured wallcovering and then paint over it. But a good alternative is to make a special feature of the ceiling by using decorative paper.

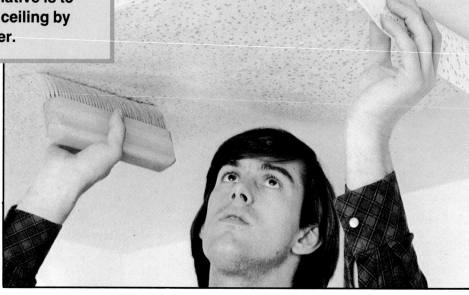

Papering ceilings can be a rather daunting prospect, even to the experienced home decorator. In fact, once you have mastered the basic technique of paperhanging, ceilings are quite straightforward and you are likely to be presented with far fewer problems than on walls. There will be no windows, few (if any) corners and not so many obstacles with which you have to deal.

If you intend to paint the ceiling it's usually best to hang a lining paper or a textured paper like woodchip first to hide the inevitable blemishes of a plaster ceiling. Or you might decide to choose a fine decorative paper and make a feature of the ceiling with it. Most of the papers that are suitable for walls can also be used for ceilings.

But before you opt for papering, it makes sense to consider the alternative: if the sole objective is to get a textured surface which will cover up cracks and bumps, you can do it just as well with a textured paint. Using a woodchip paper would only make sense if you were skilled at papering and wanted to save money; in any case, you'll still have to paint it. However, if you want a smooth ceiling or a decorative surface of distinction then papering is for you.

The equipment you'll need
You will need the same equipment as for papering walls, with the addition of a safe working platform that spans the width of the room (see *Ready Reference*). You should check with your supplier that the paper of your choice is suitable for ceilings (some heavier types may not be) and ask him to provide a suitably strong adhesive, including fungicide if it is a washable vinyl paper. Such papers are extremely suitable for high humidity environments like bathrooms and kitchens.

Preparing the surface
The surface to which you fix the paper must be clean and sound. This means washing down existing paintwork with detergent or sugar soap and then sanding it with a fine abrasive paper or pad to provide a key for the adhesive. Distempered ceilings, often found in old houses, must be scrubbed to remove the distemper, or the paper will not stick.

If the ceiling has been papered before, you should remove the old paper completely. If you try to hang another paper over it there will be blobs and bubbles where the dampness of the new paper separates the old paper from the plaster. Any surface which is at all porous, such as bare plaster, will tend to absorb moisture from the pasted paper at too fast a rate for a successful adhesion. Such surfaces should be sized by brushing them over with a proprietary size, or a diluted version of the actual paste you're going to use. Let the size dry before proceeding.

New plasterboard, often used in modern construction, needs painting with a primer/sealer before decoration. It is also wise to fix a layer of lining paper before your main decorative paper if you are hanging heavyweight or fabric wallcoverings.

Decorating perfectionists always recommend using lining paper anyway, whatever the surface. There is no doubt it does improve the final appearance, particularly on older surfaces or with thinner papers. Lining paper comes in different thicknesses or 'weights' and you should consult your supplier about a suitable grade.

One last preparation tip: don't leave cracks and dents in ceilings for the paper to cover. Fill them and sand them smooth, particularly at joins between plasterboards, and at the wall/ceiling angle. Think of your paper as a surface that needs a good smooth base, and not as a cover-up for a hideous old mess.

Planning the job
Consult the estimator panel (see *Ready Reference*) to gauge the approximate number of rolls you will need; also think about the pattern of your intended paper. Can you cope with a complex drop pattern on a ceiling, or would you be better off with a straight match? A bold paper that looks fine on walls might be a bit overpowering above your head. Is your ceiling good enough for a plainish paper, or do you need texture to draw the eye away from the ravages of time that appear in all old lath-and-plaster ceilings?

Modern papers are designed for the strips to be butted against each other, not overlapped. This means the traditional pattern of working away from, but parallel to, the main source of natural light is not essential. You will generally find it easier working across the narrowest dimension of the room. Well-applied paper will tend not to show the joins too much anyway, particularly if the pattern draws the eye.

All ceiling papering starts from a line which is strung or marked across the ceiling 10mm (⅜in) less than the width of the paper away from the wall. The 10mm (⅜in) on the length of paper which runs next to the wall allows for the walls being out of square and its overlap is trimmed off at the wall and ceiling junction. You can chalk a line and snap it against the ceiling between two tacks to make a mark, or just pin it temporarily in place and butt the first strip of paper against it.

MARKING UP AND PASTING

1 Measure in from the width of the paper minus 10mm (³/₈in), to allow for an overlap at the wall, and mark this distance on the ceiling.

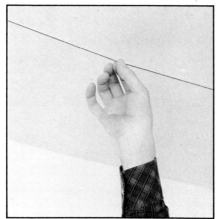

2 Make another mark at the opposite end, the same distance from the wall. Use a chalked line to link the marks, then snap the line onto the ceiling.

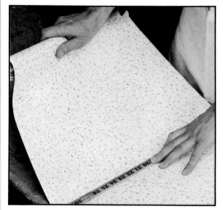

3 Cut or tear the lengths of paper. You should allow 100mm (4in) excess on each piece to give an overlap of 50mm (2in) for trimming at each end.

4 Apply paste to the back of the paper and fold it into concertina folds as you go. Paste enough lengths to allow adequate soaking time.

5 Take the last fold in the length to meet the first, short, fold so the edges meet without paste getting on the front of the paper.

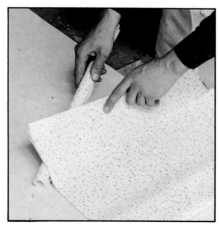

6 Slip a spare roll of paper under the folded-up length; this will serve as a support for the paper so you can carry and hold it easily.

Ready Reference

ESTIMATOR

Distance around room	Number of rolls 10.05m x 530mm (33ft x 21in)
10-12m (33-39ft)	2
12-14m (39-46ft)	3
14-18m (46-59ft)	4
18-20m (59-66ft)	5
20-22m (66-72ft)	6

TIP: WHISK YOUR PASTE
To speed up the process of mixing paste, use a kitchen whisk to beat up the mix.

A SAFE WORKING PLATFORM
Set up two stepladders and a solid plank, at a height where you can comfortably touch the ceiling with the palm of your hand.

TIP: HAVE TOOLS TO HAND
Have the necessary tools with you (in the pocket of an apron or overall) when you're on the working platform to save you scrambling up and down more than you need.

PREVENT WASTAGE
If you are pattern matching, paper in the direction which will save long bits of waste paper left over after cutting the lengths.

LINING PAPER
If you are hanging lining paper, remember that it should be hung at right angles to the paper which goes over it.

PAPERING TECHNIQUE
With the concertina-folded paper supported by the spare roll held in your left hand (if you are right-handed; vice versa if you are left-handed) pull one fold out taut and then brush it into place, working outwards from the centre to avoid trapped air bubbles. Repeat with the other folds.

TIP: TRIM ROSES NEATLY
Don't be tempted to remove the cover of a ceiling rose to trim the paper round it; inaccurate cutting may mean there are gaps when the cover is replaced. Instead:
● trim round the fitting with the cover in place leaving a slight overlap (see step-by-step photographs)
● remove the cover and press the overlap into place.

FINAL TRIMMING
When the last piece of paper has been hung you may need to spend some time on final trimming if the walls and ceiling do not meet squarely and evenly.

HANGING STRAIGHT LENGTHS

1 *Hang the first length on the 'room' side of the chalk line, not next to the wall. Brush the paper into place gently but firmly.*

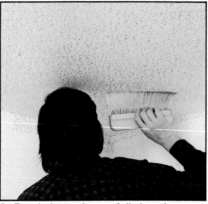

2 *Brush the ends carefully into the angles where walls and ceiling meet, and trim. Then hang the next length alongside the wall.*

3 *The lengths should be butt-jointed. Use a seam roller to ensure well-stuck edges by running it gently over the length of the seam.*

4 *Trim off the overlap at the ends and side (if necessary) of each length of paper. Use a scraper as a guide for the knife for accurate cutting.*

5 *Wipe off any excess adhesive where the overlap has been before it dries, or it will leave ugly marks on the wall surface.*

6 *You can now go ahead and hang the next length on the other side of the first piece hung. Continue until you have covered the entire ceiling.*

It makes sense to get all the lengths measured and cut out in advance, and pasted up in batches of twos or threes (depending on your speed of working) to give adequate soaking time for the type of paper you are hanging; check the manufacturer's instructions on this point. Cut all the strips, including those which will be trimmed for chimney breasts, to full room dimensions plus 100mm (4in) excess for trimming.

The concertina fold
The secret of successful ceiling papering is the correct folding technique, as you paste, so that the paper can be transferred to and laid out against the ceiling surface in a smooth manner. Each fold of the concertina should be 300mm (1ft) wide approximately, apart from the first, which can be shorter (see step-by-step photographs). It's worth practising folding with dry paper first.

Hanging the paper
Assemble the working platform securely at the correct height across the whole length of the room, beneath the area where the first strip is to be pasted. Before you get up there with a fold of wet, pasted paper, make sure you have the tools you will need to hand.

The last-to-be-pasted section of each length is first to go on the ceiling; tease off this first section and brush it into place. Continue to unfold the concertina in sections, brushing it down as you go and checking it is straight against the guideline.

Trimming and seam rolling
When you trim, you should make sure the paper butts exactly up to covings, but allow a 5-10mm (1/4-3/8in) overlap down to the surface of the walls you intend to paper later. Except with embossed papers, you should roll the butt joints between strips with a seam roller.

Light fittings or shades should always be removed, leaving just the flex hanging down. Turn the power off, to ensure safety.

If a chimney breast falls parallel to the run of the paper, you will need your scissors handy to take out an approximate piece as you work along the platform. It's worth anticipating this before you get up there; mark a rough line on the paper at the approximate position of the chimney breast. Cut out the chimney breast piece, leaving an excess of about 15mm (5/8in) for detailed trimming when the whole strip is in place.

If the strip ends at a chimney breast there are less problems. Remove any vast unwanted sections as you work and trim to fit later. External corners are dealt with by making a V-cut so that one flap of the paper can be folded down the inside alcove edge of the chimney breast (or trimmed there if you are working to a coving).

PAPERING ROUND OBSTACLES

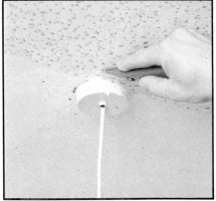

1 If there is a ceiling rose, use a knife or scissors to make a little slit in the paper so it fits round the rose; don't cut too deep.

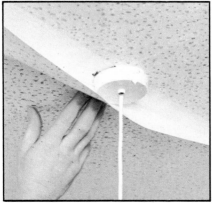

2 Hang the next length so it butts up against the previous one; at the rose take the paper over the top of the obstacle.

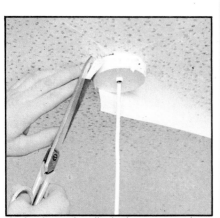

3 Again, make slits in the paper so it fits round the rose; this will allow you to brush the rest of the length of paper in place.

4 When the paper is in place, trim round the rose. Place the edge of a scraper between the knife and ceiling so there's a slight overlap.

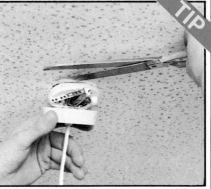

5 Turn off the power, remove the rose cover and press the overlap into place. When the cover is replaced it will conceal the cut edges completely.

6 Where the paper meets an alcove, make a slit in the paper in line with one corner of the alcove and then in line with the other.

7 You can then brush the paper into place in the normal fashion so it fits neatly into the gap between the two corners. Trim the overlap along the wall leading to the alcove.

8 Fix the next length so it butts up against the previous one. Adhesive may ooze out when seams are rolled; so long as the paper is colourfast you can remove it with a damp sponge.

9 Measure up and cut the last narrow piece, allowing for an overlap of about 25mm (1in) at the wall and ceiling junction. Paste and brush it into place; trim to complete the job.

HANGING FABRICS ON WALLS

Hessian and other fabric wallcoverings are ideal as a cover-up for less-than-perfect walls. They can give a softer, richer look to a room and provide an ideal backing for prints, pictures or other items on display.

There are many fabric wallcoverings available. Some are nubbly and tweedy; others have a delicate silky or moiré (watered silk) surface; some are like damask: woven figured material. There are wallcoverings with wool and linen strands stretched across a backing to give an overall effect of striped, half-woven cloth; fragile grasscloths (strands of natural grasses bound lightly into a mat on a paper backing); and other coverings with an Oriental effect such as raw silk and split bamboo. There are thick sound-deadening felts; wallcoverings with a leather look, including crushed and brushed velvety suedes; ones with cork slivers on a coloured, or foil, background (which glints through the cork 'skin') and last, but by no means least, ever-popular hessian which comes in a natural oatmeal colour, various dyed colours and also in a special 'sized' version intended for over-painting.

Most of these wallcoverings are paper-backed, which makes hanging easy and straightforward. Some, however, are not. Ordinary upholsterers' hessian, for example, which is only about one-third of the price of the paper-backed version, can be hung on walls; but a different hanging technique is required (see *Ready Reference*). A point to bear in mind, if you are considering hanging one of the more expensive speciality wallcoverings like silk, grasscloth or cork, is that while they come with a paper backing, which prevents stretching and wrinkling, you cannot afford to make any mistakes in measuring and cutting; also these types of wallcovering stain very easily if any paste gets onto the surface.

Real fabric of almost any type can also be hung to cover walls, so long as it is firmly woven, but usually it is not stuck into place; instead, one of two other fixing methods are used. With one method, a staple gun is used to staple the fabric to battens which are in turn stapled to the wall. With the other, special plastic fabric-fixing track is fixed to the wall and the fabric tucked into this. Either way, the fabric can be removed fairly easily for cleaning which is a delicate, but manageable operation.

Choosing and buying wallcoverings

While taste is obviously an individual matter and you will choose the type of wallcovering according to the look you want (and the amount you are prepared to pay), the different textures of the various fabric wall-coverings do tend to make them appropriate for use in particular settings. The silks, moirés and grasscloths tend to look better in a more traditional setting whereas corks, suedes, wool weaves and tweedy effects complement a modern décor and blend particularly well with exposed brickwork, timber cladding, slate and stone. Hessian usually looks right in both modern and traditional settings, is a perfect foil for pictures, prints or other exhibits and is frequently used on one specific wall area to back a prized collection.

Quite a few fabric wallcoverings have a 'random' match, which means you don't have to allow for pattern-matching when buying. However, where there is a very heavy texture or a definite striped effect running horizontally across the material, some pattern matching may be necessary if the results are not to be disappointing. Some speciality wallcoverings, like grasscloth, can have a rather untidy look when hung, but this is characteristic of the material and it is supposed to have a random-match effect. If you think this is likely to worry you, buy something a little less defined in texture.

When buying, try to see as large a sample as possible before making up your mind. If you can, see two rolls unwrapped and placed side by side and also try to see them arranged vertically as they'll be seen when hung. The more expensive wallcoverings must usually be ordered in advance from specialist decoration shops, and you may only be able to select from smallish samples. In which case, try to have an arrangement with the supplier so you can return the material for a credit if it does not match the sample to your satisfaction.

Check the width and length of roll before ordering; many fabric wallcoverings are imported and may not conform to standard sizes. So if you don't check you risk ordering too much or little.

Also remember to check carefully for colour variations between rolls. Colour differences will be only too apparent when the wallcovering is in place.

HANGING LINING PAPER

1 Measure and cut the paper, allowing for an overlap at both ends of the room. Paste the back, folding the paper into concertina folds.

2 Hang the first length horizontally across the wall. Then hang the second length so it butts against it, pulling the concertina folds out.

3 Use a wallpaper brush to smooth the paper into place and ensure an unwrinkled surface; if right-handed, you should work from right to left.

4 At the corners of the room, you will have to trim off the overlap. As a guide for the knife you can use the edge of a scraper to get a clean cut.

Preparing the surface

As with any wallcovering, the wall must be properly prepared first. This means old wallpaper should be stripped off and the wall washed clean of any old paste and size. Cracks, holes and indentations should be filled, any crumbling, or otherwise faulty plaster should be cut and filled, and the whole area should be smoothed down and then sized with a weak coat of size.

Newly-plastered surfaces must have dried out throughly; cracks should be filled, 'nibs' of plaster smoothed down and any efflorescence rubbed off with a cloth or brush. It is wise to apply a diluted coat of alkali-resisting primer, brushed well into the plaster.

Previously-painted surfaces should be washed down to remove grease and dirt and then rubbed down with glasspaper to provide a good 'key'; this is particularly important with a gloss-painted surface. Again, fill any cracks and holes and sand them down after filling.

Lining the wall

Before fixing a fabric wallcovering you should first line the wall with lining paper. The need for this is obvious with unbacked fabrics but it is equally important with other types of fabric wallcoverings since it will greatly improve the appearance of the finished result.

The lining paper should be hung horizontally (starting from the top of the wall) so there is no risk of the joins coinciding with those in the wallcovering. The edges of the paper should be butt-joined and surplus paper trimmed neatly into the corners of the room at each end. For the final length on a wall, you should trim the length roughly to size before pasting it and carry out final

Ready Reference

WALLCOVERING SIZES

Fabric wallcoverings are sometimes sold by the roll and sometimes by the metre. Sizes vary but typical widths are:
paper-backed hessian: 889mm (35in), 914mm (36in)
silk: 762mm (31in)
grasscloth: 914mm (36in)
tweed: 685mm (27in)
fine wool: 690mm (27in)
open-weave wool: 750mm (30in)
bouclé: 690mm (27in)
suede: 700mm (28in)
cork: 762mm (31in), 530mm (21in).

AVOID HEAVY-WEAR AREAS

Care and cleaning can be a problem with many fabric wallcoverings so they're best confined to areas where they won't get too much wear or be subject to grubby fingers or heating stains.

CROSS-LINE WALLS

Always cross-line the walls with lining paper first.
● if the wallcovering is very heavy, use a fairly thick lining paper
● for open-weave fabric, paint the paper first in the same colour as the fabric.

HANGING METHODS

The method of hanging depends on the type of wallcovering (check the manufacturer's instructions):
● paper-backed hessians and some other paper-backed fabrics can be hung like ordinary wallpaper. You paste the backing and, when hanging, work down from the top of the wall
● unbacked hessian and other speciality wallcoverings are hung by the paste-the-wall technique and, when hanging, you may in some cases have to work from the bottom of the wall up.
● to avoid shading, some wallcoverings should be 'reverse hung'. Each alternate length is reversed, as it is cut from the roll, and hung in the opposite direction from the previous length.

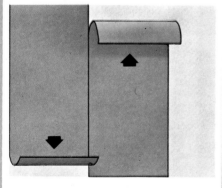

HANGING UNBACKED HESSIAN

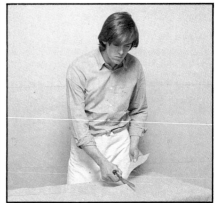

1 *Measure and cut the hessian to the required length, allowing about 100mm (4in) top and bottom. Cut enough for most of the room.*

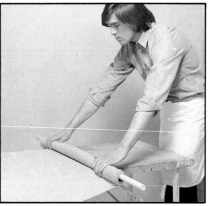

2 *Roll the first length round a stout tube or a strong stick (a piece of old broom handle is suitable) with the right side of the hessian facing in.*

3 *Using a plumbline as a guide, mark the wall vertically into strips which will be the width of the overlap narrower than the hessian width.*

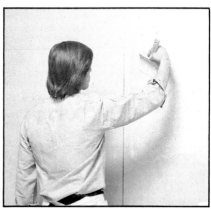

4 *Spread the adhesive on the wall with a brush, using feathered strokes, but don't apply it too thickly. Stop short of the drawn line on each side.*

5 *While the paste is still wet, start unrolling the hessian onto the wall from the roll you've made, using the lines on the wall as a guide.*

6 *To smooth the hessian into place and ensure it is securely fixed, run a clean paint roller over it when it is in place between the guidelines.*

7 *Hang the next length in the same way as you hung the first; make sure that you leave an overlap of at least 25mm (1in) between the lengths to allow enough material for trimming.*

8 *Hang hessian round the room. Before you carry out any trimming, leave the adhesive to dry to allow for shrinkage. Then trim to size at the top, bottom, and at joins.*

9 *At an internal corner, you will have to trim one length neatly into the corner, then fix the adjoining piece and trim the overlap to ensure you form a neat butt join.*

MAKING A NEAT BUTT JOIN

1 *Place a straight edge over the middle of the overlap between two lengths of hessian and then run a sharp knife through both lengths.*

2 *You can then peel off the surplus hessian; with the top waste piece removed you will be able to see and remove the piece underneath.*

3 *Paste the wall underneath the hessian on both sides of the join. Use a small brush and work carefully to ensure no adhesive gets on the front.*

4 *With a seam roller, gently run over the two edges to make a neat butt join. Make sure you don't press too hard or you risk a shiny surface.*

trimming above the skirting board when it has been brushed into place.

If you are hanging an open-weave fabric, such as furnishing hessian, it's worth painting the lining paper in the same colours as the hessian so it won't be conspicuous if it shows through the fabric.

Hanging wallcoverings
Depending on the type of wallcovering, you may be cutting and pasting several lengths or one length at a time. Or you may use the paste-the-wall technique.

If the material is to be reverse hung (see *Ready Reference*), mark the back of each length with an arrow to indicate which way each piece is to go.

If you are using paper-backed hessian, you can trim off the overlap at the top and bottom as you go along, but for an unbacked type you should leave the adhesive to dry to

allow for shrinkage before you start to trim.

Turn hessian well round external angles as you do not want a raw edge on an exposed wall area. On inside angles, cut the corner length material into two strips and butt-join them in the angle (use the overlap technique – see step-by-step photographs – if appropriate).

Looking after fabric wallcoverings
For fabric wallcoverings to look their best, they will have to be dusted every few months. Gently run the upholstery attachment of a vacuum cleaner over the wallcovering (alternatively, you can brush it down with a soft brush). If there are any stains on the fabric, use dry-cleaning fluid to remove them (after testing the fluid on an inconspicuous area like behind a picture – to make sure it doesn't cause discolouration). Loose seams should be pasted down again.

CERAMIC TILES for small areas

Ceramic tiles are easy-clean, hygienic and hard wearing. By starting with a small area in your home where these qualities are needed – like splashbacks or worktops – you'll not only grasp the basics but also gain confidence to tackle bigger things.

M odern ceramic tiles are thin slabs of clay, decorated on one side with coloured glazes. These are baked on to give the tile a hard, glassy surface resistant to water, heat and almost all household chemicals. The clay from which tiles are made, which is known as the biscuit, varies and you need to know the differences before you choose the tile to use. The thinnest ones with a pale coloured biscuit are good on all vertical surfaces (including doors where extra weight puts stress on the hinges).

If the biscuit is reddish/brown it has been high baked (vitrified). The thicker and darker coloured it is the more strength the tile has — floor tiles, for example, are usually big in size as well as thick in biscuit.

Work surfaces need tiles that are strong to withstand weights of heavy pots, while splashbacks and bathroom surfaces can take lighter, thinner ones.

Types of tiles

Within each range of tiles there are usually three types. *Spacer* tiles have small projections on each edge called lugs which butt up to the neighbouring tile and provide the correct space for grouting (with these it is very hard to vary the width of the grouting). *Border* tiles are squared off on all sides but are glazed on two adjacent edges — these give a neat finish to outer corners and top or side edges. *Universal or continental* tiles have no lugs and are square on all edges. All three can be used successfully in small areas, but do remember that if tiles do not have lugs you have to include grouting space in your calculations — the thinnest tiles need to be spaced by nothing more than torn-up pieces of cardboard, 6mm (¼in) tiles are best with a matchstick width in between.

Tiles are sold by the sq metre, sq yd, boxed in 25s or 50s, or can be bought individually. Boxed tiles usually advise on adhesive and grout needed for specific areas. When buying, if there's no written information available always check that the tile is suitable.

How to plan the layout

When tiling small areas you don't have much space to manoeuvre. The idea in all tiling is to create a symmetrical effect, using whole tiles or, if any have to be cut, making them equal.

Knowing about the different sizes of tiles helps in the planning. For example, if you know the width and height or depth of the surface you intend to tile, you can divide this by the known size of tiles until you find the one that gives the right number of whole tiles. Remember that the width of grouting has to be added to the measurement with non-lugged tiles – and except with the very thinnest tiles this can be slightly widened if it saves cutting a tile.

If you're prepared to incorporate cut tiles into the planning remember:
● on the width of the tiled area, place equal cut tiles at each end
● on the height, place cut tiles at the top edge
● on the depth (eg, window-recesses) put cut tiles at back edge
● frame a fitting by placing cut tiles at each side and the top

A mix of patterned or textured with plain tiles is best done first on metricated graph paper. This will help you see where you want the pattern to fall.

Fixings should be made in the grouting lines where possible. Some tile ranges have soap dishes, towel rails etc attached to tiles so they can be incorporated in a scheme, but if these don't suit your purposes, you can drill the tiles to screw in your own fitting (see page 53).

A working plan

All tiles should be fixed level and square so it's important to establish the horizontal and vertical with a spirit level. Draw in the lines with pencil. If you plan to tile where there is no support (eg, on either side of a basin or sink) lightly pin a length of 50 x 25mm (2 x 1in) timber below the tiling line – the batten will prevent the tiles slipping.

On doors you may have to consider adding a timber surround to keep the tiles secure as they will be subjected to movement (also see section on *Adhesives* below).

Adhesives and grouting

The choice of both of these depends on where the tiles are to be fixed. In a watery situation (eg, a shower cubicle or a steamy kitchen) it is important to use a waterproof variety of both, even though you might have

HOW TO HANG TILES

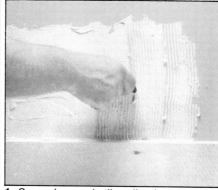

1 Spread ceramic tile adhesive to cover 1 sq metre, then 'comb' with notched spreader. To support tiles where no other support exists, pin a horizontal timber batten to the wall.

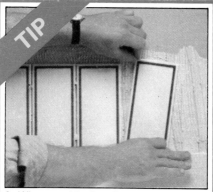

2 When positioning tiles it is important to twist them slightly to bed them. Don't slide them as this forces adhesive between joints.

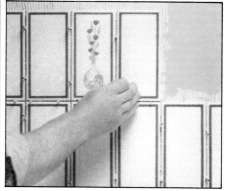

3 Form even grouting spaces between tiles without lugs with pieces of matchstick. Or you can use torn-up cardboard from the tile packaging or similar if you want only a narrow grouting space.

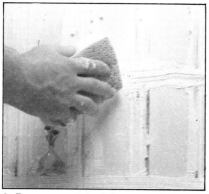

4 Remove matchsticks or card after all tiles are hung, and grout 12-24 hours later. Press grout into the spaces using a small sponge or squeegee, making sure no voids are left in either vertical or horizontal spaces.

5 After 10 minutes, wipe off excess grouting with soft cloth. Use fine dowelling (sand the end to round it) to even up and smooth the lines. Fill any voids that appear with fresh grout to prevent water penetration.

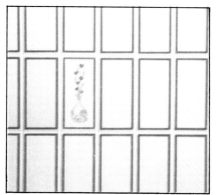

6 When grouting is dry, polish the tiles with a soft cloth so the area is smooth. All the surface needs now is an occasional wipe-down although non-waterproof grout may tend to discolour as time goes by.

Ready Reference

TILE SHAPES AND SIZES

Ceramic tiles for walls are usually square or oblong in shape. The commonest sizes are shown below. The smaller sizes are usually 4mm ($^5/_{32}$in) thick, while larger tiles may be 6mm ($^1/_4$in) or more in thickness.

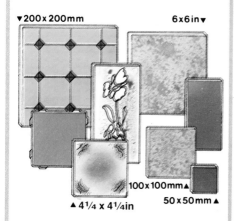

▼200 x 200mm   6 x 6 in ▼

100 x 100mm ▲   50 x 50mm ▲

▲ 4$^1/_4$ x 4$^1/_4$in

HOW MANY TILES?

Square or oblong areas
● measure lengths and width of the area
● divide each measurement by the size of tile you're using, rounding up to the next whole number if you get a fraction
● multiply the two figures to give the number of tiles needed

Awkwardly-shaped areas
● divide area into convenient squares or oblongs
● work out each one as above adding up the area totals to give the final figures

Patterns using two or more different tiles
● sketch out design on graph paper, one square for each tile (two for oblong tiles); use colours to mark where different tiles fall
● count up totals needed of each pattern, counting part tiles as whole ones

Add 10% to your final tile counts to allow for breakages

ADHESIVE/GROUT

For each square metre of tiling allow:
● 1.5kg (about 1 litre) of adhesive
● 150g of grout

TIP: AVOID NARROW STRIPS

Less than about 25mm/1in wide is very difficult to cut. When planning, if you see narrow strips are going to occur you can:
● replan the rows to use one less whole tile with two wider cut pieces at either end
● or increase the grouting space slightly between every tile in the row

to wait for 4-5 days before exposing the tile surface to use.

All ceramic tile adhesives are like thin putty and can be bought ready mixed in tubs or in powder form to be made up with water. They are what is known as thin-bed adhesives in that they are designed to be applied in a thin layer on a flat even surface. The spread is controlled by a notched comb (usually provided by the manufacturer but cheap to buy where you bought the tiles) to make furrows of a specified depth. When the tiles are pressed on with a slight twist, the adhesive evenly grips the back of the biscuit.

Special latex-based adhesives (usually, two-part products which have to be mixed before using) have much more flexibility and are good for tiles where there is any movement (eg, on doors).

Spread the adhesive on an area no more than 1 sq metre (1 sq yd) at a time, or it will lose its gripping power before you have time to place the tiles. If you remove a tile, before refixing comb the adhesive again.

Grout gives the final finish to the tiled area, filling the spaces between the tiles and preventing moisture getting behind them and affecting the adhesive. Grouting can be done 12-24 hours after the last tile has been pressed into place. Grout can be standard or waterproof (with added acrylic), and both are like a cellulose filler when made up.

If you only make up one lot of grouting, you can colour it with special grouting tints – but remember that it's hard to make other batches match the colour. Waterproof grouting cannot always take these tints.

Press grout between the tiles with a sponge or squeegee and wipe off excess with a damp sponge. Even up the grouting by drawing a pencil-like piece of wood (eg dowelling) along each row first vertically, then horizontally. Do this within 10 minutes of grouting so it is not completely dry.

Leave the tiles for 24 hours before polishing with a clean dry cloth. Wash clean only if a slight bloom remains.

Tiles should never be fixed with tight joints for any movement of the wall or fittings will cause the tiles to crack. Similarly where tiles meet baths, basins, sinks etc, flexibility is needed – and grout that dries rigid cannot provide it. These gaps must be filled with a silicone rubber sealant

Techniques with tiles

To cut tiles, lightly score the glaze with a tile cutter to break the surface. Place the tile glazed side up with the scored line over matchsticks and firmly but gently press the tile down on each side. If using a pencil press on one side, hold the other. Smooth the cut edge with a file. Very small adjustments are best done by filing the edge of the whole tile.

CUTTING TILES

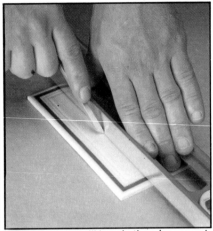

1 Before a tile will break, the glaze must be scored — on the edges as well as surface. Use a carbide-tipped cutter against a straight-edge.

2 Another type of cutter has 'jaws' which clasp the tile during breaking. (It also has a small 'wheel' for scoring through the glaze on the tile).

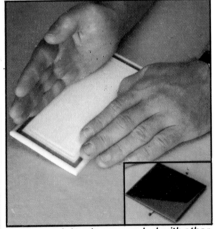

3 No special tools are needed with other tile-breaking methods. For medium thick tiles use a pencil, for thin tiles use matchsticks.

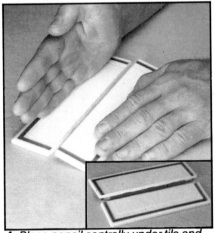

4 Place pencil centrally under tile and score line, hold one side and press firmly on other. With thin tiles, press lightly both sides.

To remove a narrow strip of tile, score the line heavily by drawing the tile cutter across the tile more firmly several times in the same place. Then use pincers to 'nibble' the waste away in small pieces and smooth the edge. Glaze on broken tiles is as sharp as glass, so be careful not to cut yourself.

Templates for awkwardly shaped tiles are not difficult to make. Cut the shape in card, place on a tile and score a line freehand with the tile cutter. Any straight score marks can be deepened afterwards, using a straight edge for support. Then nibble away the waste with pincers. If there's a large amount to be cut away, score the waste part to divide it into sections, then nibble away. A good tip is to do this on a soft or padded surface so the tile doesn't break in the wrong place.

Suitable surfaces

The ideal surface for tiling is one that's perfectly flat, dry and firm. Small irregularities will be covered up, but any major hollows, bumps or flaking, need to be made good.

Plastered walls and asbestos cement sheets: perfect for tiling, but wait a month after any new plastering to allow the wall to dry out completely. Unless surface has been previously painted, apply a coat of plaster primer to prevent the liquid in the tile adhesive from being absorbed too quickly.

Plasterboard: again, ideal for tiling as long as it's firmly fixed and adjacent boards cannot shift. (If they did the joins would probably crack). To prepare the surface, remove all dust, wipe down with white spirit

SHAPING TILES

5 Edges of broken tiles need to be smoothed off — use a special tile file mounted on wood, a wood file or rub against rough concrete.

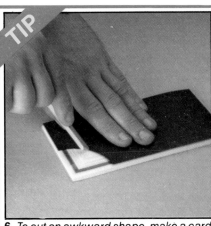

6 To cut an awkward shape, make a card template. Place it on the tile and score glaze on the surface and edges with the tile cutter.

7 On a soft surface, use pincers to take tiny nibbles out of the tile. If you're over enthusiastic you'll break off more than you intended.

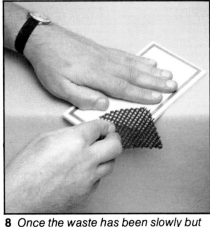

8 Once the waste has been slowly but surely nibbled away, smooth up the edge. Files are also useful when a whole tile needs a slight trimming.

Ready Reference

TOOLS FOR TILING

Tile cutter: essential for scoring glaze of tiles before breaking them. Score only once (the second time you may waver from the line and cause an uneven break).
Pincers: these are used for nibbling away small portions of tile, after scoring a line with the cutter. Ordinary pincers are fine for most jobs, but special tile nibblers are available.
Special cutter: combines a cutting edge (usually a small cutting wheel) with jaws which snap the tile along the scored line.
Tile file: an abrasive mesh, used as a file to 'shave' off small amounts.

TIP: TO DRILL A TILE

● make a cross of masking tape and mark the point where you want the hole
● drill after adhesive and grouting have set using lowest speed or a hand drill with masonry bit — too much speed at the start will craze the tile
● once through the glaze, drill in the normal way

● cut tile into two along line corresponding with centre point of pipe; offer up each half to the pipe
● mark freehand semi-circles on tile to match edge of pipe; score line with tile cutter and nibble away waste with pincers

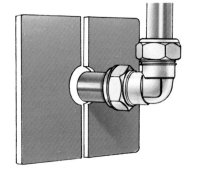

to remove grease, then treat with primer.
Paint: old emulsion-paint needs to be cleaned thoroughly with sugar soap or detergent to remove all traces of dust and grease. Gloss paint needs to be cleaned thoroughly; remove any flaking paint then roughen up whole surface with a coarse abrasive to provide a good key for the adhesive.
Wallpaper: DO NOT tile directly onto wallpaper, as this can be pulled away from the wall by the adhesive. Strip it off completely.
Wood and Chipboard: perfect for tiling as long as it is flat and adjacent boards cannot shift. Treat with an ordinary wood primer.
Laminates: joins and small, minor blemishes in the surface can be covered up so long as the entire sheet is soundly fixed and absolutely flat. Its smooth face must be roughened with course abrasive to provide a key for the tile adhesive.
Old ceramic tiles: the thin biscuit ceramic tiles are excellent for tiling over as they add little to the wall's thickness and won't protrude beyond existing fittings. Loose and cracked tiles will have to be removed. Scrape out the grouting surrounding the tile using an old, thin screwdriver or something similar, then, beginning in the centre and working outwards, remove the tile using a club hammer and cold chisel.

Small sections or mis-shapen pieces (as around a new fixture) can be built up level with neighbouring tiles with cellulose filler.

The area should then be sealed with plaster primer or emulsion paint to finish the surface.

CERAMIC WALL AND FLOOR TILES

Ceramic tiles are available in what seems like almost endless variety. To make the right choice it's important to know about the different types of tiles and the uses to which they're suited.

Ceramic tiles are not by any means a modern invention; baked and decorated clay tiles have been found in the remains of ancient civilisations going back as much as 5000 years. But whereas these early tiles were hand-made and of irregular shape and thickness, modern technology has given us perfectly-matched tiles by the million.

Ceramic tiles are mostly used on walls to provide a tough, maintenance-free and long-lasting surface finish. Cool to the touch (a boon in summer, but likely to cause condensation in winter), ceramic tiles are waterproof and stain-resistant, and can cope with reasonable extremes of temperature. As a result they are widely used in bathrooms and kitchens.

Floor tiles, on the other hand, are often used in other areas of the house. Virtually any floor in the house, and even the patio outside, can be tiled provided it is strong enough to support the weight of the tiles. Like wall tiles, they require very little maintenance apart from occasional washing, but they are much tougher and will withstand endless wear without showing signs of deterioration.

What is a tile?
The first stage in making ceramic tiles involves mixing together china clay and ball clay, sand, limestone, water (and sometimes recycled broken tiles) into a runny mixture called a 'slip'. The water is then filtered and pressed out to leave a powder which is dried at over 500°C and can then be stored until required.

This powder is eventually compressed into tile shapes under great pressure. A drier removes any moisture and then a high temperature kiln is used to bake or fire the tiles for up to 30 hours at temperatures approaching 1150°C, fusing all the particles into what is known as a 'biscuit'.

The next step is the application of the surface 'glaze' (not applied to unglazed 'quarry' floor tiles). A variety of minerals is mixed together dry and is then heated to form a substance which looks like molten glass, called 'frit'. At a later stage, china clay is added with even more ingredients. Dry colours are mixed too, if needed; these are also melted, then added to the frit, ready for application to the tiles.

For a plain colour, the biscuits pass twice through a liquid curtain of glaze. Textured and embossed effects are produced by spraying on the glaze, and designs are usually applied by a silk screen printing process. Finally the tiles are again fired at high temperatures to harden the glaze.

Shapes and sizes
Square tiles are the commonest, but many other shapes are available. Rectangular tiles can be used to achieve attractive effects, as can hexagonal or octagonal ones or interlocking Provençale shapes. Mosaics are available in a similar range of shapes.

Apart from the very small individual tiles which make up a sheet of mosaics, the smallest tiles available are 108mm (4¼in) square; these are generally for wall use. The sizes range up to 300mm (12in) square ones used on floors. In between you may find 152mm (6in) squares, 108x216mm (4¼x8½in) rectangles, 200mm (8in) and 250mm (10in) squares. Thicknesses vary from 4mm (just over ⅛in) for the smaller wall tiles to 6mm (¼in) for larger ones and up to 9.5mm (⅜in) for floor tiles.

Tile types
Ceramic tiles can also be categorised by the kind of job they do in the overall tiling scheme. Some tiles are glazed only on their faces; they are called fieldrun tiles, and have their edges concealed when fixed. Many tiles have lugs built into the unglazed edges for keeping the tiles correctly spaced apart, and these are known as **spacer** tiles.

When tiling round window reveals, external edges or when finishing halfway up a wall, you need tiles with one or two glazed edges, and these are known as **edge** tiles or **border** tiles. REX (one rounded glazed edge) tiles used to be commonly available for this purpose but have now been superseded by the **universal** tile, which (usually) has all four edges glazed and serves as both a field and edge tile. This means you can use just one type of tile, avoiding having to work out how many edge or double edge tiles will be needed. However, the terminology can vary among manufacturers; with at least one brand, a 'universal' tile is one which is glazed on two adjacent edges and has spacer lugs on the other two, unglazed, edges.

Colours and patterns
Ceramic tiles are available in a wide range of colours and patterns and with smooth or textured surfaces. Many tile ranges now include both plain and patterned tiles in matching colours so that a surface can be tiled using a mixture. The patterned tiles can be placed in blocks surrounded by plain ones; they can act as a border, or they can be randomly positioned.

Not all tiles have a complete pattern on each tile. Many are intended to be placed in squares or strips, with individual tiles making up part of a larger design. Tile shapes can, in addition, be mixed to form a pattern: for example, a square tile of one colour can be surrounded by four octagonal tiles of another colour.

tiles from Tile with Style, Tile Mart, Langley, Elon

KEY

Above: Some of the many types of decorative ceramic tiles now available:

1-6: *These square tiles (150 x 150mm/6 x 6in) are suitable for wall use only. Tiles 1 and 2 are part of a set.*

7-10: *Oblong wall tiles which have discrete designs but are part of matching sets; eg, plain ones in a set can be interspersed with matching patterned tiles.*

11-12: *Sets of wall tiles, which when placed together, building up into a pattern.*

13: *Plain square (100 x 100mm/ 4 x 4in) wall tiles.*

14-16: *Oblong plain tiles, this time of flooring quality.*

17: *Quarry-type tile with a matt finish suitable for flooring. Tiles of this type will also provide a hardwearing surface outdoors.*

18-19: *Patterned tiles which can be used for either walls or floors.*

20-22: *Hand-painted wall and floor tiles.*

23-28: *Various types of mosaics which can be used on walls and also on work surfaces.*

29: *Provençale tile suitable for wall or floor use.*

30-34: *Hexagonal floor tiles.*

35: *Square 200 x 200mm (8 x 8in) floor-quality tile.*

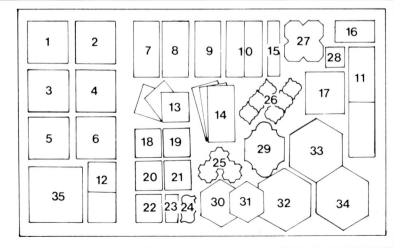

CERAMIC TILING WALL TO WALL

Ceramic tiles are an ideal decorating material for they make a room look good for years and require virtually no maintenance. But covering several walls with tiles is a large-scale job which needs a methodical and careful approach if you are to achieve the best results.

Jem Grischotti   Tiles: Rustica Roberta pattern   Flooring: GAF terra cotta cushion vinyl Coburg

The all-in-one look that wall-to-wall tiling can give has to be planned carefully to avoid expensive and time consuming mistakes. How to do this may depend on whether you want to include special patterns in the design, but following certain rules will give a desirable symmetry to the look.

One of the hardest tasks will probably be choosing the tiles for there's a vast array of shapes, sizes and colours available. Having picked out the ones you want though, don't buy until you've done the planning – for the plans of each wall should tell you whether the pattern will work in the room or would be lost in the cutting or amid the fittings.

Plans on paper also give you an instant method of working out how many tiles to buy (counting each cut one as a whole, and adding 2-5% for unintended breakage) including the number which will need to be border (two glazed edges) or mitred (on square or rectangular universal tiles) for the top row of half-tiled walls or external corners. Buy all the tiles at once, but do check each carton to make sure there's no variation in the colour (this can occur during the firing of different batches).

Planning on paper

The best possible way to start planning for a large expanse of tiling is not on the wall, but on paper. Graph paper is ideal, particularly if you intend including a mix of plain and patterned tiles, or a large motif that needs building up. Of course, advance planning is also essential if you're tiling round major features like windows, doors, mirrors, shower cubicles and so on.

You need separate pieces of graph paper for each wall you intend tiling. Allow the large (1cm) squares on the paper to represent your tiles — one for a square tile of any size, two for a rectangular tile; this will give you a scale to work to. Now mark up sheets of greaseproof paper with your actual wall sizes using the scale dictated by the tile size on the graph paper. Measure and outline on the see-through paper the exact position and in-scale dimensions of all fixtures and fittings (see the planning pictures).

At this stage, the objective is to decide how to achieve the best symmetrical layout for your tiles — the 'ideal' is to have either whole or equal-size cut tiles on each side of a fixture.

First you have to mark in the central guide lines. For instance, on *walls with a window* draw a line from the sill centre to the floor, and from the centre of the top of the window to the ceiling. If there are *two windows* also draw in the central line from floor to ceiling between them. Mark the centre point above a *door* to the ceiling and also indicate the horizontal line at the top of the door. In the same way draw in a central line from the top of a *basin or vanity unit* to the ceiling.

For all these lines use a coloured pen for you have to be aware of them when deciding where whole tiles should be positioned. But they're only the starting point — other potential problems have to be looked at too.

Place the see-through paper over the tile sizes on the graph paper so you can see how the tiles will fall in relation to the guide lines. Now take into account the following important points:
● The first row above the lowest level — either the floor, the skirting board or a wall-to-wall fitting — should be whole tiles. If necessary, change this to prevent a thin strip being cut at the ceiling.
● Check where tiles come in relation to fittings. If very thin strips (less than 38mm/ 1½in) or narrow 'L' shapes would need to be cut, move the top sheet slightly up, down, left or right till the tiles are of a cuttable size — areas to watch are around windows, doors and where one wall meets another.

Placing patterns

When you are satisfied that you have a symmetrical and workable arrangement you can tape the top sheet in the right position on the graph paper, then start to plan where you're going to position your patterned tiles. Use pencil this time in case you change your mind and want to make adjustments. These are the points to watch:
● Don't place single motif patterns at internal corners where they would have to be cut — you won't find it easy to match up the remaining piece on the adjacent wall.

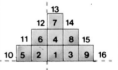
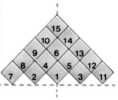

● If the pattern builds up vertically and horizontally over four or more tiles, 'centre' the pattern on the wall so that cuts are equal at both ends. If pattern loss can't be avoided with designs of this type at least it can be kept to internal corners.

● Whole tiles should be used on both faces of external corners.

Now butt each of the wall plans up to the other to make sure that the patterns relate both vertically and horizontally.

Planning on the wall

When there are no complicated tiling patterns involved and walls are free of interruptions such as windows, it's often easier to do the planning directly on the wall itself. Here, the simple objective is to place the tiles symmetrically between the corners. And to do this, all you need is a tiling gauge which you can make.

A tiling gauge is like a long ruler, except that it's marked off in tile widths. Use a long, straight piece of timber ideally about 25mm square (1in square) and remember to include the grouting gap between tiles as you rule off the gauge. If you're using rectangular tiles, mark the widths on one side, the lengths on the other.

Holding the gauge against the walls —

first vertically, then horizontally — tells you instantly where the whole tiles will fit in and where cut tiles will be needed. But first you must find the centre of each wall. Measure the width — doing this at three places will also tell you if the corners are vertical (hang a plumb line or use a spirit level to make absolutely sure) — and halve it to find the centre point. Use the tiling gauge to mark this vertical centre line with a pencil, then hold the gauge against it. Move it up or down until you have at least a whole tile's width above the floor or skirting board — this can be adjusted slightly if it avoids a thin piece of tile at ceiling height — then mark off the tile widths on the vertical line itself.

Now hold the tiling gauge horizontally, and move it to left or right of the vertical line if thin pieces of tile would have to be cut near windows, or fittings, or to make cut tiles at both ends of the wall equal. Following this adjustment, mark the wall and draw in a new vertical line if necessary. The wall can now be marked horizontally with tile widths. Keeping to the same horizontal, mark up adjacent walls in the same way.

At corners, whether internal or external, don't assume they're either square, vertical or even. An internal corner is the worst place to start your tiling for this very reason, but it

doesn't matter if you position cut tiles there. On external corners use the tiling gauge to work inwards in whole tile widths.

You can also use the tiling gauge to check that your graph plan is accurate, and make any necessary adjustments.

Putting up battens

Once you have determined that your plan is correct, fix a length of perfectly straight 50mm x 25mm (2in x 1in) battening across the full width of the wall — use a spirit level to ensure that the batten is horizontal. Use masonry nails to fix it in place but do not drive them fully home as they will have to be removed later. If using screws the wall should be plugged. The batten provides the base for your tiling and it's important that its position is correct.

If more than one wall is being tiled, continue to fix battens around the room at the same height, using the spirit level to check the horizontal. The last one you fix should tie up perfectly with the first. If there are gaps, at the door for example, check that the level either side is the same, by using a straight-edge and spirit level to bridge the gap.

Once the horizontal battens are fixed, fix a vertical batten to give yourself the starting point for the first tile. Use a spirit level or plumb line to make sure it's positioned accurately.

Fixing tiles

Begin tiling from the horizontal base upwards, checking as you work that the tiles are going up accurately both vertically and horizontally. Work on an area of approximately 1 sq metre (1 sq yd) at a time, spreading the adhesive and fixing all the whole tiles using card or matchsticks as spacers as necessary. Make sure no excess adhesive is left on the surface of the tiles.

Next, deal with any tiles that need to be cut. You may find the gap into which they fit is too narrow to operate the adhesive spreader properly. In this case spread the adhesive onto the back of the tiles.

When all the tiling above the base batten has been completed wait for 8-12 hours, before removing the battens, and completing the tiling. Take care when removing the base batten that the tiles above are not disturbed — the adhesive is unlikely to be fully set.

Dealing with corners

Your original planning should have indicated how many border or mitred tiles you will need for tiling external corners or for the top line of tiles on a half-tiled wall. You will find external corners, those which project into the room, in virtually all tiling situations — around boxed-in pipework, or around a window or door reveal, or in an L-shaped room.

Where you are using universal tiles at an

PLANNING TILE LAYOUT ON PAPER

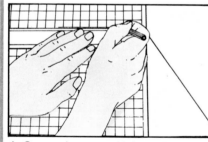

1 *On graph paper with large (eg, 1cm) squares, let each square represent one whole square tile. Strengthen the grid lines with coloured pen if necessary.*

2 *On tracing paper, draw the outline of each wall to be tiled, and mark in doors and windows. Use the scale 1cm = the actual tile size (eg, 150mm).*

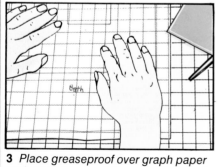

3 *Place greaseproof over graph paper and move it around till you get the most manageable size cut tiles, especially near fixtures, ceiling and floor.*

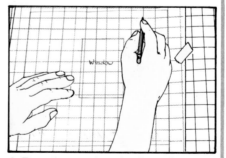

4 *Tape the top sheet in place, then mark the pattern in with pencil. Do each wall the same so that the alignment of the horizontal is correct.*

Jem Grischotti

Ready Reference

TACKLING TILING PROBLEMS

Whenever a fitting, a door or window interrupts the clean run of a wall, it becomes the focal point of the wall. So you have to plan for symmetry *round* the features. Here are some guidelines:

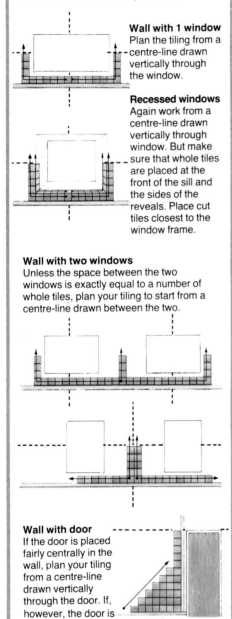

Wall with 1 window
Plan the tiling from a centre-line drawn vertically through the window.

Recessed windows
Again work from a centre-line drawn vertically through window. But make sure that whole tiles are placed at the front of the sill and the sides of the reveals. Place cut tiles closest to the window frame.

Wall with two windows
Unless the space between the two windows is exactly equal to a number of whole tiles, plan your tiling to start from a centre-line drawn between the two.

Wall with door
If the door is placed fairly centrally in the wall, plan your tiling from a centre-line drawn vertically through the door. If, however, the door is very close to a side wall, the large expanse of wall is a more prominent focal point. So plan the tiling to start one tile's width from the frame. If the frame is not exactly vertical, you'll be able to cut tiles to fit in the remaining space.

external corner, start at the corner with a whole tile — it should project by the depth of the mitre so that the mitre on the other face neatly butts up against it with a fine space for grouting in between.

With window reveals the correct method is to tile up the wall to sill level, cutting tiles if necessary. Fit whole tiles either side of the reveal, then again cut tiles to fill the space between those whole ones and the window frame. Attach whole border or mitred tiles to the sill so they butt up against the wall tiles. If using square-edged tiles the ones on the sill should cover the edges of those on the wall so the grouting line is not on the sill surface. If the sill is narrower than a whole tile, cut the excess from the back — not the front. If the sill is deeper than a whole tile, put cut tiles near the window with the cut edge against the frame. Continually check the accurate lining up of tiles with a spirit level.

Some vertical external corners are not as precisely straight and vertical as they should be and this can lead to problems of tile alignment. The use of a thick-bed adhesive will help to straighten out some irregularities where a corner goes inwards (a thin-bed helps where the wall leans outwards). Buying a 'flexible' adhesive will give you both qualities. As a general rule it is

PLANNING ON THE WALL

2 Use a plumb line to check that the wall is vertical.

1 *(inset)* Mark the tiling gauge in tile widths (and lengths if they are rectangular).

3 Draw verticals down the wall, marking off the exact tile widths to give an accurate guide.

4 Check each horizontal with a spirit level, then mark tile positions from floor to ceiling.

5 Place horizontal batten at least a tile's width above floor or a fitting using masonry nails or screws.

6 Fix vertical batten and begin to tile where the battens meet. Spread adhesive to cover 1 sq metre (1 sq yd).

Jem Grischotti

MAKE YOUR OWN TILE BREAKER

1 *Use a timber offcut wider than the tile as the base. Use 3mm (1/8in) ply for the top and sides.*

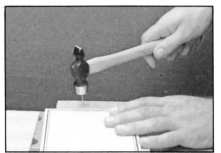

2 *Stack ply strips on both sides till the same height as the tile, then pin. Nail on the top piece.*

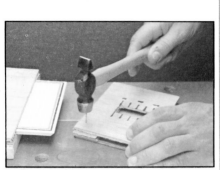

3 *The breaking part needs to be as wide and deep as the tile, with the opening on the top a half tile long.*

4 *Score the glaze on the top and edges with a carbide-tipped cutter. Put the tile into the main part.*

5 *Slip on the breaking part so the score line is between the two. Hold one side while you press the other.*

6 *The tile breaks cleanly. This aid costs nothing and will save you time when tiling a large expanse.*

TILING CORNERS

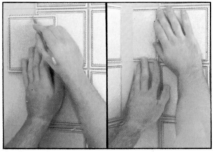

1 *At an internal corner, mark amount to be cut at top and bottom. Break the tile, then fit in position.*

2 *File the remainder until it fits the adjacent area with enough space left for a fine line of grout.*

3 *On a window sill, use a whole tile at the front and make sure that it overlaps the one on the wall-face underneath.*

4 *Mitred edges of universal tiles and glazed edges of border tiles give a better finish to external corners.*

better to concentrate on lining up your border or mitred tiles perfectly vertically with only minute 'steps' between tiles, then bedding spacer or ordinary tiles behind to correspond with the line. Don't forget that if you do have to create a very slight stepped effect, you can reduce the uneven effect between the corner tiles and others by pressing in extra grouting later.

Internal corners seldom cause serious problems as cut tiles can be shaped to suit fluctuations from the truly vertical. Don't assume when cutting tiles for a corner that all will be the same size — the chances are that they will vary considerably and should be measured and cut individually. Another point: don't butt tiles up against each other so they touch — leave space for the grouting which will give the necessary flexibility should there be any wall movement.

Tiling around electrical fittings

When tiling around electrical fittings it is better to disconnect the electricity and remove the wall plate completely so that you can tile right up to the edge of the wall box. This is much neater and easier than trying to cut tiles to fit around the perimeter of the plate. Cut tiles as described in the illustrations on page 52 and 53 and fit them in the normal way with the plate being replaced on top, completely covering the cut edges of the tiles. This same

Ready Reference

CHECK FREQUENTLY

- the vertical (with a plumb line)
- the horizontal (with spirit level)
- that tiles don't project beyond each other

TIP: MAKING TEMPLATES

Cut the card tile-size then make diagonal snips into the edge to be shaped. These pieces will be forced out of the way and an accurate cutting line can be drawn.

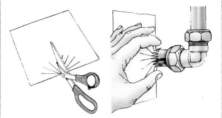

ADHESIVE AND GROUT

You need 1 litre of adhesive and 0.25kg of grout per sq metre (a little less for 1 sq yd), but for large areas buy in bulk: adhesive comes in 2½, 5 and 10 litre buckets; grout in 1.5 and 3.5kg packs.

WHEN GROUTING

- don't press mixture in with your fingers (it can abrade and irritate your skin)
- do wear light flexible gloves
- don't leave excess on tiles till dry
- do grout or caulk between tiles and window or door frames
- don't forget to grout edges of universal tiles if run finishes halfway up the wall
- use an old toothbrush to get grout into awkward places

TIP: GROUTING WALLS

On a large expanse, it's less tiring to use a rubber float to push grout between tiles – work upwards, then across; remove excess diagonally.

TILING SHOWERS

- use water resistant or waterproof adhesive and grout
- tile at least 1 row above shower head
- on ceiling use large drawing or upholstery pins to hold tiles till adhesive dries
- do floor and ceiling before walls
- don't expose tiles to water for 1 week

principle applies to anything easily removable. The fewer objects you have to tile around the better, so before starting any tiling get to work with a screwdriver.

You have the greatest control over the end result if at the planning stage you work out where you want to place fittings such as towel rails and soap dishes, shelves and the like. Some tile ranges offer them attached so it's only a matter of fitting them in as you put the tiles up.

Tiling non-rigid surfaces

On surfaces which are not totally rigid or which are subject to movement, vibration or the odd shock, tiles should not be attached using adhesive which dries hard as most standard and waterproof types do. Instead use adhesives which retain some flexibility. These may be cement-based types with a latex rubber content, or acrylic adhesives. You may have to surround a non-rigid surface with wooden lipping to protect the tiles.

TILING AROUND FIXTURES

1 At awkward corners use card to make a tile-size template. Place it on the tile and score the shape, then gently nibble out the waste with pincers — the smaller the bits the better.

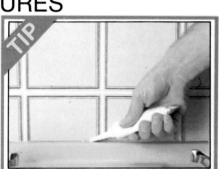

2 Where basins, baths, kitchen sinks or laundry tubs meet tiles, seal the join with silicone caulking to keep out water. Caulking comes in various colours to match fixtures.

3 After the adhesive has had time to set, the tiles are grouted both to protect them and to enhance their shape and colour.
Accessories can be bought already attached to tiles, can be screw mounted after drilling the tile, or if lightweight can be stuck on to tiles with adhesive pads.

PUTTING UP MIRROR TILES

Mirrors can create an illusion of extra space, and lining an alcove or even an entire wall can transform the look of a room. They are also very easy to install.

Mirrors have an obvious practical function but as well as this they can be used for purely decorative purposes. A wall lined with mirrors can bring a special magic to a room, making it lighter and more airy. Besides this, it creates an illusion of extra space, so that while you well know there's a wall there you feel there's something beyond. Mirrors add a touch of glamour and, quite apart from the inbuilt fascination they seem to inspire, the surface is as interesting and mobile as the scene it reflects. You can use them to decorate smaller areas as well, for example behind a set of shelves to set off a display area.

The problem with ordinary mirrors is that they are expensive and larger ones can be awkward to hang. For a large area like a wall you may decide to opt instead for mirror tiles, small mirrors which, when stuck down side by side, combine to produce a larger mirror, in fact as large a mirror as you like. They will not give the same quality image as sheet glass mirrors as the reflection will be broken up into squares, but they can perform the same decorative functions. As well as using them to line a wall or alcove you can use them to give an added dimension to other surfaces, too, such as cupboard doors, room doors, not to mention ceilings. Mirror tiles are extremely durable and also easy to look after. Though not as expensive as sheet glass mirrors, they are something of a luxury, generally costing a little more than good-quality ceramic tiles. But properly applied, they will last for years and when you bear in mind what they can do for your home, can represent real value for money.

What's available?

Although you may come across mirror tiles carrying applied designs of one sort or another, the majority are left plain, and considering how long the tiles are likely to be around, it's probably best that way; you can get awfully tired of patterned tiles after a few years. If you do want something that bit special, consider using bronzed or smoked glass tiles, rather than the normal silvered variety. They cost a little more and aren't as widely available and you'll have less choice when it comes to size, but they are very use-

ful if you want to create a slightly subdued atmosphere, or if you feel that ordinary mirrors would make the room too 'bright' for comfort.

The other choice you will have to make concerns size. Most suppliers can offer tiles 108, 150, 225 and 300mm (4¼, 6, 9 and 12in) square, with perhaps the addition of oblong tiles 300 x 150mm (12 x 6in). However, if you are prepared to order the tiles specially, larger sizes are available: up to 610mm (24in) in oblongs. Shaped tiles, mainly circles, semicircles and quadrants, are also available but you will really have to hunt round for them. You are more likely to find them part of a big mirror from mirror tiles' kit, they are rarely sold on their own.

Sheet glass mirrors are available smoked or otherwise coloured, or with patterns etched on them, and come in a very wide variety of sizes and shapes.

Working out quantities

With sheet glass mirrors, you will have to measure up the surface to be covered and then buy a mirror, or mirrors, of an appropriate size. With tiles, the simplest way to work out how many you will need is to measure the length and height of the surface to be covered, divide each dimension by the length or height of the tiles (whichever is appropriate) then, having rounded the results up to the nearest whole number, multiply them to-

PREPARING THE WALL

1 Line an uneven wall with plywood or hardboard before fixing the tiles. Mark lines at 300mm (1ft) intervals as a guide to fixing the battens.

2 Drill each end of the battens and use a bradawl to mark the fixing holes on the wall. Number the battens so they go back in the right order.

3 Drill and plug all the holes and screw the battens to the wall. Don't screw them down tightly at this stage as they may need adjusting.

4 Using a long straightedge, check in several places to see if the battens are flat. Mark which ones are too low and which are too high.

5 Use scraps of timber as shims to pack out battens that are too low, and plane down any battens that are proud. Then tighten up all the fixing screws.

6 Cut the sheets of plywood to fit and screw them in place. You must then seal the wood with a coat of primer and two coats of gloss paint.

gether to obtain an estimate of the total number of tiles.

A more accurate method, and considering the cost of mirror tiles the more accurate you can be the better, is to make a scale drawing of the wall or whatever else is to be tiled on graph paper; then you can work out the setting of the tiles and draw in the position of each individual tile. You can then count the tiles up, counting each tile as a whole tile. Finally, add on a few extra to allow for any mistakes or accidents which may occur when you're installing them.

Preparing the surface

Mirror tiles should be fixed to a flat, even surface. Use a string line stretched horizontally, vertically and diagonally at intervals across the wall to check that the surface is flat. If the wall is substantially uneven you should line it with hardboard or thin plywood

fixed to battens (see step-by-step photographs). Choose an exterior-grade board for use in kitchens, bathrooms and anywhere else likely to suffer from high humidity.

Ensure that the wall is absolutely free from damp. Make any necessary repairs and allow the structure to dry out before you go any further, bearing in mind that a very damp wall can take anything from six months to a year to dry out completely. New walls, or walls which have been recently replastered, should also be allowed to dry out; again this can take many months. Dampness in a wall can cause the mirror's silvering to deteriorate alarmingly quickly.

If you decide to use the wall's existing surface, strip off any wallcovering and make any predecoration repairs necessary to plasterwork, taking extra care to sand filler down flush with its surroundings. Self-adhesive mirror tiles must be fixed to a non-

porous surface so all surfaces such as plaster, emulsion paint, plywood, chipboard, etc must be well sealed with gloss paint (see *Ready Reference*). Then (when the paint is dry) wash the wall down to leave it spotlessly clean and ready for tiling.

To complete the preparation, make sure that the wall is resonably warm. If the room has been unused for some time, turn up the heating for a few days before tiling to take off the chill. If the wall is simply naturally cold, as it will be if it is an external solid wall, for example, warm it up by providing a little insulation behind a plywood or hardboard cladding or else line the wall with special insulated plasterboard.

Installation

There are several methods you can use to secure sheet glass mirrors to a wall or other surface. You can fit them in frames and hang

FIXING WHOLE TILES

1 Using a long straight batten and a spirit level, draw a horizontal line halfway up the wall and a vertical line halfway along it.

2 Use a tiling gauge to measure along the wall to see where the cut tiles will fall. In this case the cut tiles are too small so the guidelines are adjusted.

3 Draw new guidelines to give a symmetrical border of larger cut tiles. Then temporarily pin a batten along one of the lines.

4 Peel the protective backing off the first tile. You begin tiling in the centre, with the tile nestled in the angle between the batten and the other guideline.

5 Rest one edge of the tile against the batten, making sure its bottom edge is on the guideline. Then carefully 'hinge' it into place. Accuracy is important as the adhesive sticks very quickly.

6 To ensure a firm and long-lasting fixing, use a soft cloth and press firmly over the area of each adhesive pad. Continue fixing all the whole tiles in this way.

Ready Reference

TIP: SEAL THE WALLS
Mirror tiles must be fixed to a non-porous surface so you should seal surfaces with gloss paint first. For this:
● apply two or more coats of paint and leave it for 72 hours to dry (if you've lined the wall with hardboard or plywood give this a light sanding before you apply the primer and paint)
● don't use water-based vinyl gloss paint or you may get a reaction between the vinyl and the tiles' adhesive pads which will substantially weaken the fixing.

UNEVEN WALLS
For a wall where there is a lot of irregularity you should line the wall to even it out. Minor irregularities and undulations can, however, be accommodated by increasing the thickness of the tiles' adhesive pads. Spare pads are supplied for this purpose and you simply stick these in place on top of the pads supplied with the tiles.

PLACING TILES
Mirror tiles must be positioned accurately first time. If you have to peel a tile off the wall and try again, you'll find that when you try to re-fix it, the adhesive tabs will have lost most, if not all of their grip.

TIP: USE A SPACER
The tiles are fixed side by side but you should aim to avoid butting them too closely together. When you've finished you should just be able to squeeze a sheet of paper between each tile.

SIZE OF CUT TILES
Cut tiles should be of a reasonable size; the bigger the tile the bigger the cut tiles should be. For ease of cutting, 38mm (1½in) should be the bare minimum. To mark up tiles for cutting
● use the tile-on-tile method (see step-by-step photographs) or
● measure the gap to be filled in at least three places and then mark these measurements on the tile and draw a line through them.

TIP: LEAVE EDGE GAPS
Where the cut tiles have to abut an adjacent wall, ceiling or skirting board there will be no grout to accommodate irregularities. So if the wall, ceiling or whatever does undulate it can be best to cut the tiles short to leave a gap. When the wall is finished fill the gap around the edges with mastic or cover it with decorative wooden beading.

CUTTING TILES

1 *Place the tile to be cut over the last whole tile in the row; lay another tile against the wall and use this as a guide to mark the cutting line.*

2 *Hold a metal straightedge along the marked line, then brush over the line with a little white spirit (turps) or water. This makes cutting easier.*

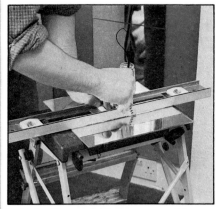

3 *Using the straightedge as a guide, score carefully along the line with a wheeled glass cutter, paying special attention to the ends of the cut.*

4 *There are many ways to break the tile. Here, the tile is held between the edge of the workbench and a wooden batten while the waste part is snapped off.*

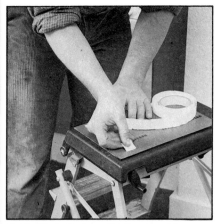

5 *It's likely that you'll have to add new adhesive pads to the back of a cut tile, and extra pads are usually supplied with the tiles for this reason.*

6 *The cut tile is aligned against the whole tile and hinged into place as before. The cut edge can be covered with beading or mastic if required.*

them like a picture, or use supports of some sort to hold them in place. There are three main types of mirror supports available: mirror screws (suitable for small or medium sizes mirrors), mirror corners (suitable for larger mirrors) which support the mirror at the corners, and mirror clips or mirror edge clips which fit at intervals at the top and bottom or round the perimeter of the mirror. Alternatively, for very large mirrors you can use a timber batten or an aluminium channel strip to support the weight of the mirror, with the other fixings simply holding it flat against the wall. (See *Ready Reference* for more information on fixing sheet glass mirrors.)

With mirror tiles, there is nothing very difficult about installing them. The majority are either fixed using separate self-adhesive tabs or are themselves 'self-adhesive', which means that the sticky tabs are already stuck to the tiles.

It is therefore simply a question of planning the setting out in much the same way as you would for ceramic tiles, peeling off the paper backing that protects the adhesive and pressing the tiles into place. You don't have to worry particularly about spacing because they sit side by side and you don't have to go through the messy business of grouting because they don't need grout. The only part of the job that may bother you is cutting tiles to fit, but really, if you can cut ceramic tiles, you should be able to cut glass and if you can cut glass you can definitely cut mirror tiles. You'll find that moistening the cutting line with water or white spirit (turps) lubricates the cutting wheel and makes cutting even easier.

Tiling ceilings

You will have to adopt a different method if you want to tile a ceiling with mirror tiles. Although the sticky pads which you use to fix them to a wall do give a very strong fixing, it isn't quite strong enough to go all out against gravity, especially if the ceiling is subject to movement, as it often is when somebody is using the room above. Here, it will be necessary to fix the tiles with screws driven into the ceiling joists, or into battens nailed between them above the ceiling. Some mirror tile manufacturers will supply pre-drilled mirrors 350 to 1200mm (14 x 48in) long and 255 to 600 (6¼ to 24in) wide which should be suitable for use in such areas.

Alternatively you can drill holes in the mirrors yourself. You'll need a special drill bit called a 'spear point' or glass drill. You need to drill very slowly so use a hand drill or, better still, a variable speed power drill. Build up a wall of putty or plasticine round the hole and fill the well with water or white spirit (turps) to cool the drill. As soon as the drill tip pierces the silvering, turn the mirror over and finish drilling the hole from the other side.

HOME REPAIRS

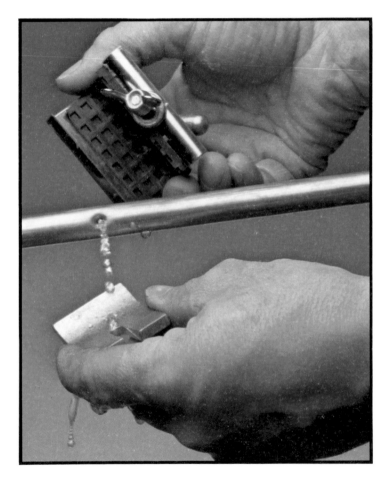

PART 2

HOME REPAIRS

ADHESIVES

To get the best results you have to pick the right adhesive for the materials you want to join, and then use it in the correct way. But the range available can make your choice extremely confusing.

The idea of an adhesive is easy to grasp: it sticks things together. In practice, however, there's a lot you need to know about the different types of adhesive on the market: how each works, what it will (and will not) stick together, how long it takes to set, whether the bond is heat-proof or waterproof, and so on. Equipped with this information, you can then begin to make the correct choice of adhesive type for the job you want to do.

Here you will find a brief description of the major types of adhesive, and a table that tells you which type to use to stick various materials together. Remember that adhesives should always be used exactly as directed by the manufacturer for the best results. They should also be treated with respect as they can damage the skin; furthermore, their fumes may be dangeous to inhale and highly inflammable.

1 Animal and fish glues

Also known as 'scotch' glues, these are the traditional woodworking adhesives, and come in either liquid form, or as solid chunks or sheets that you have to melt down. They are capable of producing a very strong bond, but have no gap-filling ability, so that woodworking joints must fit very tightly. They dry rather slowly, and are seriously weakened when exposed to dampness, however slight. They have now been almost completely replaced by modern synthetic adhesives.

2 PVA adhesives

PVA (polyvinyl acetate) adhesive is a white liquid which dries clear in under an hour, producing a strong bond within 24 hours. It is now the most important woodworking adhesive indoors, but can be used on most dry, porous surfaces. It is widely employed within the building trade as a bonding agent for concrete, and a masonry sealant. However, PVA adhesives do have limitations. They are not very good at filling gaps, so woodworking joints must have a good fit, and must be cramped until dry. The bond doesn't stand up well to stress, and is weakened by exposure to moisture. PVA adhesives also have a tendency to stain some hardwoods.

3 Casein adhesive

This woodworking adhesive comes as a powder that you mix with water, and dries to a pale yellow colour. It stands up to low temperatures and dampness better than PVA, and gives a stronger bond. However, it is weakened by water – though its strength returns as it dries out again. It can also take up to 6 hours to set so joints must be cramped. It stains many hardwoods.

4 Resorcinol Formaldehyde adhesive

An excellent woodworking adhesive, giving a strong, rigid, extremely water-resistant bond. The snag is that it comes in two parts which must be mixed together, so some wastage is inevitable. It stains most hardwoods rather badly.

5 Urea-Formaldehyde adhesive

Another two-part woodworking adhesive, urea-formaldehyde – often referred to simply as 'urea' – is the usual choice for exterior woodwork. As well as giving a very strong bond, and having the ability to bridge gaps, it stands up very well to just about everything the weather can throw at it. These qualities also makes it useful in many indoor situations. Unfortunately, it dries rather slowly and joints must be cramped for up to 6 hours. When used on hardwoods it may stain.

6 Contact adhesives

Normally based on synthetic rubber, these get their name from the way in which they are used. You apply a thin coat to both the surfaces to be joined, allow it to become touch dry, and then achieve an instantaneous bond by bringing the surfaces into contact with each other. The resulting bond will resist being pulled apart, but in time some sideways slippage may occur. For this reason, contact adhesives are not suitable for general woodwork and repairs.

Their main use is for sticking down sheet materials such as plastic laminate and cork tiles. Obviously, the fact that the adhesive bonds on contact can cause problems where accurate positioning is required, as you cannot make minor adjustments once the surfaces have been brought together. But some contact adhesives are available which have a delayed action, and so overcome this problem to a certain extent. The petroleum-based solvent used in most brands gives off vapour which is dangerous and unpleasant to inhale, and also highly inflammable. You must be sure to work in a well ventilated area, and, if this not possible, use a water-based contact adhesive instead.

7 Latex adhesives

In many ways these are similar to water-based contact adhesives, except that they use natural rubber (latex), and can either be used as a contact adhesive, or as an ordinary adhesive where you bring the surfaces together while the adhesive is wet. They are a little too expensive to be used on large areas and so are generally used for such tasks as joining fabrics, sticking down carpet, and so on – situations in which the flexible, washable (but not dry-cleanable) bond they produce is a major advantage.

8 PVC adhesives

These stick flexible PVC. The strong, flexible bond they provide makes them the ideal choice for repairing rainwear, shower curtains, beach balls, and things of that sort.

9 Cyanoacrylate adhesives

These are the adhesives ('super glues') once claimed to stick anything to everything in seconds. A cyanoacrylate adhesive will quickly bond a wide variety of materials, but it has limitations. It's expensive, and although you need very little of it, this makes it impractical to use for anything more than small repairs. Surfaces must be scrupulously clean, and a perfect fit, as it has no gap-filling ability whatsoever. Another point to remember is that when used in industry, cyanoacrylate is specially formulated to stick two specific materials together with a very stong bond. Choose two different materials and you have to use a different formula. What the handyman can buy is a compromise formula, and there are therefore some materials that it doesn't stick very well. Glass is perhaps the best example. Ordinary cyanoacrylate is degraded by the ultra-violet radiation in sunlight and glass leaves it exposed and vulnerable. As a result, a special formulation for glass has been brought out to overcome this problem.

Another problem is that cyanoacrylate reacts in a rather odd way with water. The presence of moisture actually speeds up the setting process, but, once set, exposure to water breaks down the bond. Finally, an unfortunate side-effect is that cyanoacrylate adhesive has the alarming ability to stick people to themselves or to their surroundings, so it needs to be used with great care. It is not, however, as dangerous as sometimes suggested: a lot of patient work with hot soapy water often does the trick.

In summary, a cyanoacrylate adhesive isn't as 'super' as it might appear, but it is worth keeping a tube handy for repairs where other adhesives have failed.

10 Epoxy resin adhesives
These are less convenient than cyanoacrylates as they come in two parts, a resin and a hardener, which must be carefully mixed. But epoxy resin adhesives come closer to the 'stick-anything-to everything' ideal. The strong, heat-resistant, oil-resistant, water-resistant bond that they provide makes them a good choice for small-scale repair work involving metal, china, and some plastics, as well as a variety of other materials. The surfaces must be clean, but since the resin will bridge small gaps without losing strength, a perfect fit is not essential. In fact, for repair work, epoxies have only two major snags. One is that they dry to a pale brown colour, which tends to highlight the join, though it is possible to colour the adhesive with dry pigment. The second is that they need a setting time of up to 48 hours. This can be overcome by using a fast-setting formulation, which generally holds within five or ten minutes, but still requires at least 24 hours to achieve full strength. Of course, epoxies can be used for large-scale jobs too. The reason why they tend not to be is that they are simply too expensive to use in

11 Acrylic adhesives
This is a two-part adhesive with a difference. It will join the same sorts of material as an epoxy, achieving a bond of only slightly less strength in as little as 5 minutes. You don't have to premix the adhesive and catalyst before you apply them. Instead, you can apply the catalyst to one surface, the adhesive to the other. And most important of all, the surfaces need not be clean. Even oily surfaces can be joined successfully. But it's expensive, and it is not yet widely available.

12 Plastic solvent adhesives
Although between them, epoxies, acrylics, PVC adhesives, and cyanoacrylates allow you to stick many plastics to themselves, some require a special solvent adhesive. This works by chemically 'melting' a layer of plastic on each of the surfaces to be joined, so that they merge together and produce a 'welded' joint rather like the join in a plastic model kit assembled with polystyrene cement. They work quickly, and give strong results. However, you must be sure to match the solvent to the particular type of plastic, and only two solvents are commonly available. These are UPVC solvent adhesive (for unplasticised polyvinyl chloride; used mainly for joining lengths of UPVC drain pipe) and polystyrene cement, mentioned above.

13 Cellulose adhesive
Adhesives based on cellulose aren't very strong, but they are fairly waterproof and heatproof, transparent when they dry and they do set quickly. They are most useful as an alternative to epoxy resin adhesives, or to cyanoacrylates, when repairing china and glass.

14 Vegetable gums and pastes
Based on either starch or dextrine, two plant extracts, these are useful only for sticking paper and card, and even here, these days, they tend to be restricted to the 'suitable for children' market.

15 Specialist adhesives
In addition to the general-purpose adhesives we have mentioned so far, you'll find a number of specialised adhesives, such as tile and wallpaper adhesives.

Choosing the right Adhesive...

KEY TO ADHESIVE TYPES

H Clear household	7 Latex	14 Vegetable gum
1 Animal and fish	8 PVC	**Specialist adhesives**
2 PVA	9 Cyanoacrylate	15 Wallpaper
3 Casein	10 Epoxy	16 Flooring
4 Resorcinol formaldehyde	11 Acrylic	17 Ceramic tile
5 Urea formaldehyde	12 Plastic solvent	18 Expanded polystyrene
6 Contact	13 Cellulose	

To stick ▽ to this ▷

To stick / to this	Wood	Wallpaper	Rubber	Plastic (soft)	Plastic (hard)	Plastic laminate	Plastic flooring	Plasterboard	Paper & cards	Metal	Man-made boards	Leather	China & glass	Fabrics	Expanded polystyrene	Cork tiles	Ceramic tiles	Carpet
Ceramic tiles	9 10 11	—	—	—	6 9 10 11	6	16	—	—	9 10 11	—	—	—	—	—	6	17 10	6 7
Cork tiles	6 2	15	—	—	—	6	16	—	H 2 7	—	2	—	—	7	—	6	—	7
Expanded polystyrene	18	15	—	—	—	6	—	—	—	—	2	—	—	7	18	18	—	—
China & glass	10 11	—	6 9	—	9 10 11	—	—	—	H	H 9 10 11	—	H 9 10 11	H 9 10 11 13	6 7 H	—	H	—	—
Man-made boards	1 2 3 4 5	15	9 10 11	—	9 10 11	6	16	8	H 2 7 15	6 10 11	1 2 3 4 5	6	9 10 11	6 7	18	6 16	17	6 7
Metal	9 10 11	15	9 10 11	—	9 10 11	6	—	H	9 10 11	10	6	9 10 11	6	—		6 9 10 11	9 10 11	6
Paper & cards	2	15	—	H	—	—	—	—	H 1 2 7 14 15	—	—	H	H	7	—	—	—	—
Plasterboard	2	15	—	—	—	6	16	5	2 15	—	6	6	—	2 15	18	6	17	6
Plastic flooring	—	—	—	—	—	—	16	—	—	—	—	—	—	—	—	16	17	6
Plastic (hard)	—	—	9 10 11	9 10 11 12	9 10 11 12	—	—	—	H	9 10 11	—	—	—	—	—	—	—	—
Plastic (soft)	—	—	9 10 11	8 9 10 11 12	9 10 11 12	—	—	—	—	—	—	—	—	—	—	—	—	—
Masonry	5 10	15	6	—	9 10 11	—	16	6	H 7 15	9 10 11	6 2	—	—	6 7	18	16	10 11 17	6 7
Wood	1 2 3 4 5	15	6 9 10 11	9 10 11	9 10 11	6	16	2	1 2 7 14 15	9 10 11	1 2 3 4 5	6	9 10 11	6 7	18	6 16	10 11 17	6 7

RESTORING DAMAGED DECORATIONS

You will eventually need to redecorate the walls in a room if they are not to look worn and tired, or simply old-fashioned. But in the meantime, you can repair minor or occasional damage quite simply.

In even the most well-regulated households the decorations may become damaged: paint gets chipped, paper begins to peel or gets marked and stained, vinyl can become scuffed, and wallcoverings may tear or blister. It is, however, possible to mend the damage without having to redecorate completely.

Stains on wallpaper

Before you attempt to remove a stain on wallpaper you should make sure that the paper is colourfast. Most modern ones are, unless they are handprinted, but some older papers may not be. Test a small inconspicuous corner or a spare piece of paper by dabbing it with a soft cloth which has been moistened with warm water. If the pattern blurs you should not try to clean the paper with water.

If the paper is colourfast, there are several methods you can use for stain removal. A greasy patch can sometimes be removed by rubbing gently with a piece of stale white bread, or a soft art rubber (move the rubber round in your hand so there is a clean surface to work with). You can make a cleaning 'dough' and rub this over the surface (see step-by-step photographs). For greasy blobs, make a paste with French chalk or Fuller's earth and a few drops of grease solvent (carbon tetrachloride). Press the paste onto the stain with a filling knife, leave it until it's dry and then brush it off. Sometimes grease can be blotted off; place several thicknesses of blotting paper over the stain and press lightly with a hot iron, taking care not to singe the surrounding paper.

Small marks can be removed with white spirit or grease solvent; you should dab it on gently with a clean cloth, but don't rub it. There are also proprietary aerosol dry-cleaning fluids which can be used on grease marks on walls. You spray the stain, leave the dry-cleaning fluid to dry and then brush off the resulting powder.

On vinyl or some plastic-coated papers you will need to lubricate the greasy patch with oil before you wipe it off carefully with a clean cloth or kitchen paper; then wash it with mild detergent. Washable paper and vinyl can be cleaned with mild detergent and warm water; some can be scrubbed very gently with a soft brush, but take care not to saturate the seams or the wallcovering could start to peel. When washing a wall, start at the bottom and work upwards.

Torn wallcoverings

Torn wallpaper can usually be patched fairly simply. With other wallcoverings like hessian, vinyl or grasscloths you should match the pattern with care, placing a spare piece over the tear and checking the design. Cut a piece slightly largely than the damaged area, then place it over the hole, again making sure that the pattern matches. Cut through both layers with a sharp knife to a square or oblong shape (unless there is a definite motif in the pattern, in which case you should follow the shape of this). Peel away the old wallcovering, and using a suitable adhesive stick the new piece carefully in place. Roll the patch lightly with a seam roller and leave it to dry.

Many vinyl wallcoverings have a paper backing. You should not leave the backing of the old wallcovering in place; cut right through it and strip it back to the wall surface before fixing the new piece.

Peeling or blistered paper

If your walls are coming apart at the seams – this sometimes happens because of condensation, or it may be that the wallcoverings have been overlapped instead of butt-joined – you can easily stick them back down again. If the wallcovering is vinyl you will have to use a latex adhesive to secure it.

Blisters sometimes occur if wallpaper is in-correctly pasted or if heavy paper is hung too soon, before it has absorbed enough paste; they can also be caused by a poor wall surface of condensation. One method of dealing with this is to half-fill a syringe with a suitable paste and inject the paste into the centre of the blister. Allow the paste to penetrate the back of the paper (it should take about five minutes) and then flatten the blister firmly with your fingers. Wipe away any surplus paste and then go over the area lightly with a roller until the paper lies completely flat. If you cannot get hold of a syringe, make a cross-shaped cut and peel back the tongues before using an artist's brush to push paste underneath them.

Damaged paintwork

Blisters, or cracks and chips in paintwork can be repaired as described in the step-by-step photographs. Knots in wood can sometimes cause very bad discoloration on woodwork, appearing as a brown stain under the paint film. You can sand or scrape away the paint, seal the knot with proprietary knotting and allow it to dry before you prime, sand, fill as necessary and repaint.

Damaged wall tiles

You can remove and replace a damaged wall tile. If you don't have a spare tile and cannot obtain one, you could either replace a panel of tiles with new ones so as to create a definite design, or replace just a few tiles with random patterned ones. It's also possible to tile on top of cracked or crazed tiles, using new slim universal tiles.

REMOVING STAINS FROM WALLPAPER

1 A cleaning 'dough' is made of 6 parts flour, 3 parts white spirit (turps) and 3 parts water. Make a hole in the flour and pour in the white spirit (turps).

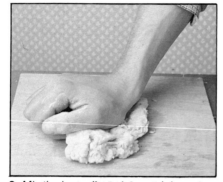

2 Mix the ingredients into a thick paste and then add the water. You should then knead the dough so the white spirit (turps) is evenly distributed.

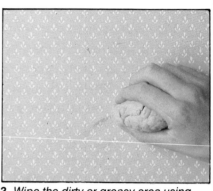

3 Wipe the dirty or greasy area using long firm strokes, and turning the dough so that you will always be working with a clean surface.

PATCHING TORN WALLPAPER

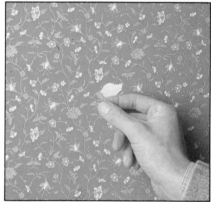

1 If there is any loose flapping paper hanging from the torn area, remove it by gently tearing it off, taking care not to enlarge the hole.

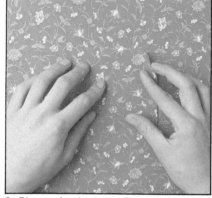

2 Place a fresh piece of wallpaper over the hole. Position it carefully so you can check that it matches the pattern of the surrounding paper.

3 To give you a flat surface on which to work, rub the bare area of wall with an india rubber or fine grade glasspaper to remove old paste and backing.

4 With the front side facing you, tear round the edges of the patch, tearing away from you so that the feathered edge will not show the backing.

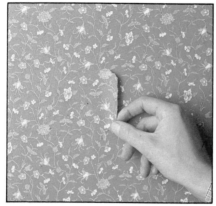

5 Paste the patch and leave it to soak for a few minutes. You can then press it into place with your fingers, making sure that the pattern matches.

6 Leave the adhesive to dry partially and then run over the patch gently with a seam roller to flatten it out so that it blends into its surroundings.

CRACKED OR CHIPPED PAINTWORK

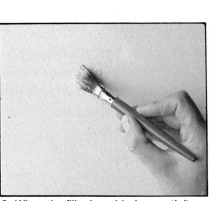

1 Cracks or chips on painted surfaces are treated in much the same way as blisters. Sand down the damaged area first to level it out.

2 You will then have to fill the holes or cracks. Use a fine-surface filler and spread it on carefully with a filling knife to even up the surface.

3 When the filler has dried, smooth it down with fine-grade glasspaper so that it is level with the rest of the wall area, and then apply paint.

REPLACING A DAMAGED TILE

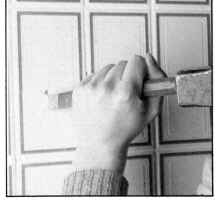

1 Gently drill a hole in the centre of the damaged tile using a masonry bit. Removal will be easier if you also rake out the grout with a skewer.

2 Place a chisel on the drilled area and tap it with a hammer, taking care not to drive it so hard that you disturb the surrounding tiles.

3 When the tile is sufficiently loose, remove the pieces. You can then dig out the old adhesive with the chisel and sand the surface smooth.

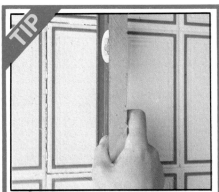

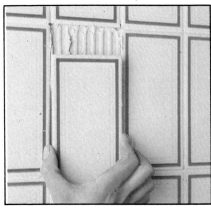

4 Place the new tile in position to check that it will be level. You may have to apply a skim of plaster or filler to bring it into line.

5 Apply the adhesive with a notched spreader and stick the new tile in place, making sure that it aligns with the other tiles on the wall.

6 Remove any excess adhesive from the front of the tiles. You can grout the newly-tiled area when the adhesive has thoroughly dried.

REPAIRING DAMAGED FLOORING

Don't despair at the first signs of damage to your floorcoverings. Carpets, vinyl, ceramic tiles and woodstrip flooring can all be repaired, patched or replaced in sections to give first class results.

Most floorcoverings have an uneven wear pattern which means that some areas will become worn or damaged before others. The area in front of the main door, the spot in front of television viewing seats, the walkway to the dining table, and the triangle between sink, cooker and worktop are all examples of areas that will come in for a lot of wear and tear. Meanwhile, other parts of the floorcovering will remain in perfectly good condition.

You'll find that it can be dangerous to leave torn carpet, broken tiles, crumbling cork or worn vinyl on the floor – a heel caught and the result could be a nasty accident. But you needn't worry about having to replace the entire floorcovering at the first sign of trouble. It's possible to carry out some first aid on damaged floors before they get too bad, and that way you'll save yourself expense and prevent accidents. In some cases, however, you won't even have to bother with first aid: you could simply change the furniture round to alter the pattern of wear and relieve areas of the floorcovering. Alternatively, you could place a rug over the most used area to take the strain. In the event of having some new floorcovering laid, remember always to save some remnants just in case you have to make repairs in the future.

Binding rug and carpet edges

The edges of both rugs and carpets often become frayed over the years and should be repaired at once. But if you have a valuable oriental rug or carpet it's advisable to have it professionally repaired and maintained.

Sealing a frayed edge on a latex-backed rug or carpet is straightforward. Start by working a 25mm (1in) wide strip of latex carpet adhesive along the back of the fraying edge. You'll probably find it easiest to use a piece of cloth to do this. Leave the adhesive to dry and then trim the carpet – preferably along the second row of carpet weave from the frayed edge – to leave a neat, straight edge. Then work more adhesive into the edge of the backing and rub it in, taking great care not to get any on to the tufts. Cut your carpet binding tape so that it's slightly longer than the rug edge and apply adhesive to it. You can then either lay the tape on the back

of the rug or carpet or, if you find it easier, lay the carpet on to the tape. Either way you must make sure that the tape overlaps the cut edge by about 3mm (⅛in); that way you'll be able to fold it upwards to secure the backing. Finally, trim off any surplus tape.

In order to bind the edge of a jute-backed carpet you'll need a proper carpet needle, some waxed thread and more hessian carpet tape. First you'll have to trim the frayed edges to make them straight. Cut the tape so that it overlaps the ends of the carpet by about 25mm (1in), and apply adhesive to the first 50mm (2in) at each end. Once the adhesive has become tacky, fold over and stick down the excess 25mm (1in) to give neat side hems. You can then line up the tape and carpet edge and fold the tape over so that it's level at the front and back. Then stitch along the edge, using the special needle and waxed thread, making sure the thread passes through both the tape and carpet. Each end should then be secured with tight overstitching.

Repairing holes in rugs and carpets

Small holes in rugs can be repaired with 4-ply rug wool or synthetic fibre of a suitable colour. First you'll have to trim any damaged tufts from the rug surface, and for this you'll probably find nail scissors best. Make new tufts by winding enough wool for the repair round the fingers of one hand. Cut through

both ends, and bunch the thread tightly together so you can cut off enough pieces to fill the hole. Each piece of wool should be slightly longer than the original pile length. Use a match stick or cotton bud to dab adhesive into the hole, and then put a bunch of strands upright in the hole, using a toothpick to work them into position on the bed of adhesive. Continue putting in more until the hole is filled. You should then leave the adhesive to set before trimming off any excess wool and using a pin to tease up the new tufts so they blend in with the colour of the surrounding material.

When carpets develop holes they, too, should be patched. It's best to use a remnant from the same carpet, if possible, but otherwise try and get some from a local stockist. Failing this, you may have to cut a piece out of the existing carpet – from an area that is covered by an article of furniture.

If you're dealing with a hessian or jute-backed carpet, you should start by marking a square round the damaged area. Paint the back of the entire square with latex adhesive, overlapping the edge by about 25mm (1in), and rub it in with a rag. Then slide a piece of wood under the damaged section before cutting through the backing with a sharp knife and removing the entire square. In the event of your carpet being patterned or having a definite texture, it's a good idea to cut out a shaped piece of carpet so that the

PATCHING RUGS AND CARPETS

1 Start to patch a hessian-backed carpet by lifting it and marking round the damaged section on the backing. Use a felt tip pen and a straight edge.

2 Paint the back of the square with a latex adhesive, overlapping by about 25mm (1in). Slip a piece of wood under the square and cut out the section.

3 Cut strips of hessian tape so that they are 50mm (2in) longer than the hole. Coat them with adhesive and fix them to the back of the carpet.

4 Match the section with a patch on a remnant of carpet and cut it out. Spread adhesive on the back of the new patch, avoiding getting it on the tufts.

5 Finally, place the patch in position and lightly hammer down the edges. Leave it to dry and tease out the edge tufts to disguise the joins.

6 If you have a hole in a rug, you'll first have to buy a suitably coloured wool with which to patch it. Trim away damaged tufts with small scissors.

7 Wind the wool round the fingers of one hand. Cut through both ends and then bunch the wool together so you can cut off strands to fill the hole.

8 Make sure that the pieces of wool are slightly longer than the pile. Dab latex adhesive into the hole using a cotton bud or match stick.

9 Press enough strands into the gap to fill it, and leave them until the adhesive has had time to set. Finally, trim off the excess wool.

REPAIRING CORK AND WOOD FLOORS

1 *If an individual cork tile has been badly stained or burnt, start by rubbing down the area with glasspaper until you have removed the mark.*

2 *After getting rid of the blemish, rub down the area with a finer glasspaper. When the surface is smooth again, brush away any dust and reseal.*

3 *If an individual strip of hardwood flooring has been damaged, you'll find it easiest to replace it. Use a chisel and mallet to remove it.*

4 *Remove any remaining debris and then use the chisel to scrape away the old adhesive. Check that the sub-floor is dust-free and level.*

5 *Apply a thin layer of the recommended adhesive to the surface. If necessary, plane down the new strip to ensure that it will fit the gap accurately.*

6 *Press in the new strip. Lay paperbacked strips with the paper uppermost; felt backing should face downwards. Rub down lightly and then reseal.*

patch will blend in better. If there is a pattern, match it on your remnant, mark it and cut it out. In all cases, it's important to ensure that the pile runs in the same direction as the original piece of carpet and that the colour is as good a match as possible.

Cut two strips of hessian tape that are each about 50mm (2in) longer than the hole and coat them with adhesive. Then slide the tapes over the hole at the back of the carpet, overlapping the edges by 25mm (1in) at each end. These strips will serve as a base on which to graft the carpet patch. Spread adhesive on the back of the patch and round the edges, taking care not to saturate the tufts. Then place the patch in position and lightly hammer down the edges. Leave the adhesive to dry, and, if necessary, tease the edge of the carpet so that the join becomes invisible.

Foam or latex-backed carpet shouldn't fray when cut, and patching it will involve techniques similar to those already described. However, you should cut the patch from the upper side of the carpet rather than from the underside. Make sure the patch is slightly larger than the hole and lay this over the damaged section, using a couple of carpet tacks to hold it in position. You can then cut through the carpet beneath using the edges of the patch as a template. Lift off the patch and remove the damaged section; then test that the patch fits accurately. Cut strips of carpet adhesive tape that are 50mm (2in) longer than the hole and stick them across the back of the carpet in a criss-cross fashion so each one overlaps the hole by half its width and by 25mm (1in) at each end. Turn the carpet the right way up, place the patch in position and press down on the tape. Lightly hammer along the join and tease if necessary.

Replacing tiles

All types of floor tiles can get damaged and will therefore need replacing. You can remove individual ceramic or quarry tiles using a hammer and chisel but, for safety's sake, you must wear goggles or safety glasses. Break up the damaged tile and then, working from the centre towards the edges, chip out the fragments and smooth the surface underneath. Put the new tile in place and check not only that it fits, but also that it sits level with the rest of the tiles Remove the tile, spread a layer of ceramic floor tiling adhesive on the floor beneath and press the new tile into position. Scrape off any surplus adhesive with the trowel and leave this area of the floor unwalked on for at least 24 hours. You can then grout the tile using either a flooring grout or a mix of one part cement to four parts sand, making sure that you wipe away the surplus with a clean sponge while it's still wet.

MENDING DAMAGED VINYL

1 Badly-stained vinyl can be quite simply cleaned. If detergent and hot water won't do the trick, try rubbing it down with steel wool.

2 If your vinyl has a tear or hole in it, you will have to patch it. Cut a patch from a remnant which matches the damaged area.

3 Cut through both layers with a sharp knife, using a straight edge. Make the cut in the imitation grout line if your vinyl has a tile pattern.

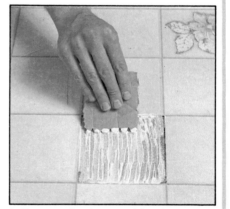

4 Remove the damaged section and scrape off any old adhesive. Then spread the recommended adhesive on the floor and the patch.

5 Carefully position the new section and press it down firmly. If necessary, trim its edges with a sharp knife to ensure a perfect fit.

6 Finally, hammer lightly over the patched area, and wipe away any surplus adhesive that oozes out from the joins with a damp cloth.

If you have a badly damaged cork tile on your floor, remove it by cutting along the edges with a sharp knife and straightedge. Prise the tile from the floor using an old chisel (bevelled side down) and a mallet. Do take care when doing this as cork can easily crumble, and surrounding tiles might get damaged. Once the tile has been removed, clean away the old adhesive from the floor surface. If you're removing the tile from a wooden floor, then you'll have to lift the paper felt and remove the panel pins. Brush out any debris left in the space, make sure that your replacement tile has straight edges and cut it to fit. If necessary, press a new piece of felt paper in position and trim the edges neatly. Apply a recommended adhesive directly to the floor and fit the tile. If the floor is wooden, hammer a pin into each corner. Remove surplus adhesive from the tile, leave to dry and then reseal.

Thermoplastic and vinyl tiles can also be replaced in much the same way. It's important to remove old adhesive on the floor, either by using a hammer and chisel or a heated scraper.

Patching sheet vinyl

Cushioned and printed vinyl can be repaired fairly easily with a patch, so it's wise always to save offcuts at the time of installation. Lay the new section over the damaged area, matching the pattern. Cut through both layers with a sharp knife, using a straight-edge and allowing a margin round the damaged area. If your vinyl has a 'tile' pattern it's a good idea to cut through the imitation grout line. Otherwise try to follow other lines in the design. Remove the damaged piece and the old adhesive and make sure the sub-floor is clean and smooth. Trim the new piece to get a good fit. Spread the recommended flooring adhesive on the back of the patch and on the floor, press the patch into position and remove any surplus adhesive that oozes out from the join. Leave the adhesive to dry and reseal, if necessary.

Replacing hardwood flooring strips

Replacement areas of hardwood strip flooring are easy to obtain, but do remember to get the correct pattern – herringbone or basket weave. Remove the damaged strip or section using a mallet and chisel and make sure you work from the centre towards the edges to avoid damaging the surrounding covering. Clean the floor thoroughly and then apply a thin layer of adhesive. Paper-backed strips should be laid with the paper uppermost, but those with felt backing should have the felt side laid downwards. Individual strips can be carefully planed to make them fit and all replacements should be gently rubbed down with glass paper, ready for sealing to match the surrounding area.

REPAIRING CONCRETE FLOORS

Rough and uneven floors? Signs of rising damp? You may discover all these problems when you start replacing your floorcovering. But if you follow our instructions you'll find correcting them relatively simple.

A solid floor often consists of concrete that has been laid on top of a layer of hardcore in the ground. This is then covered by a damp-proof membrane, which may in turn be protected by a thin layer of mortar called a screed which is levelled out and topped by the flooring. But not all solid floors are laid directly on top of the ground. You may find solid floors in flats and houses, at first floor level and above, as an alternative to framed floors which are supported by beams and structural walls and are usually · floorboards mounted on joists.

How are solid floors constructed?
You'll only find the concrete floor surface laid directly on the soil in the oldest houses. And even then you're more likely to find a heavy concrete slab beneath the surface flooring. If your floor is old, it will probably consist of hardcore with up to 150mm (6in) of concrete on top.

Surface finish, such as a 25mm (1in) terrazzo screed, quarry tiles, floorboards on slim joists, or wooden block flooring like parquet, was then laid on top.

With this older style of construction little consideration was given to rising damp. Parquet blocks were sometimes bedded in bitumen, but only if the surface of the floor came below soil level would any systematic damp-proofing be used. In that eventuality, the structural slab was covered with asphalt, which was in turn covered with a further 75mm (3in) of concrete.

The design of a modern solid floor slabs allows for a much more rigorous approach to damp proofing. A 100mm (4in) structural slab is laid over a damp-proof membrane that protects the walls as well in order to provide complete protection. On top of the structural slab may come a mortar screed suitable for carpet or vinyl laying or a direct surface finish. Damp proofing is vital because although well-laid concrete is

basically water proof, it still may allow damaging water vapour to pass through without the membrane.

What can go wrong?
Cracks are the most common fault in solid floors – and are usually due to drying shrinkage or thermal movement. But, provided the cracks are no wider than 6mm (¼in), you can repair them quite easily yourself. Minor surface damage such as roughness and unevenness is also simply repaired. If, however, the cracks are wider than 6mm (¼in), that means that something more serious is wrong with your floor – probably a crack going all the way through the slab as well as the screeding – so you should call in a builder or surveyor to advise you. A still more worrying problem, especially in a direct-to-earth floor, is rising damp. If a damp-proof membrane already exists and there is still evidence of damp, the damp is likely to be localised: the result of a small break in the membrane.

This may show up only after the old porous floor surface has been replaced with some more modern flooring. The original surface would have let damp through, so avoiding damage, but as the modern ones don't let water vapour evaporate, it tends to build up underneath and attack both the adhesive and the flooring. So, if you are going to fit new flooring on an old solid floor, first of all check that it's damp proof (see *Ready Reference*). If you do have damp, then you can put up with your existing flooring; replace it with a new flooring of the same material; or lay a damp-proof membrane.

STRUCTURE OF A SOLID FLOOR

Upper floor

Solid floors usually consist of layers of different material that are laid on top of each other. Not all solid floors are laid at ground level but those which are on the ground require a damp-proof membrane to be installed.

plaster

skirting board

floor

screed

reinforced concrete slab

Ground floor

If the floor is at ground level then the damp proof membrane must link into the damp-proof course to provide complete protection against rising damp.

outer cavity wall

skirting board

mortar screeding

floor

damp-proof membrane

damp-proof course

concrete slab

foundations

hardcore over ground

The screed is laid on top of the membrane to protect it and to provide a good finish for the floor surface to be laid upon.

Repairing localised damage.

Very small cracks and holes can be ignored: just cover them with your flooring. Larger cracks can be filled in with mortar. This should be mixed to a fairly dry consistency with a ratio of three parts sand to one part cement. A little PVA (polyvinyl acetate) building adhesive should be added, but remember to follow the instructions on the can as to how much you have to add. All you do is slightly widen the crack by using a club hammer and cold chisel, going down to a depth of 12mm (½in), undercutting the surrounding floor a little. This is very important as it allows the mortar to get a much better grip on the surface than it would if you were attempting to fill a crack with smooth, feathered edges. Clean out any dust or debris before brushing on a coat of PVA adhesive, smoothing in the mortar with a small trowel and finishing it off level with the surrounding floor. The chances are that the crack will open up again at some stage, especially if the floor on one side of it has pushed either up above or down below the rest. The only really permanent solution is to have the floor completely replaced before you lay your new floor surface.

Inserting a damp-proof membrane

The simplest way to do this is to remove the skirting boards and strip off the plaster on the walls to a point 50mm (2in) above the wall's damp-proof course. If at this stage you find your walls don't have a damp-proof course, it is advisable to get one put in before going any further. Various forms of damp-proof membrane are used, ranging from thick polythene (often known as '1000 – gauge' or 'sheet 1000'), PVC, butyl rubber or polyisobutylene for large scale work (where the sheets are loose laid or bonded to the structural slab with water-resistant adhesive), to bitumen emulsion for smaller scale jobs. These sealants are sprayed or painted on the slab in two coats, with the second one being brushed at right angles to the first to prevent thin spots and pin holes where damp could come through. To protect your room completely against rising damp you should link the membrane into the damp-proof course. This is easy if the dpc is above the floor, but it is possible that it'll be below the level of your floor. If that's the case then you will have to dig a small channel round the floor so you can gain access to it. Then all you do is paint bitumen emulsion either up or down the wall or fit the polythene sheets with more water resistant adhesive.

Some solid floors are not laid direct to earth. Some of them are cast in situ around reinforcing steel and some are precast concrete floorboards that are locked together. Others, which are made of hollow terracotta blocks that are linked together with metal

Ready Reference

CHECK FOR DAMP

Before you do any major work on a solid floor, it is vital to check if it has any protection against damp. You should:
● tape a 300mm (12in) square of polythene over part of the floor
● make sure it is airtight by smearing round the edges with petroleum jelly
● leave it untouched for a few days
● check the underside of the polythene for condensation. If any is present, dampness is rising through the floor
● repeat the test, if there is no evidence of damp, on different parts of the floor just to make sure.

LINKING INTO THE DPC

To provide completely effective protection against damp you must link the floor's damp-proof membrane into the damp-proof course in the walls.

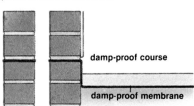

damp-proof course

damp-proof membrane

If the floor is lower than the damp-proof course you should:
● remove skirting boards and plaster
● link into the course by laying polythene sheets or painting bitumen emulsion up to the damp-proof course.

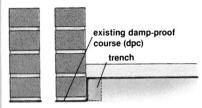

existing damp-proof course (dpc)

trench

If the floor level is higher than the damp-proof course you should:
● cut a small trench round the floor perimeter until you reach the wall dpc
● link into the exposed dpc as above
● make good the small trench.

TIP: WORK TOWARDS DOORS

When damp proofing your floor or laying a new screed, always work from the far end of the room towards the door. Otherwise you risk trapping yourself in the room.

PROTECT NEW SCREEDS

It is a good idea to dust over the surface of your newly laid screed with some sharp sand. That way, if someone walks across it while it is still tacky, the surface shouldn't pull up.

REPAIRING A CRACK

1 *Using a club hammer and cold chisel widen the crack and undercut the edges of the surrounding floor to allow the mortar a better grip.*

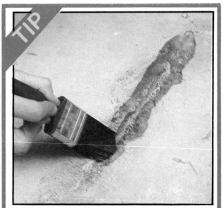

2 *Clear the crack of dust and brush on a priming coat of building adhesive and water to provide a clean surface for the mortar.*

3 *Using equal parts of water and adhesive, mix a fairly dry mortar. Then fill the crack with the mix using a small trowel.*

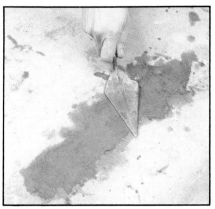

4 *Finally smooth out the mortar. Remember no repair will be permanent if you have a lot of cracks; it's best to replace the whole screed.*

rods and that have the gaps filled in with concrete, are also technically known as solid floors.

You can create a damp-proof membrane by using two coats of bitumen emulsion and applying them over the concrete slab and the exposed brickwork.

The second coat should be brushed on at right angles to the first.

Screeding a solid floor.

Screeding your floor gives vital protection to a new layer of damp proofing and is an essential preparation before replacing floor covering. It can be done in two ways. If the unevenness is slight, or you want to cover the existing flooring without lifting it, the best method to use is a self-levelling flooring compound. Make sure your floor is clean, dry and dust-free. If it is at all dusty, you should treat it with a proprietary concrete

sealer before applying the flooring compound. Mix the compound with water until it has a creamy consistency, then pour enough on the floor to cover an area just under 1 sq m (1sq yd). Using a steel float smooth it out so that nowhere is the layer thicker than 3mm (1/8in). Then move onto the next square, remembering that the compound will level itself out, so removing float marks and producing an acceptable finish. Leave it for a week or longer before laying the flooring. A second application, to smooth out slight lumps and bumps, can be applied after two or three days, but no more than three coats should be used otherwise there will be a risk of cracking at a later date.

The second method of levelling, using a mortar screed, is slightly more arduous but it does give the damp-proof membrane greater protection. Working from the far end of the room towards the door, divide the floor

DAMP PROOFING A SOLID FLOOR

1 *With a bolster chisel and club hammer remove the skirting and chop away the plaster to at least 50mm (2in) above the damp-proof course.*

2 *It's a good idea to dampen slightly the surface of the concrete slab before laying the damp-proof membrane. But don't make it too wet.*

3 *Using a coarse-fibre brush, apply the first coat of damp proofing close to the wall. Apply each coat in one stroke so they're both thick and even.*

4 *Continue the first line of damp proofing up the wall so that it links into the damp-proof course and the floor is completely sealed.*

5 *When the damp proofing has dried, apply the second coat at right angles to the first. That way no part of the floor goes untreated.*

6 *Finally, dust the membrane with sharp sand. This protects the still tacky second coat and prevents it being pulled up if walked on.*

into strips about 1m (3ft) wide using 50 x 25mm (2 x 1in) softwood battens, and use more battens around the walls. Make sure that they are level with a spirit level, and if they aren't, pack them out with scrap wood. It is vital that you get all the battens level because they serve to guide you when you start laying the screed. If you don't have them level, then your screed won't be true and that'll cause more problems when you come to lay the final surface. Cover the floor, a section at a time, with a 1:3 cement to sharp sand mortar, mixed with the minimum of water to the consistency of brown sugar. Using a stiff board, scrape it level with the battens and tamp it slightly as you go, using a steel float to give it a smooth finish.

To get the best finish to your screed keep the blade damp to stop the surface from dragging, but don't make it too wet. When you complete each section remove the guide batten furthest from you and fill in the resulting channel before tackling the next section.

If you lay a screed during a warm dry spell it's advisable to lay a plastic sheet over it for at least three days. This stops the mortar drying out too quickly and lets it cure properly. Even in milder weather it's still best to sprinkle water gently over it twice a day for a few days. If the mortar dries out too quickly it will be below strength and will probably crack as it dries. Finally make good the walls and replace the skirting.

The big drawback with this method is that it raises the level of the floor by 25mm (1in). Strictly speaking you should dig out the existing floor to the required level before starting, but this carries the risk of damaging any existing damp-proof membrane. One way of accommodating the extra thickness is to trim the bottom of the doors and build up any existing external doorsteps. Do make sure that you don't reduce the floor/ceiling height below the Building Regulations minimum of 2.3m (7ft 6in) and remember to do something about the change in level at the door thresholds: a shallow ramp is better than a shallow step.

There is another option, and that is not to lay a membrane at all. Instead you select flooring that can be laid using cement-based flooring adhesive. The former lets the damp through, so you should choose material that won't be harmed by it, and the latter acts as a sort of damp-proof membrane itself. But, as it is a makeshift solution, it will not always work and there is nothing to stop the damp rising through the walls. The floor will therefore be attacked from the edges, which can be just as harmful and the result will be that the whole floor will eventually have to be replaced, not only giving you extra work but also further expense.

SCREEDING A SOLID FLOOR

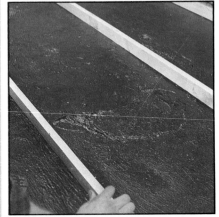

1 Divide the floor into 1m (3ft) wide strips using 50 x 25mm (2 x 1in) battens. Make sure you have battens round the walls as well.

2 Check the battens are level by laying a spirit level across them. This is important as the battens guide you when you lay the screed.

3 If the battens are not level. adjust them by packing pieces of hardboard underneath. These can be left in when the battens are lifted out.

4 The battens can be fixed with weights or nails. With nails, you must cover the holes in the membrane with more emulsion.

5 Draw a length of batten over the mortar to level it off and tamp it at the same time to make sure that it's compact and there are no air pockets.

6 The mortar should be finished off with a damp steel float that gives it the smooth surface on which the final floor is laid.

7 When you have filled up two strips, carefully remove the batten dividing them. Remember to cover the nail holes with more bitumen emulsion.

8 Using a small trowel, fill in the channel in front of you. Try not to disturb the finished mortar or you'll give yourself extra work.

9 Finally, finish off the channel with the damp steel float. The mortar should be left to cure for three days then allowed to dry completely.

REPAIRING DOORS AND WINDOWS

Over the years faults can develop in wooden windows and doors causing them to stick or sag, and the wood may rot if it is not properly protected. Luckily, most of these faults are easy to put right.

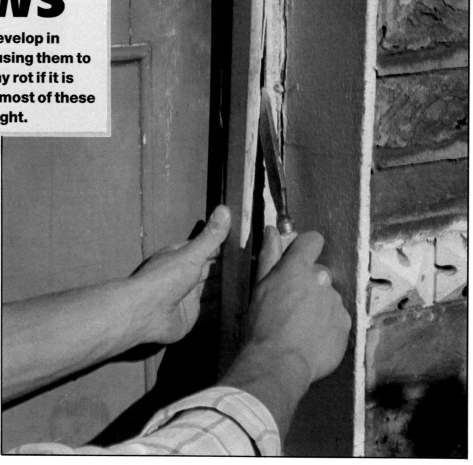

W ood is a superb material from which to make doors and windows; it is a beautiful, natural substance which is easily worked and shaped. But problems can arise as the years go by. For example, the wood may shrink or swell so joints open up or the door sticks in its frame, hinges may rust or work loose or the building may settle causing the door or window frame to distort. Usually these faults are not very serious but it's best to put them right before they get any worse.

Before describing the sort of faults you are likely to find it's worth knowing how different types of doors and frames are constructed.

Types of doors

There are three main types of door — panelled, flush and ledged-and-braced. Panelled doors consist of a timber frame that encloses a number of panels which can be of timber, plywood or glass. The frame is made up of two outer vertical members known as stiles — one is the hinge stile and the other is the lock stile. Joining the stiles is a series of horizontal members known as rails. Usually there are rails at the top, bottom and middle; the latter is sometimes known as the lock rail. Some doors have more than three. At one time the rails were mortised into the stiles, but nowadays they are just as likely to be fixed with dowels.

A flush door consists of thin sheet material such as hardboard or plywood fixed to both sides of a timber frame. This frame will have a hinge and lock stile plus a rail at the top and bottom. The void in between could be filled by other rails and diagonal braces, or instead there may be a honeycomb of toughened paper, glued to both claddings. Blocks of wood known as lock blocks are fitted to take handles and locks.

The ledged-and-braced door is nowadays used mainly on outbuildings or as a garden gate, but it was at one time regarded as a house door and is still found on older houses. It is made of matchboarding nailed to horizontal members known as ledgers. There are usually three ledgers and to add strength and stability diagonal timbers called braces are fitted. Where these braces are omitted the door is referred to as being just ledged.

Door frames consist of a timber lining nailed to timber plugs let into the masonry. A stop bead, against which the door closes, is fitted. This is usually a length of timber nailed in place, but on external doors it is often formed by a rebate, machined in place at the factory to make a one-piece frame.

Common faults in doors

If any faults arise in a door you should deal with them immediately. They are not just a nuisance; they could also be setting up stresses in the construction that could cause greater problems later on. Some of the more common faults are described below, and many of these apply to windows as well.

Doors that stick

The door may be difficult to open or close because there is too much paint on one edge or because damp has caused it to swell up. If the condition is not too bad, an easy cure is to rub candle wax on the high spots. If that doesn't work you'll have to remove some of the layers of paint and perhaps even some excess timber. Use glasspaper, a scraper, plane or Surform according to the amount

that has to be taken off. It may be easier to take the door off its hinges rather than work on it in position.

Sometimes it may not be obvious exactly where the door is sticking. Try running a knife blade between the door and frame, or rub chalk on the edges of the door — you need to plane down the bits where the chalk has rubbed off. Don't take off too much because the door will shrink in dry weather and you may then be left with a draught.

Treat any bare wood with paint or preservative to match the rest of the door. Make sure the paint is dry before you close the door because new paint, too, can cause a door to stick.

If the door is sticking at floor level it will often leave marks on the floor to indicate where the problem lies. You can sometimes cure it by placing a sheet of glasspaper under the door and then opening it and closing it a few times. If that doesn't work you'll have to take the door off its hinges. If you are dealing with a flush door and you have to remove timber from the top or bottom, always plane inwards from each side in turn to avoid splitting the wood at the stiles.

RESHAPING A DOOR STOP

1 *A gap between the door and stop will let in draughts and you should reshape the door stop for a better fit. Transfer the profile of the door onto the stop.*

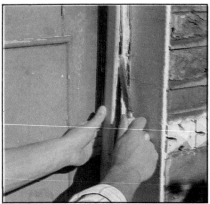

2 *Carefully prise the door stop away from the frame. If it is a factory-made one-piece frame you'll have to shape the stop as best you can in situ.*

3 *Use a saw if you have a lot of material to remove but a plane is best for small amounts. Shave off the wood until you meet the marked line.*

4 *Tack the door stop back in place with the door closed so you can position it exactly then open the door and nail it firmly to the frame.*

ADJUSTING A HINGE

1 *Before working on the hinges, prop up the door by inserting a wedge under the lock stile. There is no need to take the door down.*

2 *This hinge must be packed out to make the door hang properly – cardboard or hardboard will do. Some hinges need to be recessed deeper into the frame.*

Faulty hinges

A door can sometimes become 'hinge bound', that is, its hinge stile meets the frame before the door is properly closed, making it difficult or impossible to shut. The cause may be that the recesses for the hinges are too deep. In that case, pack them out with cardboard or hardboard. There's no need to take down the door to do this. Open it and jam a wedge under the lock stile to take the strain off the hinges. Then deal with each hinge in turn, removing all screws, pushing in the packing piece and re-inserting the screws.

The binding can also be caused by hinge recesses that are too shallow, so that the two leaves of the hinge strike each other and prevent the door from closing, or they leave a gap between the hinge stile and the door frame. In this case you should remove each hinge and chisel out the recesses to a greater depth. But check first that the screw heads are not sticking out too far as this could have the same effect. If you have difficulty driving home a screw, withdraw it and drill a pilot hole before re-inserting it.

Sagging doors

When a door is not held properly to the frame, or it droops to grate on the floor as you open it, it is said to sag. There are two possible causes for this; either the hinges are at fault, or there is a defect in the construction of the door itself.

To start with the hinges, perhaps all that's happened is the hinge screws have worked loose. In that case you could replace them with longer or thicker screws. Hinges are usually fixed with No 8 screws, so try No 10s instead (provided, of course, the countersink holes are big enough to take their heads). If this doesn't work, withdraw the screws and pack out the holes before driving them home. You can use thin dowels or spent matchsticks for this.

Another problem may be that the knuckle of the hinge is damaged so that the two leaves are not held close enough together. The hinge should in that case be replaced. Once again, there is no need to take the door down from the frame. You can replace the hinge with the door supported on a wedge under the lock stile.

These repairs will cure the immediate problem, but you ought to find out why it occurred. It may be that the hinges fitted in the first place were not strong enough. An internal door needs two 75mm (3in) – or preferably 100mm (4in) – hinges, while on a heavy external door, three hinges would be better.

If you suspect the damaged hinges were not strong enough, then you should fit replacements which are one size bigger. Alternatively you could fit an extra hinge for added strength.

Where the hinges are sound then a fault has probably developed in the door itself. Usually it will be easy to see if this is so. For instance, on a panelled door the joint between a rail and a stile may have worked loose. If the joint is a mortise-and-tenon and the tenon is actually visible on an edge, then there are two possible remedies. Basically, the loose joint is clamped shut and then fixed in some way. An easy way is to take a couple of small hardwood wedges and tap one in on each side of the tenon. Make a shallow saw cut along the length of each wedge to form a glue run, and smear woodworking adhesive on them before fixing them in place. If it is difficult to insert the wedges, open up a starting hole with a chisel and mallet.

You can also strengthen the joint by drilling holes through the face of the door into the tenon and driving in two dowels which you have grooved and smeared with adhesive.

In both cases it is best to cramp the whole door and leave it undisturbed until the glue has set. You can make an improvised cramping jig by screwing battens to a wooden floor, placing the door in the batten framework and then driving wedges between the door and the battens to hold the door tight – see *Ready Reference*.

Sometimes the tenon can be too damaged for a repair of this type to work – it might even have sheared off completely. In that case it is better to join the stile to the rail by means of repair plates. These can be fixed in a recess chiselled in the face of the door and then covered by filler. But make sure the rail is not more extensively damaged or even rotten. If it is, it will probably be much easier to buy a new door, despite the cost.

Warped and twisted doors
A common problem is that the door may be twisted. If the twist is slight, and only a problem in that it lets in draughts, the simple cure is to make the door frame conform as closely as possible to the shape of the twist. If the door stop is merely nailed in place, prise it off and reposition it to form a better fit, making up minor gaps with draughtproofing strip. If the door stop is a machined-in rebate, close the door and use a small block of wood and a pencil to trace its outline on the stop. You can then shape the stop to conform to the door, using a plane, shaper or chisel.

Where the twist is more pronounced you may need to straighten the door. Lay the door flat on a bare boarded floor, with blocks under the true corners. Then place battens across the door face and screw them down to force the door back into shape. Leave it like this for as long as possible.

If the door is bowed in the middle, place it on the floor raised on blocks at the top and bottom edges, with the bow uppermost and screw the batten across the middle.

Other faults in doors
Sometimes a crack can develop in a timber panel of a panelled door. First clean up the edges of the crack with glasspaper and smear glue along them. Drill two holes in the stile from the edge of the door towards the top and bottom of the panel, then drive in glued dowels. Tap the dowels home until the crack closes (see the step-by-step photographs). The dowels should be long enough to protrude out of the stile so that when the adhesive has set they can be cut off and planed flush.

The lock can be a source of trouble, too. It can get out of alignment so the bolt cannot enter properly. Usually only a slight adjustment is needed. The easiest cure is to slacken off the screws holding the staple or striking plate, then give it a tap in the right direction and retighten the screws. If you've had to rehang the door to correct sagging you'll have to make a bigger adjustment and you may need to cut a new mortise for the bolt. You'll also have to cut a new mortise if you've reshaped the door.

Faults in the door frame
Faults can also develop in the door frame – for example, part of it may work loose from the wall. In this case you'll have to find the heads of the nails holding it in place – they are usually visible under the paint – and drive them deeper into their timber plugs with a hammer and punch. However, if the plugs have split or shrunk this remedy will not work. So for a more secure repair drill through the timber and into the masonry behind with a masonry bit. Twist a plastic wallplug onto the end of a screw and insert the plug into the hole in the frame. Tap the screw head lightly with a hammer until the plug is fully home, then tighten up the screw. Fit as many screws as necessary to secure the frame.

Settlement of the building or loose joints may force the frame out the square, and then the door will not fit properly. The only answer is to reshape the door to fit – removing excess timber, adding a fillet here and there and shaping these until the door matches the opening as it should. An easy way to do this is to cut the top of the door to match the angle of the doorframe, add an extra piece to the bottom and then rehang the door. First transfer the angle of the frame to the top of the door using a small block of wood and a pencil, and then cut along this line. It's worth taking off a reasonable amount to make sawing easier – 12mm (½in) would be about right. Measure the gap left at the top of the door and add a batten of wood of this thickness to the bottom. Finally, move up the hinges by the same amount so the door fits correctly, and adjust the latch striker plate too, cutting a new mortise if necessary.

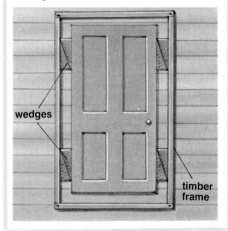

REPAIRING A CRACKED PANEL

The panels in a panelled door are usually rebated into the stiles at each side. These panels are relatively thin and can easily crack and split, perhaps because of accidental damage or simply through old age. A crack may have been filled in the past and covered up with layers of paint and it's only when you strip the door that it becomes apparent. Stripping the door can also loosen the glue holding the panels in place so the panels become free to move and the split opens up even further. A crack of this sort is impossible to fill and if you plan to leave the door unpainted you would not want to see a line of filler anyway.

The only answer is to make a proper repair which forces the crack shut.

1 Drill through the stile in two places near the top and bottom of the cracked panel. Choose a drill to match the size of dowel – 6mm ($^1/_4$in) is about right.

2 Lightly sand the crack with fine grade glasspaper; then smear a thin line of woodworking adhesive along the whole length of the crack.

3 Cut two lengths of dowelling as long as the width of the stile plus about 25mm (1in). Smear glue into the drilled holes and insert the dowels.

4 Hammer the dowels right in until they meet the side of the panel; then tap gently until the crack closes. Wipe off any excess adhesive.

5 Leave the glue to set; then cut off the ends of the dowels so that they are flush with the stile and plane the area smooth for an almost invisible repair.

External door frames can start to rot at the bottom and the rotten parts must be cut out and replaced. Probe into the timber to find out how far the rot extends, then cut out the affected portion plus a further 75mm (3in) of sound timber. You get a considerably neater finish if the new timber is scarf-jointed into the frame.

Remember to treat the ends and back of the new timber with preservative and then screw it in place into wallplugs. If the original frame was machined out of solid timber you will find it easier to make a matching section out of two separate pieces which are glued and nailed together.

If the doorstep is wooden the frame may be tenoned into it, so you will have to saw through the tenon in order to remove the defective part. There is no need to try to tenon the new timber into the step.

Treating rotten windows

The opening lights of windows often suffer from the same defects as hinged doors – loose joints, faulty hinges, etc – and the remedies are similar. However, you have to proceed with more care to avoid breaking the glass, especially on repairs that involve driving in wedges.

But the most common defect is rot, usually in the window sill. If the rotten section is not too extensive then you can make a repair, but if it has spread, you may find that the best policy is to remove the frame completely and fit a modern replacement window.

If the rot is in the middle of a sill, make a saw cut about 75mm (3in) each side of the rot. The cuts should be at an angle so that you remove a wedge-shaped piece from the sill. You will then have to cut a new piece to fit. Timber merchants sell standard sill sections but in the case of older houses you'll have to buy a rectangular section and shape it yourself.

Treat the new timber and the cut ends of the existing sill with preservative. The repair is held in place with dowels set at intervals of 100mm (4in) and fixed into the frame. Smear all meeting surfaces with adhesive before finally fixing in place. For additional strength on wider sills, fit steel repair plates to the underside of the repair. Corner repair pieces are fitted in the same way, except that they are slightly more difficult to shape to the correct profile.

Remember that the outside of any window is exposed to the weather so be sure to give any new timber a coat of primer and then a good coat of gloss paint to protect it. Older properties are more likely to have sash windows and for a complete discussion on how to repair these, see pages 24-27.

REPAIRING A ROTTEN WINDOW SILL

1 It's better to replace a damaged or rotten section of sill rather than trying to patch or fill it. Mark out a wedge-shaped section around the damage.

2 Cut carefully along the lines taking care not to cut into the rest of the frame. A tenon saw will do but is rather slow – a powered jigsaw would be easier.

3 A jigsaw could also cut along the back so you can remove the section in one piece. If you don't have one you'll have to chisel out the wood bit by bit.

4 Keep chiselling until you reach the end of the sill section. Make sure all the faces are vertical so the replacement will be easy to fit.

5 Use a sliding bevel or try square to transfer the angle of cut to the new section. Only cut one side, then mark the other while holding the wood in place.

6 Next mark the front line of the sill. It is probably easiest to plane to this line rather than trying to saw off such a narrow piece.

7 Smear adhesive over the meeting surfaces and push the wood in to place. Drill holes at intervals of 100mm (4in) and countersink the holes so the screw heads are well below the front surface.

8 For a neat and invisible fixing, insert short lengths of dowels into the screw holes to cover up the screw heads – glue them first, then plane them off flush with the rest of the sill.

9 Finally, plane the top surface of the sill until it is in line with the surrounding wood. Then prime and paint the wood to match the rest of the window sill and protect it from further rot.

REPAIRS FOR SASH WINDOWS

Almost all older houses and quite a few new ones are fitted with sash windows – handsome, but prone to faults. Here's how they work and how to repair them.

The sash (or double-hung) window was used a great deal on homes right into this century – almost to the exclusion of any other type. It's a period feature, often adding a touch of authentic charm. Unfortunately sash windows can be very difficult to keep in good working order.

Sash windows actually consist of two separate windows – sashes is their proper name – each sliding vertically in its own channel. When both are closed, the sash in the outer channel is at the top, and the inner sash is at the bottom.

The channels are formed by three sets of beading, running round the inside of the frame. These are known (starting with the outermost one) as the *outer*, *parting* and *staff* beads. The outer and staff beads lie flat on the window frame, but the parting bead is fixed on its edge. The outer bead, in fact, may well form part of the frame itself; the other two are always separate pieces, nailed in place. For easy removal they should never be glued, or maintenance of the window becomes impossible.

How sashes work

Counterbalancing weights, each pair of which weighs the same as the sash they're attached to, ensure that the sashes stay in whatever position you choose and don't come crashing down – perhaps with such force that the glass is shattered. There's a weight on each side of each sash, hidden in a compartment inside the frame. Each weight is attached to its sash by a cord that passes over a pulley at the top of the frame and is nailed to the side of the sash.

The drawback of sash windows is that it's almost impossible to make them fully draught-proof, although some success can be achieved with brush-type draught excluders. The only sure way is to install secondary double glazing – the type that fits within the window reveal and is hinged to, or slides in, its own frame. You can't attach fixed double glazing panels directly to each sash because they won't slide past each other. And even if you could, the extra weight would throw the sashes out of balance, preventing the inner one from remaining in the open position and the outer one from remaining closed.

Minor repairs

However, many lesser faults can easily be cured if you know what to do. Often you needn't even dismantle the window.

Hacking out and replacing old, crumbling putty, and renewing a cracked pane of glass, for example, are two jobs where dismantling the window is unnecessary. And if a pulley squeaks – just oil it.

You can even repair a sash corner joint that has begun to open up, provided you wedge the sash firmly in place while you're working on it. All that's needed is a flat, L-shaped metal plate which you can easily buy: you just screw it across the corner. It looks a bit unsightly if left exposed; but you can conceal it by first chiselling out a shallow L-shaped recess to take it, and afterwards covering it with paint (not emulsion paint), cellulose filler and then a top coat of paint – in that order, so that the water in the filler doesn't rust the metal and discolour the paintwork.

Filler will also take care of minor cracks, dents and other blemishes in the wood. You can do a certain amount of redecorating, too, without removing the sashes, but you'll find it hard to get a neat edge as you approach the concealed parts.

Major repairs

Some jobs, however, do call for taking the window to pieces – a procedure that's far easier than it sounds. One such task is silencing a rattle; the root of the trouble in this case is that the beads are too far apart and need repositioning.

Prise off first the staff bead and then the parting bead on each side of the frame. There's usually no need to interfere with the sections of beading at top and bottom, but you'll have to take out the inner sash to get at the parting bead. To remove a bead, cut down the angle with a sharp knife first to break the paint seal and avoid tearing off flakes. Then push a chisel between it and the frame, as near the nails as you can, and spring it out gradually.

The various beads may well have become damaged over the years. In that case you can simply replace them with new ones, bought from a timber merchant (ask for them by their proper names, and he'll understand). To lessen the risk of splitting, drill pilot holes for the nails – oval nails are best. When re-fixing the beads, position them close enough to each sash to cure the rattle, but not too close, or you'll bring about the second common fault: sashes which won't slide freely, or at all.

The other and more likely reason for that, however, is a build-up of paint in the channels. You can't just go on putting coat upon coat of paint when you redecorate them, and the only remedy when they jam is to sand or scrape off the paint where the

DISMANTLING THE WINDOW

1 Remove the staff bead at each side by levering it off gently with a broad-bladed chisel, inserted as near as possible to each of the nails.

2 After lowering the inner sash, hold on to the cord to stop it escaping, and cut it. A long piece of string tied on to it first, above the cut, will help to thread the cord.

3 Once you've cut the sash cord on the opposite side of the frame as well, you'll be able to lift out the inner sash and place it to one side, out of the way.

4 The parting bead holds the outer sash in place; remove it as you did the staff bead. Then cut the cords on the outer sash and remove that too.

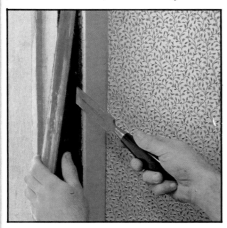

5 Lever off the pocket covers which conceal the weights in the sides of the frame (sometimes there are two on each side) and lift out each weight.

6 Pull the cord until the string appears. Remove the cord and weight and tie the ends of the string together so it won't slip off the pulley.

Ready Reference

PARTS OF A SASH WINDOW

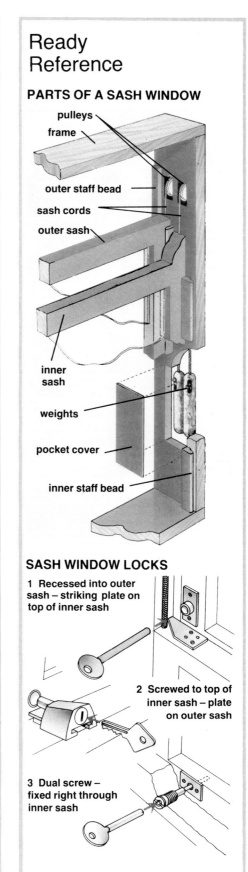

pulleys
frame
outer staff bead
sash cords
outer sash
inner sash
weights
pocket cover
inner staff bead

SASH WINDOW LOCKS

1 Recessed into outer sash – striking plate on top of inner sash

2 Screwed to top of inner sash – plate on outer sash

3 Dual screw – fixed right through inner sash

REPAIRING SASHES

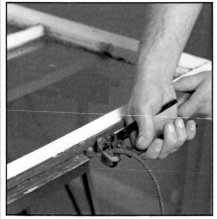

1 *Use a pair of pincers to remove the nails and the remaining bits of old sash cord from the grooves which run down each side of the sash, near the top.*

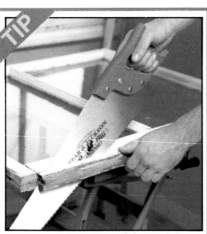

2 *If one of the edges of the sash is damaged, remove it altogether by sawing it off – ready for the fixing of a replacement piece of new timber.*

3 *Sash corner joints that have begun to part but aren't loose can be filled before re-painting. This will stop rain getting into them and rotting the timber.*

4 *A really rickety joint needs more extensive repairs. Begin by cramping it tightly together – but not so tightly that you crack the glass.*

5 *For a dowel repair, drill a hole right through the joint, running from top to bottom through the tenon. Glue and insert the dowel and tap it gently home.*

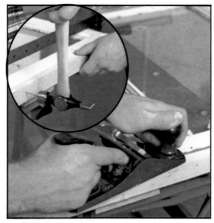

6 *Replace the sawn-off piece with one near the right size, and planed to the exact width. Glue and nail it (inset), then plane it flush with the rest of the sash.*

sashes are binding, leaving room for the primer and one or two further coats that will have to be re-applied to the bare wood.

Taking out sashes
By far the most serious possibility, however, is that eventually a sash cord will break and need replacing. When this happens you should replace all four, because if one goes the rest are sure to be near breaking-point. In any case the hardest part of the job is dismantling everything; fitting four new cords is very little more trouble than fitting one.

Begin by levering off the staff bead. Swing the lower sash inwards, tie a length of string to each sash cord just above the sash, and cut each cord below the knot, letting the weights down gradually to the bottom of their compartments. With the string now attached to the cord, there's no danger of being unable to retrieve the weights from their pockets. Lift out the lower sash, remove the parting bead, pull down the upper sash and repeat the process. Lift that out too, and remove the old cord and fixing nails from each sash.

Now that you've got the sashes out, you can take the opportunity to do major surgery on them if necessary. Where a corner joint is rickety, dowels make a neater and more professional repair than a metal plate. You'll need to cramp the sash firmly in place on a workbench first, both to hold it steady and to keep the joint tight while you drill the dowel holes. The joint will almost certainly be a mortise and tenon, so the best place to run strengthening dowels is sideways through the tenon, or perhaps lengthwise on either side of it.

If one of the sash members is cracked or rotten, it may be possible to remove the bad piece by sawing lengthwise, and to replace it with new timber – cut slightly too large, glued, nailed and finally planed off flush. For both these jobs, use urea-formaldehyde adhesive, which resists damp.

Sometimes a sash sticks in its channel because it has warped or swollen. In this case, removing a few shavings from the offending part with a plane may be the answer.

The only really tricky job (one you'll be well advised to leave unless you're quite skilled) is renewing the glazing bars which divide individual panes of glass within a sash. And if a sash is in bad enough condition to call for other major repairs, if may be more practical to replace it altogether. Getting a joinery shop to copy the old one is generally far wiser than substituting a modern window which may be quite out of keeping with the character of the house.

With the sashes removed, you also have the opportunity to make a thorough job of re-painting the sashes and the frame. Use a

REPLACING SASH CORDS

1 *All four sash cords are renewed in the same way. First untie the string, and tie the new cord to the end which hangs on the visible side of the frame.*

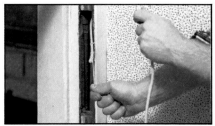

2 *Pull the other end of the string to draw the new cord over the pulley and right down inside the frame to the bottom of the weight compartment.*

3 *Thread the new cord through the weight and tie a secure knot to keep it there. Then repeat these steps for the weight on the other side of the sash.*

4 *After measuring the length of the groove down each side of the sash, mark each side of the frame the same distance from the top of the pulley.*

5 *Pulling each cord so that the weight dangles 50mm (2in) above the base of its compartment, cut the cord at the mark – but don't let go of it.*

6 *After working on the outer sash, you should replace the parting bead. Nail it on edge, but don't glue it in case you need to remove it in future.*

7 *Nail the cord into the groove in the sash. Don't nail the cord right to the top of the groove, or the sash won't run right up.*

8 *The final step is to replace the staff bead, nailing each length flat in position after mitring both ends. Don't glue this one either, for the same reason.*

9 *For a thorough job, and a neater appearance, renew the staff beads at the top and bottom of the frame, as well as those at each side.*

blowlamp or chemical paint stripper to remove layers of old paint if it's in bad condition, and then coat the timber with wood primer. Alternatively just sand the old paint-work down and spot-prime any bare patches. Then apply the rest of your paint system in the usual way.

Renewing sash cords

Whether or not you've had to pause in order to repair a sash or to repaint everything, you're now ready to carry on and fit new sash cords.

The first step is to remove the weights. To get at them, you have to take out the one or two pieces of wood covering each weight compartment – the pocket pieces. These are usually just a push fit, and you prise them out with an old chisel or screwdriver; in some

cases, however, there's also a retaining screw. Lift out each weight, untie the cord from it, and attach it to the free end of the string, making a complete loop. If there's rust on the weight, you can rub it off with abrasive paper at this stage, but there's no need to paint it.

You can buy new sash cord from almost any builder's merchant or hardware store, but ask for it by name – don't just use any old cord. To fit the new cord, untie the loop of string, tie the cord to it, and use it to thread the cord over the pulley and down into the weight compartment. Then tie the cord to the weight with a strong knot. At this stage don't try cutting the cord to the correct length – leave it too long.

Most sashes have a groove, near the top of each side, in which the cord is fixed with

small galvanised round-head nails. Either nail the cord into the groove and trim off the excess, or mark the groove length on the frame and trim the cord to the mark. Which-ever you do, the weight should hang 50mm (2in) above the base of its compartment when the sash is at the top of the frame. It's the same for each sash. Note that the cord shouldn't be fixed right to the top of the groove, or the sash won't run all the way up. The topmost nail should be as far down from the top as the top of the pulley is from the top of the frame opening.

After fixing the cords at both sides of the outer sash, replace the parting bead. Then repeat the whole process for the inner sash, and lastly replace it and the staff bead in position. When fixing the beads, make sure the sashes have room to slide freely.

EMERGENCY PIPE REPAIRS

A leaking pipe is no joke. First you have to stop the water – so you need to know where to turn if off – and then to make some kind of emergency repair, even if it's just a holding operation.

Leaks in domestic plumbing systems have a nasty habit of happening at the most inconvenient of times, often when it isn't possible to carry out a proper permanent repair. What you need is a plumbing emergency first aid kit, and there are now several proprietary products available that will at least enable you to make a temporary repair and get the water flowing again.

With any leak, the vital first step is to stop the flow of water. Even a small leak can create a surprisingly large pool of water in no time. Stopping the flow in any pipe is relatively easy provided that you know the locations of the various stop-taps or valves that isolate parts of your water system, or cut it off completely from the mains supply.

Water comes into the house through a pipe known as the rising main, and because

water in this pipe (and others leading from it) is under mains pressure, leaks from it will be particularly serious. It enters the house underground, and from there leads either to all the cold taps and a water heating system, or to just the cold tap in the kitchen and to a cold water storage tank.

Leaks can result from a number of causes. Pipework may have been forced or strained at some point, resulting in a leak at one of the fittings connecting the lengths of pipe together, or in a fracture at a bend.

Corrosion within pipes may lead to pinholes in pipe lengths, while frost damage can lead to bursts and splits in pipes and to leaks at fittings caused by ice forcing the fitting open. Whatever the cause, cutting off the water supply to the affected pipe is the first vital step.

Where to turn off the water

1 Cold water supply pipes connected directly to the mains: in the UK these pipes usually only supply the kitchen cold tap, the cold water storage tank and sometimes instantaneous water heaters. In Australia and other countries, the pipes may supply *all* cold water taps and the hot water storage cylinder. The simple way of deciding whether any pipe or tap is supplied directly by the mains is by the pressure – taps supplied from a tank are what's known as gravity-fed and the pressure of water is relatively low compared to mains pressure.

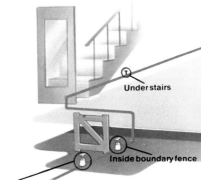

Under stairs

Inside boundary fence

Under footpath outside boundary fence

2 Cold water supply pipes from a cold water storage tank: in the UK these pipes usually supply the bathroom cold taps, the WC cistern and the hot water cylinder.

To close off the water supply in these pipes there's often a stop-valve immediately alongside the cold water tank where the pipe exits. Turn this off first and then open all cold water taps. They'll run dry almost immediately. If there isn't a stop-valve, you have to drain the whole tank. So first you stop water entering the tank by either turning off the mains (as above) or by tying up the ball-valve in the tank so that it remains closed. Then you open all the taps in the house.

3 Hot water pipes: these are all supplied from a hot water cylinder, which in turn gets its cold water either from the cold tank or from the mains.

Since hot water leaves the hot water storage cylinder from the top, it's only the pressure of water going in at the bottom of the cylinder that forces the water out. Turn off the supply of cold water (either at the cold water tank, or at the mains) and you stop the flow. In this sort of situation the hot water cylinder remains full. If for any reason you need to drain this as well, use the drain cock near the bottom. It's essential in this case to turn off either the immersion heater or boiler.

To turn off the water, look for the mains stop-valves. There may, in fact, be two: one inside the house where the mains pipe enters (under the kitchen sink, in the utility room, or even under the stairs); the other outside – either just inside the boundary of the property (near to a water meter, if you have one), or under the footpath outside the garden fence. Outdoor stop-valves may be set as much as a metre (3 ft) down beneath a hinged cover or metal plate, and you may need a special 'key' which is really just a long rod with a square socket on the end which fits over the tap to turn it. In most cases, however, it's simply a matter of reaching down to turn it off by hand or with a wrench. Some outdoor stop-valves also control a neighbour's water supply, so do warn them if you're turning it off.

The stop-valve inside will either be a wheel type or an ordinary T-shaped type. The only possible complication is if it hasn't been touched for years and is stuck fast. A little penetrating oil and tapping it with a hammer will usually loosen it sufficiently. (It's worth closing the stop-valve now and again to see that it doesn't get stuck.)

Ready Reference

TURNING OFF THE STOP TAP

Make sure the family knows where the mains stop tap is.

● do not force the handle if it has seized up — it could break it off.
● use hammer or wrench to tap the fitting while pouring penetrating oil down spindle.
● if you can't free it call the water authority emergency service — they can turn the water off where your supply pipe leaves the mains.
● don't reopen stop valve fully when turning on the supply until a permanent pipe repair is made. This reduces water pressure on a temporary seal.

TIP: MAKESHIFT REPAIRS

If you don't have the right materials to hand (see next page) try this:
● bandage insulating tape round the pipe and hole
● cover with a 150mm (6in) piece of garden hosepipe slit along its length and tie with wire at each end, twisting ends of wire together with pliers
● wrap more tape tightly over this

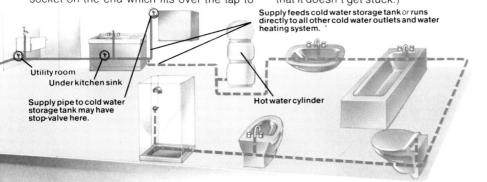

Supply feeds cold water storage tank *or* runs directly to all other cold water outlets and water heating system.

Utility room
Under kitchen sink
Supply pipe to cold water storage tank may have stop-valve here.
Hot water cylinder

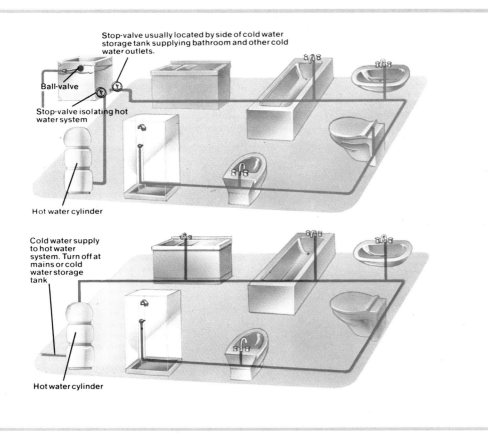

Stop-valve usually located by side of cold water storage tank supplying bathroom and other cold water outlets.

Ball-valve
Stop-valve isolating hot water system
Hot water cylinder

Cold water supply to hot water system. Turn off at mains or cold water storage tank

Hot water cylinder

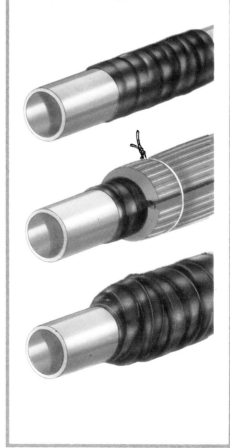

EMERGENCY REPAIRS

● One type of repair kit is based on a two-part **epoxy resin plastic putty** supplied as two strips of differently-coloured putty in an airtight pack. When the strips are thoroughly kneaded together the putty is packed firmly round the pipe, where it will harden to form a seal. However, this hardening process takes up to 24 hours and the water supply will have to remain off for this period. (If you don't need to use all the pack in one go, reseal it immediately).

Equal amounts of putty should always be used and mixed together thoroughly until a uniform colour results, otherwise it won't harden properly. It's also essential that the pipe or joint is scrupulously rubbed down and cleaned with methylated spirit or nail polish remover. This will ensure a good bond between the putty and the metal.

● One of the most valuable aids is a multi-size **pipe repair clamp** which has the added advantage of being reusable. It consists of a rubber pad which fits over the hole (for this repair it's not necessary to turn off the water) and a metal clamp which draws the rubber tightly against the pipe when it is screwed in place.

Position the pad and one side of the clamp over the hole, and link the two parts of the clamp together, making sure that the pad is still in place. Tighten the wing nut fully. If the position of the hole makes this difficult, use blocks of wood to hold the pipe away from the wall. This method of repair cannot, of course, be used to mend leaks occurring at fittings.

● Another proprietary product uses a two-part **sticky tape** system which builds up waterproof layers over the leak — in the true sense this does form an instant repair. The area round the leak should be dried and cleaned and then the first of the tapes is wrapped tightly round the pipe, covering the leak and 25mm (1in) either side of it. Then 150mm strips of the second tape, with the backing film removed, are stuck to the pipe and stretched as they are wound round, each turn overlapping the previous one by about half the width of the tape. This covering should extend 25mm beyond either end of the first layer of tape. The job is completed by wrapping the first tape over all the repair.

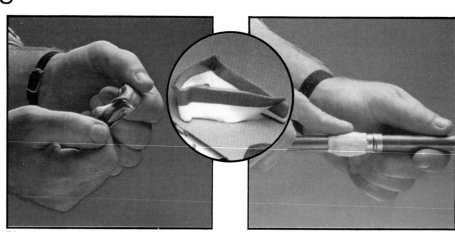

Plastic putty *Using your fingers, mix together equal amounts of the two putty strips. It's ready for use when the colour is even all through.*

Thoroughly clean area round the leaking pipe, then pack putty round fitting. It can be sanded smooth when it's completely hard.

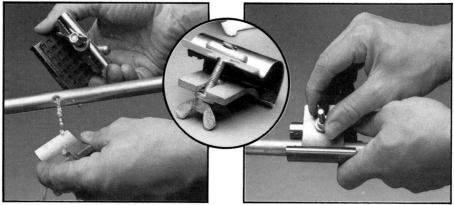

Pipe clamp *Place rubber pad and one side of metal clamp directly over leak in pipe. There's no need to turn off the water with this type of repair.*

Link the two parts of clamp togther, being careful to keep it in position. Screw down wing nut to secure rubber pad against pipe.

Sticky tape *Start winding first tape round pipe about 25mm (1in) from the leaking fitting. Continue over the joint and for 25mm on other side.*

Stretch and overlap 150mm strips of second tape round pipe. Continue 25mm (1in) either side of first tape. Finish off with layer of first tape.

STOPPING TAPS LEAKING

Although taps are in frequent use, they rarely need maintenance. But if one starts to leak don't ignore it. Leaking taps are not only annoying and wasteful, but also, if they are hot taps, expensive — you've paid to heat the water going down the drain.

A tap is a device for controlling the flow of water at an outlet point, and is opened and closed by turning a handle. This may be a 'tee' or 'capstan' type (so called because of the shape) fitted onto a spindle rising from the body of the tap. Or it may be a 'shrouded head', covering all of the upper part of the tap.

Turning the handle clockwise forces a jumper unit down onto a valve seating in the waterway of the tap and stops the flow of water. Because metal against metal doesn't make a very tight seal, a synthetic rubber disc — a washer — is attached to the base of the jumper so that it beds firmly onto the seating.

Turning the handle anti-clockwise raises the jumper from the seating and allows water to flow. An exception to this is the Supatap where the nozzle is rotated to control the flow. When you open a tap water pressure will also force water round the jumper unit and, unless there is some way of preventing it, this would escape from round the spindle. To get round this problem some taps have 'O' ring seals fitted to the spindle while older taps have greased wool packed tightly in a gland around the spindle. More modern taps have rubber tube for packing.

Mixers work in exactly the same way as ordinary taps except that they have only one spout that combines the flow of water from the hot and cold supplies. On kitchen mixers particularly this spout can be swivelled so that it can be pushed to one side to give better access to the sink or can supply a double sink.

When a tap starts to leak, there's a strong temptation either to ignore it or to try to stop it by closing it as tightly as you can. Such action is invariably ineffective and could lead to the valve seating being permanently damaged.

Where leaks occur

Basically there are three places a tap can leak: at the spout, in which case the washer and perhaps the seating will need looking at; at the spindle when the tap is turned on, which means either the packing in the gland or the 'O' ring has failed; or at the swivel point at the spout of a mixer tap, which means that the 'O' ring is at fault. All these repairs are easy to deal with. But first you must know the type of tap and the terminology related to it.

How washers are replaced

Conventional pillar tap This is the basic type of tap design and provides a good example of the procedure to follow when replacing a washer. These taps are commonly used for the hot and cold water supply over the kitchen sink and in this position they are probably the most frequently used taps in the house. It's quite likely that sooner or later the washers will need replacing.

To do this you'll first have to turn off the water supply either at the mains or, if you're lucky, at isolating stop-valves under the sink which when shut cut off the supply either to the hot or cold tap without affecting the rest of the system (see section on emergency repairs on pages 28-30). Turn on the tap fully so it is drained before you start work.

Usually with a pillar tap the spindle rises out of a dome-like easy-clean cover, which you should be able to unscrew by hand. If this proves too difficult, you can use a wrench, but pad the jaws thoroughly with rag to avoid damaging the finish on plated taps.

With the tap turned on fully you can then raise the cover sufficiently to slip the jaws of a wrench under it to grip the 'flats' of the headgear — the main body of the tap which has a nut-shaped section to it. If you can't do this you'll need to take off the tap handle and easy-clean cover. First you'll have to remove the tiny grub-screw in the side of the handle which can then be lifted off. If this proves difficult a good tip is to open the tap fully, unscrew, then raise the easy-clean cover and place pieces of wood (a spring-loaded clothes peg will do) between the bottom of the easy-clean cover and the body of the tap. By turning the tap handle as if you were trying to close it the upward pressure on the easy-clean cover will force it off the spindle. However, you then have to replace it over the spindle just sufficiently to enable you to turn the tap on. When this is done take it off again and remove the easy-clean cover. While you are doing all this make sure you hold the tap steady. If the headgear is stiff and the entire tap turns you could damage the part of the sink into which the tap fits.

You can now put the headgear to one side. You should be able to see the jumper, with the washer attached, resting on the valve seating within the body of the tap (though sometimes it gets stuck and lifts out with the headgear). Often the washer is held in position on the jumper by a tiny nut which has to be undone with pliers before the washer can be replaced. This may be easier said than done, and rather than waste time attempting the all-but-impossible, it's probably better to fit a new washer and jumper complete rather than just renewing the washer. Once this has been done the tap can be reassembled, and as you do this smear the screw threads with petroleum jelly.

Others: Folkard Bolding   Blue enamelled taps: Zazzeri   Supatap: Deltaflow   Jem Grischotti

Bib with capstan handle

Pillar with capstan handle

Supatap

Pillar with shrouded head

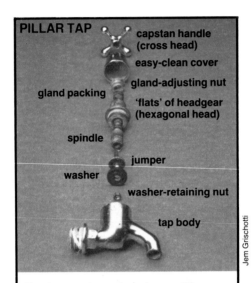

PILLAR TAP
- capstan handle (cross head)
- easy-clean cover
- gland-adjusting nut
- gland packing
- 'flats' of headgear (hexagonal head)
- spindle
- jumper
- washer
- washer-retaining nut
- tap body

Jem Grischotti

New taps rarely need repairs – and the actuality is more likely to be taps like these which won't be bright and clean inside. In hard-water areas lime scale will have accumulated which can cause the tap to jam so remove it with wire wool when the tap's dismantled. This will also help you identify the parts.

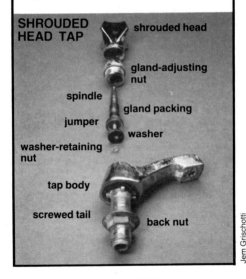

SHROUDED HEAD TAP
- shrouded head
- gland-adjusting nut
- spindle
- gland packing
- jumper
- washer
- washer-retaining nut
- tap body
- screwed tail
- back nut

Jem Grischotti

Tap with shrouded head This is basically a pillar tap where the spindle is totally enclosed by an easy-clean cover that also acts as a handle to turn the tap on and off. Some shrouded heads are made of plastic and care is therefore needed when using wrenches. But the mystery of this tap is how

to get to the inside — and methods vary with the make of tap.

Some shrouded heads can simply be pulled off, perhaps after opening the tap fully and then giving another half turn. Some are secured by a tiny grub-screw in the side. But the commonest method of attaching the head is by a screw beneath the plastic 'hot' or 'cold' indicator. Prise the plastic bit off with a small screwdriver to reveal the retaining screw (normally a cross-headed screw). When the shrouded head has been removed you'll find that you can unscrew the head-gear to reach the interior of the tap in the same way as with an ordinary pillar tap. Rewashering can then be done in the same way.

If the jumper is not resting on the valve seating in the body of the tap, but is 'pegged' into the headgear so that it can be turned round and round but can't be withdrawn, it's slightly more of a problem to remove the washer-retaining nut. The easiest way is to fasten the jumper plate in a vice (although pliers will do) and turn the nut with a spanner. Some penetrating oil will help to free the thread. If after this you still can't loosen the nut, a good tip is to slip the blade of a screwdriver between the plate of the jumper and the tap headgear and lever it to break the pegging. A new jumper and washer can then be fitted complete, although the stem should be 'burred' or roughened with a file to give an 'interference fit' when it is slipped into the headgear.

Bib taps These taps are treated in exactly the same way as a conventional pillar tap. You might find with a garden tap that there's no easy-clean cover, so the headgear is already exposed.

Ready Reference

KNOW YOUR TAPS

Bib taps have a tee-shaped or capstan handle and a horizontal inlet.

Pillar taps have a vertical inlet, can be made of metal or plastic with capstan or elbow-action handles or shrouded head. Made to fit holes in sinks, basins and baths.

Supataps are a patented pillar tap. The water control is on the nozzle and a washer can be changed without turning off the supply.

Mixers are pillar units in which hot and cold water meet and come out through a central spout.
● kitchen mixers have a divider in the spout – a regulation to stop mains (cold) and stored water (hot) mixing in one plumbing fitting
● bath mixers can have a shower attachment to divert mixed water up to a sprinkler.

TOOLS FOR TAP REPAIRS

● **thin screwdriver** is useful for prising off clipped on coverings, separating washer from jumper, removing 'O' rings, grub-screws
● **cross-headed screwdriver** might be needed for retaining-screw on some shrouded or mixer taps
● **adjustable wrench or spanner** is needed to remove the headgear.

Bathroom mixer

Kitchen mixer

REPLACING A PILLAR TAP WASHER

1 *Pillar taps should be opened fully after turning off the water supply. Now unscrew the easy-clean cover.*

2 *Lift up the easy-clean cover so you can slip an adjustable spanner or wrench in to undo the headgear.*

If there isn't enough space for the spanner or wrench, undo the grub-screw and then remove the handle.

If the handle won't come out, put a wedge under the cover and try to close the tap and force the cover up.

3 *With the handle fully opened, the headgear can be removed and the jumper unit pulled away.*

4 *Some taps have the washer fixed to the jumper unit by a nut; in others it has to be prised off.*

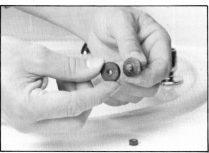

5 *Push a washer of the correct size over the end of the jumper unit. If held by a nut clean it with steel wool before replacing it.*

6 *Push the jumper unit back onto the headgear and replace in the tap. Turn the handle to half close the tap, then restore the mains supply.*

SHROUDED TAP

1 *With a shrouded head tap, you can either pull it off or prise off the indicator cap with a screwdriver after turning the water supply off and the tap on.*

2 *Undo the retaining screw (probably a cross-headed type so you'll need the right screwdriver) and then you will be able to pull off the head.*

3 *Hold the spout to prevent damaging the basin while you unscrew the headgear either using a spanner or an adjustable wrench.*

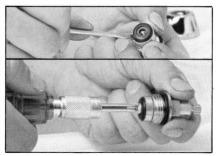

4 *Unscrew the retaining nut, remove the old washer and replace with one of the correct size. Reassemble the tap, then restore the water supply.*

WHAT'S GONE WRONG?

Check out the problem first.
Washers may be worn or disintegrating. Replace with 12mm (½in) or 18mm (¾in) synthetic rubber washers, available from hardware stores. A good tip for a temporary repair is to reverse the old washer.

'O' rings that look worn may also cause leaks. Choose the same size so they fit snugly.

Valve seating is damaged if rough and uneven. You can:
● use a domed, not a flat, washer

● fit a washer and seating set which covers up the damage

● buy or hire a reseating tool to grind the damaged seat smooth

TIPS TO SAVE TIME AND TROUBLE

● If you can't undo the nut holding the washer to the jumper, buy an all-in-one jumper and washer set.
● If a metal easy-clean cover is stuck pour very hot water over it. It should then unscrew.
● After repairing a tap, leave the water to run gently for 15 minutes to remove any air trapped in the pipes.

RE-WASHERING A SUPATAP

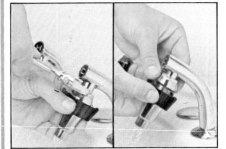

1 *Turn on the tap slightly and hold it while you undo the top nut. Open the tap fully, then turn the nozzle to unscrew it from the headgear.*

2 *As the nozzle comes away in your hand, a valve in the tap will automatically cut off the water so that you can make the repair.*

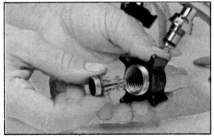

3 *Tap the nozzle on a hard surface so you can shake out the antisplash device to which will be attached the jumper unit and the washer.*

4 *Prise the old washer and jumper unit from the antisplash device and press in a new complete unit. Now you can reassemble the tap.*

Jem Grischotti

Supataps Changing the washer on this type of tap can be carried out in minutes, without the need to cut off the water supply first. Before you begin, check that you have a replacement Supatap washer and jumper unit. Once you've undone the retaining nut at the top of the nozzle you have to open up the tap fully — and then keep on turning. At first the flow will increase, but then, just before the nozzle comes off in your hand, a check-valve inside the tap will fall into position and stop the flow. You can separate the anti-splash device, (containing the washer and jumper unit) from the nozzle by turning it upside down and tapping the nozzle on a hard surface — not a ceramic sink or basin. The washer and jumper unit then need to be prised from the anti-splash device — you can use a knife blade or the edge of a coin to do this. A new washer and jumper unit can then be snapped in. When reassembling the tap it's necessary to remember that the nozzle has a left-hand thread and so has to be turned anti-clockwise to tighten it.

Repairing a poor seating

Sometimes a tap will continue to drip although you've changed the washer. This is usually because the valve seating has become scored and damaged by grit from the mains, so the washer can't make a water-tight connection.

You can use a reseating tool to put the problem right. This entails removing the headgear after the water has been turned off, inserting the tool into the body of the tap and turning it to cut a new seating. It won't be worthwhile buying one of these tools for what is a once-in-a-lifetime job, but you may be able to hire one from a tool hire company.

An alternative method, and certainly one that's a lot easier, is to use a nylon 'washer and seating set'. Again with the water supply off, the headgear and the washer and jumper are removed from the tap end and the nylon liner is placed in position over the seating. The jumper and washer are then inserted into the headgear, which is screwed back onto the tap. The tap handle is then turned to the off position. This action will force the liner into and over the old seating to give a watertight joint.

You can't, of course, use one of these sets to reseat a Supatap. However, the makers (Deltaflow Ltd) will supply a reseating tool on request, but these taps very rarely need reseating.

You can also use a domed washer to cure a poor seating. It increases the surface area in contact with the waterway and so

LEAKAGE UP THE SPINDLE

1 *If the tap has a stuffing box round the spindle, first try to tighten the gland-adjusting nut.*

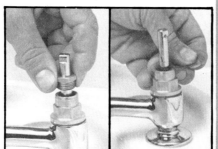

2 *If this fails to stop the leak, remove the nut and then pick out the old greased wool stuffing.*

3 *Smear petroleum jelly on a length of knitting wool, then wind it around the spindle, packing it down tightly.*

4 *Alternatively you may be able to use a rubber packing washer which just has to be slipped on.*

REPLACING 'O' RING SEALS

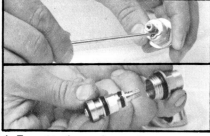

1 *To get to the seals on a tap, remove the headgear and prise off the circlip which holds the spindle in place.*

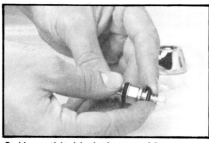

2 *Use a thin-bladed screwdriver to work off the worn 'O' rings and then replace them with new ones.*

3 *At the swivel point of a spout, first undo any grub-screw. Now twist the spout to one side and gently ease it from the mounting.*

4 *Prise off the worn seals with a screwdriver and then slip new ones into position. Replace the spout back in the mounting, restore water.*

effectively cuts off the flow when the tap is turned off even though the top of the valve seating may not be smooth.

Repacking a gland
This is necessary when you turn the tap on and water bubbles up the spindle towards the handle. At the same time the tap can be turned on and off far too easily — you might even be able to spin the handle with a flick of the fingers. This fault is a common cause of water hammer — heavy thudding following the closure of a tap or float-valve — that can result in damage to the plumbing system.

Leakage up the spindle is most likely to occur in rather old fashioned — but still very common — taps in which the spindle passes through a gland or 'stuffing box' filled with greased wool. It's inevitable that water containing detergent will be splashed onto the tap and this may result in the grease being washed out of the gland. The leakage can also be created if you run a garden or washing machine hose from the tap.

Fortunately, to make a repair you don't have to cut off the water supply to the tap, but you must be able to get at the gland-adjusting nut. This is the first nut through which the spindle passes.

Giving the gland-adjusting nut about half a turn may be enough to stop the leakage up the spindle, but eventually all the adjustment available will be taken up and you'll then have to repack the gland. When the gland-adjusting nut has been unscrewed and removed, the old gland packing material can be taken out and replaced with knitting wool saturated with petroleum jelly. The wool is wound round the spindle and packed down tightly before the gland-adjusting nut is put back and tightened until the tap handle can be turned fairly easily but without any leaks occurring.

Replacing an 'O' ring
Many modern taps have 'O' ring seals instead of a packed gland or stuffing box. If an 'O' ring fails the remedy is simply to undo the gland-adjusting nut, pick out the old 'O' ring and replace it with a new one. Leaks from taps with this fitting are rare. 'O' rings are also found at the swivel point of many mixer taps and if a leak occurs here you have to remove the spout to make the change – but this is usually only held with a grub-screw.

Older Supataps aren't fitted with an 'O' ring seal but if water leaks from the top of the nozzle you can fit a ring round the valve casing. Modern Supataps have an 'O' ring already fitted and if it needs replacing, it's a simple matter of slipping it off and pushing on another — but choose one that fits snugly and doesn't move about. If this doesn't cure the leak you'll have to replace the anti-splash device which could have become worn.

STOP-VALVES AND BALL-VALVES

The valves that control your household water system aren't difficult to understand – or to fit or repair. So the next time one of yours goes wrong, be prepared to put it right yourself.

S top-valves, gate-valves and ball-valves are all plumbing fittings that in different ways do precisely the same thing, which is to regulate the flow of water through pipes. Each of the three types of valve performs an important function in your water system, and it is therefore in your interest to know not only what they do and how they do it, but also how to put right any of the faults to which they are prone.

Stop-valves

Your main stop-valve is perhaps the single most important plumbing fitting in your house. In the event of almost any plumbing emergency the very first thing that you should do is turn it off. This will stop the flow of water into your house and reduce the extent of any damage. Looking like a very basic brass tap, your main stop-valve will be found set into the rising main not far from the point where this pipe enters your house. Often it will be located under the kitchen sink.

If your house is fairly old then it could be that it won't be provided with a main stop-valve. If this is the case, then you will have to use the local water authority's stop-valve instead. You will find it under a hinged metal flap set into your garden path or the pavement outside your property. This sort of stop-valve usually has a specially-shaped handle that can only be turned with one of the water authority's turnkeys. So that you can deal promptly with any emergency you should make sure that you either have one of these turnkeys, or at least that you have ready access to one. However, both for the sake of convenience and because specialist gadgets like turnkeys have a habit of disappearing when they're most needed, you may decide to install a main stop-valve yourself – not a difficult task if the rising main is made of copper pipe.

The internal construction of a stop-valve is identical to that of an ordinary tap, and so it is prone to the same types of faults (see *Ready Reference*). But one further trouble that may afflict your stop-valve – which doesn't crop up with ordinary taps – is that of jamming in the open position as a result of disuse. It's a problem cured simply by applying penetrat-

ing oil to the spindle. However, you can prevent this happening by closing and opening the stop-valve regularly, and by leaving it fractionally less than fully open – a quarter turn towards closure will do.

Gate-valves

Whereas stop-valves are always fitted to pipes that are under mains pressure, gate-valves are used on pipes that are only subject to low pressure. They are therefore found on hot and cold water distribution pipes and on those of the central heating system. Gate-valves differ from stop-valves in as much as they control the flow of water through them, not with a washered valve, but by means of a metal plate or 'gate'. You can distinguish them from stop-valves by the fact that their valve bodies are bigger, and by their wheel – as opposed to crutch – handles. Due to the simplicity of their internal construction gate-valves require little attention (see *Ready Reference*). Unlike stop-valves, which have to be fitted so that the water flowing through them follows the direction of an arrow stamped on the valve body, you can install a gate-valve either way round.

Mini stop-valves

Mini stop-valves are useful little fittings that you can insert into any pipe run. Their presence enables you to re-washer or renew a tap or ball-valve (see below) or repair a water-using appliance such as a washing machine without disrupting the rest of your

water system. They can also be used to quieten an excessively noisy lavatory flushing cistern that is fed directly from the rising main, since by slowing down the flow of water to the ball-valve you can reduce the noise without materially affecting the cistern's rate of filling after flushing. You usually fit a mini stop-valve immediately before the appliance that it is to control; and they can be turned off and on either with a screwdriver, or by turning a small handle through 180°.

Ball-valves

Ball-valves are really just self-regulating taps designed to maintain a given volume of water in a cistern. While there are a number of different patterns they all have a float – not necessarily a ball these days – at one end of a rigid arm which opens or closes a valve as the water level in the cistern falls or rises. There are basically two types of ball-valves: the traditional type, generally made of brass, in which the water flow is controlled by a washered plug or piston; and the type that has been developed more recently in which the flow is controlled by a large rubber diaphragm housed within a plastic body.

Croydon and Portsmouth ball-valves

The oldest of the traditional types of ball-valves is the Croydon pattern. You can easily recognise one of these by the position of its piston, which operates vertically, and by the fact that it delivers water to the cistern in two insufferably noisy streams. Due to their noisi-

VALVE TYPES

Apart from the float arm the only moving part on a diaphragm-type valve is a small plunger. When prompted by the float arm this plunger presses a large rubber diaphragm against the valve nozzle to close it.

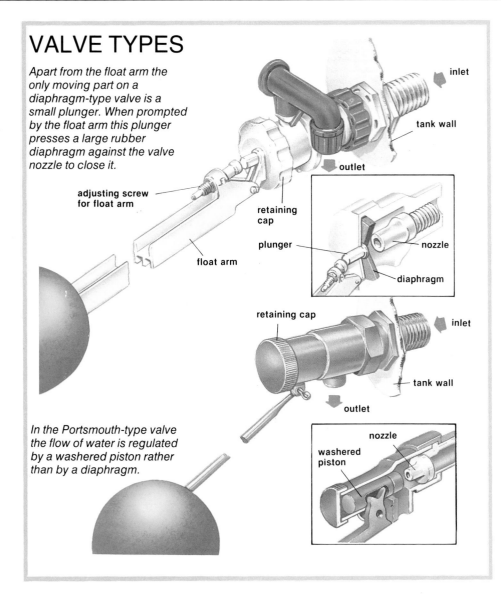

adjusting screw for float arm

retaining cap

float arm

plunger

inlet

tank wall

outlet

nozzle

diaphragm

retaining cap

inlet

tank wall

outlet

nozzle

washered piston

In the Portsmouth-type valve the flow of water is regulated by a washered piston rather than by a diaphragm.

Ready Reference

HOW A STOP-VALVE WORKS

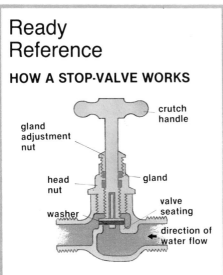

crutch handle

gland adjustment nut

head nut

washer

gland

valve seating

direction of water flow

Because a stop-valve works in the same way as an ordinary tap its washer and gland are also subject to wear. You can:
● remove headgear to replace a worn washer
● deal with a worn gland by tightening the adjustment nut, or by re-packing the gland.

HOW A GATE-VALVE WORKS

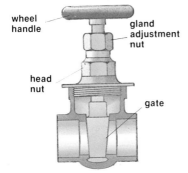

wheel handle

gland adjustment nut

head nut

gate

A gate-valve requires little attention. The only thing that may give trouble is the gland, which sometimes needs adjusting or renewing.

DEZINCIFICATION

In areas where the water supply is unusually acidic the zinc content of pipe fittings made of brass (an alloy of copper and zinc) can be dissolved by the water. This phenomenom is known as dezincification, and it results in the fittings losing their structural strength. When it presents a problem, fittings made of gunmetal (an alloy of copper and tin) are usually used though cheaper corrosion-resistant brass fittings are also available. These usually have CR stamped on the valve body.

ness, Croydon valves are now by and large obsolete, and if you do come across one you will almost certainly want to replace it. The traditional type of valve that superseded the Croydon pattern was the Portsmouth valve (see illustration). You can distinguish it from the former type by the fact that its piston operates horizontally; and as it is still popular with plumbers despite the development of more sophisticated diaphragm type valves, it is a pattern that you may well find in your home.

When one of your ball-valves goes wrong the first thing you will notice is water dripping from an outside overflow pipe. If the valve is a Portsmouth pattern then it is likely to have developed one of three faults. First, it could have jammed partially open as a result of the build-up of scale or the presence of grit; or, secondly, it could need re-washering. In either of these cases this will necessitate you turning off the water supply so that you can either clean the ball-valve or fit a new washer

to it (see step-by-step photographs). Lastly, the valve could have been incorrectly adjusted to maintain the proper water level in the cistern – which should be about 25mm (1in) below the overflow pipe. Even modern Portsmouth valves are rarely provided with any specific means of adjusting the water level, so if you need to do so you will have to resort to bending the float arm.

Noise can be a problem with Portsmouth valves. It is caused either by the inrush of water through the valve nozzle, or by vibration created by the float bouncing on ripples on the surface of the water ('water hammer'). As silencer tubes are now banned by water authorities, you will have to try other methods to deal with this problem. Reducing the mains pressure by closing the rising main stop-valve slightly may help, and as vibration can be magnified by a loose rising main it is worth making sure that this pipe is properly secured with pipe clips. Another measure

REPAIRING A BALL- VALVE

1 *The first thing you do when faced with a faulty Portsmouth valve is examine the piston. In order to get at it you will first have to remove the float arm.*

2 *If you can't get the piston out or if you suspect that your ball-valve needs a clean rather than a new washer, then you will have to remove the whole valve body.*

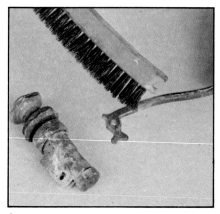

3 *If a build-up of scale does turn out to be the cause of your problem, clean the valve and the end of the floam arm with a wire brush.*

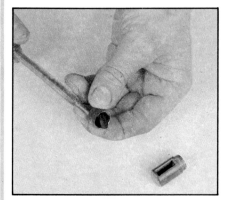

4 *You'll find the old washer seated in the cap. Poke it out and substitute a new one. Smear the piston with petroleum jelly before replacing it in the valve.*

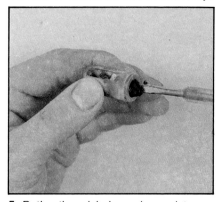

5 *Rather than risk damaging a piston that refuses to unscrew, pick out the old washer with a point and force a new one back in its place.*

6 *Debris caught in the valve nozzle can interrupt the water flow. Cure this problem by dismantling the valve and removing the debris with a nail.*

you could take would be to improvise a stabiliser for the float using a submerged plastic flowerpot tied to the float arm with nylon cord. However, if all the above measures fail you will have to consider replacing the Portsmouth valve with one of the modern diaphragm types.

Diaphragm ball-valves

Diaphragm ball-valves, which are also referred to as BRS or Garston ball-valves, were specially developed to overcome the noisiness and inherent faults of the Croydon and Portsmouth valves. Since the moving parts of a diaphragm valve are protected from incoming water by the diaphragm (see illustration) there is no risk of them seizing up as a result of scale deposits; and the problem of noisy water delivery is often overcome nowadays by an overhead sprinkler outlet which sprays rather than squirts the water into the cistern. Should you need to adjust the water

level in a cistern fitted with a diaphragm valve, then invariably you can by means other than bending the float arm. The only problems you are likely to encounter with diaphragm valves are jamming of the diaphragm against the valve nozzle, and obstruction of the space between the nozzle and diaphragm with debris from the main. You remedy these problems by unscrewing the knurled retaining cap and either freeing the diaphragm with a pointed tool or removing the debris.

High and low pressure water supply

The water pressure under which a ball-valve operates is an important factor, as the size of the hole in the nozzle of the valve will be either smaller or larger according to whether it is under high pressure (ie, mains pressure) or low pressure (ie, supplied by water from a storage tank). Older Portsmouth valves have either HP (high pressure) or LP (low pressure) stamped on their bodies, and will only operate

satisfactorily under the pressure for which they are designed. Modern valves, on the other hand, have interchangeable nozzles which allow you to convert them from low to high pressure or vice versa. If you fit a high-pressure valve (or nozzle) in a situation where a low-pressure one is required this will result in an agonisingly slow re-fill. A constantly dripping overflow may be the sign of a low-pressure valve that has been fitted to a cistern that is fed by the mains.

In some areas, mains pressure varies considerably throughout a 24-hour period. During the day, when demand is high, pressure will be low, whereas in the evening as demand falls off the pressure increases. These fluctuations in pressure don't affect low pressure valves but they do affect high pressure ones, which can perform erratically as a result. You can overcome this problem if it affects you by replacing your high pressure ball-valves with equilibrium valves.

REPLACING TAPS

Changing the old taps on your basin is a bright and practical way of making your bathroom more attractive. It may also be a good idea if they are old and inefficient. Here's what is involved.

There may be a number of reasons why you wish to replace the taps supplying your sink, basin or bath. They may continually drip or leak, where new taps would give efficient, trouble-free service. Perhaps you want the advantages that mixers have over individual taps or perhaps it is simply that the chromium plating has worn off leaving the taps looking incurably shabby.

It is more likely, however, that appearance, rather than malfunction, will be your reason for changing. There are fashions in plumbing fittings as in clothing and furniture. Taps of the 1950s or 60s are instantly recognisable as out-of-date in a bathroom or kitchen of the 1980s. Fortunately, fashions in sinks, basins and baths have changed rather less dramatically over the past three decades. There is probably no more cost-effective way of improving bathroom and kitchen appearance than by the provision of sparkling new taps or mixers.

Choosing taps

When you come to select your new taps you may feel that you are faced with a bewildering choice. Tap size, appearance, the material of which the tap is made, whether to choose individual taps or mixers and – for the bath – whether to provide for an over-bath shower by fitting a bath/shower mixer: all these things need to be considered.

Size is easily enough dealt with. Taps and mixers are still in imperial sizes. Bath tap tails are ¾in in diameter, and basin and sink taps ½in in diameter. There are, however, a few suppliers who are beginning to designate taps by the metric size, not of the taps themselves, but of the copper supply pipes to which they will probably be connected. Such a supplier might refer to bath taps as 22mm and sink and basin taps as 15mm.

Most taps are made of chromium-plated brass, though there are also ranges of enamelled and even gold-plated taps and mixers. Although taps and mixers are still manufactured with conventional crutch or capstan handles, most people nowadays prefer to choose taps with 'shrouded'

heads made of acrylic or other plastic. In effect, these combine the functions of handle and easy-clean cover, completely concealing the tap's headgear. A still popular alternative is the functional 'Supatap', nowadays provided with plastic rather than metal 'ears' for quick and comfortable turning on and off.

There is also a very competitively priced range of all-plastic taps. These usually give satisfactory enough service in the home, but they cannot be regarded as being as sturdy as conventional metal taps, and they can be damaged by very hot water.

So far as design is concerned the big difference is between 'bib taps' and 'pillar taps'. Bib taps have a horizontal inlet and are usually wall-mounted while pillar taps have a vertical inlet and are mounted on the bath, basin or sink they serve.

Taking out old basin taps

When replacing old taps with new ones the most difficult part of the job is likely to be – as with so many plumbing operations – removing the old fittings. Let's first consider wash basin taps.

You must, of course, cut off the hot and cold water supplies to the basin. The best way of doing this will usually be to tie up the float arm of the ball valve supplying the cold water storage cistern so as to prevent water flowing in. Then run the bathroom cold taps until water ceases to flow. Only then open up the hot taps. This will conserve most of the expensively heated water in the hot water storage cylinder.

If you look under the basin you will find that the tails of the taps are connected to the water supply pipes with small, fairly accessible nuts, and that a larger – often

Ready Reference

EQUIPMENT CHECKLIST

For replacing existing taps, you will need the following tools and equipment:
● new taps of the right type and size
● an adjustable spanner
● a basin wrench ('crowsfoot')
● an adjustable wrench
● penetrating oil
● plastic washers (see below)
● plumber's putty
● PTFE tape

You may also need tap tail adaptors (if the new taps have shorter tails than the old ones) and new tap connectors (if your new taps have metric tails instead of imperial ones).

WHAT ABOUT WASHERS?

With ceramic basins, use a plastic washer above and below the basin surface (A) so you don't crack the basin as you tighten the back-nut. You can use plumber's putty instead of the upper washer.

On thin basins, use a special top-hat washer between basin and back-nut (B).

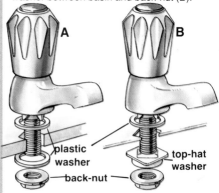

The lugs at the top of the tap tail are meant to stop tap turning in square tap holes. Use special anti-rotation washers to stop new taps with smaller lugs from turning in old tap holes.

TIPS TO SAVE TROUBLE

● to undo stubborn back-nuts, add extra leverage to the crowsfoot by hooking a wrench handle into its other end
● if this fails, squirt penetrating oil around the back-nuts. Leave for a while and try again
● in really stubborn cases, remove the basin completely, and turn it upside down on the floor so you have more room to work
● grip the tap body with an adjustable spanner to stop it turning as you use the crowsfoot; otherwise the tap lugs could crack the basin

REMOVING OLD TAPS

1 *It's best to change taps by removing the basin completely. Loosen the two tap connectors carefully with an adjustable spanner.*

2 *Disconnect the waste trap connector using an adjustable wrench. Take care not to damage the trap, particularly if it is lead or copper.*

3 *Undo any screws holding the basin to its brackets on the wall, and lift it clear of the brackets before lowering it carefully to the floor.*

4 *Check the condition of the back-nuts, which may be badly corroded. It's a good idea to apply penetrating oil and leave this to work for a while.*

5 *Use the crowsfoot (with extra leverage if necessary) to undo the back-nut. If more force is needed, grip the tap itself with a wrench to stop it turning.*

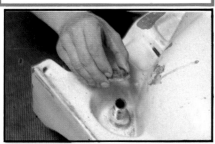

6 *Remove the back-nut and any washers beneath it and the basin. Old washers like these should always be replaced with new washers.*

inaccessible – back-nut secures the tap to the basin. The nuts of the swivel tap connectors joining the pipes to the taps are usually easily undone with a wrench or spanner of the appropriate size. The back-nuts can be extremely difficult – even for professional plumbers!

There are special wrenches and basin or 'crows foot' spanners that may help, but they won't perform miracles and ceramic basins can be very easily damaged by heavy handedness. The best course of action is to disconnect the swivel tap connectors and to disconnect the trap from the waste outlet. These are secured by nuts and are easily

undone. Then lift the basin off its brackets or hanger and place it upside down on the floor. Apply some penetrating oil to the tap tails and, after allowing a few minutes for it to soak in, tackle the nuts with your wrench or crowsfoot spanner. You'll find they are much more accessible. Hold the tap while you do this to stop it swivelling and damaging the basin.

Fitting the new taps

When fitting the new taps or mixer, unscrew the back-nuts, press some plumber's putty round the tail directly below the tap body or fit a plastic washer onto the top tail.

FITTING NEW TAPS

1 Remove the tap and clean up the basin surround, chipping away scale and any old putty remaining from when the tap was originally installed.

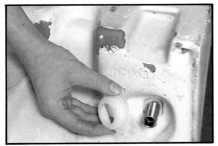

3 Twist the tap so that it's at the correct angle to the basin and is firmly bedded on the putty. Then push a top-hat washer onto the tail.

5 Tighten up the back-nut until the tap assembly is completely firm, using the crowsfoot or an adjustable spanner. Repeat the process for the other tap.

7 When all is secure, remove any surplus putty from around the base of the taps, wiping it over with a finger to leave a smooth, neat finish.

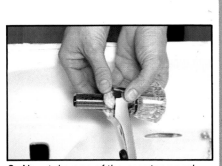

2 Now take one of the new taps and fit a washer or plumber's putty around the top of the tail before pushing it into the hole in the basin.

4 With the top-hat washer firmly in place, take the new back-nut and screw it up the tail of the tap by hand.

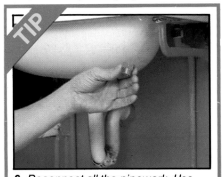

6 Reconnect all the pipework. Use tap-tail adaptors if the new taps have shorter tails than the old ones.

8 Turn the water back on. Check that the flow from the taps is regular and that the waste trap is not leaking. If it is, tighten up its connectors slightly.

Push the tails through the holes in the basin. Slip flat plastic washers over the tails where they protrude from beneath the basin, screw on the back-nuts and tighten them up. Make sure that the taps or mixer are secure, but don't overtighten them. To make tightening easier, (and undoing, if ever necessary) use top-hat washers.

All that remains to be done is to connect the swivel tap connectors to the tails of the new taps or mixer. You will see that a tap connector consists of a lining – with a flange – that is inserted into the tap tail and is then secured by the coupling nut. This nut is provided with a washer to ensure a watertight connection. When renewing taps you may well need to renew this small washer.

It is possible that when you come to connect the water supply pipes to the taps you will get an unpleasant surprise. The tails of modern taps are slightly shorter than those of older ones and the tap connectors may not reach. If the water supply pipes are of lead or of copper it is quite likely that they will have enough 'give' to enable you to make the connection but, if not, there are extension pieces specially made to bridge the gap.

Bib taps

If you're replacing existing bib taps with those of a more modern design, it's a relatively simple matter of disconnecting and unscrewing the old ones and fitting the new taps in their place. However, it's quite possible that you'll want to remove the bib taps altogether and fit a new sink with some pillar taps. This will involve a little more plumbing work. To start with, turn off the water supply and remove the taps and old sink. If the pipework comes up from the floor, you'll need to uncover the run in the wall to below where the new sink will go. You should then be able to ease the pipes away from the wall and cut off the exposed sections. This will allow you to join short lengths of new pipe, bent slightly if necessary, to link the pipe ends and the tap tails. Alternatively, if the pipes come down the wall you'll have to extend the run to below the level of the new sink and use elbow fittings to link the pipe to the tap tails. In either case it's a good idea to fit the taps to the new sink first and to make up the pipework runs slightly overlong, so that when the new sink is offered up to the wall you can measure up accurately and avoid the risk of cutting off too much pipe. Rather than having to make difficult bends you can use lengths of corrugated copper pipe. One end of the pipe is plain so that it can be fitted to the 15mm supply pipes with either a soldered capillary or compression fitting; the other end has a swivel tap connector.

REPLACING A RADIATOR

If one of your existing radiators is malfunctioning in some way, or else just out of character with the decor of your home why not replace it with a brand new one? You'll find this job straightforward if you follow our instructions.

There are a number of reasons why you may want to replace an existing radiator in your home's central heating system. These can range from the aesthetic to the purely practical. At one time radiators were ugly and cumbersome, and if you have any still in use like this it's quite likely that they'll clash with the decor of your home. On the practical side, you may well find that a radiator in your system has developed leaks. This will mean both water and heat loss, as well as the inconvenience of cleaning up the mess. And, of course, you may simply feel that a modern radiator would produce more heat, and so improve the comfort in your home. Whatever your reasons for replacing a radiator, you'll have to choose a new one to go in its place, before actually removing the existing one.

Choosing a new radiator

Modern radiators are usually made of 1.25mm (about 1/16in) thick pressed steel, and are designed to be space-saving, neat and attractive. For a simple replacement job, size will be among the most important considerations. If the new radiator can be successfully connected to the existing fittings, you won't need to alter or modify the circulating pipes. Consequently, the job will be that much easier. Radiators are available in a wide variety of sizes, ranging in height from 300mm (12in) to 800mm (30in) and in length from 480mm (19in) to 3200mm (10ft 6in) – so you shouldn't have too much difficulty in finding one that will fit into the space left by the old one. Special low, finned radiators are also available. These are usually fitted along the skirting and are both neat and unobtrusive – yet can be turned into decorative features in their own right.

But size isn't the only important consideration. After all, a radiator's job is to provide heat, so you'll have to shop around and find the one which, for its size, will produce most heat. A radiator's heat output is measured in Btu – British Thermal units – so you should look for the one with the highest Btu rating for its size. Remember, it's always possible to turn off a radiator that makes a room too warm; it's far less easy to increase heat output in a room which, with the radiator

THE FITTINGS

A typical panel radiator is fitted with a flow control valve (below), a lock-shield valve (bottom right), an air-bleed valve (right) and a blanking-off plate (far right).

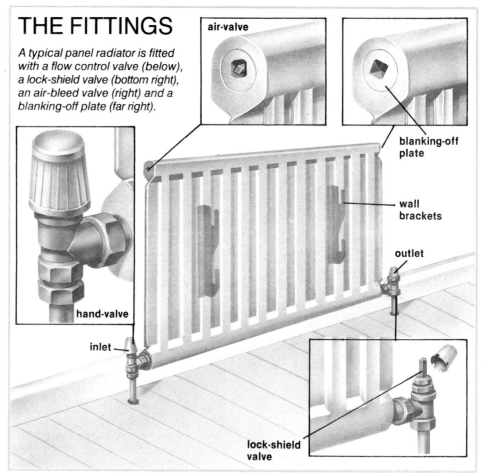

air-valve

blanking-off plate

wall brackets

outlet

hand-valve

inlet

lock-shield valve

REMOVING THE OLD RADIATOR

1 *Turn off the flow control valve by hand, and the lock-shield valve by turning its spindle with pliers. Note how many turns are needed to close it completely.*

2 *Hold the lock-shield valve body with a wrench so you don't bend the pipework, and undo the valve coupling carefully with an adjustable spanner.*

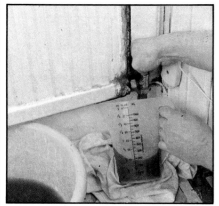

3 *Open the air-bleed valve, pull the coupling away and allow the radiator to drain into a convenient container. Have rags and a larger bowl handy too.*

4 *Having drained most of the water, undo the other coupling, lift the radiator off its brackets and drain out the dregs. Then remove the old brackets.*

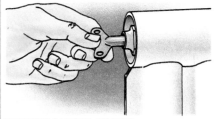
turned fully on, remains uncomfortably chilly.

However, one way of increasing heat output, while retaining the same sized radiator, is to install a double-panel radiator. This is, literally, an ordinary radiator with two panels for the hot water to fill instead of the usual one and therefore has virtually double the heat output. So, while a single panel radiator 685mm x 1150mm (27in x 45in) will have a heat output of 3575Btu, a double panel one of the same size will be rated at 5990Btu.

Although modern radiators are likely to provide more heat than the older variety, they do have one drawback. Because of the thinness of their metal, they are more prone to internal corrosion and this will ultimately produce leaks.

Dealing with internal corrosion
Internal corrosion in modern radiators arises from an electrolytic reaction between the steel of the radiators and the copper circulating pipes of the central heating system. This results in the production of a corrosive black iron oxide sludge (magnetite) and hydrogen gas. In a similar fashion, if the original installation of your heating system was somewhat messily done, then copper swarf, produced when the pipes were cut, could have been retained within the circulating pipes. This will also corrode the steel at any point where the two come in contact – usually within a radiator. Because the raw material from which the sludge is produced is the metal of the radiators, eventually they will leak and need to be replaced. And as the sludge is also attracted by the magnetic field of the circulating pump, its abrasive qualities are a common cause of early pump failure.

Early indications of serious internal corrosion are a need to vent one or more radiators at regular intervals, and cold spots on their surfaces. If in doubt, the diagnosis can be confirmed by applying a flame to the escaping gas when the radiator is being vented. If it burns with a blue and yellow flame, you can be sure that hydrogen is in the system and will have been produced by the chemical reaction of the two metals.

Once you've confirmed that corrosion is present within the system, you'll have to flush it through and introduce a reliable corrosion preventative chemical into the feed and expansion tank. By doing this, you should be able to prevent further corrosion and so save your system.

Removing the old radiator

One of the great deterrents to anyone wanting to remove a radiator is the prospect of having to drain the whole system. However, this won't be necessary provided the radiator to be replaced has a valve at both the hot water inlet and the outlet. Once these are closed, you'll be able to keep virtually all the system's water isolated in other parts.

At the inlet end you're likely to find the hand-valve which is the control by which you open and close the radiator. At the outlet end you'll find what is termed the lock-shield-valve. When you come to inspect your radiator, don't worry if their positions are reversed – they will still be equally effective.

The first thing to do when removing a radiator is to close these valves. The hand-valve is straightforward, but you'll have to remove the cover to get at the lock-shield valve. You'll be able to close this valve using a spanner or an adjustable wrench with which to grip its spindle.

As you turn it, it's a good idea to note carefully how many turns it takes to close. And you'll find this task slightly easier if you mark the turning nut with a piece of chalk before you begin. The reason for all this is to maintain the balance of the system. After it was first installed, your system would have been balanced. The lock-shield valves of all the radiators were adjusted to give an equal level of water through-flow so that they were all heating up equally. So, by noting the number of turns taken to close the lock-shield, when you come to fit the new radiator you can simply open it up by the same amount – so avoiding the somewhat tedious task of re-balancing the whole system.

Once you've closed both valves, you can unscrew the nuts which connect the valves to the radiator inlet and outlet. Do these one at a time after having placed a low dish under each end to collect the water and protect the floor. Use an adjustable wrench to undo the coupling nuts. It's wise to hold the circulating pipe securely in place with another wrench. Otherwise, if you apply too much pressure to the coupling nut you risk fracturing the flowpipe, and this would cause

FITTING THE NEW RADIATOR

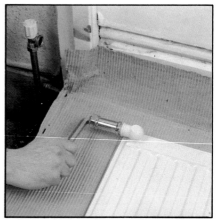

1 To ensure watertight connections to the new radiator, wrap PTFE tape round all threaded fittings and then smear on some jointing compound.

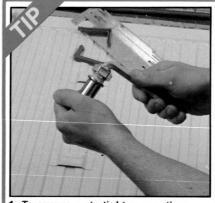

2 Screw in the valve couplings with a hexagonal radiator spanner. Use extension pieces if the new radiator is slightly narrower than the old one.

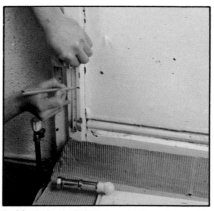

5 Mark the height taken in 4 on the wall above each valve, and join up the marks at each end with a pencil line. This marks the level of the new brackets.

6 Transfer the measurements taken in 3 to the wall to indicate the vertical position of each bracket. Accuracy is not so vital here as in 5.

9 Lift the radiator into place on its brackets. You can move it slightly from side to side to align the valve couplings with the inlet and outlet valves.

10 Wrap the coupling threads in PTFE tape and jointing compound, and do up the couplings. Again, use a wrench to support the valve body and prevent strain.

you a lot of extra work and expense to mend – as well as causing quite a mess. As you unscrew each nut, the water from the radiator will flow out. If the system has been previously treated with corrosion proofer, it's well worth saving the water. That way you can pour it back into the feed-and-expansion tank when the job is complete.

Once the water has drained out, remove the tail pieces and coupling nuts from each end. Then block up each hole with a rag and lift the radiator from the brackets that hold it to the wall. It's a good idea to get the radiator out of your home as soon as possible – just in case it leaks any remaining dirty water on to your carpet.

Fitting a new radiator

Your new radiator will probably have four holes or tappings – one at each corner – and each one will have a female screwed thread. How you connect the radiator up to your system depends on the way in which the old one was fitted. Nowadays it is usual for the flow and return connections to be made to the bottom two holes but, of course, if your system had the flow pipe at a higher level then you'll have to reconnect it in the same way.

Fit an air-valve into one of the top tappings. First wrap PTFE thread sealing tape anti-clockwise round the male thread of the valve and then use a radiator key that grips inside the body of the valve to screw it home. Unless your radiator has a top inlet the other top tapping must be plugged with a blanking off plate. This should also be wrapped with PTFE tape and screwed home in the same way as the air vent.

You'll then have to fit tail pieces and coupling screws (either new ones, or the ones from the original radiator if you can remove them) on to the new one. Again wrap each thread with PTFE tape before fitting them. It's a good idea to buy new wall brackets for your replacement radiator. After all, you can't be sure the old ones will be suitable. You should drill and plug the wall and then fix the brackets in place. Fit the radiator so that the inlet end is a few millimetres higher than the outlet valve. This will make venting easier. You can now fix the radiator in place and connect the coupling nuts to the hand-valve and lock-shield valve and screw them up tightly.

You'll have to open the air-valve at the top of the radiator so that the air in it can be displaced as it fills with water. All you do is slowly open the hand-valve and allow the radiator to fill. When water starts to flow from the air-valve you'll know all the air has been displaced and you should immediately close the valve. Finally, open the lock-shield valve by the same number of turns and part turns it took originally to close it.

3 Lay the radiator down in line with the two valves, and measure the distance from each valve coupling to the centre of the nearest bracket mounting.

4 Next, measure the height of the base of the radiator brackets from a line joining the centres of the inlet and outlet valves.

7 Hold the bracket against the wall in line with the vertical and horizontal marks you've made, and draw in the positions for the fixing screws.

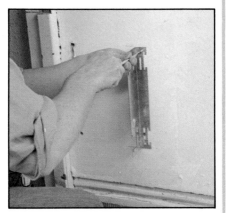

8 Drill and plug the four holes – two to each bracket – and fix the brackets in position. Make sure the wallplug is well below the plaster to avoid cracking.

11 After connecting up the couplings, use a bleed key to open the air-bleed valve slightly so that air can escape as the radiator fills with water.

12 Open the inlet valve, allow the radiator to fill and then close the air-bleed valve. Finally open the lock-shield valve by as many turns as you took to close it.

SEALING ROUND A BATH

Cracked seals round baths and basins can cause damage to floors and walls, while stains can ruin the best bathroom suites. Here's how to overcome these difficulties.

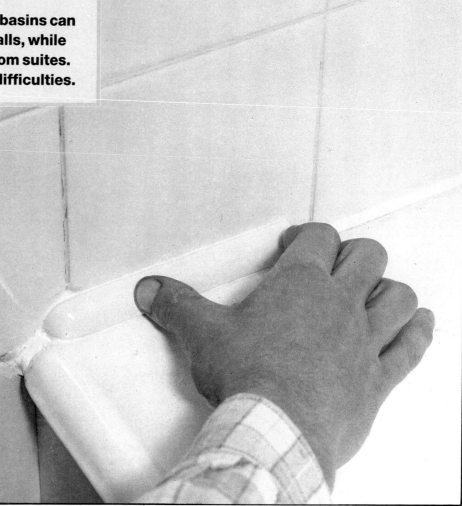

One of the commonest problems associated with baths, shower trays and wash basins is the difficulty of sealing the gap between the edges and the walls. It is extremely important that this is done effectively as, apart from being an unsightly dirt trap, water continually splashing through the gap can lead to attacks of rot in floor timbers, as well as damaging decorations in the room below.

Filling the gap

An ordinary cellulose filler will be adequate, but you'll probably find that it won't last for very long. After all, repeated soakings are bound to start it crumbling. And even if this can be avoided, the chances are that the movement of the bath relative to the wall – as it fills with hot water or as someone climbs in or out – will have the same result.

The answer is to use a special kind of filler, one that is both waterproof and flexible, called silicone mastic. This is frequently sold as bathroom sealant in small tubes, or, for larger jobs, in cartridges that fit into a special mastic gun. In addition to white, it is available in a selection of colours to match the variety of coloured bathroom suites now on the market.

If you are faced by a crack up to 3mm (⅛in) wide, then filling it is a straightforward job. All you do is squeeze a bead of mastic along the gap, holding the nozzle at an angle of about 45°. If you are using a cartridge gun, you can cut the nozzle to produce a bead of the correct size. If the mastic ends up on surfaces where it's not required, wipe it off with a damp cloth before it sets. With the bead in place you'll have to finish it off with a piece of dowel or narrow piping. Dip it in water to prevent the mastic from sticking and don't be tempted to use your fingers – you won't get as neat a finish and you could run the risk of inadvertently getting mastic in your eyes.

However, if the gap is wider than 3mm (⅛in) or so, you'll find it increasingly difficult to apply the bead smoothly and neatly, and to prevent it sagging once in place. The solution is to caulk the gap before applying the mastic. This involves filling the crack with soft rope or twists of soaked newspaper to provide a base that will help the mastic to bridge the gap until it sets. Provided you finish off with a good covering of mastic, there's no reason why this shouldn't last. However, it is a fiddly job and you might prefer to use an alternative method.

Tiling the gap

If your bathroom is tiled, or if there is a tiled splashback around the bath, the simplest solution is to bridge the gap with quadrant tiles – the ceramic equivalent of wooden quadrant beading. These are normally available singly as straight lengths with both ends cut square, or with one end finished in a bullnose, and in mitred pairs for coping with internal corners. One drawback with quadrant tiles is that they are becoming difficult to obtain, and it's worth bearing in mind that not only can they work out quite expensive, but they also come in only a limited range of colours (designed to match existing bathroom suites rather than modern tile ranges).

If you're going to seal the gap in the course of actually tiling the wall or splashback, then you can fix the quadrant tiles in position and grout them in the normal way, 12-24 hours after the last tile has been pressed into place. In order to accommodate any movement, however, you should make sure that the tiles are bedded in a thick layer of silicone mastic where they rest on the bath's lip. On the other hand, if you're faced with existing tiling round the edge, simply bed the quadrant tiles in mastic from start to finish, using mastic instead of grout as well.

Quadrant tiles can be used successfully in situations where the wall is not tiled – perhaps painted, papered or timber-clad instead.

USING SILICONE MASTIC

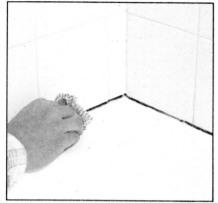

1 Clean round the gap using a soft cloth and methylated spirits to ensure that surfaces are free of soap and grease. Dry the edges carefully.

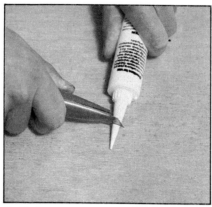

2 Make sure you use a silicone mastic to seal the gap: it is both waterproof and flexible. Cut the nozzle to produce a bead of the correct size.

3 Hold the tube at an angle of 45° to both the tiles and the bath edge. Apply continual pressure to the plunger to give a smooth, uniform bead.

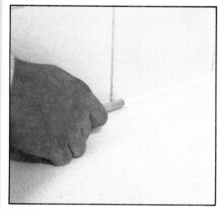

4 If the mastic has a rippled finish you should carefully smooth it out. Use a piece of dowel or narrow pipe dipped in water to prevent sticking.

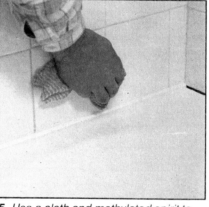

5 Use a cloth and methylated spirit to remove any unwanted mastic before it goes off. If it has already set, use a razor blade or sharp knife.

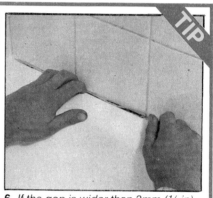

TIP

6 If the gap is wider than 3mm (⅛in) you should caulk it to prevent the mastic from sagging. Use soft rope or twists of soaked newspaper.

However, in the last case it's worth considering the use of timber quadrant beading as an alternative. All you have to do is pin it to the cladding or fix it to clean, bare plaster using an epoxy resin adhesive. Again, make sure that the timber is bedded in mastic where it rests on the lip of the bath, shower tray or basin. Do remember to treat the timber with a good-quality preservative (one that can be painted or varnished over) and then paint or varnish it all round, including any cut ends, before fixing it in place.

Dealing with stains

Another problem with taps and baths is staining just below the taps. This tends to be at its worst in hard water areas and, so far, nobody has come up with a really effective way of removing these stains once they've formed. As always, prevention is better than cure, so you should make sure that the

staining doesn't build up in the first place. Dripping taps and shower roses should be repaired as soon as possible, and if they're old enough to introduce the additional problem of rust staining you should consider having them replaced (see *Replacing Taps* pages 40-43). You can work to minimise the build-up of stains by wiping out the bath immediately after use and cleaning it regularly with a proprietary cleaner. However, if the bath surface has got to the point where even the most thorough cleaning cannot help, then you'll have to think about giving it a facelift.

Painting your bath

Bath enamel – a hard-wearing version of ordinary enamel paint – was originally used for covering up badly stained enamelled surfaces. However, over the years this has acquired an unfortunate reputation for failure:

not only is it unable to withstand the sort of treatment it gets in a bath, but also extreme care is required during both preparation and application in order to produce acceptable and lasting results. It is still available, but usually only in white, and it is worth considering only if you want to touch up the scratched surface of a cooker, fridge or washing machine.

For baths and other bathroom fittings, a recent development has proved to be a better option. This is an epoxy resin coating that will provide a very hard, heat-resistant and chemical-resistant finish on most of the non-porous surfaces to be found in the bathroom. It comes in a number of different colours that will match the colouring of most modern bathroom fittings with the exception of white. It cannot be used on plastics or on surfaces that have already been painted. The only possible disadvantage is that it can

USING QUADRANT TILES

1 *If you're using quadrant tiles to seal the gap, you should bed them in silicone mastic rather than tile adhesive. Apply this to both long edges of each tile.*

2 *Start by dealing with the internal corners. Use the specially mitred tiles and ensure that they butt tightly up to each other.*

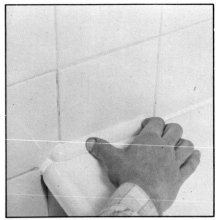

3 *Turn your attention to the front corners of the bath and fix the bullnose tiles in position. You should bed them in extra mastic if necessary.*

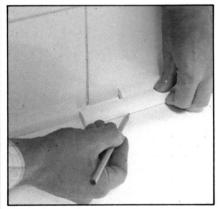

4 *Work your way inwards towards the centre of each edge of the bath. If you have to cut a tile, first hold it in place and mark the cutting line.*

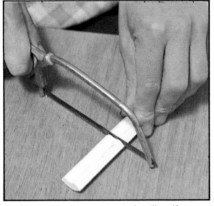

5 *Use a hacksaw to cut the tiles if you don't have a special tile-cutter. Saw from the unglazed side and cut through to just above the glazing.*

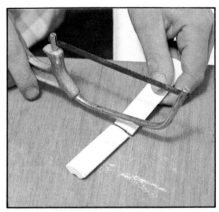

6 *Turn the tile over. Hold it on a firm surface and tap is smartly with the edge of a hacksaw above the line of the saw cut to break the tile.*

7 *Before fixing the cut piece of tile in position you should smooth the edge. Use an old rasp, and complete by using glasspaper to achieve a fine finish.*

8 *You will find that mastic will almost certainly be squeezed out from the edges of the tiles. Wait until it's set and then remove it with a sharp blade.*

9 *Finally, you should clean up the tiles by rubbing over them with a soft cloth dipped in methylated spirits or nail varnish remover.*

APPLYING NEW BATH COATING

1 Clean the bath surface thoroughly with hot washing soda to remove all traces of grease and scum; otherwise the new coating will simply peel off again.

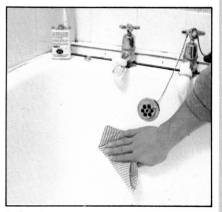

2 Scrape off any hard scale from round the taps, overflow and waste outlet, using wire wool if necessary to clean parts the scraper cannot reach.

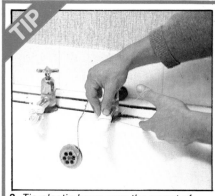

3 Tie plastic bags over the spout of each tap to catch any drips that might spoil the coating before it has completely hardened.

4 Dry the entire bath surface carefully (a hair dryer or fan heater will speed up the process) and then wipe the bath over with the special brush cleaner.

5 Start applying the coating at the bottom of the bath side furthest from you; work up the side towards the rim and along towards the head of the bath.

6 Continue applying the coating area by area, using a smaller brush to touch in awkward parts. A second coat may be needed when the first is touch dry.

sometimes work out a bit expensive, though it will obviously be considerably cheaper than buying a new bathroom suite.

Using resin coatings

Epoxy resin coating for baths comes in a kit consisting of coloured resin, a chemical hardening agent, and a can of special brush cleaner. All you do is mix the resin with the hardener and, following the manufacturer's instructions closely, brush it on.' There are, though, a number of points to bear in mind.

First, you must be very careful about the preparation. The bath surface must be scrupulously clean, dry, and free from grease; otherwise the coating will simply peel off. Lime scale and hard water staining should be removed as far as possible, and then the bath must be vigorously scrubbed with a warm solution of washing soda. Pay particular attention to soap holders, the 'tide-mark' line and the area round the waste outlet where soap deposits tend to be at their worst. Allow the bath to dry and then, as a final precaution against grease, wipe over the surface with a little of the special brush cleaner on a soft, lint-free cloth. Again, allow the bath to dry and tie plastic bags round taps and shower roses to contain any unexpected, and potentially damaging, drips splashing the coating before it is dry.

Secondly, great care must be taken with the application; provided you use a good quality brush, you shouldn't find it too difficult to achieve a smooth, even coverage – though you might find a second coat necessary. For a really professional finish you might consider using a spray gun. Make sure you mask off areas that you don't want painted and check that there is nothing plastic in the gun that is likely to be corroded by the mixture.

Finally, always follow the safety rules. Two-part coatings of this type are normally highly inflammable, so be sure to work in a well-ventilated room. Keep naked flames well away from the solution and, of course, don't smoke while you're doing the job. If any resin comes into contact with your skin or eyes, wash it off immediately with cold water.

Start on the floor of the bath and work up towards the rim, tackling the half furthest from you first. As soon as you have finished, clean your equipment with the cleaner provided and then rinse the brushes or gun with warm soapy water. It's also a good idea to throw away any resin/hardener mixture you have left over as it will set solid, even in a sealed container. Finally, you should ensure that you take good care of the newly coated bath. Don't use it for at least 48 hours, don't use acid-based cleaners on it and keep soap in a soap tray or it might stain the surface. If you get any coating on your hands, you should use brush cleaner on them and then rinse them in warm, soapy water.

BOXING IN PIPEWORK

Exposed pipework can look extremely ugly and ruin your home's decor, so the answer is to conceal it. There are a number of ways of doing this but the simplest is to box it all in.

E very home has a multitude of pipes in it; without them there could be no hot or cold water system, no sewage disposal and no gas supply, but the fact remains that pipework look unsightly if exposed to view Older houses suffer in this respect far more than modern ones.

Builders used to leave ugly pipes on display all over the place, especially in kitchens and bathrooms. In many older homes, the supply pipes that take water to the bath, basins, sinks and WCs are there for all to see, and there'll often be waste and soil pipes fully exposed en route from upstairs rooms to the drains.

The demands of modern plumbing in a home can make this problem still more aggravating. It's amazing, for example, just how much pipework is needed to give even a small home central heating. Just a single pipe running through a room can ruin its appearance.

However, it's possible to take full advantage of modern plumbing equipment without having an array of ugly, different-sized pipes on view throughout your home, providing you put a little forethought into what you are doing.

Installing and concealing new pipes

If you're installing new pipe runs, you'll probably find that horizontal ones don't pose as many problems as vertical ones. Provided you don't have a solid floor, pipes can usually be run under the floorboards. If, on the other hand, you're laying a new concrete floor, you could make channels in it to accept the new pipes. You will need to embed some timber battens or, better still, some scaffolding poles in the new floor until it is almost dry. When they are removed, the pipes can be laid in the channels they have formed. The pipes should then be covered with mortar, ready for the final floorcovering to be laid. It is important in laying such channels to ensure the continuity of the damp-proof membrane in the floor.

Vertical pipes can be more of a headache, and you should aim to conceal these in an understairs cupboard, if you can, or to run them up through the hall. Whatever you do, you'll want to keep the pipes out of the living

BOXING IN PIPES

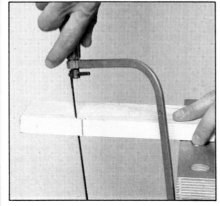

1 *Take a floor-to-ceiling length of 75x25mm (3x1in) timber, scribe one end to fit over the skirting board and cut out the waste with a coping saw.*

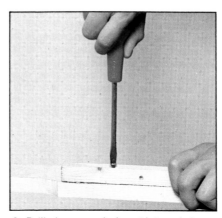

2 *Drill clearance holes at intervals in a 25mm (1in) square batten, and glue and screw it to the main timber flush with its rear edge.*

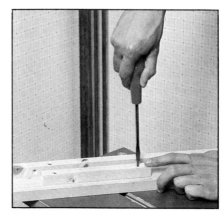

3 *Add short lengths of 25mm square batten to the main timber, recessing them from its front edge so that the cladding panel will be a flush fit.*

4 *Mark the position of a second pre-drilled 25mm square batten on the other wall, and drill and plug the holes before fixing it in position.*

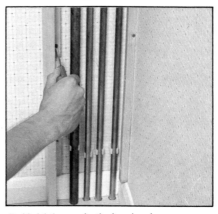

5 *Hold the main timber in place, mark the positions of the fixing screws, drill and plug the holes and fix the timber in its final position.*

6 *Finally, drill clearance holes in the cladding panel and screw it into place. Note how it fits flush with the edge of the main 75x25mm timber.*

room if at all possible. However, if this proves difficult, a good position for them is at the side of the window: they won't be immediately visible and you can easily hide them behind ceiling-to-floor curtains extending beyond the sides of the window opening. The pipes are likely to protrude from the wall by as much as 25mm (1in) or so. which means the curtains will have to be carefully put up to allow them to operate in front of the pipes. The best solution is to fix a horizontal batten of say, 50x25mm (2x1in) timber to the wall at ceiling height above the window and each side of the pipes and then screw the track to that. That way the curtains will clear the pipes and hide them from view. Alternatively, you could use a curtain pole, which projects that much further from the wall than the track.

Curtains can conveniently be used elsewhere to conceal pipes. If you've had to run vertical pipes through the hall, it's probably best to keep them to one side of the front door where they are not obvious. Ceiling-to-floor curtains could be used to cover the pipes, as well as to provide extra draught-proofing, comfort and privacy – especially if you have a completely glazed front door.

Another place to site the vertical pipes in the living room is in a group down the side of the chimney breast furthest away from the door. This is one of the last places in the room likely to be noticed by anyone entering it.

Once the pipes reach the first floor concealing them is not so critical, as they may pass within fitted wardrobes; in any case not so many people will be seeing them. You may also be able to keep many of them out of view by running them through the airing cupboard. Even so, a lot of pipes are going to be on view in parts of your home where they'll look ugly and out of place, and boxing them in is one of the best ways of concealing them.

Simple boxing in

For many people a simple boxing-in of their existing pipes to keep them out of sight is all that they require. This is a straightforward task and the materials are easily available.

You'll need softwood battens, usually 50x25mm (2x1in), with a cladding of hard-board or 3mm plywood for the simplest job. Before you go ahead. however, you should check whether any hot water passes through the pipes to be hidden. If this is the case and you're using hardboard for your cladding, you'll have to condition it first or it will warp as the heat in the pipework dries it out. This is not a difficult technique: all you'll have to do is brush water onto the reverse (mesh) side and leave it flat for 48 hours in the room where it is to be fixed. The softwood battens should also be left lying flat in the room for a few days so that they, too, will adjust to the moisture content of the air. Once

DEALING WITH PROBLEM PIPES

Boxing-in your exposed pipes is straightforward, and there are a number of different ways of dealing with the various types that you'll find in your home. All the materials you'll need are readily available.

For pipes near the floor you can neatly fit plywood cladding to battens to hide them.

batten

pipe clip

plywood

Alternatively, the pipes can be disguised behind skirting clipped to the pipe.

draught-proofing strip

Soil and waste pipes are much bigger than ordinary water supply pipes, but they can be disguised in the normal way with battens and plywood or chipboard cladding, although they will remain more obtrusive.

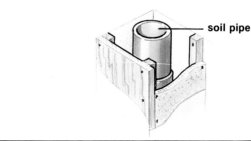

soil pipe

soil pipe

It's important to have access to any stop-valve on a pipe run, and you can provide this by fitting an inspection hatch.

stop-valve

Waste pipes in the bathroom where you're short of space can be disguised in a specially-built narrow cupboard.

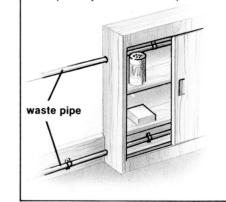

waste pipe

You can fix 50x25mm (2x1in) battens edge-on using, angle brackets and then attach cladding to cover the pipes.

plasterboard strip

Pipes are often run down the side of a chimney breast. Rather than just boxing them in you can increase the width of the chimney breast to hide them completely.

In corners, fit the cladding to chamfered battens or else use special clips to fit it to the pipe itself.

cornice

Narrow pipes that run at the top of a wall can be concealed neatly behind coving or cornices.

the wood has been conditioned, the two battens should be screwed to the wall on each side of the pipes and the cladding attached to the battens.

Fixing battens edge-on to the wall is not always the perfect answer but by doing so you'll be able to cover adequately a few pipes that project up to 25mm (1in) or so from the wall, and the cladding will, in any case, hold the battens steady. Remember that you should never use glue to fix the cladding to the battens because you might need access to the pipes for repairs or modification at some stage in the future. Pins punched in at 150mm (6in) centres, with their heads covered with filler, should prove adequate; this way the cladding can be prised off if necessary.

Boxing in pipes running in a corner will require two 25mm (1in) battens which have been chamfered at the front to provide an angled edge. These are screwed to the two walls and the cladding, also with chamfered edges, is then fixed to the battens. For larger pipes you'll need just a single larger batten fixed to one of the smaller ones; the cladding will be pinned to this and the smaller batten.

Another method is to use a spring clip attached to a piece of 19mm (⅝in) thick timber. Its edges should be planed and chamfered to allow it to fit neatly into the corner, and the spring clip is then fixed to the pipe itself.

If the pipes are in the alcove of a chimney breast you can box them in and then finish off the boxing so that it looks like an extension of the existing wall (see Ready Reference). The boxing for horizontal pipes down near the floor can often be made to look like wide and deep skirting. A 25mm (1in) batten should be fixed to the floor itself and one should also run above, but parallel to, the pipe. To the upper batten an additional 50x25mm (2x1in) batten should be fixed; the cladding is then attached to this and the batten on the floor.

Gaining access to the pipes
You might find you need access to a particular part of a pipe. In that case you should cut out a section of the cladding and fit it with screws to create what is in effect a little trap door.

If you're boxing in a length of pipe that has a stop-valve on it you should again make a little trap door, but this time fix it on with hinges so that access can be immediate. You can fix a small handle or touch latch on to it to facilitate opening.

Concealing pipes with furniture
If you find pipes exposed in a number of rooms in your home, one method of concealing them, which will provide you with extra storage space as well, is to install built-in furniture. An ideal location for this is that living room alcove mentioned above. The pipes would be largely unnoticed if you fitted a waist-high cupboard with book shelves on top, for example. The construction of such a cupboard is straightforward (for further details see Ready Reference).

If the pipes are on the back wall, the shelves can be supported on an adjustable shelving system in which brackets lock into uprights. The uprights should be fitted to vertical battens; that way the shelves will be thrown well clear of the pipes. Alternatively, if you have the pipes running up the side of the chimney breast, you can carefully cut notches out of a corner of each shelf so you won't disturb any of the pipes.

The bathroom is an obvious place where unsightly plumbing can be concealed behind built-in furniture. A built-in cupboard, beneath the washbasin, for instance, will provide extra storage space as well as acting as a neat disguise. If you live in a flat that has the upstairs neighbour's soil pipe passing through your bathroom, you can disguise it neatly with shelves at the end of a built-in washbasin unit or with a built-in vanity unit.

Another way of concealing pipes is to construct a false wall. This is especially useful if your plaster is in very poor condition. You simply fix timber cladding, probably match-boarding or veneered plywood, to battens running down edges of the walls. Water pipes will go conveniently behind such cladding providing you never forget their location and try to drive nails into the timber!

A more sophisticated version of this that is especially suited to the kitchen or living room, is done with timber panelling. However, if the pipes are running up and outside the wall, it would be wise to allow for some air holes or a small gap at both the top and the bottom. This will ensure that warm air can circulate.

If you find that for some reason you cannot conceal your pipes then it's worth thinking about going to the opposite extreme and making a feature out of them. Pipes that have been painted with bright colours, for example, can look extremely attractive in their own right. And copper pipework, polished and lacquered to stop it tarnishing, can be a really eye-catching feature. You'll have to make sure that the pipes are in good condition to warrant either painting or polishing up, and that their new colour won't clash with your existing decor. Ideally they should be lightly rubbed down to clean them before being given a coat of special enamel radiator paint. You should also take care not to apply too thick a coat of paint – especially on any vertical pipes, as you could end up with unsightly drips, which would be difficult to get rid of once the paint has dried.

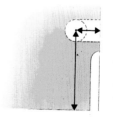
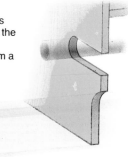
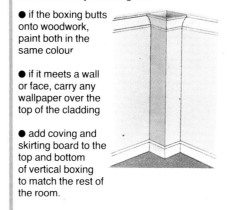

CLEARING BLOCKAGES

There are few plumbing emergencies quite as unpleasant as a blocked drain or waste pipe. However, it's usually possible to cure the problem if you know what to do when you've tracked down the blockage and you have the right equipment.

P rofessional plumbers rarely relish being called out to deal with a blockage. There *are* specialist drain clearance firms, but they can't always be contacted quickly in an emergency – and their charges reflect what can sometimes be the unpleasantness of the job. Drain or waste-pipe clearance is usually well within the capacity of the householder, and there are certainly few more cost-effective do-it-yourself jobs about the house.

Coping with blocked sinks

The outlet of the sink, usually the trap immediately beneath the sink itself, is the commonest site of waste-pipe blockage. Usually the obstruction can be cleared quickly and easily by means of a sink-waste plunger or force cup. This is a very simple plumbing tool obtainable from any do-it-yourself shop, ironmongers or household store. It consists of a rubber or plastic hemisphere, usually mounted on a wooden or plastic handle. Every household should have one.

To use it to clear a sink waste blockage, first press a damp cloth firmly into the overflow outlet, holding it securely with one hand. Then pull out the plug and lower the plunger into the flooded sink so that the cup is positioned over the waste outlet. Plunge it up and down sharply half a dozen or more times. Since water cannot be compressed, the water in the waste between the cup and the obstruction is converted into a ram to clear the blockage. The overflow outlet is sealed to prevent the force being dissipated up the overflow.

If your first efforts at plunging are unsuccessful, persevere. Each thrust may be moving the obstruction a little further along the waste pipe until it is discharged into the drain gully or the main soil and waste stack.

Should plunging prove unsuccessful you'll have to gain access to the trap. Brass and lead U-shaped traps have a screwed-in plug at the base. With plastic U-shaped and bottle traps the lower part can be un-screwed and removed – see *Ready Reference*. Before attempting this, put the plug in the sink and place a bucket under the trap; it will probably be full of water unless the blockage is immediately below the sink

WHERE BLOCKAGES OCCUR

Blockages can occur in several different places around your home's waste and drain systems. The commonest sites are:

1 *traps under basins, baths and sinks;*

2 *WC traps;*

3 *waste pipes running to soil stacks, hoppers or gullies;*

4 *rainwater or yard gullies;*

5 *underground drain runs between house and manhole;*

6 *intercepting chambers (see Ready Reference);*

7 *underground drain runs between manhole and sewer.*

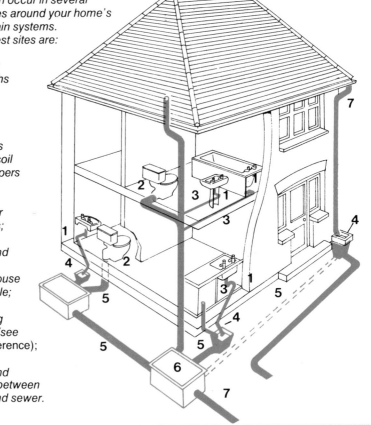

CLEARING BLOCKED TRAPS

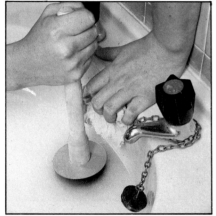

1 *Try using a plunger to clear blocked sinks, basins, baths or WCs. Cover the overflow with a damp cloth, then push the plunger down sharply several times.*

2 *If the blockage persists, you will have to open up the trap. Put the plug in the basin and have a bucket handy to catch the trap contents.*

3 *In a confined space like this, you may find it easier to remove the next push-fit elbow before tackling the connection to the waste outlet itself.*

4 *With the trap fully dismantled, wash each component thoroughly to remove the blockage and any scum clinging to the pipe sides. Leave the plug in.*

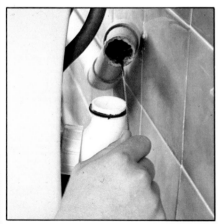

5 *Before reassembling the trap fully, check that the next section of the waste pipe is clear by poking a length of wire down it as far as you can reach.*

6 *A build-up of hair and scum can often block basin wastes just below the outlet. Fish out as much as possible with a slim wire hook passed through the grating.*

Ready Reference

TYPES OF TRAP

On old plumbing systems you may still come across lead traps, which have a removable rodding eye in the base. On more modern systems plastic traps will have been installed, and it is easy to unscrew part of the trap to clear a blockage.

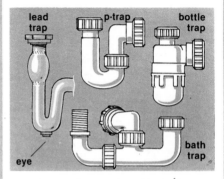

TIP: SUPPORT LEAD TRAPS

Lead traps are very soft, and may bend or split if you use force to open the rodding eye. To avoid this:
● insert a piece of scrap wood into the U-bend of the trap
● undo the rodding eye with a spanner, turning it in the direction shown while bracing the trap with the scrap wood
● reverse the procedure to replace it.

RODDING INTERCEPTING TRAPS

The manhole nearest the main sewer may be an intercepting trap, designed to keep sewer gases out of the house drains. To clear a blockage between it and the sewer,

feed your rods into the rodding arm. To prevent the stonware plug from being dislodged and causing a blockage you can have a glass disc fitted.

outlet, and the chances are that opening the trap will release it. Having done so, probe into the trap, and into the waste pipe itself. You can buy purpose-made sink waste augers for this purpose, but you'll find that a piece of expanding curtain wire, with a hook on the end, can be equally effective.

Blocked baths and basins

Basin and bath wastes are less likely to be totally blocked than sink wastes but, when blockages do occur, they can usually be cleared in the same way. They are, however, very subject to partial blockage. The waste water is often found to run from the bath or basin ever more slowly. This may be due to a build-up of scum, scale and hair on the inside of the waste pipe, and the use of a proprietary drain-clearing chemical will usually clear it. These frequently have a caustic soda base, so they should be kept away from children and handled with care, strictly in accordance with the manufacturer's instructions. Before spooning them into the bath or basin waste outlet it is wise to smear petroleum jelly over the rim of the outlet to protect the chromium finish, especially with plastic baths or fittings.

Partial blockage of a wash basin waste may often be caused by hair suspended from the grid of the outlet. This may be all but invisible from above, but probing with a piece of wire (the old standby of a straightened-out wire coathanger is useful) can often produce festoons. If you can't clear the hair by this means, unscrew the nut that connects the threaded waste outlet to the trap and pull the trap to one side. Now use a pair of pliers to pull the hair away from beneath the grid.

Overflows from gullies

Where waste pipes and downpipes discharge into gullies, the first signs of trouble may be when the gully overflows and the surrounding area is flooded as a result. The gully trap has probably become blocked, either by blown leaves or other debris, or by a build-up of grease and scum on the sides of the trap. Raise the gully grid if one is fitted (and get a new one if it's broken or missing). Then scoop out any debris with a rubber-gloved hand or an improvised scoop, scrub the gully out with caustic soda and flush it through with plenty of clean water before replacing the grid.

Blockages below ground

A blockage in the underground drains may be shown up by a WC which, when flushed, fills with water almost to the rim and then very slowly subsides, or by dirty water seeping from under a manhole cover. You'll need a set of drain rods to clear any underground blockage. It is best to hire these from a local

CLEARING BLOCKED GULLIES

1 Both surface-water and yard gullies are easily blocked by wind-blown debris such as waste paper and dead leaves. First lift off the gully grating.

2 Try to scoop out as much debris as possible from the gully trap, either by hand or with an improvised scoop such as an old tin can.

3 If the blockage is cleared and the water flows away, scrub out the sides of the gully with a brush and detergent. Clean the gully grating too.

4 Finally, hose the gully out thoroughly with running water. If you are unable to clear the blockage, you may have to rod the drain run from a nearby manhole.

tool hire firm if and when the emergency arises. A drain that blocks sufficiently frequently to justify the purchase of a set of rods undoubtedly has a major defect that needs professional advice and attention.

Raising the manhole covers will give you an indication of the position of the blockage. If, for instance, the manhole near your front boundary is empty, but the one beside the house into which the soil pipe and yard gully discharges is flooded, then the blockage must be between these two manholes. Screw two or three lengths of drain-rod together, add the appropriate accessory to one end and then lower it into the flooded manhole. Feel for the drain half-channel at its base and push the rod end along it and into the drain towards the obstruction. Screw on extra rods as necessary until you reach and clear the blockage. You may find it easier to push the rods into the drain – and to extract them

again – if you twist them as you do so. *Always* twist in a clockwise direction. If you twist anti-clockwise the rods will unscrew and one or more lengths will be left irretrievably in the drain.

Many older houses have intercepting traps. These traps, which were intended to keep sewer gases out of the house drains, are the commonest site of drain blockage. You can see if your drains have an intercepting trap by raising the cover of the manhole nearest to your property boundary before trouble occurs and looking inside. If there is an intercepting trap the half-channel of the gully will fall into what appears to be a hole at the end of the manhole; actually it is the inlet to the trap. Immediately above this hole will be a stoneware stopper. This closes the rodding arm giving access to the length of drain between the intercepting trap and the sewer.

A blockage in the intercepting trap is

RODDING BLOCKED DRAINS

1 *Raise manhole covers carefully. If the hand grips are missing, use an old brick bolster to lift one edge, and then slide in a piece of wood.*

2 *With the wood supporting one end of the cover, grasp it securely and lift it to one side. Bend from the knees so you don't strain your back.*

3 *Select one of the drain rod heads (a rubber disc is being fitted here) and screw it securely onto the threaded end of the first drain rod.*

4 *Screw a second rod onto the end of the first, and lower the head into the half-channel in the bottom of the chamber. Push the rods towards the blockage.*

5 *Screw on further rods as necessary and work the head in and out to clear the blockage. Never turn the rods anticlockwise, or they may unscrew and be lost.*

6 *When you have cleared the blockage, hose down the sides and base of the manhole with running water, and let water run through the drain for a while.*

indicated when all the drain inspection chambers are flooded. It can usually be cleared quite easily by plunging. To do this, screw a drain plunger (a 4in or 100mm diameter rubber disc) onto the end of a drain rod. Screw on one or two other rods as necessary and lower the plunger into the flooded manhole. Feel for the half-channel at its base and move the plunger along until you reach the inlet of the intercepting trap. Plunge down sharply three or four times and, unless you are very unlucky, there will be a gurgle and the water level in the manhole will quickly fall.

Very occasionally, there may be a blockage between the intercepting trap and the sewer, and the point must be made that this length of drain is the householder's responsibility, even though much of it may lie under the public highway. To clear such a blockage the stoneware cap must be knocked out of

the inlet to the rodding arm (this can be done with the drain rods but it isn't the easiest of jobs) and the rods passed down the rodding arm towards the sewer.

Intercepting traps are also subject to a kind of partial blockage that may go unnoticed for weeks or even months. An increase in pressure on the sewer side of the trap – due to a surge of storm water, for instance – may push the stopper out of the rodding arm. It will fall into the trap below and cause an almost immediate stoppage. However this will not be noticed because sewage will now be able to escape down the open rodding arm to the sewer. The householder usually becomes aware of a partial blockage of this kind as a result of an unpleasant smell, caused by the decomposition of the sewage in the base of the manhole.

The remedy is, of course, to remove the stopper and to replace it. Where the trouble

recurs it is best to discard the stopper and to lightly cement a glass or slate disc in its place. In the very unusual event of a stoppage between the intercepting trap and the sewer, this disc can be broken with a crowbar and replaced after the drain has been cleared – see *Ready Reference*.

After any drain clearance the manhole walls should be washed down with a hot soda solution and a garden hose should be used to flush the drain through thoroughly.

Blocked gutters
Roof rainwater gutters may become obstructed by leaves or other objects. An overflowing gutter isn't an instant catastrophe but, if neglected, it will cause dampness to the house walls. An inspection, removal of debris and a hose down of gutters should be a routine part of every householder's preparations for winter.

REPLACING SKIRTING & ARCHITRAVES

Wood trim is functional, decorative and found in almost every home. But it often gets damaged or just shabby. Luckily, repairing and renewing it are among the easiest of all do-it-yourself jobs.

Various types of timber mouldings are standard features of all houses, however plain. Although each performs a specific job, they also provide ornamentation and a chance to vary decoration.

As the years pass, they're bound to come in for a few knocks – and will most likely be covered in several layers of paint, which not only get chipped but also eventually clog up their profiles. Skirting boards, in particular, are also prone to rot if walls or floors are damp. However, since wood trim is in no way part of the house's structure, repairs and even replacement should create no major problems.

Slight dents and cracks can often be repaired with cellulose filler – or perhaps glass fibre repair paste for larger or more accident-prone areas. In most cases you'll have difficulty blending in the filler by hand with an ordinary filling knife. Instead, you can use a template cut to the profile of the moulding from plastic sheet (a large plastic ice-cream container is ideal), or hardboard or cardboard; run it along to smooth the surface after applying the filler.

If the damage is more serious, you may be able to saw and/or chisel out the bad part to leave clean edges, and glue and pin in a small piece or pieces of prepared moulding, or else plain timber shaped to fit.

If patching and filling won't work, you need a completely new piece. This, however, can be a snag if your existing moulding is one of the scores of obsolete types, because you won't be able to match it off the shelf.

You may occasionally be able to buy something suitable – on site where an old house is being demolished or renovated, or perhaps from a demolition contractor who stocks secondhand timber. Otherwise, many joinery firms will cut a moulding specially if you take in a sample of the pattern; but that's likely to prove very expensive.

Your next option is to substitute a readily available pattern of moulding throughout the room. But that's a pity – not to say a lot of trouble – if most of it is sound. A third possibility, probably the most attractive if you only need a small piece, is to make it yourself. You can mould the shape with a power router, or perhaps a plough plane, or

combination plane or scratch stock.

A scratch stock consists of a piece of steel (for example part of a hacksaw blade) ground and/or filed to the profile you want. It is then clamped with screws between two pieces of hardwood in an improvised stock, and scraped along the timber till the desired shape emerges.

Externally curved mouldings, such as plain chamfered skirting and architrave, can of course usually be formed with an ordinary bench plane and glasspaper. Lastly, it's sometimes possible to make the moulding up in sections from smaller ones, glued together and filled where necessary.

Skirting boards

Skirting boards are generally the widest and longest mouldings around the house. They're fixed, of course, along the bottom of walls, where they prevent damage to wall coverings and make a neat join with the floor.

Sometimes plain square-edged timber – say 150x25mm (6x1in) planed – forms a skirting, but moulded pieces are more usual. Nowadays 'torus', 'ovolo', 'ogee' and the plain chamfered and rounded types are by far the commonest. Plastic skirting boards are another modern development.

A gap between the skirting and the floor

surface can easily be hidden with a quadrant moulding – nailed to the skirting, not the floor, so any shrinkage or swelling in the floor won't open up cracks visible from above.

If a skirting board has simply come loose, use a torch to look behind it for any wooden battens or plugs (described below) into which the original fixings may go. Then nail through into these. If the plaster continues to the floor, nail through it into the masonry behind. But if there's bare brickwork without such battens or plugs – or if your nailing loosens previously sound fixings – you'll have to use countersunk screws and wallplugs, inserted into holes made with a masonry drill.

If, however, actual damage or rot demands the removal of one or more whole sections, a bolster chisel makes a good lever for prising boards off. The best place to begin removal is at an external corner; otherwise take the overlapping board at an internal corner, or start at the point where the skirting meets the doorway.

Usually skirting boards are nailed in place, but you must be alert for screws (their heads may be covered with filler or even wooden plugs). Unscrew them first, or, if that's impossible, cut away a little plaster above the skirting board and slip a cold chisel behind the skirting to chop through them before you finish prising the board off.

RENEWING SKIRTING BOARDS

1 *If you have to saw out the board before removal, a flooring saw is the best tool to use. But it will still require plenty of pressure.*

2 *If the plaster overlaps the top of the skirting, start by driving a bolster horizontally, to make a clean break and leave the plaster intact.*

3 *Work right along the wall this way, then drive the bolster downwards to force the board out. If possible, wedge it out as well.*

4 *Finally, pull the board carefully away from the wall, while at the same time levering it off with a bolster, crowbar or similar tool.*

5 *Avoid injury by always removing the nails from old boards. Knock them through from the back before pulling them out with a claw hammer.*

6 *Measure the length, and use a sliding bevel to gauge the exact angle at which you'll have to cut the end butting against the door architrave.*

7 *Saw the board to length and cut butt joints to the gauged angle. External corners need mitring; internal ones are scribed for a sure fit.*

8 *Where necessary insert packing pieces – at 400 to 450mm (16 to 18in) centres – of a thickness which will bring the board out to the right level.*

9 *Mark on the board face where the packing pieces are, and nail it on. If nailing through both board and packing, use masonry nails.*

RENEWING ARCHITRAVES

1 *Starting at the bottom, carefully lever and pull off all three pieces of moulding, working from both sides of each piece for easier removal.*

2 *Cut the moulding squarely into three over-long pieces, position the uprights and mark off the height. The distance from the opening is equal all round.*

3 *If possible, use a mitre box or other jig to cut the upper end of each upright off at 45°. Do check that the cut slopes the right way each time.*

4 *Nail each of the uprights lightly in position (parallel to the frame or lining, with its outer edge against the skirting at the bottom).*

5 *Place the top piece upside down on the uprights, and mark it at both ends. Cut one mitre, position it, re-check the length and cut the other.*

6 *After adjusting the uprights' positions (and shaving the mitres) if necessary, nail all three pieces firmly, and pin the mitres lightly.*

Failing that, a hacksaw should do the job.

In certain places – eg, the backs of alcoves – the skirting board is held in position by the two pieces at right angles to it. So, unless you remove at least one of those first, sawing the board out is your only option. A flooring saw may work. Otherwise drill a series of holes in line down the face of the skirting, and use a chisel to chop out the waste between the holes so you can prise out the two ends of the board. Pipework and other obstacles sometimes force the same solution.

If a length of skirting refuses to come away completely, you may still be able to make sawing easier by levering enough of it out to push timber wedges behind it. In all cases, it's best to saw at an angle of 45° across the thickness. If you're just removing a section, cut the new piece to the same angle when you come to fix that in place.

Always use 45° cuts, rather than butt joins, if you have to make up a long piece from two shorter ones. They'll be less conspicuous, especially if you site the join near an out-of-the-way corner.

Fixing new skirting

For a tight fit, you should only measure and cut a skirting board after fixing the adjacent one in position. What's more, neatness dictates that the ends have to be cut in the right way.

External corners are always mitred. You can use either a deep mitre or box, or a circular saw which should be set to a 45° bevel, and drive light nails through the completed joint. Where walls meet at odd angles (eg, round bay windows) you'll have to gauge each angle with a sliding bevel, and measure it with a protractor. Then re-set the bevel to half the angle, and mark the pieces accordingly.

On internal corners, however, a mitre will tend to separate and show a gap – because, when you fix the second board against the wall, it will tend to move away slightly from the first board. The answer is to scribe the profile of the moulding onto the second board – see opposite. Cut it out so that its end fits snugly into position over the first board. Then cut it to length at the other end. (Plain boards, of course, can just be butt-jointed.)

The fixing itself depends largely on what's behind the old skirting. If it's fairly recent, the plaster will probably run right down to the floor, the skirting being simply nailed on top of it. Nail the new piece on in the same way, using masonry nails long enough to pass through both layers of plaster and into the brickwork – say 63mm (2½in).

For a hollow timber-framed stud partition, use ordinary oval or lost-head nails, making sure they pass through the cladding and into the timber sole plate (into the studs, too, in the case of wide skirtings). Ordinary nails will also do for solid walls of soft blocks, and for

SCRIBING AND FIXING SKIRTING

Use an offcut of skirting to scribe the profile on the back of the board (below left). An end cut to this line will fit snugly into the corner (below right).

Fix skirtings in the order shown below, to ensure that any slight gaps in scribed joints aren't immediately obvious from the middle of the room.

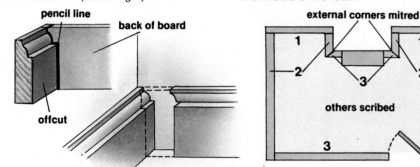

pencil line
back of board
offcut

external corners mitred
others scribed

medium-hard blocks you can use cut nails. If for any reason nails don't hold, use screws and wallplugs.

Older skirtings can present more problems, because the plaster usually doesn't go right to the floor. In fact, it sometimes overlaps the top of the skirting – which means you need special care during removal, so as not to dislodge too much of it.

Obsolete types of skirting are often very wide, and sometimes even made in two sections across the width. If, as is almost certain, you're replacing them with something narrower, you'll have to be prepared to extend the plaster downwards accordingly.

The skirting will usually have been nailed either into timber plugs wedged into the mortar joints, or to short vertical battens ('grounds') on the face of the brickwork. There may also be a continuous batten along its upper edge. Your best plan is to make use of these existing plugs or battens. However, you may well have to add packing pieces of your own to bring the skirting forward – the aim being to get its back as nearly as possible flush with the face of the plaster. You may also have to replace plugs or battens that have split or been riddled by woodworm.

Here again, nailing right through is the quickest method. But you may find you can only get a secure fixing and the right alignment by screwing or nailing the packing on first, then nailing or even screwing the skirting to that.

A very uneven floor may mean you have to scribe the lower edge of the board to fit, but such gaps are usually noticeable only when very thin sheet floorcoverings are laid; carpets will usually hide them.

Architraves

The idea of an architrave is to hide the join between a door or window frame or lining and the surrounding plaster.

A loose architrave can be nailed back in place to the door frame, or even screwed to the surrounding masonry if you drill right through it with a masonry bit and insert wallplugs to take the screws. But removal and fixing are both easier than for skirting, so replacement is usually the sensible alternative to major repairs. You just lever the existing architrave off, and nail the new one on.

On a brick or block wall, you usually nail through the moulding's inner edge and into the doorframe, lining or 'wrought grounds' with 25 mm (1 in) oval nails; lost-head nails or panel pins can also be used. But if necessary you can nail through the middle of the moulding and into the wall itself, using cut nails for medium-hard blocks if you like, and masonry nails for bricks and hard blocks. If you find that there are rough (concealed) grounds between the plaster and the frame or lining, then nail into those. On a stud wall, nail into the studs.

At the bottom, the upright pieces butt against the floor and the ends of the skirting. At the top the corners are mitred. A good idea is to start by cutting off three pieces of moulding which are manageable but still slightly too long. Then you can mark off the heights of the two upright ones (which may of course differ a bit, depending on whether the floor is flat or level), mitre their top ends and fix them loosely to the wall.

This makes it easy to mark off the exact length of the top piece. Mitre its ends, position it, and make any adjustments – by moving the uprights slightly, and even shaving the mitred ends with a sharp chisel or block plane if necessary. Then nail all three pieces finally in place, and pin the mitres from the top as for skirting boards.

When mitring, always make quite sure you're cutting the right way round. That sounds silly, but you'll find it's all too easy to waste whole pieces by mistake.

Ready Reference

SHAPES OF MOULDINGS

Skirtings
Common profiles include A: chamfered ('splayed and rounded'); B: torus; C: ogee and D: pencil round. E is another common type. Skirtings are often made with a different moulding each side, so you can use either.

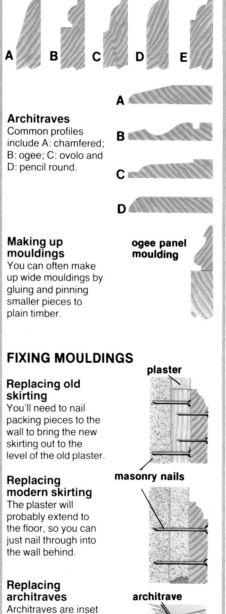

A B C D E

Architraves
Common profiles include A: chamfered; B: ogee; C: ovolo and D: pencil round.

A
B
C
D

Making up mouldings
You can often make up wide mouldings by gluing and pinning smaller pieces to plain timber.

ogee panel moulding

FIXING MOULDINGS

Replacing old skirting
You'll need to nail packing pieces to the wall to bring the new skirting out to the level of the old plaster.

plaster
masonry nails

Replacing modern skirting
The plaster will probably extend to the floor, so you can just nail through into the wall behind.

Replacing architraves
Architraves are inset slightly from the edge of the door (or window) frame or lining, and conceal the join with the plaster.

architrave

REGLAZING A WINDOW

Windows may be a vital barrier against the elements but they're also quite fragile and can be broken easily. When this happens the glass has to be replaced. It's not a complicated job and few specialist tools are required – it does, however, need a degree of care.

Windows may be all shapes and sizes but basically all have a main frame containing one or more fixed or opening frames. The glass is held in a rebate – a narrow 'shelf' – on the outer face of the window, and is kept in place with either angular metal nails called sprigs (on wooden frames) or wire clips (on metal frames). These are then covered with putty, a pliable material which hardens when exposed to the air and provides a water-proof bedding for the glass (see *Ready Reference*).

The technique for reglazing a window depends mainly on what the window frame is made from – and wooden ones are by far the most common.

Removing the glass
Obviously, this has to be done carefully. If necessary, tap the old pane with a hammer until it is sufficiently broken to let you pull out most of the pieces by hand – you should wear thick gloves for protection. Any tiny fragments embedded in the putty can be tugged out with pincers, but don't worry if they refuse to budge. They can wait until the putty is removed.

Preparing the frame
The professional glazier uses a tool called a hacking knife to chop out the old putty. It's an inexpensive tool to buy. If you have an old chisel, you could use this in conjunction with a mallet. If the putty is very old it can be quite stubborn, so take care not to damage the window frame. On multi-paned windows, you should also avoid using so much force

that surrounding panes crack.

As soon as the rebate is clear, brush it out. Rub it down with medium grade glasspaper until it is clean and smooth, then give it a coat of ordinary wood primer – not paint because this will prevent the putty drying.

PREPARING A WOODEN FRAME

1 Tap out most of the broken glass with a hammer, then remove the remaining splinters by hand – but wear thick gloves for protection.

2 Chop out the old putty from the rebate using a hacking knife. Tap it with a hammer if necessary. Be careful not to damage the window frame.

3 Pull out the old glazing sprigs with a pair of pincers. If the sprigs aren't damaged you can re-use when fitting the new pane of glass.

Buying new glass

It's important to choose the right type of glass, but don't try to cut it to size yourself. Your local glazier will do a much better job, and is less likely to break the pane in the process. There's also no financial advantage to doing the job yourself for you'll be left with unusable off-cuts. And don't think you can use up that odd piece of glass you may have lying about. Old glass does not cut well at all, and tends to break in the wrong place even when you've scored it with a carbide-tipped glasscutter.

So measure the width and height of the rebate into which the glass must fit; double check the measurements to be sure, and order the glass to be cut 3mm (⅛in) smaller on each dimension. This allows for any slight inaccuracy in your measurements, and avoids the risk of the glass cracking due to expansion or contraction of the frame. If you need patterned glass, make a note of which way the pattern runs.

The fixing process

First you must line the rebate with putty. You can either take a ball of putty in the palm of your hand and squeeze it out between thumb and forefinger using your thumb to press it in; or you can roll the putty into finger-thick sausages and press these into place. Wet your hands before handling putty to prevent it sticking to your fingers, and knead it until it is pliable and any surface oils are thoroughly mixed in.

Next, press the pane into the puttied rebate with the palms of your hands, so that putty oozes out, around and behind the glass. Apply pressure around the edges rather than in the centre of the pane and check that, when you've finished, the glass is separated from the frame on the inside by a bed of putty which is 2mm to 3mm (up to ⅛in) thick.

Now for the unnerving part – nailing the glass in place. It's best to use glazing sprigs,

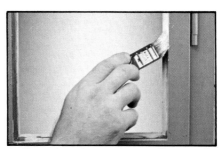

4 *Clean the rebate using medium-grade glasspaper, then remove any dust and prime the rebate with a narrow paintbrush.*

but you could make do with 19mm (¾in) panel pins that have had their heads nipped off with pliers. You'll need at least two per side, spaced no more than 230mm (9in) apart, and you must be sure to drive them squarely into the wood so they don't pinch and crack the glass. When you've finished, just over 6mm (¼in) of pin should be showing.

The final stage is to fill the rest of the rebate with a triangular fillet of putty that neatly covers the pins. Apply the putty in the same way as when lining the rebate, and use a putty knife or an ordinary filling knife to do the shaping, mitring the corners of the fillet as neatly as possible. Wet the knife blade to prevent the putty sticking to it as you draw it over the fillet.

Clean off the excess putty – including any that oozed out inside the pane earlier – and allow to dry hard before painting.

When you need to reglaze a window that isn't at ground level, you'll have to work from a ladder. Obviously you'll have to be organised when working at a height. Tap out most of the glass first from inside – and make sure there's no one standing below as you do so. Put all the tools and equipment in a bucket which you can hang on a hook attached to the ladder at the top. Don't try to carry the glass – it's best to get someone to pass it through the window.

Modern windows

Conventional steel-framed windows are reglazed in almost the same way as wooden ones, except that the glass is fixed with wire clips fitting into holes in the frame, rather than with glazing sprigs. Remove these and re-use them to fix the new pane – along with the right type of putty – after priming with a metal primer.

Because putty needs paint to protect it, and because modern aluminium and plastic windows aren't meant to be painted, a different method is used to hold the glass. Normally, it's a variation on the rubber gasket system used to keep the windows fixed in a car.

Just how easy these windows are to reglaze depends on the design; different manufacturers have their own systems and unless it is obvious how the glass fits in, all you can do is ask the window manufacturer for his advice. In some cases, he will prefer to do the repair himself.

Replacing double glazing

There are few problems where secondary double glazing is involved. This system uses a completely separate window frame to hold the extra pane of glass. All you do is treat each element of the system as a single glazed window. One complication you may come up against is where a do-it-yourself

PUTTING IN NEW GLASS

Cross-pein hammer Stanley Tools

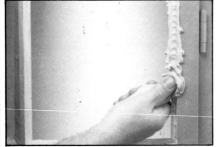

1 When the primer is dry line the rebate with putty. Hold the putty in the palm of your hand and squeeze it out between your forefinger and thumb.

2 Position a new pane of glass in the rebate. Press it in place gently from the sides to avoid pressure on the centre, which could shatter the glass.

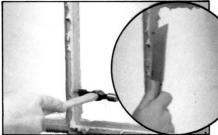

3 Knock in glazing sprigs using a cross-pein hammer or (inset) the back of a hacking knife. Slide the tool across the surface of the glass.

4 When all the glazing sprigs have been inserted, apply putty to the rebate to cover the edges of the glass. Press it into the angle with your thumb.

5 Shape the putty fillet into a slope using the straight edge of a putty knife. The slope shouldn't extend beyond the rebate line on the inside of the frame.

6 When you've shaped the putty into a slope, mitre each corner with the square edge of a filling knife, laying the blade on lightly to smooth out any ridges.

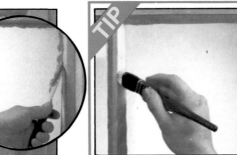

7 Trim off any surplus putty – from the surface of the glass and (inset) from the inside face of the pane – by running the putty knife along the rebate.

8 Leave the putty to dry for about a fortnight, then prime, undercoat and top coat. Allow the paint to extend 2 or 3mm (1/8in) onto the glass surface.

double glazing kit has been used. In this case the extra 'frame' may be no more than plastic channelling clipped over the edge of the glass, so it's more a case of remaking this frame than reglazing it.

Replacing double glazing where both panes are mounted in the same frame is more involved, and how you approach it depends on whether factory-made sealed units or two ordinary panes of glass have been used.

In the latter case, you merely fix two new panes in the same way as if reglazing an ordinary window. Just be sure you don't get marks on the panes facing into the double glazing's air gap – you can't clean them off once the second pane is in place.

Factory-made sealed units are also sometimes fitted like a single pane of glass but, more often, you'll have a modern gasket system to contend with. In any case, the most important thing is to order the new sealed units to exactly the right size. They cannot be trimmed if you make a mistake.

Dealing with leaded lights

Strictly speaking, to reglaze a leaded light, you must remove the putty and glazing sprigs from the main window frame and lift out the entire glass and lead latticework, so it can be worked on flat. You may, however, get away with working in situ if you get a helper to hold a sheet of hardboard or something similar against the other side of the pane, to keep it flat while you carry out the repair.

Whichever approach you adopt, you must lever away the lip of lead (called the 'came') holding the glass in place by using an old chisel. Cut the lead near the corners of the pane with a knife to make this easier. Remove the broken glass, clean out the putty from the channel in the lead, apply new putty and then fit the new pane – this should be cut to fit the dimensions of the rebate exactly. Finally, smooth back the lead with the handle of the chisel to hold it in place. To finish, make good the knife cuts with solder, or with a proprietary plastic repair compound.

There's more about this type of repair in another section.

Why glass?

You may be wondering why nobody has come up with a glass or glass substitute that never breaks. Well, they have. Leaving aside bullet-proof glass and the like, there are a host of plastic glazing materials on the market ranging from the familiar Perspex to compounds with complicated chemical names. But they all have two major drawbacks – they are comparatively expensive to buy, and they scratch so easily that they lose their transparency.

Jem Grischotti

HOME ELECTRICS

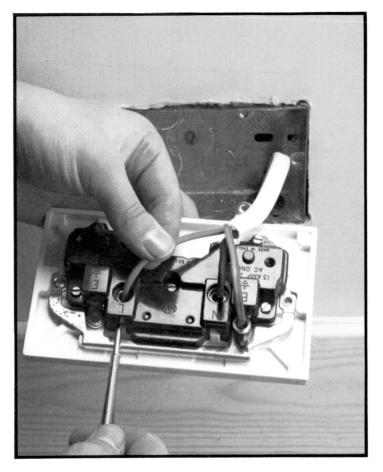

PART 3

HOME ELECTRICS

PLUGS & FUSES

Fuses and plugs are the two parts of a home's electrical system that most closely concern the householder and it's important to know what they do and how to use them.

FUSES

A fuse is a safety device inserted into an electrical circuit to protect the mains wiring or any appliance from damage by overloading. This can be caused by anything from too many appliances overloading a particular circuit to a short circuit within an appliance, its plug or in some other part of the system. Basically the fuse is a thin wire that melts ('blows') and breaks the circuit if too much current flows through it. Circuit fuses are located in the house's main fuse box or consumer unit. Fuses are also fitted in modern plugs.

Circuit fuses

Circuit fuses protect the fixed wiring and apparatus, and if they 'blow' no equipment will operate on the circuit affected.

Every circuit fuse has a current rating in amps (A) appropriate to the rating of the circuit, and is colour-coded: white is for a 5A fuse (for lighting circuits), blue for a 15A, yellow for a 20A, red for a 30A (ring mains) and green for a 45A (cooker circuit).

There are two types of circuit fuse – rewirable and cartridge. A rewirable fuse is the least sensitive method of protection, but it can be mended easily by connecting fuse wire of the correct rating between the terminals of the fuse carrier.

In a cartridge fuse, the fuse wire is enclosed in a clip-in ceramic cartridge filled with quartz powder (sand) and if it blows you simply replace the whole cartridge. Unlike the rewirable fuse where it's possible to fit the wrongly rated fuse wire, it's impossible to fit a larger amperage cartridge as the size of fuse holder usually depends on the rating of the circuit to which it is fitted. The only exception to this is with 15A and 20A fuses which are the same size, but as the cartridges are colour-coded, a mistake is avoidable.

BE PREPARED

● Make a list of which circuit does what (eg, no 1: downstairs lighting) and keep it by the main fuse box or consumer unit

● Keep a fuse wire card containing adequate lengths of each rating, a small screwdriver and a torch near the fuse box or consumer unit ready for emergencies

● If the consumer unit contains cartridge fuses, always keep at least two spare fuses of each current rating in a plastic bag and hang it nearby.

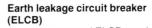

FUSE WIRE

Craig Warwick

Miniature circuit breaker (MCB)

MCBs can be fitted instead of circuit fuses in modern consumer units. An MCB is a switching device that is activated by the surge of current caused by overloading or a short circuit. It has the advantage that it can be reset at the push of a button or the flick of a switch – unless the fault that caused it to switch off in the first place is still present.

MCBs are more sensitive and faster reacting than circuit fuses. Some kinds have the same colour-coding as conventional circuit fuses; others are labelled with the circuit rating.

Earth leakage circuit breaker (ELCB)

A current-operated ELCB may be fitted in conjunction with the house's earthing system, and usually protects all circuits in the house. It cuts off the power supply if it detects an electric current flowing to earth – this is what happens when someone receives an electric shock, or insulation fails on a mains cable. An ELCB is activated by far less current than is necessary to blow a fuse or trip an MCB, and operates within a fraction of a second.

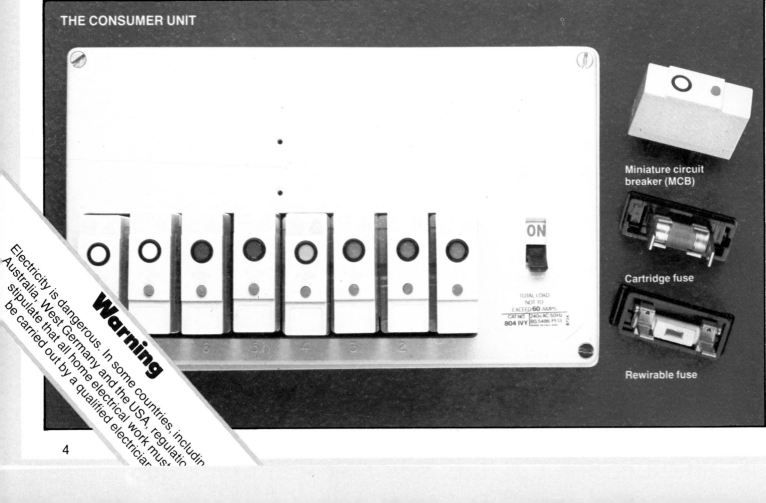

THE CONSUMER UNIT

ON

TOTAL LOAD NOT TO EXCEED **60** AMPS
CAT NO. 240v AC 50Hz
804 IVY BS 5486 Pt 13

Miniature circuit breaker (MCB)

Cartridge fuse

Rewirable fuse

Jem Grishotti

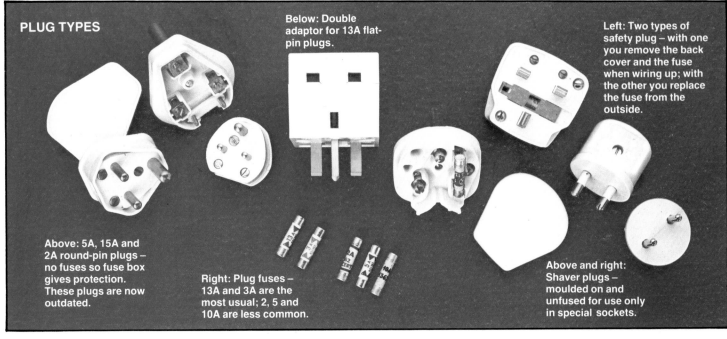

PLUG TYPES

Below: Double adaptor for 13A flat-pin plugs.

Left: Two types of safety plug – with one you remove the back cover and the fuse when wiring up; with the other you replace the fuse from the outside.

Above: 5A, 15A and 2A round-pin plugs – no fuses so fuse box gives protection. These plugs are now outdated.

Right: Plug fuses – 13A and 3A are the most usual; 2, 5 and 10A are less common.

Above and right: Shaver plugs – moulded on and unfused for use only in special sockets.

Jem Grischotti

Circuit fuses and faults

If a circuit fuse blows immediately after it has been mended, the cause could be a fault in an appliance, in the circuit wiring or in a socket outlet. A fixed appliance such as a shower unit or immersion heater (which has no plug or intermediate fuse) could also be to blame. Such faults should be investigated by a qualified electrician.

Continuous blowing of a lighting circuit fuse is probably caused by a short circuit in the flex or lampholder of a pendant light.

Plug fuses

Modern 13A flat-pin plugs contain fuses that protect the individual appliance and its flex in case a fault occurs. When they blow they only isolate the appliance concerned, so other appliances plugged into the main circuit will still function.

Plug fuses are of the cartridge type which fit neatly into a carrier in the plug, but are a different size to circuit cartridge fuses. The two standard ones have current ratings of 3A and 13A and are colour-coded red and brown respectively. Fit a 3A fuse for appliances rated at less than 700 watts, a 13A fuse otherwise (and always for colour TV sets). Plug fuses can also be fitted into connection units used to supply fixed appliances such as a night storage heater or a freezer.

When a plug fuse blows

If an appliance doesn't work, the most likely cause is a blown plug fuse. Replace it with a new one of the correct rating for the appliance (see above), then put the plug back in the socket and switch on. If nothing happens, check that the socket is live by plugging in an appliance that you know is working. Should this not work, check the circuit fuse.

PLUGS

The function of a plug is to connect a portable appliance (eg a lamp or power tool) to the fixed wiring via a socket outlet anywhere around the house.

The modern standard plug is a 13A fused three-pin plug, which has flat pins. There is also a moulded-on unfused two-pin plug used exclusively for electric shavers in conjunction with a special socket outlet. In older installations, instead of 13A plugs, round-pin plugs with current ratings of 2A, 5A and 15A are used. These are not fused.

A recent development is a 13A fused plug that is moulded onto the PVC sheathing of the flex and can't be dismantled. However, it's possible to change the fuse by lifting up a flap between the pins of the plug. It's also possible to change the fuse in some conventional plugs without removing the plug top. If you ever need to replace a moulded-on plug you have to cut off the flex as close to the plug as possible and replace it with a conventional 13A plug.

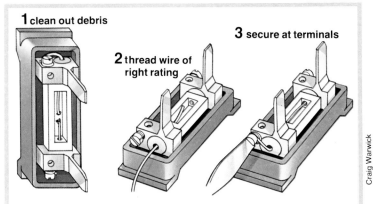

1 clean out debris

2 thread wire of right rating

3 secure at terminals

Craig Warwick

Replacing circuit fuses

Turn off the main on/off switch on the fuse box or consumer unit before tackling the repair. With a rewirable fuse, you may have to remove each in turn to locate the one that's blown. Always use fuse wire of the correct rating for the circuit when you make the repair – don't be tempted to use a higher rated one even if the fuse continues to blow. Don't make the wire taut between the terminals as this will reduce the current rating, resulting in over-heating and premature failure of the fuse wire. NEVER fit any other metallic object into a fuse carrier.

If a cartridge fuse blows, and you've no list of the circuits (or it is not obvious which circuit has been affected), turn off the main switch and remove each cartridge in turn. Test it by holding it across the open end of a switched-on metal torch, with one end of the fuse on the casing and the other on the end of the battery. A sound fuse will light the torch. Alternatively, use a continuity tester (available from electrical stores). Replace the blown fuse with a new one of the correct rating.

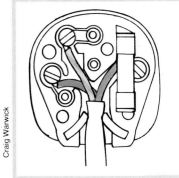

Craig Warwick

Plugs and earthing

Most electrical appliances are Fitted with three-core flex (see pages 6 and 7). When plugged in, the earth wire (green/yellow) is linked to the house's earthing and ensures that the appliance is properly earthed. Two-core flex is for double-insulated appliances. Left: A correctly-wired 13A plug.
REMEMBER
BL (Bottom Left) = BLue
BR (Bottom Right) = BRown.

CABLE & FLEX

Two types of wiring are used in the domestic electrical circuits. Fixed cables are normally concealed, and carry electrical current to switches, ceiling lights, and socket outlets. Flexible cords (flexes) connect portable appliances and light fittings to the fixed wiring.

Fixed wiring

This consists mostly of PVC-sheathed cable containing three copper conductors (cores). The core insulated in red PVC is the 'live' and the one in black the 'neutral' though in lighting circuits in the cable to the switch both the black and red are live. (The black core is required to have a piece of red sleeving on it to indicate this, although this is often omitted by incompetent electricians. Cables having two red conductors are made for contract work, but rarely stocked and sold retail). The third core is the earth and this is uninsulated, but when exposed after the sheathing is removed ready for wiring up it must be sleeved in green/yellow striped PVC before being connected to the earth terminal. In some wiring circuits PVC-sheathed cables having one core only are used, for example, where a live core is looped out of a switch or a neutral core is looped out of a light, to supply an additional light or lights. Three-core and earth cable is used for two-way switching. The conductors are insulated in red, blue and yellow; the colour coding is for purposes of identification only.

Cables

PVC-sheathed and insulated, two-core and earth

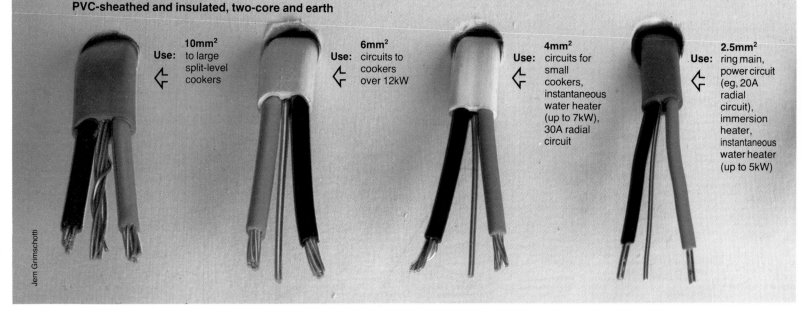

Jem Grimschotti

Use: 10mm² to large split-level cookers

Use: 6mm² circuits to cookers over 12kW

Use: 4mm² circuits for small cookers, instantaneous water heater (up to 7kW), 30A radial circuit

Use: 2.5mm² ring main, power circuit (eg, 20A radial circuit), immersion heater, instantaneous water heater (up to 5kW)

Flexible cords

Flexible cords are made in various sizes and current ratings and the types you'll most often come across are: *parallel twin unsheathed, circular PVC-sheathed, circular braided, unkinkable* and *heat-resisting*. Each conductor is made up of a number of strands of copper and it is this which gives the cord its flexibility.

The insulation used round the conductors now conforms to an international colour coding standard – brown denotes the live wire, blue the neutral, and green/yellow the earth, when it is part of the flex. Transparent or white insulation is used for a flex that carries a low current and where it doesn't matter which wire is connected to the live and neutral terminals of an appliance. It is used mainly for table lamps that need no earth.

Parallel twin unsheathed

Circular PVC sheathed two-core, and two-core and earth

Circular braided (rubber insulated)

Use: 0.5mm² and 0.75mm² — plain lighting pendants (two-core) 1.0mm² and 1.5mm² most appliances (three-core), power tools and other double-insulated appliances (two-core)

Use: 1.00mm² and 1.25mm² electric heaters and fires

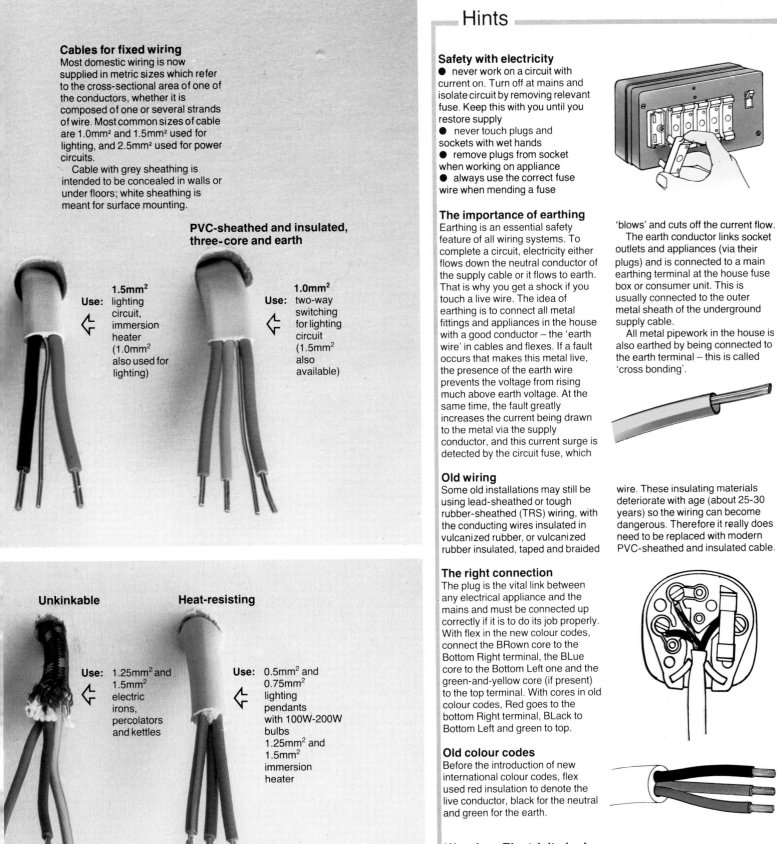

Cables for fixed wiring

Most domestic wiring is now supplied in metric sizes which refer to the cross-sectional area of one of the conductors, whether it is composed of one or several strands of wire. Most common sizes of cable are 1.0mm² and 1.5mm² used for lighting, and 2.5mm² used for power circuits.

Cable with grey sheathing is intended to be concealed in walls or under floors; white sheathing is meant for surface mounting.

PVC-sheathed and insulated, three-core and earth

1.5mm²
Use: lighting circuit, immersion heater (1.0mm² also used for lighting)

1.0mm²
Use: two-way switching for lighting circuit (1.5mm² also available)

Unkinkable
Use: 1.25mm² and 1.5mm² electric irons, percolators and kettles

Heat-resisting
Use: 0.5mm² and 0.75mm² lighting pendants with 100W-200W bulbs 1.25mm² and 1.5mm² immersion heater

Hints

Safety with electricity
● never work on a circuit with current on. Turn off at mains and isolate circuit by removing relevant fuse. Keep this with you until you restore supply
● never touch plugs and sockets with wet hands
● remove plugs from socket when working on appliance
● always use the correct fuse wire when mending a fuse

The importance of earthing
Earthing is an essential safety feature of all wiring systems. To complete a circuit, electricity either flows down the neutral conductor of the supply cable or it flows to earth. That is why you get a shock if you touch a live wire. The idea of earthing is to connect all metal fittings and appliances in the house with a good conductor – the 'earth wire' in cables and flexes. If a fault occurs that makes this metal live, the presence of the earth wire prevents the voltage from rising much above earth voltage. At the same time, the fault greatly increases the current being drawn to the metal via the supply conductor, and this current surge is detected by the circuit fuse, which 'blows' and cuts off the current flow.

The earth conductor links socket outlets and appliances (via their plugs) and is connected to a main earthing terminal at the house fuse box or consumer unit. This is usually connected to the outer metal sheath of the underground supply cable.

All metal pipework in the house is also earthed by being connected to the earth terminal – this is called 'cross bonding'.

Old wiring
Some old installations may still be using lead-sheathed or tough rubber-sheathed (TRS) wiring, with the conducting wires insulated in vulcanized rubber, or vulcanized rubber insulated, taped and braided wire. These insulating materials deteriorate with age (about 25-30 years) so the wiring can become dangerous. Therefore it really does need to be replaced with modern PVC-sheathed and insulated cable.

The right connection
The plug is the vital link between any electrical appliance and the mains and must be connected up correctly if it is to do its job properly. With flex in the new colour codes, connect the BRown core to the Bottom Right terminal, the BLue core to the Bottom Left one and the green-and-yellow core (if present) to the top terminal. With cores in old colour codes, Red goes to the bottom Right terminal, BLack to Bottom Left and green to top.

Old colour codes
Before the introduction of new international colour codes, flex used red insulation to denote the live conductor, black for the neutral and green for the earth.

Warning: Electricity is dangerous.
In some countries, including Australia, West Germany and the USA, regulations stipulate that all home electrical work must be carried out by a qualified electrician.

EXTENDING FLEX SAFELY

Ideally, electrical appliances should be linked to the mains via an unbroken length of flex. However, there are times when you may need a longer flex — which means extending the one that's fitted, or else using a separate extension lead with its own plug and socket.

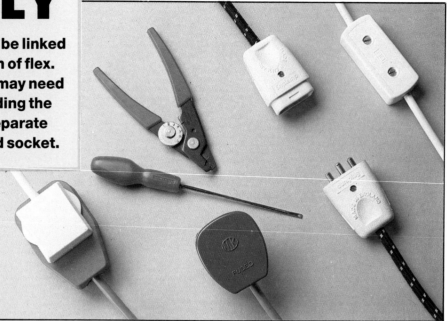

If you've got enough socket outlets in your home, you should be able to plug in most of your appliances to a nearby socket without any problem. But there are often situations where the length of flex that's fitted just isn't long enough. For example, few vacuum cleaners have enough flex to allow uninterrupted cleaning without you having to keep unplugging the appliance and moving to another socket outlet to plug it in. And most power tools come with annoyingly short leads – fine if you always use them at your workbench, but not much use elsewhere.

There are two ways round the problem. The first is to fit a longer flex – the right answer for cases like the vacuum cleaner. The second is to use a separate extension lead into which appliances with short flexes can be plugged whenever the need arises.

Extension leads

An extension lead is just a length of flex with a plug on one end (to plug into the mains) and a socket on the other (into which you plug the tool or appliance you're using). You can buy one ready-made, complete with connectors and packed loose in a bag (in which case it will have what is called a trailing socket at the 'appliance' end of the lead), or complete with a drum onto which the flex is wound when the lead is not in use (here the socket is actually mounted on the drum). Alternatively, you can buy the various components and connect them up yourself.

Earthing and current rating

Any extension lead must serve the same purpose as the flex on the appliance whose reach it is extending, and this means that above all it must provide earth continuity. Many power tools (especially those intended for use out of doors, such as lawnmowers) are double-insulated, which means that they do not need an earth connection and are fitted with two-core flex. So, in theory, you could use an extension lead with just two cores as well.

However, the extension lead you intend to use with your lawnmower may end up being used with another appliance instead – one that *does* need earthing. So any extension

lead you use should, for safety's sake, always have three-core flex. It will still work with any double-insulated appliance too, of course.

The other important thing about extension leads is the current rating of the flex used. You may have intended your lead to be used only for a power drill using, say, 400 watts – well within the capacity of a 3A 0.5mm² flex. But suppose someone unknowingly uses that same flex to power a fan heater rated at 3kW. The flex will then be heavily overloaded and unless a 3A fuse has been fitted in the lead's plug the flex will overheat and could start a fire. So play safe: always use 1.25mm² flex for an extension lead, whatever you intend to use it for.

If you're going to use the extension lead out of doors, it's best to choose an orange or white sheathed flex rather than a black one, so you can see it better and avoid tripping over it or cutting it with your hedge trimmer.

Safety with extension leads

There are two points to remember about using extension leads safely. The first is always to uncoil the lead from the drum before you use it, especially if it's powering a high-rated appliance. If you don't it may overheat and eventually melt. The second point is never to use a lead out of doors when it is raining, or after rain when foliage is wet and moisture could get into the socket.

Making up your own lead

The flex should, as already described, be 1.25mm² two-core and earth PVC-sheathed flex. The plug can be any conventional plug that suits your house sockets. However, a toughened plastic or moulded rubber one will stand up to knocks better.

The socket should also be toughened plastic or rubber. There's the same choice of pin type and colour as with moulded plugs, and you can have one, two or four outlets on the one socket.

It's best to keep your lead on a drum of some sort so it doesn't get kinked when coiled up. An empty cable reel is ideal, or you can make a simple drum from plywood and softwood offcuts – see *Ready Reference*.

Extending flex

On appliances like vacuum cleaners and lawnmowers, you may prefer to extend the appliance flex permanently instead of using an extension lead. The best way of doing this is to replace the existing flex completely, wiring the new flex into the appliance itself. But provided you use the right method, you can also extend the existing flex by adding on an extra length with a flex connector.

For most household appliances a one-piece connector is ideal – see the step-by-step photographs opposite. This simply links the old and new flex within a one-piece moulding. Make sure you use the right size – a 5A one for appliances rated at less than 1200 watts, a 13A one otherwise.

If you'll want to disconnect the flex extension for any reason, use a two-part connector instead. Fit a two-pin one to double-insulated appliances, a three-pin one otherwise. Remember always to connect the plug part to the appliance flex and the socket part to the extension flex. If you do it the other way round the plug pins will be live when the flex is plugged into the mains. For leads of this type being used out of doors, go for a weatherproof type with a shroud that locks the two parts together.

ASSEMBLING THE COMPONENTS

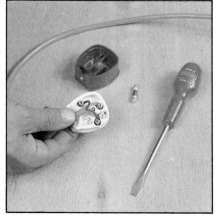

1 *If you're making up an extension lead, use orange or white 1.25mm² three-core flex and a toughened plug. Make sure the cord grip holds the flex securely.*

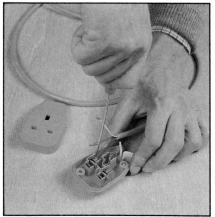

2 *Connect the other end of the flex to the correct terminals within the trailing socket. Again, make sure the cord grip is secure before fitting the cover.*

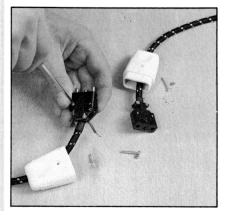

3 *With a two-part flex connector, prepare the cores. Thread the flex through the shrouds, connect up the cores and tighten the cord grips.*

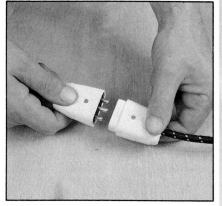

4 *Fit the shrouds over the terminal blocks. Check that you have connected the plug part to the appliance flex, the socket part to the mains flex.*

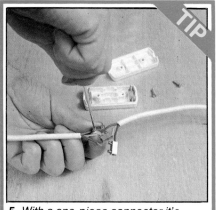

5 *With a one-piece connector it's easier to link the cores if you remove the terminals first. You may have to cut each core to a different length.*

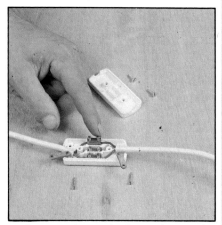

6 *Open up the cord grips and press the terminal blocks into place, laying the cores in their channels. Do up the two cord grips and fit the connector cover.*

Ready Reference

READY-MADE LEADS

You can buy extension leads ready-made and wound on plastic drums, complete with a carrying handle. Before you buy one
● check that the flex is rated at 13A rather than 5A
● check the flex length; it may be anything from 9 to 20m (30 to 66ft).
Look too for extra features like switched sockets with neons, hanging hooks and somewhere to stow the plug.

PICK THE RIGHT FLEX

For extension leads, always choose 1.25mm² two-core and earth PVC-sheathed cable – preferably orange or white rather than black. Fit a 13A fuse in the plug.
If you're extending an appliance flex via a flex connector, use the same type of flex and make sure you choose the right current rating, according to the wattage of the appliance.

Core size	current rating	max. wattage
0.5mm²	3A	720W
0.75mm²	6A	1440W
1.0mm²	10A	2000W
1.25mm²	13A	3000W

EXTENDING OLD FLEX

The flex you're extending may have the old colour codes on its core insulation. To make sure you connect the cores correctly, remember that
● live cores were colour-coded red, but are now coded brown
● neutral cores were black, are now blue
● earth cores were green, are now green/yellow striped.

TIP: UNCOIL DRUM FLEXES

If you're using a ready-made extension reel, it's safest to uncoil the flex fully before using it. Otherwise there is a risk of the flex overheating and melting, especially if a highly-rated appliance is being used.

MAKING A REEL

If you've made up your own extension lead, it's a good idea to store it on a makeshift or home-made drum so it doesn't become kinked or knotted. You can either use an empty cable reel (A), or make up a simple drum from plywood and softwood offcuts (B).

TRACING ELECTRICAL FAULTS

When the lights go out or an electrical appliance won't work, the reason is often obvious. But when it isn't, it helps to know how to locate the fault and put it right.

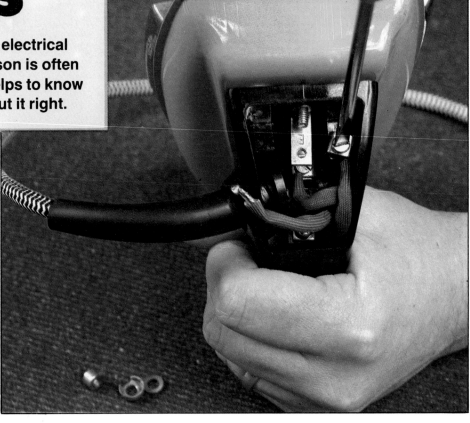

Most people's immediate reaction to something going wrong with their electricity supply is to head for the meter cupboard, muttering darkly about another blown fuse. Fuses do blow occasionally for no immediately obvious reason, but usually there is a problem that needs to be pin-pointed and put right before the power can be restored. It's no use mending a blown fuse, only to find that when the power is restored the fuse blows again because the fault is still present.

Tracing everyday electrical faults is not particularly difficult. You simply have to be methodical in checking the various possible causes, and eliminating options until you find the culprit. More serious faults on the house's fixed wiring system can be more difficult to track down, but again some careful investigation can often locate the source of the trouble, even if professional help has to be called in to put it right.

Safety first
Before you start investigating any electrical faults, remember the cardinal rule and switch off the power at the main switch. When fuses blow, it is all too easy to forget that other parts of the system may still be live and therefore dangerous, and even if you know precisely how your house has been wired up it is foolish to take risks. If the fault appears to be on an electrical appliance, the same rules apply: always switch off the appliance *and* pull out the plug before attempting to investigate. Don't rely on the switch to isolate it; the fault may be in the switch itself.

It's also important to be prepared for things to go wrong with your electrics; even new systems can develop faults, and in fact a modern installation using circuit breakers will detect faults more readily than one with rewireable or cartridge fuses, so giving more regular cause for investigation. Make sure that you keep a small emergency electrical tool kit in an accessible place where it won't get raided for other jobs; it should include one or two screwdrivers, a pair of pliers, a handyman's knife, spare fuses and fuse wire, and above all a *working* torch. There is nothing more annoying when the lights go out than finding the torch does not work.

Check the obvious
When something electrical fails to operate, always check the obvious first – replace the bulb when a light doesn't work, or glance outside to see if everyone in the street has been blacked out by a power cut before panicking that all your fuses have blown. Having satisfied yourself that you may have a genuine fault, start a methodical check of all the possibilities.

A fault can occur in a number of places. It may be on an appliance, within the flex or plug linking it to the mains, on the main circuitry itself or at the fuseboard. Let's start at the appliance end of things. If something went bang as you switched the appliance on, unplug it immediately; the fault is probably on the appliance itself. If it simply stopped working, try plugging it in at another socket; if it goes, there's a fault on the circuit feeding the original socket. If it doesn't go, either the second socket is on the same faulty circuit as the first one (which we'll come to later) or there may be a fault in the link between the appliance and the socket – loose connections where the cores are connected to either the plug or the appliance itself, damaged flex (both these problems are caused by abuse of the flex in use), or a blown fuse in the plug if one is fitted.

Plug and flex connections
The next step is to check the flex connections within the plug and the appliance. The connections at plug terminals are particularly prone to damage if the plug's cord grip or flex anchorage is not doing its job; a tug on the flex can then break the cores, cutting the power and possibly causing a short circuit. If the connections are weak or damaged, disconnect them, cut back the sheathing and insulation and remake the connections. Make sure that the flex is correctly anchored within the body of the plug before replacing the cover.

If the plug contains a fuse, test that it has not blown by using a continuity tester, or by holding it across the open end of a switched-on metal-cased torch – see *Ready Reference*. Replace a blown fuse with a new one of the correct current rating; 3A for appliances rated at 720W or below, 13A for higher-rated appliances (and all colour televisions).

Next, check the flex connections within the appliance itself. Always unplug an appliance before opening it up to gain access to the terminal block, and then remake any doubtful-looking connections by cutting off the end of the flex and stripping back the outer and inner insulation carefully to expose fresh conductor strands. If the flex itself is worn or

REWIRING A PLUG

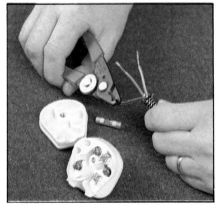

1 *Strip the outer sheathing carefully, cut each core 12mm (¹/₂in) longer than is necessary to reach its correct terminal and then remove 12mm of core sheathing.*

2 *Twist the strands of each core neatly and form a loop that will fit round the terminal screw. Connect the cores as shown here and screw down the studs.*

3 *Check that the core insulation reaches right to each terminal, and that there are no loose strands visible. Then fit the flex securely in the cord grip.*

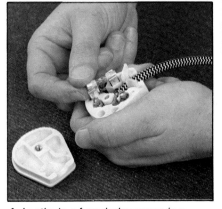

4 *Lastly, in a fused plug press in a cartridge fuse of the correct rating for the appliance concerned, and screw the plug top firmly on.*

damaged, take this opportunity to fit new flex of the correct type and current rating – see *Ready Reference*, step-by-step photographs and pages 6 and 7 for details. Make sure you re-use any grommets, heat-resistant sleeving, special captive washers and the like that were fitted to the appliance.

Lastly, check the flex continuity; it is possible that damage to the flex itself has broken one of the cores within the outer sheathing. Again use a continuity tester for this, holding the two probes against opposite ends of each core in turn, or use your metal-cased torch again, touching one core to the case and the other to the battery. Replace the flex if *any* core fails the test; the appliance may still work if the earth core is damaged, but the earthing will be lost and the appliance could become live and dangerous to anyone using it in the event of another fault developing in the future.

Lighting problems

Similar problems to these can also occur on lighting circuits, where the pendant flex linking ceiling roses to lampholders can become disconnected or faulty through accidental damage or old age. If replacing the bulb doesn't work, switch off the power at the mains and examine the condition of the flex. Look especially for bad or broken connections at the ceiling rose and within the lampholder. Replace the flex if the core insulation has become brittle, and fit a new lampholder if the plastic is discoloured (both these problems are caused by heat from the light bulb). See *Cable and Flex* on pages 6 and 7.

Mending blown fuses

A circuit fuse will blow for two main reasons, overloading and short circuits – see *Ready Reference*. Too many appliances connected

Ready Reference

COMMON FAULTS

Many electrical breakdowns in the home are caused by only a few common faults. These include:
● overloading of circuits, causing the circuit fuse to blow or the MCB to trip
● short circuits, where the current by-passes its proper route because of failed insulation or contact between cable or flex cores; the resulting high current flow creates heat and blows the plug fuse (if fitted) and circuit fuse
● earthing faults, where insulation breaks down and allows the metal body of an appliance to become live, causing a shock to the user if the appliance is not properly earthed and blowing a fuse or causing the ELCB to trip otherwise
● poor connections causing overheating that can lead to a fire and to short circuits and earthing faults.

TIP: TESTING FUSES

You can test suspect cartridge fuses (both circuit and plug types) by holding them across the open end of a switched-on metal-cased torch, with one end on the casing and the other on the battery. A sound fuse will light the torch.

CHOOSE THE RIGHT FLEX

When fitting new flex to an appliance, it's important to choose the correct type and current rating. The table below will help:

Size (mm²)	Rating amps	watts	Use
0.5	3	720	Light fittings
0.75	6	1440	Small appliances
1.0	10	2400	Larger appliances
1.5	15	3600	
2.5	20	4800	

If you are buying flex for pendant lights, remember that the maximum weight of fitting that each size of twin flex can support is
● 2kg (4¹/₂lb) for 0.5mm² flex
● 3kg (6¹/₂lb) for 0.75mm² flex
● 5kg (11lb) for larger sizes.

Select circular **three-core PVC-insulated flex** for most appliances, **unkinkable** or **braided flex** for irons, kettles and the like, **two-core flex** for non-metallic lamps and light fittings and for double-insulated appliances, and **heat-resisting flex** for powerful pendant lights and for heater connections.

to a circuit will demand too much current, and this will melt the fuse. Similarly, a short circuit – where, for example, bare live and neutral flex cores touch – causes a current surge that blows the fuse.

If overloading caused the fuse to blow, the remedy is simple: disconnect all the equipment on the circuit, mend the fuse and avoid using too many high-wattage appliances at the same time in future. If a short circuit was to blame, you will have to hunt for the cause and rectify it before mending the fuse – see photographs on the next page.

When a circuit fuse blows, turn off the main switch and remove fuseholders until you find the one that has blown. Then clean out the remains of the old fuse wire, and fit a new piece of the correct rating for the circuit – 5A for lighting circuits, 15A for circuits to immersion heaters and the like, and 30A for ring circuits. Cut the wire over-long, thread it loosely across or through the ceramic holder and connect it carefully to the terminals. Trim the ends off neatly, replace the fuseholder in the consumer unit and turn on the power again. If the fuse blows again, and you have already checked for possible causes on appliances, flexes and lighting pendants, suspect a circuit fault – see below.

If you have cartridge fuses, all you have to do is find which cartridge has blown by removing the fuseholder and testing the cartridge with a continuity tester or metal-cased torch. A blown cartridge fuse should be replaced by a new one of the same current rating. Again, if the new fuse blows immediately, suspect a circuit fault.

If you have miniature circuit breakers (MCBs) you will not be able to switch the MCB on again if the fault that tripped it off is still present. Otherwise, simply reset it by switching it to ON or pressing in the centre button.

Earth leakage circuit breakers (ELCBs)

If your installation has an ELCB, it will trip off if an earthing fault occurs – for example, if a live wire or connection comes into contact with earthed metal. Like an MCB, it cannot be switched on again until the fault is rectified – a useful safety point. However, it will not trip off in the event of a short circuit between live and neutral, or when overloading occurs.

The high-sensitivity current-operated ELCB, in addition to detecting earth faults, also protects against the danger of electric shocks by tripping off if it detects current flowing to earth through the human body. It can do this quickly enough to prevent the shock from causing death.

Tracing circuit faults

If you have checked appliances, flexes, plug connections and pendant lights, and a fault is still present, it is likely to be in the fixed

REPLACING FLEX

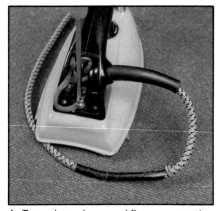

1 *To replace damaged flex, remove the appropriate cover plate or panel from the appliance. Make a note of which core goes where before undoing it.*

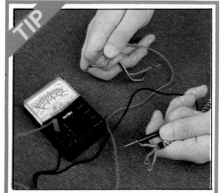

2 *Loosen the cord grip within the appliance and withdraw the old flex. Here heat-resisting sleeving has been fitted; save this for re-use.*

3 *If you suspect that the cores within apparently undamaged flex are broken, test each core in turn with a continuity tester.*

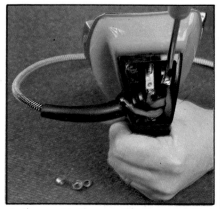

4 *Connect in the new flex by reversing the disconnection sequence, re-using grommets, sleeving and washers. Make sure each connection is secure.*

wiring. Here, it is possible to track down one or two faults, but you may in the end have to call in a professional electrician.

The likeliest causes of circuit faults are damage to cables (perhaps caused by drilling holes in walls or by nailing down floorboards where cables run), ageing of cables (leading to insulation breakdown, and overheating) and faults at wiring accessories (light switches, socket outlets and so on). Let's look at the last one first, simply because such items are at least easily accessible.

If the cable cores are not properly stripped and connected within the accessory, short circuits or earth faults can develop. To check a suspect accessory such as a socket outlet, isolate the circuit, unscrew the faceplate and examine the terminal connections and the insulation. Ensure that each core is firmly held in its correct terminal, and that each core has insulation right up to the terminal,

so that it cannot touch another core or any bare metal. There is usually enough slack on the mains cable to allow you to trim over-long cores back slightly. Check that the earth core is sleeved in green/yellow PVC, and try not to double over the cable as you ease the faceplate back into position; over-full boxes can lead to short circuits and damage to cable and core insulation ... and more trouble. You can carry out similar checks at light switches and ceiling roses. Any damaged accessories you find should be replaced immediately with new ones.

Damage to cables is relatively easy to cure provided that you can find where the damage is. If you drilled or nailed through a cable, you will of course be able to pin-point it immediately. Cable beneath floorboards can be repaired simply by isolating the circuit, cutting the cable completely at the point of damage and using a three-terminal junction

REPAIRING A CIRCUIT FUSE

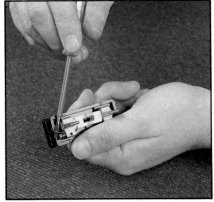

1 *Switch off the mains and locate the blown fuse. Then remove the remains of the old fuse wire and clean off any charring that has occurred.*

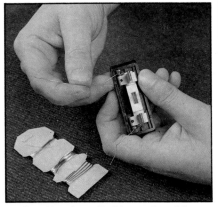

2 *Feed in a length of fuse wire of the correct rating and wind each end round the terminal before tightening up the screw. Don't pull the wire taut.*

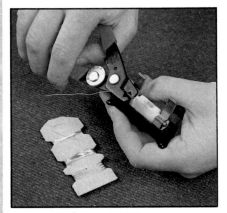

3 *Trim off the unwanted ends of fuse wire neatly with wire strippers, then replace the fuse carrier in the fuse box and restore the power.*

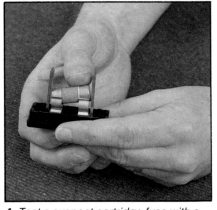

4 *Test a suspect cartridge fuse with a continuity tester or torch (see Ready Reference) and replace it by pressing in a new fuse of the correct rating.*

box to link the cut ends. Cable buried in plaster must be cut out and a new length of cable inserted between adjacent accessories to replace the damaged length. Where this would involve a long length of cable (on a run to a remote socket, for example) it is acceptable to use junction boxes in nearby floor or ceiling voids to connect in the new length of cable. You will then have to make good the cutting-out.

Tracking down a break in the cable elsewhere in the installation is a difficult job best left to a qualified electrician. If, however, you find that your house is wired in rubber-sheathed cable and faults are beginning to occur, don't waste time and effort trying to track them down: you need a re-wire. For information on the different cables and flex available and their uses, see pages 6 and 7.

If you are unable to trace an electrical fault after checking all the points already de-scribed, call in a professional electrician who will be able to use specialist test equipment to locate the fault. Do *not* attempt to bypass a fault with a makeshift wiring arrangement, and NEVER use any conducting foreign body such as a nail to restore power to a circuit whose fuse keeps blowing. Such tricks can kill.

Regular maintenance
You will find that a little common-sense maintenance work will help to prevent a lot of minor electrical faults from occurring at all. For example, it's well worth spending a couple of hours every so often checking the condition of the flex on portable appliances (especially those heavily used, such as kettles, irons, hair driers and the like) and the connections within plugs. Also, make a point of replacing immediately any electrical accessory that is in any way damaged.

UNDERSTANDING ELECTRICS

In theory, you could do electrical jobs knowing nothing about electricity, given accurate step-by-step instructions. But you can't deal with any part of an electrical installation in isolation — everything is linked. And unless you understand how each part of the system works you have no way of knowing if you are making a mistake. With electricity, ignorance is dangerous.

We're all familiar with lights and power sockets, but how does the electricity reach them so we can use it? In fact, electricity enters your home along one thick cable (the service cable), passes through a large 'service fuse' and into a meter which records the amount you use. Everything up to and including that meter belongs to the electricity board, and is their responsibility. Everything beyond is the householder's property, which is perhaps why installations vary so much.

In a modern installation — one wired in the last 30 years — there are two wires carrying electric current that lead from the meter to what is called the consumer unit. These wires are known as the meter tails — one is termed live, the other neutral.

On the inlet side of the consumer unit there's a switch with which you can turn off the power altogether, but the unit's principal job is to divide up the power and send it round your home through a network of cables.

These cables are organized into circuits. There are circuits for lights, power sockets and so on, each with its own fuse in the consumer unit. The cables themselves run under the floor, above the ceiling and may even be visible on wall surfaces, although more often they are buried within them.

In older installations, instead of a consumer unit there may be individual fuse boxes protecting separate circuits. And each of these fuse boxes will have an isolating switch to cut off power to the circuit it controls. These fuse boxes are connected direct to the meter by

live and neutral meter tails. Alternatively the fuse boxes may be supplied from a distribution board which in turn is connected to the meter.

Sometimes, even with a consumer unit you may find separate fuse boxes. This is normally the result of the system having been extended.

What are circuits?

If you take a battery, and connect a wire to the positive (+) terminal, and another to the negative (−), then bring the free ends of the wires together, electricity will flow from positive to negative along them. That's a circuit. You can build a torch bulb and holder into it to prove it works. Break the circuit by cutting one wire, and the light goes out (the flow of current has stopped), and it will stay out until the cut ends are rejoined. That's a simple switch.

Of course, the circuits in your home are a good deal more complex than that, and their design varies according to whether they supply lights, power sockets or whatever. Even the electricity is different. Instead of flowing in one direction, it goes back and forth 50 times a second — hence its name *alternating current*, or AC for short.

But the principle is the same. Think of 'live' as positive, 'neutral' as negative, and you will see that for any appliance such as an electric fire to work it must have wires connecting it to the live and neutral terminals in the consumer unit. Those wires may be contained in a single cable, but the link must always be there, with switches *en route* to make or break it, and for safety reasons, switches are on the live wire.

What are fuses?

The main service cable has its fuse; the various circuits have theirs in the consumer

unit or fuse box and if you remove the back of a flat-pin plug you'll find a fuse in there.

Think of an electric light bulb. It gives out light because electricity passing through the filament (the fine wire just visible inside the bulb) makes it very hot. If you pass enough electricity through any wire, it will also heat up. If that wire happens to be a circuit cable, an appliance flex, or the service cable to the meter, then the consequences would be serious. So, to protect them, a weak link called a fuse is built into the circuit.

Most fuses are just thin pieces of wire. They can be fitted to rewirable fuse carriers, in which case you can replace them, or they may be in ceramic cartridges, in which case you throw them away and fit another. In any event, the fuse's thickness is described in terms of how much electricity — expressed in amps — is theoretically needed to melt it.

The word 'theoretically' is important because, in fact, fuses aren't particularly accurate or reliable. For this reason, a more sensitive device called a miniature circuit breaker (MCB) may be used instead. It's just a switch that turns off automatically when danger threatens. Once the fault responsible for the overload is put right, you switch on again.

Why cables?

It would be far too complicated to wire a house like a battery and bulb circuit using individual wires. Instead, the copper wires carrying the electricity are encased in PVC insulation to stop them touching and making their circuit in the wrong place — what's called a short circuit — and then bound together in PVC sheathing to form a cable. In this way, the live, neutral and earth wires can be run as one, even though each one is still connected up separately.

Different kinds of cable are used for different jobs. For full details of the most common types see pages 6 and 7.

Earthing

The purpose of the earth wire within the cable is to make up the earth continuity conductor (ECC). This is an essential safety feature of any electrical installation. Its role is to act as a 'safety valve' in the event of a fault, causing a fuse to blow or an MCB to trip to isolate a faulty circuit or faulty appliance from the mains supply. In doing so it could prevent the risk of fire or someone being electrocuted.

Earth wires are connected to the metal parts of switches, socket outlets, fittings and appliances (and even plumbing) in a really up-to-date system. Electricity will flow along the line of least resistance, so that if by some mishap any of these parts became live (by coming into contact with a live conductor) the earth wire would offer a line of 'less' resistance. In effect the faulty current would travel along the earth wire rather than through a person touching the live metal part. And the extra current passing through one circuit would

be sufficient to blow the fuse or activate the MCB.

Unfortunately this doesn't always happen — so, for added safety, a special device called an earth leakage circuit breaker (ELCB) can be fitted to detect the slightest leakage of current to earth. It shuts off the power within milliseconds — quickly enough to save a life — at the first sign of a fault.

ELCBs can be added to an existing system, or included within the consumer unit in a new installation. They usually protect all the circuits in the house and also act as a mains on/off switch.

Ring circuits

For getting electricity to the power points, the most common system of wiring is what's called a 'ring' circuit. Wired in 2.5mm² two-core and earth cable, most homes have one such circuit for each floor of the house.

The two-cores and the earth wire are connected to their terminals in the consumer unit (or fuse box) and then pass through each power socket in turn before returning to their respective terminals in the consumer unit (fuse box). The circuit is protected by a 30A

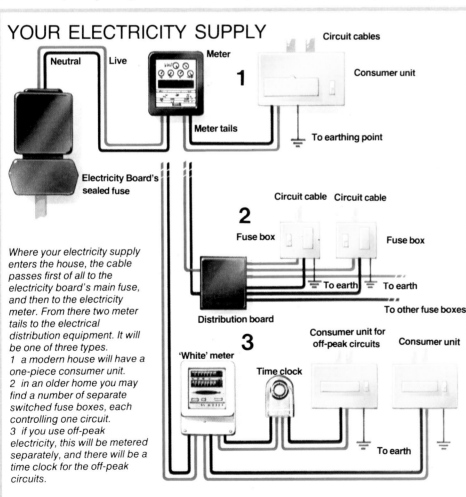

YOUR ELECTRICITY SUPPLY

Neutral | Live | Meter | Circuit cables
Consumer unit | **1**
Meter tails
To earthing point
Electricity Board's sealed fuse

Where your electricity supply enters the house, the cable passes first of all to the electricity board's main fuse, and then to the electricity meter. From there two meter tails to the electrical distribution equipment. It will be one of three types.
1 a modern house will have a one-piece consumer unit.
2 in an older home you may find a number of separate switched fuse boxes, each controlling one circuit.
3 if you use off-peak electricity, this will be metered separately, and there will be a time clock for the off-peak circuits.

Circuit cable | Circuit cable | **2**
Fuse box | Fuse box
To earth | To earth
To other fuse boxes
Distribution board
Consumer unit for off-peak circuits | Consumer unit | **3**
'White' meter | Time clock
To earth

Trevor Lawrence

fuse. The advantage of this system is it allows the cable to cope with more sockets than if it made a one-way trip (as with radial circuits). In fact, you are allowed as many sockets as you like on the ring, so long as the floor area served by the circuit doesn't exceed 100 sq metres (1,080 sq ft). What's more, you can increase the number of sockets by adding 'branch lines' off the ring. These are called 'spurs' and break into the ring via a junction box, a spur connection unit, or an existing socket. You are allo-

wed as many spurs as can feed one single socket, one double socket, or one fixed appliance via a fused connection unit. Until a recent change in the IEE wiring regulations, a spur could feed two single sockets, and you may find such spurs on your existing circuits.

Of course, with all those sockets, there is a risk of overloading the circuit, but in the average family home it's unlikely that you'll have enough sockets in use at any one time. The circuit may carry up to 30 amps of current

which is equivalent to having appliances and portable lamps using 7,200 watts of power all switched on together. It's doubtful that you would want all this on at the same time, but it's wise not to go above this level of power use. If the circuit does overload, the fuse will blow. or the MCB will switch off.

Radial circuits

Unlike ring circuits, radial circuits consist of a single cable that leaves the fuse box and runs to one or more sockets. In older homes in the UK, before ring circuits were introduced, all power circuits were wired as radials. Since homes had (and needed) only a few sockets, individual circuits were usually run to each one from the fuse box. The sockets themselves were rated at 2A, 5A or 15A, and had round holes to accept round-pin plugs. Such circuits will probably have been wired in rubber- or lead-sheathed cables, which deteriorate with age (see pages 6 and 7) and are not able to satisfy the far greater electrical demands of a modern household. It's wise to have such circuits examined by a qualified electrician. and best of all to have them replaced.

Radial circuits are, however, also used in modern wiring systems where a ring circuit could be inappropriate for some reason. There are two types, with different current-carrying capacity.

A 20A radial circuit uses 2.5mm² cable and

A ring circuit originates from a 30A fuseway in the consumer unit. Protection may be by an MCB rather than a rewirable or cartridge fuse.

Spurs are sometimes added when the ring circuit is installed to save on the wiring runs. They are usually connected at a three-terminal junction box.

Socket outlets on a ring circuit take the fused 13A flat-pin plug. They can be one- or two-gang (ie, take one or two plugs); the best have switches.

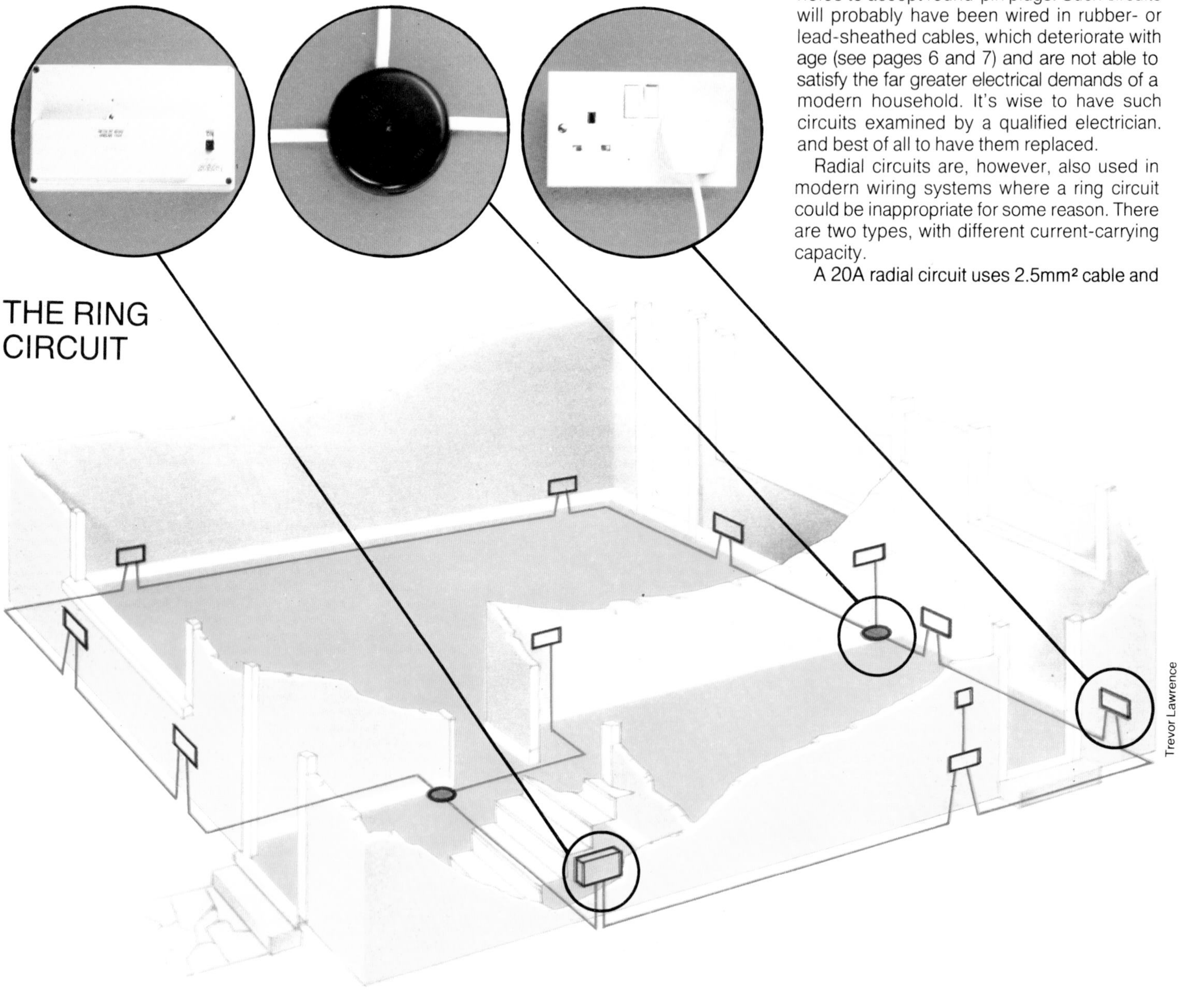

Jem Grischotti

THE RING CIRCUIT

Trevor Lawrence

is protected by a 20A fuse (rewirable or cartridge) or an MCB in the consumer unit (or fuse box). It can supply an unlimited number of 13A socket outlets and fixed appliances using 3kW of power or less, providing they are within a floor area not exceeding 20 sq metres (about 215 sq ft).

The other type of circuit is the 30A radial which is wired in 4mm² cable and can feed a floor area of up to 50 sq metres (540 sq ft). It can be protected by a 30A cartridge fuse or MCB, but *not* by a rewirable fuse.

These restrictions on floor area mean that several radial circuits would have to be installed to cover the same area as a ring circuit. This is one of the reasons why the 'ring' is now the most common method of wiring in the UK, but radial circuits can supplement an overworked ring circuit.

Special purpose circuits

In addition to rings and radials, your home may have special circuits which supply only one outlet or appliance. Cookers, immersion heaters, instantaneous showers and the like are wired in this way and each has its own individual fuse. In effect, these circuits are just radials that have had both the cable and fuse sizes 'beefed up' to cope with the often heavy demands of the appliances they supply — for example, a large family-size cooker might need a 45A fuse, and 6mm² or even 10mm² cable.

Because electric night storage heaters all come on together they could overload a ring circuit; consequently each one is supplied by

The various radial power circuits originate from fuseways in a consumer unit or from individual fuse boxes. They are protected by rewirable fuses.

Modern radial circuits have sockets that take 13A flat-pin plugs. Older radials with lead or rubber-sheathed cable take round pin plugs.

Even if you have ring circuit wiring, radial circuits are used for special purposes, such as supplying a cooker. It may also contain a 13A socket outlet.

A fused connection unit sometimes supplies a fixed appliance on a radial circuit. This could be a wall mounted heater or an immersion heater.

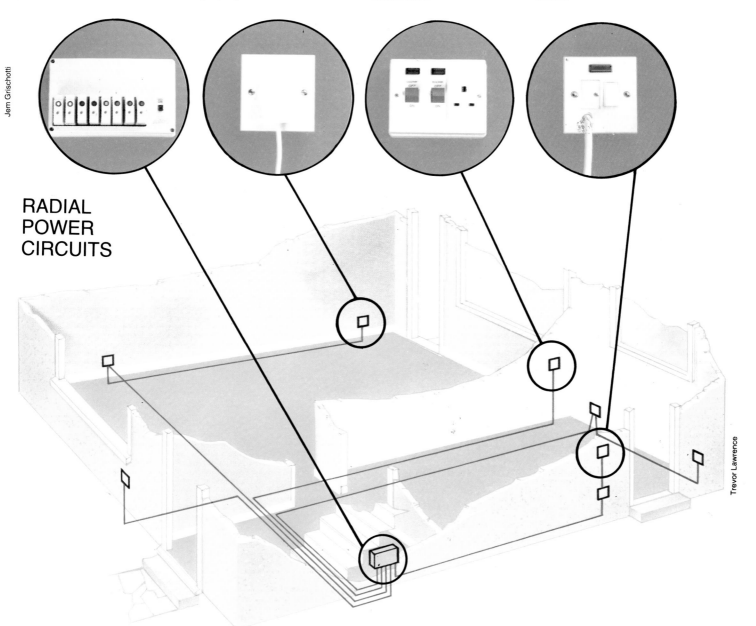

RADIAL POWER CIRCUITS

Jem Grischotti

Trevor Lawrence

LIGHTING CIRCUITS

LOOP-IN LIGHTING

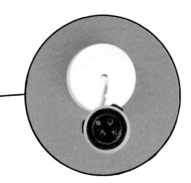

The cable on a loop-in lighting circuit links each ceiling rose in turn. The switch cable also connects into the rose as does the flexible cord for the lampholder.

JUNCTION BOX SYSTEM

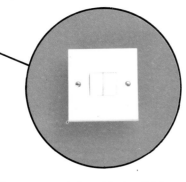

A two-gang switch enables two lighting points to be controlled individually from the same point. Switches can be surface-mounted or flush.

Trevor Lawrence

Jem Grischotti

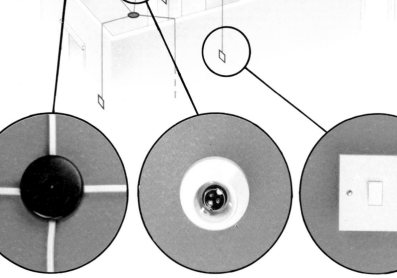

With junction box wiring the main cable runs between four-terminal junction boxes. The other cables go to the lighting point and the switch.

Batten holders are used to fit a light close to the ceiling. In bathrooms, they must have a 'skirt' to prevent contact with metal on the fitting or bulb.

The simplest switch is a one-gang type mounted on a face-plate. They can be either surface mounted or recessed to be flush with the wall.

a separate radial circuit protected by a 20A fuse. The fuses are housed in a separate consumer unit which is linked to a sealed time clock and uses off-peak electricity.

Lighting circuits

Two systems of wiring lighting circuits are in common use, and it is not unusual for an installation to contain a little bit of each. One is called the loop-in system; the other the junction (or joint) box system.

With the loop-in system, a cable (normally 1.0mm² but sometimes 1.5mm²) leaves a 5A fuse in the consumer unit (or fuse box) and is connected to the first in a series of special loop-in ceiling roses. From this rose, one cable goes onto the next in the series, and another takes the power down to the switch controlling the light and back up through the light itself.

The junction box system uses the same idea but, instead of going from rose to rose, the cable from the consumer unit (or fuse box) passes through a series of junction boxes. From each box, one cable goes to the ceiling rose or light, and another to the switch that controls it. This system is particularly useful, for example, when fitting wall lights as there is little space at the back of a wall light fitting for looping-in.

Lighting circuits are rated at 5 amps, which means they can take a load of up to 1,200 watts. In effect, they could supply 12 lamp-holders containing bulbs of 100w each or smaller. But as you may want to fit bulbs with higher wattages, it is usual for a lighting circuit to supply up to eight outlet points, so separate circuits are required for each floor.

Strictly speaking it's better to arrange the circuits so that there is more than one on each floor — this means that you won't be in total darkness if a fuse in the consumer unit blows.

LIGHTING DESIGN – THE BASICS

There is more to lighting your home than meets the eye, and well-designed lighting schemes can enhance every room in the house. To start with, you need to grasp some of the basic principles.

In most homes the standard of room lighting leaves something to be desired. Interior design generally has made immense strides in recent years, yet even new homes are built with a lighting specification left over from the dark ages – literally. Builders still follow what is known quaintly as the Builder's Norm – one pendant light in the centre of each room, switched by the entrance door – a standard that hasn't changed since the days of gas lighting, although in small rooms the gas light would often be a wall bracket fitting. You may be lucky enough to find the occasional wall light – in the lounge or bedroom, for example – but even homes that have been extensively modernised are unlikely to have anything much more adventurous.

This is a pity, because there is now a very wide range of attractive and versatile light fittings available, and a glance around many public buildings will show you some of the effects they can produce if used with a little flair. Installing fittings like these in your home isn't difficult, and the difference that well-designed lighting can make to every room in the house has to be seen to be believed.

How much light do you get?

Electric lamps – tungsten-filament bulbs and tubes and fluorescent fittings – are rated in watts (W). This tells you how much electricity the lamp uses when lit; it doesn't directly indicate how much light the lamp gives off (although it's obvious that a 100W lamp will be brighter than a 40W one), nor does it tell you how much useful light is provided or in what direction. The amount and quality of light needed for different tasks or effects varies widely; lighting to illuminate the dining table, the kitchen worktops or the family silver will differ from lighting for reading, sewing or lulling a child to sleep.

The actual amount of light emitted from a lamp is measured in units called lumens. Some lamps burn more efficiently that others, emitting more lumens per watt. Generally speaking, coiled-coil pear-shaped clear and pearl bulbs will tend to have the highest efficiency in lumens/watt; next come mushroom-shaped bulbs, double-life bulbs and finally single-coil bulbs. What's

more, the actual wattage of the bulb is also a factor; a 40W coiled-coil bulb has an output of 390 lumens (9.75 lumens/watt) while a 100W bulb of the same type emits 1260 lumens (12.6 lumens/watt).

Fluorescent tubes, as is widely known, are much more efficient light emitters than tungsten filament lamps. For example, a 40W warm white tube gives out 1950 lumens (48 lumens/watt) and an 80W tube of the same colour gives 3730 lumens (44 lumens) watt). On average, fluorescent tubes give about four times as much light as light bulbs of the same wattage.

How much light do you need?

When you're planning a lighting scheme these figures (see *Ready Reference* for a summary) will come in very useful. The other figure you need to know is how much light to provide in a given area. A rough and ready figure to work to for general lighting is 22 watts per sq m (2W/sq ft), and if seeing what you are doing was the only criterion for satisfactory illumination, it could be used without variation. However, several other factors have to be taken into account, including the type and position of the light fitting chosen, whether the lighting of a surface or object is direct or indirect, and the colour and reflectivity of the surface being lit. So as a general guideline it's a good idea to take the 22W/sq m figure as the minimum overall lighting required in each room, and to regard any additional local lighting as being supplementary to this. To

WHERE THE LIGHT GOES

Below: How light is emitted from various lamp types – GLS (A), ISL (B), CS (C), PAR (D), small spot (E) and fluorescent (F).

Below: The direction of light emitted may be modified by the type of fitting chosen. Shown here are a pendant (1), close-

ceiling fitting (2), wall light (3), track spotlight (4), downlighter (5), wall washer (6), eyeball (7) and uplighter (8).

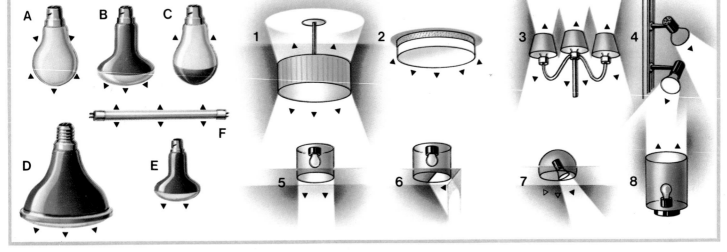

give a worked example, a living room measuring 6x4m (20x13ft) would need an overall lighting level of 6x4x22 = 528 watts.

The other point you need to take into account is that the amount of illumination you get – the amount of light falling on a surface – depends on how far it is from the light source. Double the distance and the level of illumination is halved.

Light bulbs and tubes

We tend to think of light bulbs and tubes as emitting light at random in all directions, and this is certainly true of the ordinary (GLS) bulb and the standard tungsten or fluorescent tube. But other types of lamp are available that emit light only in certain directions because the bulb or tube surface is coated with reflective or opaque material. For example, the internally-silvered (ISL) bulb has an internal reflector that covers the neck and sides of the bulb, resulting in a controlled beam that is ideal for projecting light onto walls and for spotlighting objects. The crown-silvered (CS) bulb has the reflector on the crown of the bulb, so that light is projected backwards into the fitting; when used with a parabolic reflector dish, the result is a parallel beam of light like that produced by a car headlamp. The PAR (parabolic aluminised reflector) lamp combines the CS optics into a single sealed unit that can provide spot or flood lighting.

Types of light fitting

There are four principal types of light fitting with which these various lamps can be used, and the type of fitting chosen may further modify the beam of light that the lamp itself emits, so giving you additional flexibility in

the design of your lighting effects. The four types are: ceiling-mounted (pendant or close-fitting); wall-mounted; concealed (including 'downlighters' and 'wall-washers'), and free-standing (table, or standard lamps and 'uplighters').

Pendant fittings, the most familiar type, range from a plain lampholder carrying a decorative shade to multi-light fittings suspended from a ceiling plate by chains or a rod. Some give a general light output, others mainly direct downward and/or upward depending on the style of shade chosen. Rise-and-fall fittings are simply pendants with a spring-loaded flex extender concealed in the ceiling plate.

Close-ceiling fittings are mounted on the ceiling surface as an alternative to pendant fittings, and so by definition emit light in an overall downward direction only. They are usually fitted with a translucent glass or plastic cover, which may be coloured. Fluorescent fittings of various types also come into this category.

Wall-mounted fittings can range from simple brackets holding plain or decorative bulbs, with or without shades, to spot and flood fittings. Uplighters (see below under 'Free-standing fittings') can also be wall-mounted.

Concealed fittings include downlighters and wall-washers, both of which are usually recessed into the ceiling. Downlighters are cylindrical housings and usually contain an ISL bulb, so providing a fairly well-defined beam pointing to the floor. Wall-washers have either an adjustable aperture or an eyeball-type fitting that directs light downwards *and* to one side, allowing a ceiling-mounted

fitting to 'wash' a nearby wall with light.

Free-standing fittings need little description – table and standard lamps come in a very wide range of models and offer general or local lighting according to type. The one comparatively unfamiliar member of this group is the uplighter, which bounces reflected light off ceilings and walls and is an excellent source of background or concealed light.

The effect of colour schemes

The colour scheme used in any room can have a profound effect on the level of lighting it requires. It goes without saying that dark wallcoverings and carpets will absorb a lot of light, so that a greater light wattage will have to be provided than if the room has white walls and pale furnishings.

The colour of walls and ceilings is particularly important when you plan to use a lot of indirect lighting, although this doesn't mean you have to have pale surfaces; you simply need more wattage. It's certainly true that you can achieve more dramatic lighting effects (at the expense of the general level of illumination) in rooms decorated in rich, deep colours.

Light and shadow

Before we begin to deal with the more detailed planning of lighting schemes, the last ground rule to remember – and one of the most important, too – concerns the problem of positioning lights to avoid glare and the creation of hard shadows. This is mainly solved by the correct choice of fitting for the job, and its careful positioning in the room. The illustrations opposite summarise some of the commonest problems and show how they can be overcome.

AVOIDING GLARE AND HARD SHADOWS

Living rooms *A central light is no good for reading as it casts shadows on the page.*

Position a reading lamp behind you, and provide indirect lighting near TV sets.

Dining rooms *Avoid fittings where the naked lamp is close to eye level and glares diners.*

Fit a rise-and-fall fitting, and provide two fittings above long tables.

Workrooms *A wrongly-positioned lamp means that you are working in your own shadow.*

Fit a concealed lamp above the work surface, adding an adjustable one for typing.

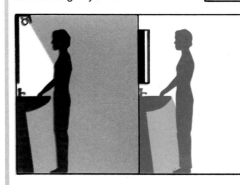

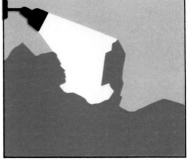

Bathrooms *Concealed lighting above mirrors leaves faces in shadow. Better illumination is provided by fittings at each side of the mirror.*

Bedrooms *Position reading lights on the wall above your head (and switch them at the bedside).*

Children's rooms *If night-time light is needed, provide it indirectly, or install a dimmer switch.*

LIGHTING DESIGN – THE PLANNING

Once you're familiar with the basic principles of lighting design, you can go on to some more detailed planning of your lighting and start to turn ideas into reality.

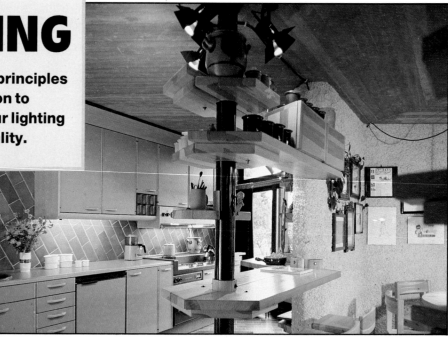

The lighting you choose for your home should meet two criteria: it should be functional, giving you light where you need it (and in the right quantity), and it should be decorative, enhancing the looks of the room concerned while conserving its character. The type of fitting chosen for each light source is of great importance. Certain fittings excel at particular jobs (as discussed on pages 19 to 21) but the fitting is ultimately responsible for helping to create exactly the effect you want.

Above all, the aim must be to provide a balanced mixture of light and shadow; uniformly bright lighting is stark and cheerless, while deep shadows are simply depressing. You can do this for the most part using fittings with tungsten light bulbs, or with fluorescent tubes concealed in some way and used for perimeter lighting. An unshielded fluorescent fitting, whether linear or circular, gives an overall flat lighting effect with no shadows, which robs a room of its character and makes it appear almost two-dimensional – satisfactory in a kitchen or garage, perhaps, but not for visual comfort in a living room.

Lamp positions

There are a few simple guidelines to bear in mind when planning the positions of light fittings. The first golden rule is to ensure that naked bulbs cannot be seen by anyone in the room, whether standing, sitting or even lying (after all, you'll see most of your bedroom lighting effects from the bed). You can avoid this by judicious choice of fittings and shades, and also by thinking about the height of the fitting; examples are using a rise-and-fall fitting over a dining table, and setting wall lights low rather than high above bedheads.

Secondly, aim for an acceptable level of lighting throughout the room, even when local lights are providing extra illumination at individual points. This avoids creating pools of hard, dark shadows.

Thirdly, use lighting to highlight special features in the room; these can range from the obvious – an attractive fireplace or a group of pictures – to the sort of feature often ignored, such as a run of beautiful curtains that could be lit from above by perimeter

LIGHT EFFECTS

You can create various effects by 'washing' walls with light. For perfect and graded washes, use wallwashers with reflector floods – all 150W for a perfect wash, in decreasing wattages for a graded one. For spill and scallop washes, use downlighters to graze the wall with light.

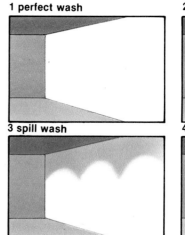

1 perfect wash

2 graded wash

3 spill wash

4 scallop wash

lighting (behind pelmets) or wallwashers.

Lighting for special jobs

One activity needing good localised lighting is reading, and here a reflector lamp, table or standard lamp placed behind the chair gives the best illumination without glare. Where sewing is involved, even brighter illumination is needed, and a spotlight (wall-mounted or freestanding) is the best choice. For writing at a desk, a fluorescent or tungsten tube concealed behind a pelmet above the desk (or below its top shelf) will illuminate the whole desk surface and eliminate hand shadows; if a typewriter is being used, add an adjustable lamp to one side of the desk to illuminate the keyboard without creating glare. Lastly, amongst leisure pursuits,

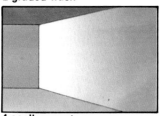

television watching comes fairly high, and here the aim should be to reduce contrast glare from the tube by providing low-level lighting behind the set – a dimmed wall light in an alcove, or a table lamp or standard lamp behind and to one side of the set.

In the kitchen, the first priority is good task lighting over work areas, and the best solutions are a ceiling-mounted fluorescent tube or track-light fitting over the sink and hob areas, and lighting above worktops concealed behind battens fixed to the underside of wall cupboards.

In the bedroom, the specific needs are bedhead lighting (two directional lights in shared bedrooms allow one person to read, the other to sleep) and good lighting at dressing tables, where the light should shine

LIGHTING FOR DOWNSTAIRS ROOMS

The best way to plan and co-ordinate your home lighting scheme is with a simple floor plan on which the position of fixtures and fittings are marked. This example is intended to show the scope you have for planning alternative lighting effects. In the living room the range of fittings allows general and task lighting, while wallwashers, track lighting and perimeter fittings allow a choice of lighting effects to be achieved. In the kitchen a central spotlight group back up the general and task lighting provided by fluorescent fittings on the ceiling and over the worktops.

KEY
1 Centre pendant fitting
2 Close-ceiling fitting
3 Fluorescent tube fitting
4 Rise-and-fall fitting
5 Recessed downlighters
6 Recessed wallwashers
7 Table lamps
8 Standard lamps
9 Track fitting with spotlights
10 Picture strip light
11 Perimeter lighting
12 Strip lighting over worktops
13 Ceiling-mounted spot group
14 Outside light

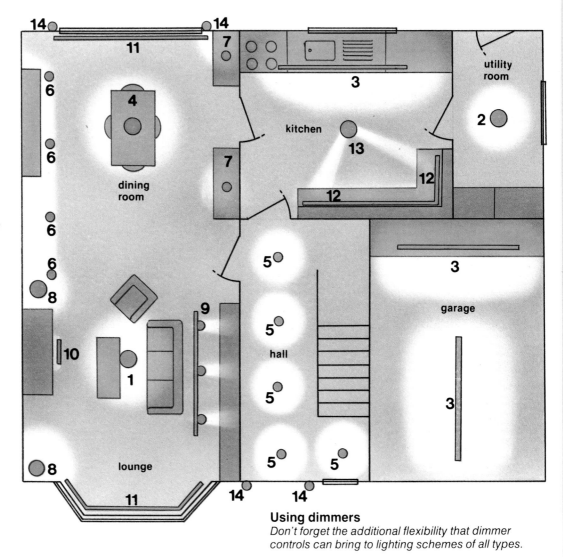

Using dimmers
Don't forget the additional flexibility that dimmer controls can bring to lighting schemes of all types.

on the face, not the mirror. Table lamps or striplights at each side of the mirror offer the best lighting balance. The same point also applies to lighting next to mirrors in the bathroom, but make sure any lights chosen are switched from a point out of reach of bath, basin or shower.

One other specific form of task lighting is worth considering, and that is lighting in wardrobes and storage cupboards. Strip lighting positioned above the inner face of the door frame, or down each side if shelves would be in shadow, is the simplest answer, and control can be automatic if door switches are used. Remember that the circuit to such lights also requires an ordinary plateswitch, wired into the spur between the mains supply and the automatic switch/switches.

Room lighting
Apart from individual task lighting, every room needs more general illumination, and this can be provided in many different ways. Here are some of your options.

In the living room, the central pendant light (if fitted) should be an attractive feature unlit as well as lit. The same applies to wall lights, table and standard lamps too. Other forms of lighting tend to be more functional in their appearance – wallwashers and downlighters recessed into the ceiling, track lighting carrying spotlights above a display unit or a range of pictures, or perimeter fluorescent lighting hidden behind cornices or pelmets. Remember that an open-topped pelmet allows light to travel upwards and reflect off the ceiling. Where you are installing a run of

downlighters or wallwashers, it's a good idea to have them individually switched so you can vary the areas of the room that are illuminated.

In the dining room the use of rise-and-fall fittings over dining tables has already been covered. What is needed in addition is some fairly subdued background lighting – say, wall lights or wallwashers illuminating the sideboard/serving area, or perimeter lighting throwing light downwards over curtains.

The landing, hall and stairs is one area of the home where good, bright lighting is essential; safety must take preference over 'mood', so that all parts of the stairwell are clearly lit without glare. Light should fall on the treads, with the risers in shadow. Suspended fittings must not be so low as to

23

LIGHTING FOR UPSTAIRS ROOMS

As with the downstairs, a simple floor plan makes it much easier to decide on what sort of lighting to provide for the various rooms. There is obviously less need for flexibility in bedrooms and bathrooms, but still plenty of scope for practical or restful effects to be achieved.

The most important points shown here include good lighting on landing and stairs (with the stair treads illuminated and the risers in shadow), adjustable light fittings at bedheads and over desks and dressing tables, and additional lighting in the bathroom for shaving, making up and showering.

KEY
1 Centre pendant fitting
2 Close-mounted ceiling fittings
3 Adjustable wall light
4 Adjustable table lamp
5 Recessed downlighters
6 Ceiling-mounted spot group
7 Wall-mounted strip light
8 Picture strip light
9 Strip lights for cupboard interiors (with door switches)

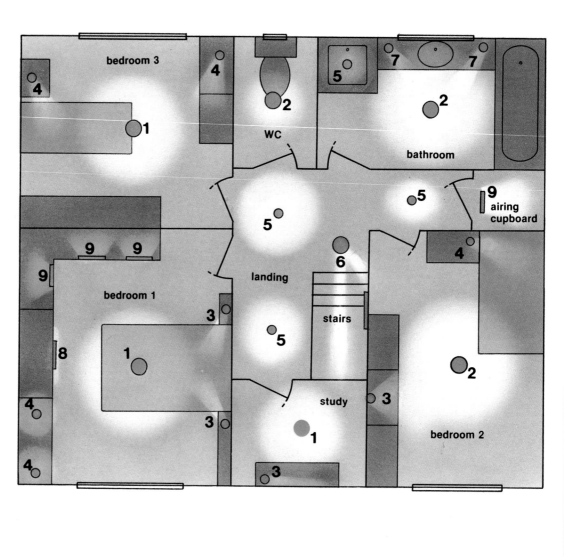

impede passage on the staircase. Downlighters can work extremely well if installed in the landing ceiling above an open flight; otherwise aim to light the flight from at least two positions so that it is evenly illuminated.

In kitchens you will need some sort of general lighting in addition to 'task' lighting over work surfaces. In a small kitchen this could be provided by the main ceiling-mounted fluorescent fitting, but you could experiment with either a close-ceiling fitting (easy to clean) or even track lighting carrying a number of spotlights directed towards the walls. If you eat in your kitchen too, add a rise-and-fall fitting over the table so you can turn off the fluorescent tube at meal-times and enjoy a softer light. Island bars are best illuminated with downlighters mounted directly above the bar surface.

Bedroom background lighting can be as simple or as sophisticated as you wish – ornate pendants, simple centre fittings, perimeter lighting or wall lights. However, do include two-way switching of whatever arrangements you choose, so that you aren't having to leap in and out of bed to turn lights on and off.

Lastly, in bathrooms a close-ceiling light, or even a fitting recessed into the ceiling itself, is the best way to provide even lighting over the whole room.

Drawing up your plans
The simplest way to plan your home lighting is to use sketch plans on which you can mark the positions of major pieces of furniture and the locations where task lighting will be required. The examples shown here illustrate the principle and help to give some idea of the scope and flexibility you have.

As you work out your requirements, don't hesitate to experiment with portable lamps and dummy fittings to see what effects you can achieve. For example, you can make up an extension cable carrying three or four lampholders with cardboard shades to try out the effect of a row of downlighters and wallwashers, or get a helper to hold spotlights in various positions in the room while you decide on the best angle and fitting height to choose. Light fittings and lamps are comparatively expensive, and a little time spent experimenting in this way will be worthwhile in the long run.

CEILING LIGHTS AND SWITCHES

Most ceiling lights are positioned centrally in a room to give general lighting. But by adding another light, or changing the position of an existing fitting, you can highlight particular areas and enhance the decoration.

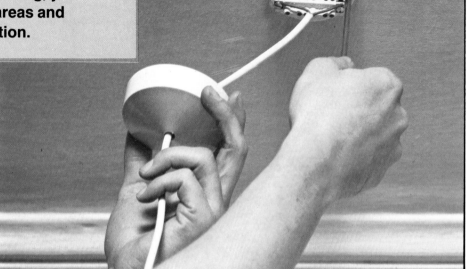

Keith Morris

Putting in a new pendant ceiling light and switch, or changing the position of an existing one, usually presents few problems – even if you have little or no experience of electrical work.

A pendant is the most common ceiling light and consists of a lampholder wired to a length of flexible cord which hangs from a ceiling rose. Another type can be plugged into the ceiling rose – in this case the flexible cord has to have a special fitting which slots into a batten holder.

Know your system

Installing a new ceiling light requires making a simple connection into a nearby lighting circuit either by inserting a junction box or at an existing loop-in rose and then running a cable to a switch. In order to connect into the circuit you'll first need to know how the lights in your house are wired and which lights belong to which circuit. Then you'll be able to work out whether you can actually add another light to the circuit that is nearest to the new light's position.

There are two principal methods of wiring a lighting circuit. In the loop-in method the cable runs from ceiling rose to ceiling rose, stopping at the last one on the circuit, and the switches are wired into the roses. With the junction box system the cable runs to a number of junction boxes each serving a switch and a light. You may well find that both methods have been used in the same circuit to simplify and reduce the cable runs.

It's possible to connect into a nearby rose provided it's a loop-in type. You can check this simply by turning off the power and unscrewing the rose cover. A loop-in rose will have more than one red insulated wire going into the central terminal bank of the three in-line terminal banks. However, it can be quite fiddly to fit another cable, given that the terminal banks are very small, so you might find it easier to insert a junction box in the main circuit. And if there isn't a loop-in rose you'll have to use this method anyway.

Earthing for lighting circuits

Modern lighting circuits are protected by an earth. But if you've got a fairly old system (it's

likely to be based on junction boxes), you might find that it doesn't have one. So when you're extending such a circuit, you're now required to protect the new wiring, light fitting and switch by installing an earth. Consequently, you have to use two-core and earth cable for the extension, which will most probably connect into the existing circuit at a junction box. You then have to run a 1.5mm^2 earth cable from this point to the main earthing point.

Circuit additions

Usually there's a lighting circuit for each floor of a house and in a single storey dwelling there are likely to be two or more. But it's easy to identify the individual circuits simply by switching on all the lights, turning off the power and taking out a 5A fuse from the consumer unit or switching off an MCB. When you restore the power you'll know that the lights that remain off all belong to the same circuit.

Generally speaking, a lighting circuit serves six to eight fixed lighting points. In fact it can serve up to 12 lampholders provided the total wattage of the bulbs on the circuit doesn't exceed 1,200 watts. This means that unless other lights have previously been added – wall lights for example – there shouldn't be a problem of connecting in another light.

Remember, when adding up the bulb wattages, a bulb of less than 100 watts counts as 100 watts and not its face value.

The place for lights

Apart from bathrooms, where special regulations apply, you can position lights and switches in any place you like inside the house. But bear in mind they are there to fulfil a function, so switches, for example, should be conveniently located – by a door is often the most satisfactory position. Usually they are set on the wall 1.4 metres (4ft 6in) above floor level. But they can be higher or lower to suit your needs.

You mustn't install pendant lights, especially plain pendants with exposed flexible cords, in a bathroom. This is for your safety. Flexes can become frayed, and if, say, you tried to change a bulb while standing in the bath and touched an exposed conductor you could electrocute yourself. Consequently, all light fittings here must be of the close-mounted type and preferably totally enclosed to keep off condensation. If instead you use an open batten lampholder it must be fitted with a protective shield or skirt which makes it impossible for anyone changing the bulb to touch the metal clamp.

A wall-mounted switch must also be out of reach of a person using the bath or shower. In modern small bathrooms, however, this is often impossible. The alternative is to place the switch just outside the room by the door, or to fit a special ceiling switch operated by an insulating cord which doesn't have to be out of reach of the bath or the shower.

Ready Reference

LIGHTING BASICS

● Extensions to lighting circuits are usually wired in 1.00mm² two-core and earth PVC-sheathed and insulated cable.
● You can extend from an existing rose only if it is of the loop-in variety with three banks of terminals; such roses can accommodate up to four cables. If you have older roses, extensions must be made via a junction box.

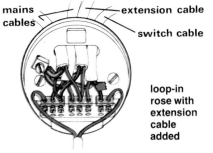

mains cables

extension cable

switch cable

loop-in rose with extension cable added

TOOLS FOR THE JOB

Electrician's pliers have cutting edges on the jaws and insulated handles.
Wire strippers can be adjusted to the diameter of the insulation to be stripped.
Handyman's knife – ideal for cutting back the sheathing of the cable.
Screwdrivers – a small one is best for the terminal fixing screws and a medium sized one for the fixing screws on the rose and switch.

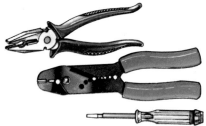

HOW TO STRIP CABLE

● Use handyman's knife to cut sheathing between neutral and earth cores.
● Use wire strippers to remove core insulation.

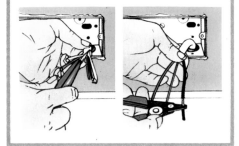

PREPARING THE CABLE RUN

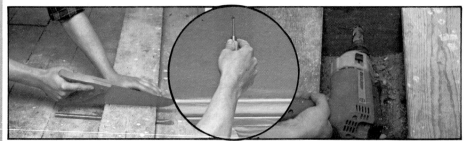

1 Raise the floorboard above the proposed location of the new light and any others necessary for laying the power supply and switch cables.

2 Mark the position of the new rose, then bore a 12mm (¹/₂in) hole. Where the cable crosses a joist, drill a 16mm (⁵/₈in) hole 50mm (2in) below the top.

3 If the new rose can't be screwed to a joist, drill a 12mm (¹/₂in) hole in a wooden batten to coincide with the hole in the ceiling and fix the batten in position.

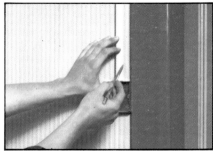

4 If flush-fitting the switch and chasing in the cable, use a mounting box and a length of conduit to mark their positions on the wall.

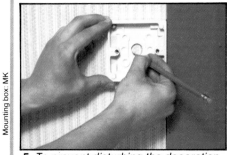

5 To prevent disturbing the decoration in one room, you can bring the switch cable down the other side of the wall and surface-mount the switch.

6 Use a small bolster chisel and club hammer to channel out a groove in the wall to take the switch cable and to chop out the recess for the switch.

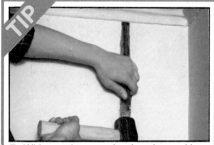

TIP

7 With cornices, make the channel in the wall first, then drive a long cold chisel gently up the back.

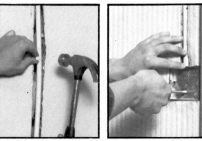

8 Fix the conduit in place with old nails, although you can also use clout nails. Drill and plug the fixing holes for the box and screw it into place.

Mounting box: MK

Keith Morris

LAYING THE CABLE

1 Run the cable from where it joins the existing circuit to the new rose and lay in the switch cable. Allow 200mm (8in) for connections.

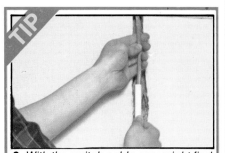

2 With the switch cable, you might find it easier to pull down the required length and then slide on the conduit before fixing it in place.

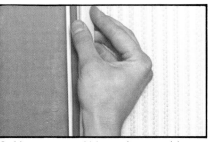

3 It's not a good idea to leave cable exposed on a wall. When surface-mounting, the cable should be laid in PVC trunking with a clip-on cover.

4 If the cable is brought down on the other side of the wall to the switch, you'll need to drill a hole through so the cable enters the back of the box.

FIXING THE SWITCH

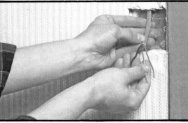

1 After making good, strip back about 100mm (4in) of sheathing; take off 15mm (5/8in) of insulation and bend over the exposed wire; sleeve the earth wire.

2 Because the switch is wired into the 'live' of the circuit, the black wire is live and not neutral; mark it as such with red PVC tape.

3 Connect the earth wire to the earth terminal of the metal box and the two conductors to the terminals on the back of the faceplate.

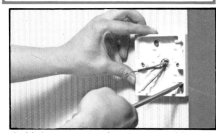

4 Make sure a surface-mounted box is square before connecting the switch. With a flush fitting squareness can be adjusted when attaching the faceplate.

Putting in switches

There is a great variety of switches available, but all perform the same function of breaking or completing an electrical circuit so you can turn the light off or on. Modern switches are of the rocker type; a one-gang switch has a single switch on the faceplate; a two-gang switch has two switches on the same faceplate, and so on. Dimmer switches are slightly different in that you can vary the power flowing to the bulb (so reducing or increasing its brightness) by rotating a control knob.

With a new light, you can either connect it into an existing switch position (fitting a two-gang switch in place of a one-gang one, for example) or a new switch. Depending on how you connect into the existing circuit, you'll have to run the switch cable above the ceiling from a rose or a junction box down the wall to where you are going to locate it. If you want to conceal the cable on the down drop you'll have to cut a shallow channel — which will damage the existing decoration. Or, you can surface-mount it in trunking.

Making the connection

Once you've decided where you want to put the light fitting and switch, you then have to decide where it's best to make the connection into the existing circuit.

Wiring runs may require some detective work to find out what each cable is doing — you don't want to connect into a switch cable by mistake. This may mean climbing into the roof space or raising a few floorboards. You'll need to do this anyway to run in the new cables to the required positions. As cable is expensive, it's best to plan your runs to use as little as possible. But when you measure along the proposed route, don't forget to allow about 200mm extra at the switch, rose and junction box for stripping back the conductors and joining in.

Changing the position of a ceiling light is even easier than adding a new one. If after you've turned off the power you undo the existing rose you'll see immediately the type of lighting circuit you are dealing with.

If there is only a black, a red and an earth wire going into it on the fixed wiring side then you have a junction box system. All you have to do is to disconnect the wires from the rose and reconnect them to the respective terminals of a new three-terminal junction box that you'll have to put in directly above the old fitting. You can then lead off another cable from this junction box to the re-positioned ceiling rose. The switch remains unaffected.

If the rose is a loop-in type, you have to carry out a similar modification, but this time the switch wires have to be incorporated in the new junction box, which must be a four-terminal type.

FITTING THE NEW ROSE AND LAMPHOLDER

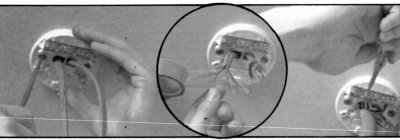

1 Fix the new rose to the ceiling. Strip back 75mm (3in) of sheathing and 8mm (¹/₃in) of insulation from the conductors, and sleeve the earth wires.

2 With loop-in wiring you'll need to wrap red PVC tape round the black wire (inset) then make the connections to the terminals as illustrated.

3 With junction box wiring, the earth is connected to the earth terminal, the black conductor goes to the neutral bank and the red to the SW terminal.

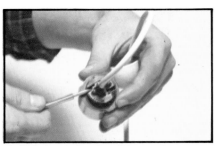

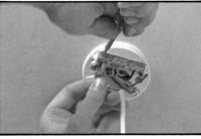

4 Strip back the sheathing and insulation of one end of the flex and connect the blue and brown conductors to the two terminals of the lampholder.

5 Screw on the cap and then slip the rose cover over the flex. Cut the flex to length and prepare the free end for connecting to the rose.

6 At the rose, connect the blue conductor to the terminal on the neutral side and the red to the SW side. Hook the wires over the cord grips.

CONNECTING INTO THE CIRCUIT

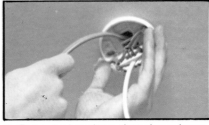

1 When connecting into a loop-in rose, undo the fixing screws and pull the fitting a little way from the ceiling. But keep all the wires in place.

2 Tap out a knockout, then draw down through it about 200mm (8in) of the cable that leads to the new ceiling rose, or else feed the cable up from below.

3 Prepare the cable by stripping back about 75mm (3in) of sheathing and 10mm (³/₈in) of insulation from the conductors. Sleeve the earth wire.

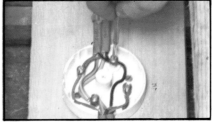

4 Connect the earth to the earth terminal, the black to the neutral terminals and the red to the central in-line terminals.

5 When connecting in at a junction box, use a four-terminal type mounted on a batten. Connect the wires to the terminals as shown.

6 When taking out an old loop-in rose, disconnect the switch and feed cables and connect up the two feed cables as shown in a three-terminal junction box.

INSTALLING WALL LIGHTS

Ceiling lights are simple and effective, but if you want a lighting scheme that is a little more exciting, more decorative and more versatile, they are not enough. One solution is to fit wall lights. Here's how.

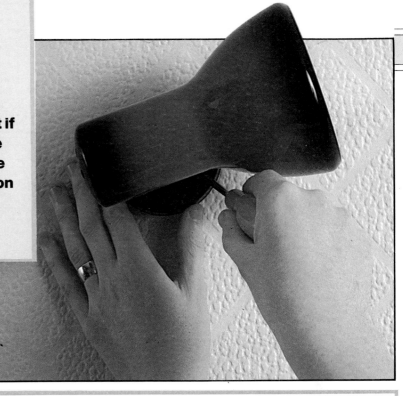

There are two keys to a really successful lighting scheme: variety and versatility. Variety, because having a uniform level of light throughout a room is just plain boring. And versatility because your lighting needs change from one part of the room to another. In a living room, for example, you may prefer the overall lighting level to be fairly low and restful, but you will still need pools of intense light for reading, or perhaps simply to show off decorative feature like pictures, plants or ornaments. That's where wall lights come in. They are very good at creating interesting pools of light.

Choosing a light

With so many wall lights to choose from where do you start? It really depends on what you want the light to do. Few provide a light you can put to practical use. Most are purely decorative.

The traditional wall light is a good example. It normally has a low wattage, candle-shaped lamp, mounted on a wooden base, and concealed behind a pretty parchment shade, so that it spreads a fan of soft light across the wall.

More recent versions take the imitation candelabra and gaslight theme still further, having ornate brass, copper, and aluminium stems, and, instead of shades, translucent bowls in plain, coloured, frosted, smoked, and sculpted glass or plastic. They tend to use more powerful bulbs, and can be made to light the top or bottom of the wall, but the net result is the same. They are for looking at, rather than seeing by.

This is also true of many modern wall light designs. There are, for example, cylindrical fittings open at top and bottom to spread a shaft of light in two directions, either vertically or horizontally.

Still attractive, but producing a more useful light, there are the fully enclosed fittings. 'Opals', for example, create a beautifully soft, even light, and look rather like round, square or rectangular blocks of milky glass or plastic. For those who prefer more ornate lights, sculpted glass versions (they look like cut crystal) are also available. Enclosed fittings are particularly handy

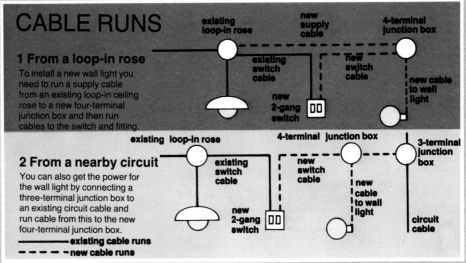

CABLE RUNS

1 From a loop-in rose
To install a new wall light you need to run a supply cable from an existing loop-in ceiling rose to a new four-terminal junction box and then run cables to the switch and fitting.

existing loop-in rose · new supply cable · 4-terminal junction box · existing switch cable · new switch cable · new cable to wall light · new 2-gang switch

2 From a nearby circuit
You can also get the power for the wall light by connecting a three-terminal junction box to an existing circuit cable and run cable from this to the new four-terminal junction box.

existing loop-in rose · 4-terminal junction box · 3-terminal junction box · existing switch cable · new switch cable · new cable to wall light · new 2-gang switch · circuit cable

—— existing cable runs
- - - - new cable runs

where space is limited – in a hallway, perhaps – and since many are weatherproof, they are an excellent choice for the humid atmosphere of a bathroom or an outside porch.

More useful still are the spotlights. Usually mounted on adjustable arms away from the wall, they can be used to send a strong beam of light almost anywhere – back onto the wall, say, to light a picture, or out into the room to illuminate a desk or sitting area. Their only real snag is that they need careful shading, if they are not to dazzle you. Mounting them on the ceiling may overcome this problem.

And finally, don't forget fluorescent lights. Slimline fluorescent tubes, though inhospitable looking, give off little heat and are easily concealed. Use them to spread a sheet of light over a wall. The light assembly can be mounted on a wooden batten and

shaded by a pelmet or baffle. If you wish, the pelmet can be painted or papered to match the wall. Miniature fluorescents are also handy for lighting pictures and shelves, but whatever the size, be sure to use a 'de luxe' warm white' tube, or the light will look cold and harsh.

Positioning the fitting

Choosing a light is only half the battle. To give of its best it must be carefully positioned. With the exception of enclosed fittings, which stand very well on their own, most need to be arranged at least in pairs, and sometimes even in a group. Traditional wall lights and mock candelabra, for example, tend to look best when arranged symmetrically in pairs – say, on each side of a chimney breast. Spotlights, on the other hand, are often most effective in a cluster.

Of course, there are no hard and fast

Ready Reference

POSITIONING WALL LIGHTS
● fix ordinary wall lights about 1.5m (5ft) above floor level
● bedside lights are best set about 1.2m (4ft) above floor level.

WHAT SWITCH TO USE
Use a one-way plate switch for the wall light. Set it on a metal mounting box sunk into the wall or on a plastic box mounted on the surface.
● a separate switch is needed to isolate a wall light from the main circuit even if it has a built-in switch of its own

● alternatively you can use an existing switch position to control an extra wall light by replacing a one-gang switch unit with a two-gang unit.

FITTING THE WALL LIGHT
The wires of the fitting are linked to the circuit cable using insulated cable connectors. These are housed in a BESA box or an architrave box which is sunk into the wall and hidden by the light fitting.

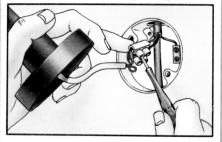

INSTALLING THE FITTING

1 Mark the position of the BESA box on the wall where the light is to go. Use a through box if the light's switch is to be immediately below the BESA box.

2 With a club hammer and bolster chisel, chop out the hole to take the box, and channels to take cables up to the ceiling and down or across to the switch.

3 Fix the box in place with screws and wall plugs, then run in the cables for the light and switch. Note that the switch cable passes straight through the box.

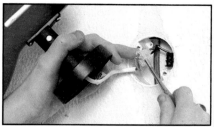

4 Connect the light cable to the light with insulated cable connectors Tuck the earth wire out of the way if it is not needed.

INSTALLING A SWITCH

1 To install a new switch, mark out the position of the switch mounting box (a plaster-depth box) and chop out the hole to receive it.

2 Drill and plug the wall, then screw the mounting box in place, checking it is level. Next, feed in the cable coming from the new circuit's junction box.

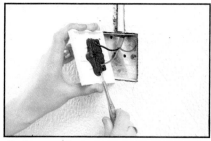

3 Connect the cable to a one-gang one-way switch. Ensure the terminal marked 'TOP' is at the top. Connect the earth wire to the box terminal.

4 If using an existing switch position, insert a new two-gang plate switch. Connect existing cable to one set of terminals, new cable to the other.

ALTERNATIVES

1 If the light switch is not to be vertically below the light position, use a single entry BESA box instead of a through one, fitting it in the same way.

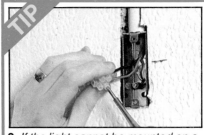

2 If the light cannot be mounted on a BESA box, connect the wires in an architrave mounting box. Knockouts let this act as a single entry or through box.

LIGHTING CIRCUIT CONNECTIONS

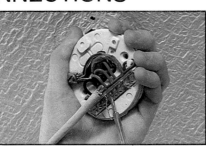

1 Turn off the power at the mains, unscrew the rose and ease it away from the ceiling so you can pull through new 1.0 or 1.5mm² cable.

3 Run the cable to a junction box between the switch and light. Then run one cable to the light, another to the switch position.

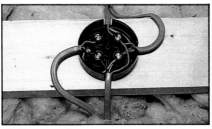

2 Connect the cable to the rose's loop-in terminals; the red wire to the centre terminal block, the black to the neutral block, and the earth to the earth block.

4 If you can't connect to the rose, insert a junction box at some point along one of the rose's feed cables. Run cables down to the light and switch as before.

CONNECTING TO A RING CIRCUIT

1 The easiest way to link a lighting spur to the ring circuit is to connect a 2.5mm² cable to the back of a socket. Ensure the socket isn't already on a spur.

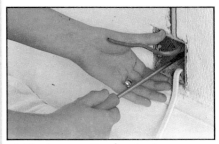

4 Fix the mounting box for the connection unit into the whole, and then run the cable into it from the power socket or three-terminal junction box.

2 Alternatively, cut the ring circuit cables and connect them to a three-terminal junction beneath the floor; then run the spur cable into that.

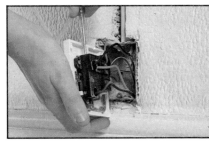

5 Having run the cable to the light position (or four-terminal junction box), fit the connection unit with a 5A fuse and connect it up.

3 Mark the position of the fused connection unit. Cut through the wallpaper with a sharp knife before you chisel out the hole for the mounting box.

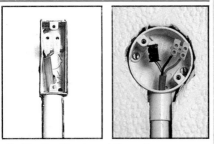

6 Finally, fit an architrave box or a stopped BESA box at the light position and install the light as before. Note the cable will now enter from below.

Ready Reference

WIRING THE CIRCUIT

The easiest way to provide wall lights with power is to run a 1.0mm² two-core and earth, PVC-sheathed and insulated cable from a loop-in ceiling rose.

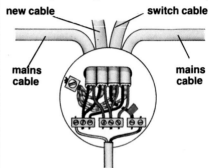

new cable | switch cable

mains cable | mains cable

● run a cable from the rose to a junction box. Two cables then run from the box – one to the light and one to its switch (A)
● rather than connecting into the main lighting circuit at a rose, you can break into the main feed cable and install a junction box (B).

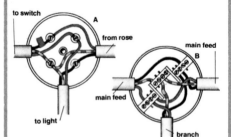

to switch
A
from rose
main feed
B
main feed
to light
branch

ALTERNATIVE WIRING

Wall lights can also take their power from a ring circuit.
● install a three-terminal junction box (A). Then run a 2.5mm² cable to a fused connection unit fitted with a 5A fuse (B). Continue the wiring to the light (C) and a switch (D) as if the power had been taken from the lighting circuit (ie, use 1.0mm² cable)

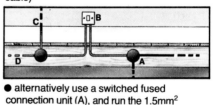

C | B
D | A

● alternatively use a switched fused connection unit (A), and run the 1.5mm² cable straight to the wall light. The unit then acts as an isolating light switch.

A

rules. In the end, it's all down to what looks and works best in your particular situation. Try to imagine how the lights will affect the room – not only the lights themselves and their position, but also the direction of the light they will give out.

You ought to pay particular attention to the light's height above the floor. The general rule is to place the light at just below eye level – about 1,500mm (5ft) – but you can vary this as necessary to stop the light getting in your eyes or to help direct it where it's needed. Wall lights used as bedside lamps, for example, should be about 1,220mm (4ft) above the floor and positioned so they can't get knocked as someone walks past them.

Installing the light

Having mastered the basic electrical techniques covered in previous sections you shouldn't find it hard to fit the light. But remember electricity can be dangerous if abused, so follow the instructions to the letter. If they don't tie in with your home's existing wiring, or if you're unsure about what you're doing, don't take chances – get expert advice.

The first step is to find a power source, though it is best to leave the connections into the existing circuit until last. That way, you can do almost all the work with your home's electrics working normally; you'll have to turn off the power at the mains only for the few minutes needed to make the final connection.

In most cases, taking a spur off the existing lighting circuit is your best bet. Do check, though, that the wall light will not overload it. Isolate the circuit in question by removing the fuse carrier from the consumer unit, or by turning off its MCB, and add up the total wattage of the bulbs it feeds – those that are now dead, in other words. Bulbs rated at 100W or more count at face value; less powerful bulbs count as 100W. When you've done that, add on the wattage of the new light and make sure the grand total is less than 1,200 watts.

Assuming this is so, there are two ways to break into the circuit. In theory, the simplest is to connect a 1.0 or 1.5mm² two-core and earth cable to a loop-in ceiling rose, and run it to a four-terminal junction box above the ceiling. In practice, it's often hard to fit the extra wires in, so, as an alternative, trace a mains feed cable out of the rose, and connect the junction box into this cable.

Once you've got power to the junction box, wire up the wall light and its switch on the conventional junction box system (see pages 14-18 and 25-28) with one cable going to the light, and another to the switch. The switch can be anywhere convenient, either close to the light or away from it. You can use the switch position by

the room's door if you wish. It's a simple matter to convert the existing one-gang switch there (for ceiling light) to a two-gang (for ceiling light and wall light).

Many wall lights have a built-in switch, so you may wonder why a switch is necessary. Although these are fine for everyday use, you ought to be able to isolate the wall light completely so an additional ordinary plate switch is required.

Though fitting a wall light is not complicated there are two problems you may meet. The first is in fixing the light to the wall. Many can be screwed to the holes provided in the BESA box housing connections between light and cable. Failing that, you can fix the light to the wall using screws and wall plugs, and house the connections in a metal architrave mounting box sunk into the wall behind it.

The second problem is earthing. Even if the wall light doesn't need to be earthed, the earth wire in the new cables must be linked to your home's main earthing point at the fuse box or consumer unit. (Never connect earth wires to water or gas pipes.) You can, of course, do this by connecting it to the earth wire in the existing wiring, but, if the existing wiring is old, it may not have an earth wire. In this case, you should run a single sheathed earth core from the new junction box back to the earthing point.

Connecting to a ring circuit

If it's inconvenient or impossible to take power from the lighting circuit, you can connect the wall light to a ring circuit. Essentially, you run a spur to the wall light's junction box (see *Fluorescent Lighting* pages 62-64). You break into the ring by either connecting a 2.5mm² two-core and earth cable to the back of a power socket, or by joining it to a three-terminal junction box and connecting this to the ring circuit cable beneath the floor.

However, there is a snag. The ring circuit fuse has too high a rating for a lighting circuit (remember, these need a 5A fuse). To get round this, you have to run the 2.5mm² cable into a fused connection unit fitted with a 5A fuse, and continue the circuit to a four-terminal junction box and then on to the light and switch junction box with 1.0 or 1.5mm² cable.

Obviously, this involves considerable extra work and expense; but there is a short cut. You can do away with the junction box and separate switch, and use a switched fused connection unit to control the wall light. It sounds appealing, but it too has its drawbacks. The connection unit will not match the other light switches in the room, and it needs to be as close as possible to the light – an unnecessarily complex cable run would be needed to control the light from the far side of the room.

INSTALLING TRACK LIGHTING

Track lighting allows you plenty of scope in lighting your home. It's efficient, versatile and attractive and, what's more, extremely easy to install.

Track and fittings : Rotaflex

The time is bound to come when you want to alter the lighting in your home. You may want to highlight certain features, such as paintings, or merely provide yourself with extra light. You may want to change your wall lights or depart from the traditional concept of a ceiling rose and pendant light. In all these cases you should think about installing track lighting.

What is track lighting?
Track lighting consists of individual light fittings of various types that are mounted on special tracks fixed to ceilings or walls. This enables you to move the lights into whatever position you like and, in addition, to adjust them so their light is thrown in whichever direction you want.

The track itself is a metal casing, usually square or tubular in cross-section, that contains twin electrical conductors. These live and neutral conductors are bare and extend from one end of the track to the other. They function in much the same way as the conductor rails of an electric railway, with the light fittings instead of the trains picking up electric current from the live rails. The conductors are shielded from touch, while the lights are fitted with special adaptors for making contact with the conductors inside the track and which also serves to hold the lights in place.

Once the track has been fixed in position and the electrical connections made, then the adaptors are placed on to the track and the spotlights moved along to exactly where you want them. You can then lock them into position.

Obtaining the power supply for your track lighting is very simple. You're really faced with two options. On the one hand you can simply connect the 'live' end of the track to the existing ceiling rose, after removing the flex of the original lampholder, or you can run in an entirely new lighting circuit. For track lights mounted on the wall, power can be supplied either by an existing light circuit or the room's socket outlet circuit. The best method, however, is to wire the lights through a fused connection unit, as if it were a wall light linked to the power circuits.

Any number of lights can be fitted onto any one track, provided you don't exceed the track's current rating. With a 10A track, the most suitable for a domestic situation, this will be 2400W and with a 16A track, 4000W. In other words, with a 10A track you could, in theory, fit up to 24 100W spotlights. In practice the limiting factor is more likely to be the circuit wiring. Remember, lighting circuits are actually rated at 5A which means that each one can take a load of up to 1200W or, in effect, can supply twelve lampholders containing lamps of 100W each or smaller. So when you are adding track lighting to an existing circuit, check that the extra lights won't mean exceeding this figure. If they will, run a spur from a nearby power circuit (via a fused connection unit) instead see pages 35.

Choosing your lighting track
Lighting track for commercial purposes comes in various standard lengths. The domestic variety usually only comes in two lengths, 1000mm (39in) or 1500mm (59in). Once you've decided on the approximate lengths of track that you'll need, visit your local stockist to see exactly what is available. When making your choice of track, it's a good idea to check what type of light fittings are available

with it and whether they'll meet your requirements. After all, the track itself is usually available in only a few finishes – white, brown, polished brass and polished silver are the commonest – while there are probably over a hundred different types of light fitting available. If you find that you can't get the exact length you require, don't worry; it can easily be cut to size with a hacksaw and if longer lengths are required, special connectors are available. And there are 90° angle connectors for when a track is required to turn a corner.

Choosing the lights
There are so many different types of fitting available that you're bound to find one that will suit the decor of your home and do the job you want it to. The number you fit on any one track will depend largely on what you want to light. As a rule, though, track lighting would prove expensive for just one or two fittings.

Installing the track
There are a number of ways of fixing the track to your ceiling or wall. It can be fixed almost flush to the surface with the help of small clips. Alternatively, you can use a special mounting canopy that will fit conveniently and neatly over an existing ceiling rose or

Ready Reference

MOUNTING METHODS
There are three methods of fixing lighting track to a ceiling:

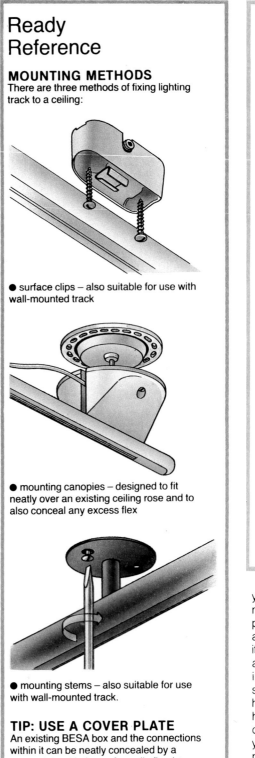

● surface clips – also suitable for use with wall-mounted track

● mounting canopies – designed to fit neatly over an existing ceiling rose and to also conceal any excess flex

● mounting stems – also suitable for use with wall-mounted track.

TIP: USE A COVER PLATE
An existing BESA box and the connections within it can be neatly concealed by a cover plate with the surface clip fixed on top. You might well find that the mains outlet point is not immediately above where you want to position the lighting track. One solution is to use a cover plate and to run the connecting cable to the track in mini-trunking.

PREPARING THE CEILING

1 *Switch off the electricity supply at the mains and unscrew the existing ceiling rose cover. You can then remove the old pendant flex and lampholder.*

2 *Site the first surface clip so that the live end of the track will sit close to the power source. Make sure the clip has a secure fixing.*

3 *Measure the position of the second clip: with a 1m (39in) track it should be 600mm (2ft) away; with a 1.5m (39in) track it should be 800mm (32in) away.*

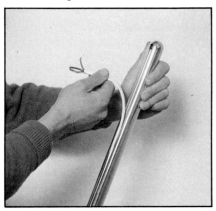

4 *Before fixing the track in place you'll have to free the flex. This is housed in a channel on the top side of the track and can be pulled clear.*

you can use mounting stems, which are merely short rods on backplates. You'll probably find that your lighting track will have a length of special flex already connected to its live end. This is likely to be the same length as the track. An advantage of these mounting methods is that in addition to providing a simple means for fitting the track itself, they help to conceal the track flex – so you won't have to cut it to length. The flex is fitted into a channel on the ceiling face of the track and you may well have to remove the shorter plastic end piece so you can free it. If you're going to use a mounting canopy and obtain power from an existing ceiling rose then the excess flex can be simply tucked into the canopy. Using surface clips will enable you to thread the flex up into the ceiling so that it can be neatly connected to a BESA box or a junction box. Only the mounting stems don't actually conceal the flex. But in their case all

you do is run the flex in its channel and leave only a short section exposed where it runs up to the ceiling rose or BESA box.

Before installing the lighting you'll have to finalise the position for the track on the ceiling or the wall. Ideally you should make sure that the mains outlet of your existing light coincides with the live end of the track. This could mean altering the position of the outlet, or even installing some new wiring, and if this is the case it should be done before you fix up the track.

Mounting track on the ceiling is perfectly straightforward but it will require solid fixings. It's best to use the joists, but if these don't coincide with the fixing holes drilled in the square cross-sectioned track you can easily drill some new holes in it to match your joist spacings. Alternatively, secure a piece of chipboard between the relevant joists and fix the track to this. Most mounting canopies

MAKING THE CONNECTIONS

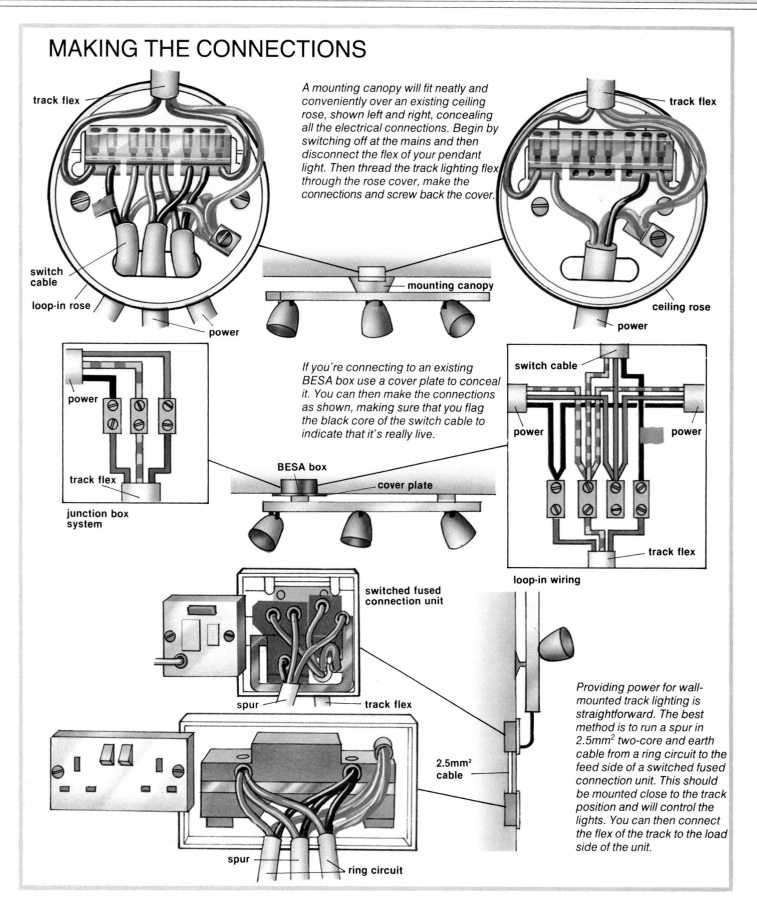

track flex

A mounting canopy will fit neatly and conveniently over an existing ceiling rose, shown left and right, concealing all the electrical connections. Begin by switching off at the mains and then disconnect the flex of your pendant light. Then thread the track lighting flex through the rose cover, make the connections and screw back the cover.

track flex

switch cable

loop-in rose

mounting canopy

ceiling rose

power

power

power

If you're connecting to an existing BESA box use a cover plate to conceal it. You can then make the connections as shown, making sure that you flag the black core of the switch cable to indicate that it's really live.

switch cable

power

power

track flex

junction box system

BESA box

cover plate

track flex

loop-in wiring

switched fused connection unit

spur

track flex

Providing power for wall-mounted track lighting is straightforward. The best method is to run a spur in 2.5mm² two-core and earth cable from a ring circuit to the feed side of a switched fused connection unit. This should be mounted close to the track position and will control the lights. You can then connect the flex of the track to the load side of the unit.

2.5mm² cable

spur

ring circuit

35

INSTALLING THE TRACK AND FITTINGS

1 *Offer up the track to the surface clips, making sure that it will be centrally positioned and that the clip grub screws are slackened.*

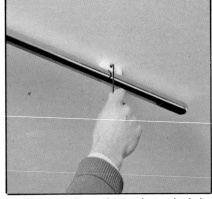

2 *When you have the track precisely in position, secure it in place by tightening up the clip grub screws with the hexagonal key provided.*

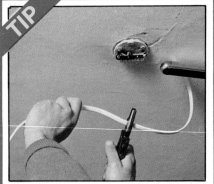

3 *Before making the electrical connections, cut the flex to length. If you're using a mounting canopy, you can safely tuck the excess inside.*

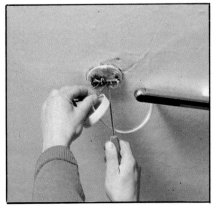

4 *Next, make the connections. Link the brown core to the bank of live terminals, the blue core to the neutral bank and the green/yellow core to the earth terminal.*

5 *Most track lights are stepped on one side so you can't fit them incorrectly. Move the lever through 90° to retract the contacts and fixing levers.*

6 *Then fix the lights onto the track. Simply hold them in place, reposition the lever and lock the lights in the desired position on the track.*

have fixing holes 51mm (2in) apart. In other words, the canopy will be able to fit over an existing rose, and the connection to the circuit can then be completely concealed. However, where the existing rose is old and has different spacings between its fixing holes you'll have to discard it and use an alternative method of connecting to the circuit.

This method involves fixing a BESA box flush with the surface of the ceiling. Inside the BESA box the flying leads of the lighting track are connected to the existing circuit wires with insulated cable connectors. The box itself has two screwed lugs that are spaced at 51mm (2in) centres, so the canopy will fit perfectly in place. If you're using stems, you'll find that the procedure is virtually the same although there could well be slight differences between the various systems currently on the market. Fixing track to walls is much the same as fixing it to the ceiling.

However, you'll probably find that you have to drill and plug the wall to get a really secure fixing, and you'll also have to cut a channel in the plaster to run in the cable unless your track reaches right up to the ceiling and the cable can be concealed within it.

Obtaining power for track lighting
One of the major advantages of track lighting is that it can often be connected to an existing lighting point without any alteration of the circuitry. However, new wiring will be necessary when there is no convenient lighting which can be used to supply the track; where the addition of track lighting is likely to overload the lighting circuit, and where track lighting is to be used in addition to the existing lighting. If you're going to have to run in a new circuit for the track you should use 1.0mm two-core and earth cable rated at 5A. This will be able to supply power for up to 12

spotlights on three or four tracks. The circuit will be the same as an ordinary lighting circuit and you'll probably find it easiest to use junction boxes as each track will need to be controlled by a wall switch. That way you can use BESA boxes in which to make the connections to the track. For further details on using a BESA box see *Ready Reference* on page 34.

Track lighting fixed to the wall will be able to obtain its power supply from the existing lighting point if it is replacing wall lights. However, if you're mounting new lights then you're faced with two options. You can either break into the lighting circuit in the ceiling void above and run cable down to the track or you can break into the socket outlet circuit. In the latter case you should take a spur to a switched fused connection and then run 1.0mm^2 two-core and earth cable to the track itself.

PLANNING TO UP-DATE YOUR ELECTRICS

Rewiring your home can be very straightforward but it still requires detailed planning and careful consideration. If you know exactly what you want from your home's circuits and where you want to site your power outlets and lights, then you're halfway to completing the job.

Completely rewiring your home is a job that sounds more difficult than it really is. If you've mastered such techniques as running cable, fitting new lights and installing new socket outlets then it certainly won't pose you any major problems.

Making the decision to rewire is perhaps the biggest step you'll have to take and, as with any electrical installation, you should never undertake the job without knowing exactly what you want and where you want it. Detailed planning is crucial to the final results and overlooking one important socket outlet or light can cause considerable inconvenience and, in the long run, extra work. Before making any decision about rewiring your home it's a good idea to examine the existing circuitry thoroughly to make sure that it really does need replacing.

When to rewire

There are two basic reasons for rewiring your home: first, because the existing fixed wiring is past its useful and safe life; and second because the number of power outlets and lights no longer meets your requirements. There are certain tell-tale danger signs which you might come across when you inspect your circuitry. The use of rubber-sheathed cable ended in the early 1950s, so if you find this used in your circuits you'll know that they're quite old. If the insulation is worn and perished, then it's clear that the cable will have to be replaced to avoid the risk of fire or shocks. And, if you find that fuses in your consumer unit are blowing with alarming regularity, it's obvious something is seriously wrong.

You'll also have to consider whether the existing circuitry provides adequate lighting points and power outlets. Again there are a number of tell-tale signs. If you have to use adaptors to cope with all your appliances you'll know you don't have enough sockets; long trailing flexes will indicate that those existing outlets are not correctly sited. If you find you have to move lamps around to provide yourself with decent lighting, then it's clear that your lighting system is also inadequate.

Having examined your existing power and lighting systems, you're left with two alterna-

tives. You can either adapt the existing circuitry (provided, of course, that the cable is in good enough condition) to give yourself extra power outlets and lighting points, or else you can completely rewire it. If you are in any doubt, then it's best to rewire; the chances are that it'll have to be done at some stage anyway and, by doing so immediately, it's likely to give you a safer and more efficient system cheaply and to increase the value of your home.

The circuitry

Before planning the number of sockets and lighting points you want, you'll have to decide exactly how you're going to run the circuits. Most modern homes are fitted with one ring circuit and one lighting circuit per floor. However, this is not necessarily the best arrangement. It's worth considering dividing your home up vertically, so that you have one ring circuit supplying one half of the house and another the second half. It'll mean a little more work, but, if one of the circuits blows at any time, you'll still have light and power left on each floor. It's a good idea to have your kitchen supplied by its own ring or radial circuit as, of all the rooms in the home, it uses most power.

Remember that certain electrical appliances, such as a cooker or immersion heater,

should be connected exclusively to a separate radial circuit. Whatever you decide, you'll probably find that two ring circuits plus an extra radial or ring circuit for the kitchen, and additional radial circuits for certain fixed appliances, will suffice. Your next step will be the detailed siting of individual power outlets and lighting points in each room.

Living areas

The increase in electrical gadgetry and appliances over the past decade means that the average home now requires many more socket outlets. What with stereos, TVs, digital clocks and video games, as well as standard and table lamps, living rooms are going to need about ten sockets rather than the two or three usually fitted. Dining rooms are unlikely to need as many, unless you are in the habit of using toasters, coffee percolators, food warmers and so on at every meal, but remember that it's better to provide too many rather than too few.

For reasons of economy and convenience it's best to fit switched double sockets throughout, and you can, of course, re-use those from the previous circuits if they are in good condition. Flush-mounted ones are neatest, but require a bit of extra work to fit them.

Most living rooms and dining areas are

REWIRING YOUR LIVING AREAS

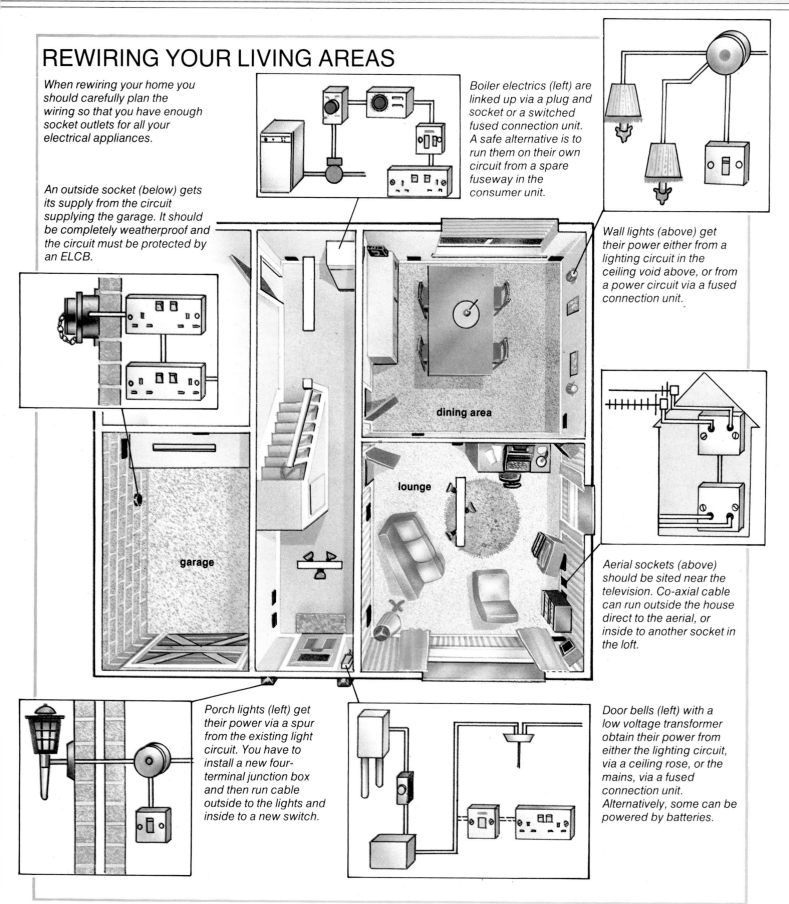

When rewiring your home you should carefully plan the wiring so that you have enough socket outlets for all your electrical appliances.

An outside socket (below) gets its supply from the circuit supplying the garage. It should be completely weatherproof and the circuit must be protected by an ELCB.

Boiler electrics (left) are linked up via a plug and socket or a switched fused connection unit. A safe alternative is to run them on their own circuit from a spare fuseway in the consumer unit.

Wall lights (above) get their power either from a lighting circuit in the ceiling void above, or from a power circuit via a fused connection unit.

Aerial sockets (above) should be sited near the television. Co-axial cable can run outside the house direct to the aerial, or inside to another socket in the loft.

dining area

lounge

garage

Porch lights (left) get their power via a spur from the existing light circuit. You have to install a new four-terminal junction box and then run cable outside to the lights and inside to a new switch.

Door bells (left) with a low voltage transformer obtain their power from either the lighting circuit, via a ceiling rose, or the mains, via a fused connection unit. Alternatively, some can be powered by batteries.

REWIRING BEDROOMS AND BATHROOMS

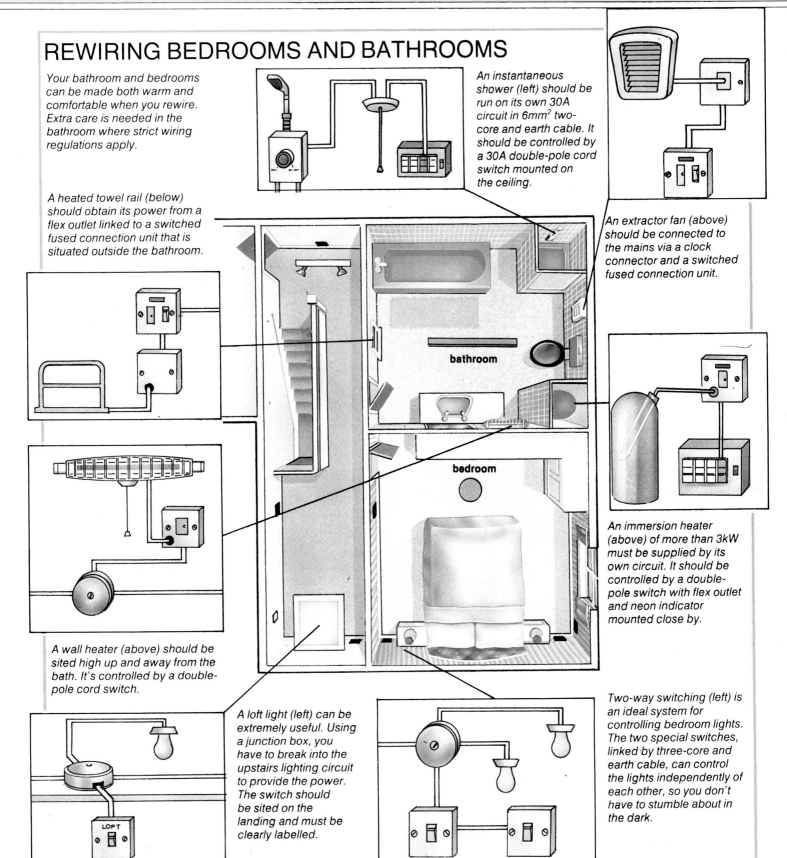

Your bathroom and bedrooms can be made both warm and comfortable when you rewire. Extra care is needed in the bathroom where strict wiring regulations apply.

A heated towel rail (below) should obtain its power from a flex outlet linked to a switched fused connection unit that is situated outside the bathroom.

An instantaneous shower (left) should be run on its own 30A circuit in 6mm² two-core and earth cable. It should be controlled by a 30A double-pole cord switch mounted on the ceiling.

An extractor fan (above) should be connected to the mains via a clock connector and a switched fused connection unit.

An immersion heater (above) of more than 3kW must be supplied by its own circuit. It should be controlled by a double-pole switch with flex outlet and neon indicator mounted close by.

A wall heater (above) should be sited high up and away from the bath. It's controlled by a double-pole cord switch.

A loft light (left) can be extremely useful. Using a junction box, you have to break into the upstairs lighting circuit to provide the power. The switch should be sited on the landing and must be clearly labelled.

Two-way switching (left) is an ideal system for controlling bedroom lights. The two special switches, linked by three-core and earth cable, can control the lights independently of each other, so you don't have to stumble about in the dark.

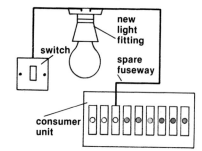
fitted with a central light and if you decide to reposition this you must make sure that the new rose can be fitted securely to a joist or a wooden batten fitted between two joists. If you decide to install a fluorescent fitting instead, you'll have to alter the wiring only if you already have a loop-in system, in which case you'll have to install an extra junction box.

Spotlights or wall lights can provide a more specific light on particular areas of the room, or for special tasks such as reading or sewing. A point to remember, however, is that wall and table lights can be run from the power circuit to avoid the risk of overloading the lighting circuit. They should be connected to a fused connection unit or plug fitted with a 5A fuse.

Halls and passageways
Sockets for plugging in a vacuum cleaner are necessary in the hall or on the landing, but the lighting is likely to be your most important consideration. Adequate lighting over the stairs is vital as every year many people injure themselves by falling down badly-lit stairs. But, whilst lighting should be adequate, it shouldn't be so bright as to dazzle you as you're going up or down the stairs; so it's worth considering the use of downlighters or carefully directed spot-lights. Incidentally, don't forget about two-way switching: it will prevent you ever having to use the stairs in the dark. If you have a cupboard under the stairs it's a good idea to run in power for a light there; it'll make a lot of difference when you're looking for things. Fit the light on its own circuit. As most consumer units are kept under the stairs, it will enable you to replace the fuse without having to work in the dark. At the same time as rewiring the hall, it's also worth installing a porch light. This will make your home that much more welcoming, deter burglars and can be connected to an ordinary lighting circuit. Also, as you'll be running cable in the roof space, it's a good idea to install a light in the loft.

Bathrooms
Bathrooms require special consideration as they are potentially the most dangerous room in which to use electricity. However, there are a number of regulations that apply to them and if you bear these in mind when planning the rewiring you shouldn't experience any difficulty.

The only socket outlets permitted in the bathroom are double-isolated shaver sockets so that means the only portable appliance you can use is an electrical shaver. Any other appliance plugged into this socket will trip the thermal overload device and cut off the current.

All switches must be cord-operated and any lights they control must either be completely enclosed, to prevent the use of

the lightholder for any other appliance, or else be fitted with a protective skirt. They must, of course, be out of reach of anyone using the bath or shower.

Fixed appliances may be installed in the bathroom, but again you must proceed with caution. A towel rail, for example, can be connected to a fused connection unit, but the unit itself must be outside the bathroom and you'll have to use a simple flex outlet near the appliance. A wall heater or fire must be fixed high on the wall, away from the bath or shower, and must also be controlled by a cord switch, preferably with a neon indicator. An electric shower requires its own 30A radial circuit, and should be controlled by a double-pole cord switch to isolate it from the mains.

Bedrooms
Along with the living room and the kitchen, the bedroom is likely to be where you'll make most use of electric appliances – after all, you're going to want to make it as comfortable as possible. By the time you've plugged in the tea-maker, the radio/alarm, the electric blanket and two bedside lights you're already up to five sockets, and that's four more than most builders seem to think are necessary! When planning the siting of the socket outlets you should also bear in mind that the needs of a teenager are quite different from those of a young child, while those of an elderly parent staying permanently are different from those of an occasional guest. So you shouldn't necessarily install the same number of sockets in the same position in each room; but it's always better to install more than you immediately need. Once again, two-way switching is a useful way of avoiding stumbling around in the dark and is particularly suited to the bedroom. It's also important to have some kind of bright overall light so that you'll find it easier to look for something, should a small item, like jewellery, drop on the floor.

Outside the house
When you rewire your home you are advised to run a special circuit so you can have power and light in your garden, garage or shed. This will be classified as a sub-main cable and under new wiring regulations must be protected by an earth leakage circuit breaker (ELCB). This legislation also applies to simple extension cables which are only in use while the appliance they supply is being used. Special waterproof and hard-wearing accessories are available and these should be connected up with great care before being used.

Only after you've carefully considered the state of your home's electrics and determined exactly what your requirements are can you proceed with the actual re-wiring. As this can be a complicated undertaking it may be wise to call in a professional.

IMPROVING KITCHEN ELECTRICS

An old kitchen can be transformed and updated simply by adding extra socket outlets and additional lighting. Supplying the power is not complicated, and existing circuits can be easily adapted or completely rewired.

The kitchen is one of the most frequently used rooms in the home and as a result should be as efficient and streamlined as possible. A modern one ought really to be able to take full advantage of the growth in electrical appliances and the improvement in artificial lighting that has been seen over the past decade or so. If you cast a critical eye round your kitchen you'll probably find that the electrics certainly leave something to be desired. A couple of socket outlets and a central light are painfully inadequate in this day and age: if you were to equip your kitchen with many of the available labour-saving devices you certainly wouldn't be able to power them from individual socket outlets. And a single central light will mean that you're likely to have to prepare food and wash dishes in your own shadow.

If you're not satisfied with the electrics in your kitchen, to improve them you can either rewire the whole kitchen or else extend the existing circuits.

Planning your needs

Before you start work on your kitchen you must decide exactly what you want from it. You'll have to decide how many socket outlets you're going to need and just what sort of lighting you'll want. The best way of deciding on sockets is to make a list of electrical appliances and tick off those you own, or are likely to own. Then decide upon other things, such as a radio or television, which you might also want to use in the kitchen occasionally. In your calculations you shouldn't forget that some appliances, like a cooker hood or a waste disposal unit, are better connected to a fused connection unit rather than a socket outlet. However, it's still a good idea to allow more socket outlets than you think are necessary. That way you'll do away with the need for adaptors (never, in any case, to be recommended from a safety point of view) and the temptation of trailing flexes for long distances over worktops. And though you may think that you could use one socket for several different pieces of equipment, it's better, in fact, to have one per appliance so that you minimise the amount of plug changing. Moving appliances around is

specially risky in a kitchen where you might be tempted to change plugs with wet hands and so risk getting a nasty shock.

There's only one electrical appliance used in the kitchen which can't get its power from an ordinary 13A socket outlet or fused connection unit and that's the cooker. Both freestanding and split-level cookers must be connected exclusively to their own radial circuits. For further information on the most suitable types of cable to use when connecting up a cooker see pages 6 and 7.

Planning your lighting needs is just as important, and you'll probably find that you'll need two sorts of artificial lighting to make your kitchen completely practical. It's a good idea to have some kind of general lighting and to complement that with more specific 'task' lighting on certain areas.

General lighting will be adequate for the kitchen as a whole, so you can eat and work in comfort, while the specific lighting will provide the more intense local light needed on worktops, sinks and sometimes the cooker. You might find that simply replacing your existing light with a fluorescent tube provides you with adequate lighting, and this will certainly be true if your kitchen is not very large. However, if you've a fairly sizeable kitchen you might well require spotlights or downlighters in addition to two or more fluorescent tubes on the ceiling. And if

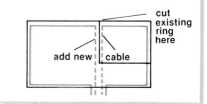

you feel the light from fluorescent lights is too harsh, you might decide to fit an illuminated ceiling or recessed lights. None of this is beyond the ordinary do-it-yourselfer, and will all go towards transforming your kitchen into a modern one of which you can be proud.

Identifying the circuits

When you've decided exactly how you want to modify your kitchen you'll have to turn your attention to the existing circuitry. First of all you must establish whether the kitchen is supplied by its own ring circuit, whether it's part of a larger ring circuit serving a whole floor, or whether it's supplied by a radial circuit. The chances are that it'll be on a large downstairs ring circuit, but if you're not sure, it's quite easy to check. You'll have to switch on an appliance in the kitchen and then remove the fuse for the ring circuit from the consumer unit. Its fuse should be labelled but if it isn't, you can identify it by virtue of the two cables leaving the fuseway. If the appliance still doesn't work, you'll know it's on the ring and if the removal of the fuse doesn't affect electrical appliances in any other rooms you'll know the kitchen has its own ring circuit. If you find the kitchen circuit has only one cable leaving the consumer unit then that shows it is supplied by a radial circuit.

Remember that there are limitations imposed on both types of circuit. There is no limit to the number of sockets and fused connection units you can install on any new circuit, but you must make sure that the non-fused spurs do not outnumber them. However, there are limitations to the area which each new circuit can serve. A new ring circuit must on no account exceed 100sq m (1075sq ft), while an equivalent 30A radial circuit is limited to an area of 50sq m (540sq ft) – although this is still considerably larger than the average kitchen. A 20A radial circuit is restricted to an area of 20sq m (215sq ft). While those referring to the area each circuit supplies are unlikely to restrict you, they are worth bearing in mind, especially if you have a very large kitchen.

Adapting the circuitry

Once you've established exactly what kind of circuit you have you'll find that there are a number of options open to you. If your power needs are not going to be too demanding you simply fit new socket outlets onto your existing circuit. Alternatively you can modify it so you can provide new power outlets or, if you want, replace it completely with a new circuit for the kitchen's exclusive use.

Simply fitting new sockets onto an existing circuit is not difficult and the only inconvenience will involve disturbing the decorations in the kitchen. For further details

PROVIDING POWER FOR APPLIANCES

Electrical appliances in the kitchen can obtain their power from the ring circuit, a spur or a radial circuit. Double socket outlets are best and switched fused connection units provide extra safety and convenience.

Instantaneous water heater
This is useful mounted close to a sink where there is no regular hot water supply. It should obtain its power through a fused connection unit.

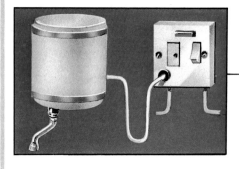

Double socket outlet
This kind of power point is specially suited to use in the kitchen because of the large number of electrical appliances. Switched sockets are safest.

Chest freezer
It's best to use an unswitched fused connection unit as the outlet. That way you avoid the risk of the freezer being accidentally switched off.

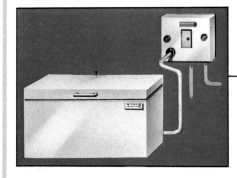

Washing machine
This can be supplied by a spur from the ring circuit. It's a good idea to use a switched fused connection unit so it can't be accidentally disconnected.

utility room

Dishwasher

A switched fused connection unit on a spur is the best way to provide the power. A neon indicator shows at a glance if the power is on or off.

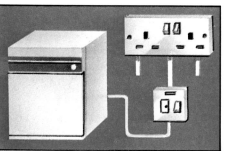

Waste disposal unit

The switched fused connection unit can be sited under the worktop where it will be easily accessible if it is needed, but also neatly out of sight.

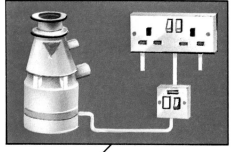

Extractor fan

A switched fused connection unit on a spur from the ring circuit lets you control the fan. A clock connector links the flex from the fan to the spur cable.

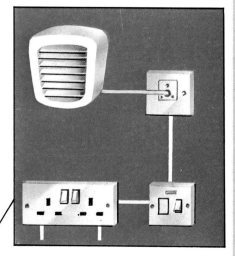

Cooker

This is the only appliance that requires an exclusive radial circuit. This should run from the consumer unit via a cooker switch and connector unit.

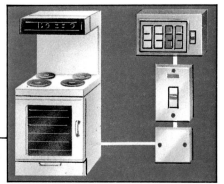

Refrigerator

This can be simply plugged into a socket outlet which should be below the worktop but where it can be easily reached without moving the appliance.

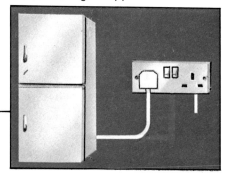

kitchen

IMPROVING YOUR KITCHEN LIGHTING

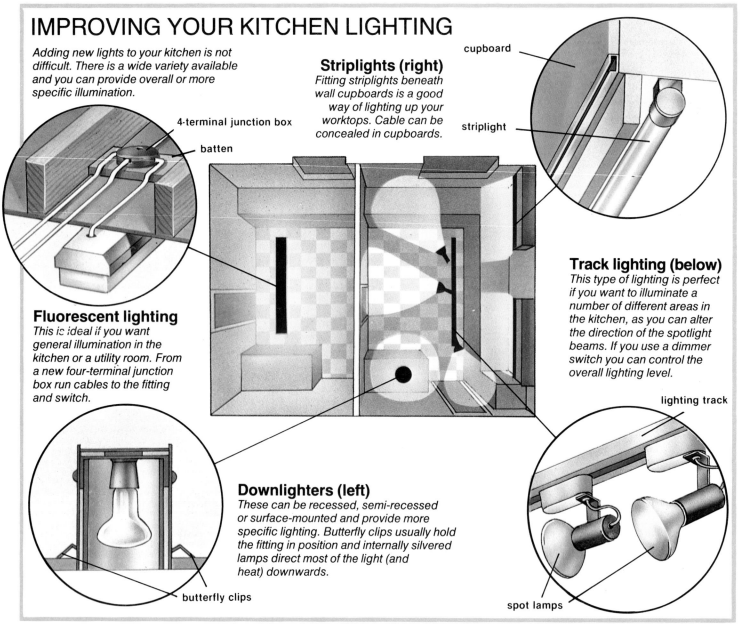

Adding new lights to your kitchen is not difficult. There is a wide variety available and you can provide overall or more specific illumination.

4-terminal junction box

batten

Striplights (right)
Fitting striplights beneath wall cupboards is a good way of lighting up your worktops. Cable can be concealed in cupboards.

cupboard

striplight

Fluorescent lighting
This is ideal if you want general illumination in the kitchen or a utility room. From a new four-terminal junction box run cables to the fitting and switch.

Track lighting (below)
This type of lighting is perfect if you want to illuminate a number of different areas in the kitchen, as you can alter the direction of the spotlight beams. If you use a dimmer switch you can control the overall lighting level.

lighting track

Downlighters (left)
These can be recessed, semi-recessed or surface-mounted and provide more specific lighting. Butterfly clips usually hold the fitting in position and internally silvered lamps direct most of the light (and heat) downwards.

butterfly clips

spot lamps

on installing a new socket see *Adding a Power Point*, pages 46-49.

If you have a radial circuit in your kitchen this can easily be extended provided you don't exceed the limitations on area mentioned earlier. You'll have to break into the circuit at the last outlet. With the power off, you should then remove the outlet and connect the equivalent sized cable to it. Then extend the circuit's route so that it supplies as many extra sockets and fused connection units as you want to install. Otherwise you would install a new radial circuit to supplement an existing circuit. For further information see *Cable and Flex*.

A third option is to split a large ring circuit into two smaller ring circuits. That way you still use most of the existing cable and all of your existing power outlets. To do this sounds much more complicated than it actually is. After you've switched off the power at the mains, you should trace the cable run of the existing circuit. At the point at which it leaves the adjacent room to enter the kitchen you'll have to break into it. Using 30A cable connectors you should then attach enough 2.5mm² two-core and earth cable to the cable in the adjacent room to enable you to run it back to the consumer unit. On the way, of course, you can add extra power outlets where you need them. You'll have to do exactly the same in the kitchen extending the existing cable so that it, too, returns to the consumer unit via whatever extra power outlets you wish to install. You'll probably find that you'll have to make a couple of alterations

in the arrangements of fuses and cable in the consumer unit. Each circuit will require its own 30A fuse where the circuit both starts and ends. Unless you already have a spare 30A fuseway, you'll probably have to fit a new MCB or fuse in your consumer unit. If there isn't enough room in the unit then you will have to fit another switchfuse unit to sit alongside the existing consumer unit.

The ultimate way to provide power for your new socket outlets and fixed appliances is to run in a completely new ring circuit. This is undoubtedly the best way, for not only does it satisfy all your power requirements but it also means that, should a fuse blow in the other circuit, you'll still have some power on the same floor.

Siting the sockets

The best position for the socket outlets in your kitchen will depend largely on how it is laid out. Sockets for portable appliances such as kettles, toasters, food mixers and so on should be on the wall above the work surfaces so flexes are not stretched and connections strained; switched fused connection units for fixed appliances such as refrigerators, freezers and washing machines and other appliances like cooker hoods or extractor fans can be fixed at a similar height or just below the work surface if you want them out of sight. But remember they should be accessible so they can be turned on and off without any trouble. If you fit them just above skirting board level, you'll conceal them neatly behind the appliance but they'll be extremely awkward to get at.

If the appliance is fitted with flex, you'll need a unit with a special flex outlet and it should be sited as near as possible to the appliance and fitted with the appropriate fuse – 3A for loads of up to 720W and 13A for loads up to 3kW.

There is a considerable range of socket types available. Most are rated to indicate the amount of current the fitting can carry to assist you in your choice.

Rewiring your lights

Having considered the power circuits, you'll probably want to turn your attention to the lighting in your kitchen. It's no good getting all sorts of marvellous electrical gadgetry and then not being able to see to use it!

As a rule, you'll find there's one lighting circuit for each floor and each one supplies eight or nine lampholders. If there's any danger of overloading the circuit by adding new lights then you should install a new circuit. And an additional circuit means that should a fuse blow, the downstairs of the house won't be left in the dark! For further details on installing a new light circuit see *Understanding Electrics*.

However, you might find that modifying your existing lighting will be sufficient for your needs. For instance, replacing an existing tungsten filament lamp with a fluorescent fitting is simple and effective. If your lighting circuit is wired on the junction box system then all you have to do is remove the existing light, fit the new tube holder and make the connections. If, however, you've got loop-in wiring you'll have to modify the wiring a little as there are no loop-in facilities on a fluorescent fitting (for further details see *Fluorescent Lighting*). With quite a large kitchen you can be more adventurous in your choice of lighting and there is a wide variety of fittings available, including conventional pendant or ceiling-mounted lights, illuminated ceilings, spotlights, downlighters and concealed striplights.

Choosing your lights

Pendant lights are probably not a particularly good idea in small kitchens. Not only do they cause more shadow than other types, but their flexes tend to get quickly covered in grime. However, a pendant light fitted on a rise-and-fall fitting is perfectly suited for use over an eating area in a larger kitchen.

Fluorescent lights are ideal for general lighting in a kitchen because they cast virtually no shadows. Although they don't give a particularly attractive sort of light, diffusers and coloured tubes make them much more acceptable, while their efficiency and relative cheapness are factors strongly in their favour.

If you find fluorescent lighting ugly and too 'cold' you could incorporate it in an illuminated ceiling. With this method two or more fluorescent lights are fitted to the original ceiling and a second 'ceiling' of translucent plastic panels is fitted below. This is not difficult to do. A lattice or grid of metal bars has to be fitted below the level of the existing ceiling and the panels are then laid on top. These panels can be of different colours to provide a slightly softer effect. A partly illuminated ceiling can be achieved by cutting out sections of the existing ceiling between a pair of joists and replacing them with translucent panels. For further details on fluorescent and other lighting see *Lighting Design*, pages 19-21.

Spotlamps provide a concentrated light which is ideal for focussing on a particular area. They can be mounted on the ceiling, on the wall and singly or in groups on a track. Fitting track lighting is ideal for a kitchen as you can pick out a number of specific areas, as well as providing general lighting. For further details see *Track Lighting*, pages 33-36.

Downlighters are ideal for a kitchen as they will give a concentrated beam of light on a worktop. They are usually the recessed type and therefore lie flush with the ceiling. To fit one you'll have to cut a circular hole in the ceiling to take the tubular fitting. Remember it's a good idea to fit a heat-resisting pad to the underside of the floorboards above and that way you will avoid any possible risk from the rising heat of the bulb. However, semi-recessed and surface-mounted types are also available, and are rather easier to fit. For further details on recessed lighting see *Up-date Your Electrics*, pages 37-40.

Finally, **striplights** provide a very effective method of lighting worktops that lie under wall cupboards and are therefore often poorly lit. The striplights are fitted to the underside of the cupboard along with a batten to cut out the glare.

Remember, the rewiring of a kitchen or the adapting of existing circuitry are not such daunting tasks as they first seem, and the results can be both rewarding and satisfying.

Ready Reference

ENLARGING SOCKET OUTLETS

Changing a single socket outlet into a double one is easy. How you do it depends on how the existing socket is mounted.

For flush-mounted sockets
you should:
● remove the mounting box
● enlarge the hole
● fit the new double box.
If you don't want to chop out a larger hole you should:
● buy a surface-mounted double box
● attach it to the lugs of the existing single box.

For surface mounted sockets
you should:
● remove the existing single box
● fit a surface-mounted double box, or
● chop out a new hole
● fit a flush-mounted double box.

TYPES OF LAMP

Spotlights and downlighters can be fitted with a number of different lamps. The 'general service' lamp gives a wide spread of light.

The internally silvered lamp is silvered round the base and sides so the light is thrown forward. It gives a broad beam.

The crown silvered lamp controls the amount of glare and produces a narrow beam suited to lighting specific features in a room.

The parabolic aluminized reflector is made from armoured glass, lasts longer than most lamps and is mainly used outside.

TIP: RUNNING CABLE

Cable that is chased into the wall should never be run horizontally. This is only acceptable:
● if it is surface mounted, or
● if it is concealed in mini-trunking.
Remember, you can always hide cable runs behind kitchen units.

ADDING A POWER POINT

Electrical equipment is now used more and more in the home, so an extra power socket is always useful. Here's how to fit one.

Keith Morris

There's nothing really difficult about installing a new power point. It's easier than putting in a new light as you don't have to worry about a switch cable.

The circuitry

Ever since the early 1950s, the power supply to the sockets has almost always been wired as a ring circuit, where the cable starts and ends at the consumer unit. Houses rewired since then will almost certainly have had this system installed. This means that once you've decided where you want the new outlet point – by a shelf in the living room for a hi-fi system, or over a worktop in the kitchen, for example – all you then have to do is to run a 'branch' or 'spur' to it from a convenient point on a nearby ring circuit.

The connection could be made at any socket on the ring (unless it already has a spur coming from it), or by using a three-terminal junction box inserted into the cable run. Each spur can have either one single or one double socket fitted to it.

Checking your circuits

Although it's very likely that your house has ring circuits for the power supply, it's important to make sure. A ring circuit serves a number of 13A power outlets, and the sockets themselves take the familiar three-pin plugs with flat pins. But having this type of socket doesn't necessarily mean you've got a ring circuit – a new radial circuit may have been installed with these fittings, or an old radial circuit may simply have been modernised with new socket outlets. If in doubt, get an electrician to check the circuit.

Inspecting your fuseboards

First you've got to check whether you've got a modern consumer unit or separate fuse boxes for each of the circuits. Having a consumer unit is a fair indication that you've got ring circuit wiring, and if two cables are connected to each individual 30A fuseway in the unit this will confirm it. Normally each floor of the house will have a separate ring circuit, protected by a 30A fuse or MCB.

If you have separate fuse boxes, look for the ones with 30A fuses. If they have one supply cable going into them and two circuit cables coming out, this indicates a ring circuit.

It's easy to identify the sockets on any particular circuit simply by plugging in electrical appliances, such as table lamps, turning off the power and then removing a 30A fuse from the fuse box or consumer unit, or switching off a 30A MCB. When you restore the supply, the equipment that remains off will indicate which sockets are on the circuit.

Dealing with radial circuits

Where a house hasn't got ring circuits, then the power sockets will be supplied by some form of radial circuit. Because there are different types of radial circuit, each governed by separate regulations controlling the number and location of sockets on the circuit, the size of cable to be used and the size of fuse protecting it, it's not possible to connect a spur to a nearby radial circuit. In all probability you'll have to install a new circuit starting at a new, separate fuse box or else at a spare fuseway in a consumer unit.

If you've still got unfused 15A, 5A and 2A round-pin plugs, then this is a sure sign of very old radial circuits, which were installed more than 30 years ago. Rather than extending the system you should seriously consider taking these circuits out and replacing them with ring circuits, as the wiring will almost certainly be nearing the end of its life. You'll then be able to position the new sockets exactly where you want them. If you're in any doubt about the circuitry in your house you should contact your local electricity authority or a qualified electrician before carrying out any work.

Adding a spur to a ring

Once you've established you're dealing with a ring circuit and what sockets are on it, you'll need to find out if any spurs have already been added. You can't have more spurs than there are socket outlets on the ring itself. But unless the circuit has been heavily modified, it's unlikely that this situation will arise. You'll also need to know where any spurs are located – you don't want to overload an existing branch by mistake.

You can distinguish the sockets on the ring from those on a spur by a combination of inspecting the back of the sockets and tracing some cable runs (see *Ready Reference*). But remember to turn off the power first.

When you've got this information, you can work out whether it's feasible to add to the ring circuit. And you'll have a good idea where the cable runs.

Installing the socket

It's best to install the socket and lay in the cable before making the final join into the ring, since by doing this you reduce the amount of time that the power to the circuit is off.

You can either set the socket flush with the wall or mount it on the surface. The latter is the less messy method, but the fitting stands proud of the wall and so is more conspicuous.

FLUSH FITTING IN A BRICK WALL

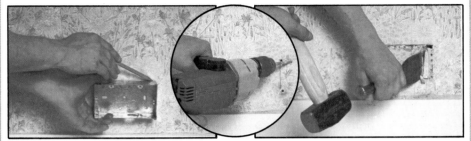

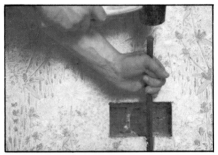

1 *Decide where you want to position the socket, then pencil round the mounting box as a guide for where to chop out the wall.*

2 *Drill slightly within the pencil lines to the depth of the mounting box, then work along the lines with a bolster chisel before chopping out the recess.*

3 *Channel a cable run down the back of the skirting using a long, thin cold chisel. Alternatively, use a long masonry bit and an electric drill.*

4 *Thread the cable up from under the floor, through some PVC conduiting behind the skirting and into the mounting box.*

5 *Push the box into position, then use a bradawl to mark where the fixing holes are to go in the recess. Remove the box and drill and plug the holes.*

6 *Set the box back into place and screw it tightly into the recess. Check that it is level, and then make good if necessary with plaster or filler.*

Keith Morris

Keith Morris

Flush-fixing a socket on a plasterboard wall is a little more involved.

If you choose to surface-mount the socket, all you have to do is to fix a PVC or metal box directly to the wall after you've removed the knockout (and, if metal, use a grommet) where you want the cable to enter. The socket can then be screwed directly to this.

Laying in the cable

Because cable is expensive, it's best to plan the spur so that it uses as little cable as possible. When you channel cable into a wall you'll need to chase out a shallow run, fix the cable in position with clips, then plaster over it. But the best method of all is to run the cable in oval PVC conduiting. It won't give any more protection against an electric drill, but it'll prevent any possible reaction between the plaster making good and the cable sheathing. Always channel horizontally or vertically, and never diagonally, so it's easier to trace the wiring run when you've completed decorating. You can then avoid the cable when fixing something to the wall.

Normally the cable will drop down to below floor level to connect into the circuit. Rather than remove the skirting to get the cable down

Ready Reference

WARNING
The power supply to the sockets will probably be wired as a ring circuit. You can add a spur to this provided the number of spurs doesn't exceed the number of sockets on the ring.

CABLE SIZE
New spurs should be in 2.5mm^2 cable

CHECKING OUT A RING CIRCUIT
These instructions assume that your installation conforms to the Wiring Regulations. If it seems to have been modified in an unauthorised way, get a qualified electrician to check it.

TURN OFF THE POWER SUPPLY. Start by undoing a socket near where you want to install the new socket.

AT A SINGLE SOCKET
One cable entering
Socket is on the end of a spur. There could be another single socket on the branch.
Action: trace cable. If it goes to another single socket and this socket has only two cables going to it, then you have found an intermediate socket on the spur. It it goes to a double socket where there are three cables, then the single socket is the only socket on the spur. It's the same if the cable goes to a junction box.

Two cables entering
Socket could be on the ring, or it could be the intermediate socket on a spur.
Action: You'll need to trace the cable runs. If the cable is the only one going to another single socket, then the socket is on a spur. If the cable makes up one of two cables in another socket then it's on the ring.

Three cables entering
Socket is on the ring with a spur leading from it.
Action: to check which cable is which you'll need to trace the cable runs.

AT A DOUBLE SOCKET
One cable entering
Socket is on a spur. You can't connect a new socket from this.
Two cables entering
Socket is on the ring. You can connect a spur into this.
Three cables entering
Socket is on the ring with a spur leading from it. Checking to see which cable is which is the same as for a single socket with three cables. You can't connect a spur from this socket.

FLUSH FITTING IN A PLASTERBOARD WALL

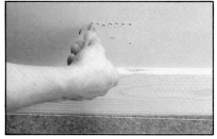

1 *Knock along the cavity wall to locate a stud near where you want the socket. Pierce the wall with a bradawl to locate the centre of the upright.*

2 *Position the box centrally over the stud and pencil round it. Be as accurate as you can because eventually the box should fit neatly in the opening.*

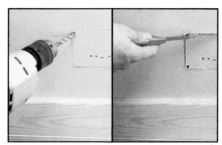

3 *Drill the corners of the guidelines. Push a pad saw (or keyhole saw) into one of them and cut along the lines. The plasterboard will come out in one piece.*

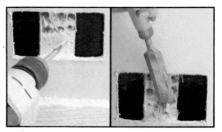

4 *Once you've exposed the stud, you'll need to remove some of the wood so the box can be fully recessed. You can do this with a drill and chisel.*

5 *Use a long drill bit to drill down through the baseplate of the stud partition. Try and keep the drill as upright as possible.*

6 *Lay the cable from the point where it joins the main circuit and thread it up through the hole in the baseplate and into the box.*

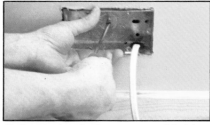

7 *Set the box in the recess and fix it in place by screwing to the stud. The cable end can now be prepared and connected to the socket terminals.*

8 *Where there is no stud to fix to, fit special lugs to the box sides. These press against the plasterboard's inner face when the faceplate is attached.*

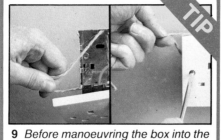

9 *Before manoeuvring the box into the recess, thread some string through the front so you can hold it in position.*

Jem Grischotti

CONNECTING THE NEW SOCKET

1 *Strip back the sheathing of the cable by running a sharp knife down the side of the uninsulated earth. Avoid damaging the other cores.*

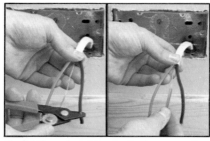

2 *Set the wire strippers to the correct gauge and remove about 9mm (³⁄₈in) of insulation from the cores. Sleeve the earth core in green/yellow PVC.*

3 *Connect the three cores to the relevant terminals of the socket, making sure no exposed core is showing. Then screw the socket into position.*

Keith Morris

the back you can use a long steel cold chisel to chip out a groove. You'll then have to drill down through the end of the floorboard with a wood bit. Alternatively, you can use a long masonry bit with an electric drill to complete the task.

But if the floor is solid, the ring is usually in the ceiling void above, in which case the branch will drop down from the ceiling. And this will involve a considerable amount of channelling out if you want to install the new socket near floor level.

Stud partition walls also present a few problems. If the socket is near the floor, you should be able to get a long drill bit through the hole you cut for the socket to drill through the baseplate and floorboard. You can then thread the cable through. But if the socket is to be placed higher up the wall, noggings and sound insulation material may prevent the cable being drawn through the cavity. In this case you will probably have to surface-mount the cable.

In fact, surface-mounting is the easiest method of running the cable. All you do is fix special plastic conduit to the wall and lay the cable inside before clipping on the lid. But many people regard this as an ugly solution.

When laying cable under ground floor floorboards you should clip it to the sides of the joists about 50mm (2in) below the surface so that it doesn't droop on the ground. Cable in the ceiling void can rest on the surface.

When you have to cross joists, you'll need to drill 16mm (5⁄8in) holes about 50mm (2in) below the level of the floorboards. The cable is threaded through them and so is well clear of any floorboard fixing nails.

Connecting into the circuit

If you use a junction box, you'll need one with three terminals inside. You have to connect the live conductors (those with red insulation) of the circuit cable and the spur to one terminal, the neutral conductors (black insulation) to another, and the earth wires to the third. Sleeve the earth wires in green/yellow PVC first.

You might decide that it's easier to connect into the back of an existing socket rather than use a junction box, although this will probably mean some extra channelling on the wall. Space is limited at the back of a socket so it may be difficult to fit the conductors to the relevant terminals. However, this method is ideal if the new socket that you're fitting on one wall is back-to-back with an existing fitting. By carefully drilling through the wall a length of cable can be linked from the old socket into the new.

CONNECTING INTO THE CIRCUIT

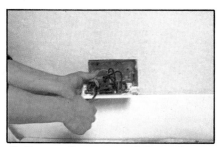

1 *Unscrew a nearby socket to check that it's on the ring – normally there'll be two red, two black and two earth wires. Sometimes the earths are in one sleeve.*

2 *Usually it's easier to push the new cable up into the mounting box from below the floor, although you might prefer to take it the other way.*

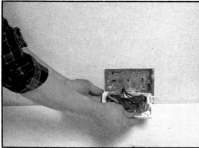

3 *Prepare the cores and sleeve the earth of the new cable, then connect them into the appropriate terminals on the back of the socket.*

4 *If installing a junction box use a three-terminal type. Connect the red conductors to one terminal, the blacks to another and the earths to a third.*

Keith Morris

Ready Reference

SOCKET MOUNTINGS

Metal boxes are recessed into the wall and provide a fixing for the socket itself. Knockouts are provided in the back, sides and ends to allow the cable to enter the box. Rubber grommets are fitted round the hole so the cable doesn't chafe against the metal edges.

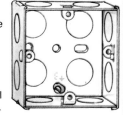

Elongated screw slots allow box to be levelled when fixed to wall.

Adjustable lugs enable final adjustments to level of faceplate on wall.

Boxes are usually 35mm deep, but with single-brick walls boxes 25mm deep should be used, along with accessories having deeper-than-usual faceplates.

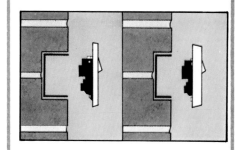

Lugs can be fitted to a metal box so that it can be fitted into stud partition walls.

Surface-mounted boxes (usually white plastic) are 35mm deep, and are simply screwed to the wall surface where required.

TIP: FIT SAFETY PLATES

Safety plates can be fitted to sockets to prevent young children playing with them.

PROBLEMS

● **Crumbly plaster** There's little that can be done other than cutting back to sound area. Position box and socket as required then make good surrounding area.

● **Poor bricks** Because of soft bricks you can quite easily chop out too big a recess for the box. Pack the recess with dabs of mortar or plaster.

● **Cavity Walls** To prevent breaking through into the cavity only chop out a recess big enough to take a shallow box, about 25mm (1in).

RUNNING CABLE

The hardest part of the average electrical job is running the cables: it takes up a lot of time and a lot of effort. But there are certain techniques used by experts which can make it much easier.

Before you get involved in the details of how to install the wiring, there's one simple question you must answer. Does it matter if the cable runs show? This is because there are only two approaches to the job of running cable. Either you fix the cable to the surface of the wall, or you conceal it. The first option is far quicker and easier but doesn't look particularly attractive; it's good enough for use in, say, an understairs cupboard. For a neater finish, using this method, you can smarten up the cable runs by boxing them in with some trunking. Many people, however, prefer to conceal the wiring completely by taking it under the floor, over the ceiling, or in walls.

TYPICAL CABLE RUNS

More and more electrical equipment is now being used in the home. And the chances are that sooner or later you will want to install a new power point, wall or ceiling light, or another switch. In which case you will have to get power to your new accessory. To do that will involve running cable from an existing circuit or installing a completely new one. Running cable to a new appliance can be the hardest part of any job and, as the illustration on the right shows, you will be involved in trailing cable across the roof space or ceiling void, channelling it down walls and threading it behind partitions as well as taking it under floorboards. But it's much easier than it seems. There are a number of tricks of the trade that will make any electrical job simpler and less time consuming. For example, once you can 'fish' cable, the daunting task of running it under a floor is simple.

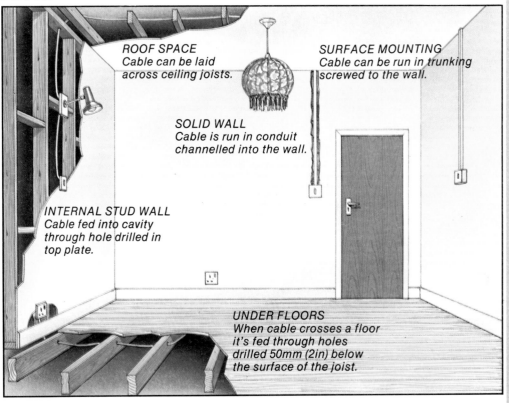

ROOF SPACE
Cable can be laid across ceiling joists.

SURFACE MOUNTING
Cable can be run in trunking screwed to the wall.

SOLID WALL
Cable is run in conduit channelled into the wall.

INTERNAL STUD WALL
Cable fed into cavity through hole drilled in top plate.

UNDER FLOORS
When cable crosses a floor it's fed through holes drilled 50mm (2in) below the surface of the joist.

SURFACE MOUNTING CABLE

1 *To run cable in trunking, cut the trunking to length and fix the channel half to the wall with screws and wall plugs at 450mm (18in) centres.*

2 *Run the cable and press it firmly into the channel as far as it will go, carefully smoothing it out to avoid kinks and twists.*

3 *Next, snap the trunking's capping piece over the channelling, tapping it firmly along its length with your hand to lock it into place.*

4 *If the cable is to be on show, merely secure it every 225mm (9in) with cable clips. Fit them over the cable and drive home the fixing pins.*

Planning the route

Having made your decision you must now work out a suitable route for the cable to follow.

If it is to be surface-mounted – with or without trunking – run the cable around window and door frames, just above skirting boards and picture rails, down the corners of the room, or along the angle between wall and ceiling. This not only helps conceal the cable's presence, but also protects it against accidental damage. This last point is most important, and is the reason why you must never run cable over a floor.

With concealed wiring, the position is more complicated. When running cable under a floor or above a ceiling, you must allow for the direction in which the joists run – normally at right angles to the floorboards – and use an indirect route, taking it parallel to the joists and/or at right angles to them.

When running cable within a wall, the cable should *always* run vertically or horizontally from whatever it supplies, *never* diagonally.

Surface-mounting techniques

If you are leaving the cable on show, all you need do is cut it to length, and fix it to the surface with a cable clip about every 225mm (9in), making sure it is free from kinks and twists. With modern cable clips, simply fit the groove in the plastic block over the cable and drive home the small pin provided.

Surface mounting cable within trunking involves a bit more work. Having obtained the right size of PVC trunking, build up the run a section at a time, cutting the trunking to length with a hacksaw. Once each piece is cut, separate it into its two parts – the

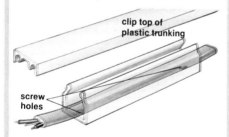
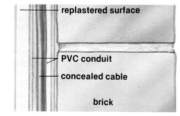

channelling and capping – and fix the channel to the wall with screws and wall plugs at roughly 450mm (18in) intervals (you may have to drill screw clearance holes in the channelling yourself).

Continue in this way until the run is complete. Turn corners by using proprietary fittings or by angling the ends of two pieces of trunking to form a neatly mitred joint, then run the cable. Press this firmly into the channel, and finish off by snapping the capping pieces firmly into place.

Concealing cables in walls

There are two ways to conceal cable in a wall. With a solid wall, chop a channel (called a 'chase') out of the plaster using a club hammer and bolster chisel, carefully continuing this behind any skirting boards, picture rails, and coverings. You could now run the cable in this chase and plaster over it. However, to give the cable some protection, it is better to fit a length of PVC conduit into the chase and run the cable through this before replastering.

To continue the run either above the ceiling or through the floor before you position the conduit, use a long drill bit so you can drill through the floor behind the skirting board. If a joist blocks the hole, angle the drill sufficiently to avoid it.

With a hollow internal partition wall, the job is rather easier, because you can run the cable within the cavity.

First drill a hole in the wall where the cable is to emerge, making sure you go right through into the cavity. Your next step is to gain access to the timber 'plate' at the very top of the wall, either by going up into the loft, or by lifting floorboards in the room above. Drill a 19mm (¾in) hole through the plate, at a point vertically above the first hole, or as near vertically above it as possible.

All that remains is to tie the cable you wish to run to a length of stout 'draw' wire – single-core earth cable is often used – and then to tie the free end of this wire to a length of string. To the free end of the string, tie a small weight, and drop the weight through the hole at the top of the wall. Then all you do is make a hook in a piece of stout wire, insert it in the cavity, catch hold of the string and pull it (and in turn the draw wire and cable) through the hole in the room below.

What are the snags? There are two. You may find that, at some point between the two holes, the cavity is blocked by a horizontal timber called a noggin. If this happens, try to reach the noggin from above with a long auger bit (you should be able to hire one) and drill through it. Failing that, chisel through the wall surface, cut a notch in the side of the noggin, pass the cable through the notch, and then make good.

The second snag is that you may not be

CHASING OUT SOLID WALLS

1 *Mark out the cable run using a length of conduit, and chop a channel ('chase') in the wall to receive it, using a club hammer and a bolster chisel.*

2 *Continue the chase behind any coving, skirting board, or picture rail by chipping out the plaster there with a long, narrow cold chisel.*

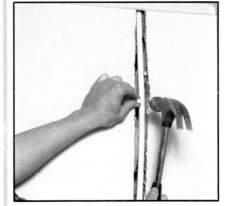

3 *Cut a length of PVC conduit to fit, and lay it in the chase, securing it temporarily with clout nails driven into the wall's mortar joints.*

4 *Pull the cable through the conduit, then make good the wall by filling in over the conduit with plaster or cellulose filler.*

able to reach the top plate to drill it. In which case, either give up the ideas of having concealed wiring, or try a variation on the second method used to run cable into the cavity from below the floor.

Here, it is sometimes possible to lift a couple of floorboards and drill up through the plate forming the bottom of the wall. Failing that you have to take a very long drill bit, drill through the wall into the cavity, then continue drilling through into the timber plate. You can now use the weighted string trick to feed the cable in through the hole in the wall, and out under the floor.

Running cable beneath a floor

The technique for running cable beneath a suspended timber floor depends on whether the floor is on an upper storey and so has a ceiling underneath, or is on a ground floor

with empty space below. If it's a ground floor, it may be possible to crawl underneath and secure the cable to the sides of the joists with cable clips, or to pass it through 19mm (¾in) diameter holes drilled in the joists at least 50mm (2in) below their top edge. This prevents anyone nailing into the floor and hitting the cable.

If you cannot crawl underneath, then the cable can be left loose in the void. But how do you run it without lifting the entire floor? The answer is you use another trick, called 'fishing'.

For this, you need a piece of stiff but reasonably flexible galvanised wire, say 14 standard wire gauge (swg), rather longer than the intended cable run, and a piece of thicker, more rigid wire, about 1m in length. Each piece should have one end bent to form a hook.

Lift a floorboard at each end of the

COPING WITH STUD WALLS

1 Drill a hole in the wall where the cable is to emerge, then bore a second hole in the wooden plate forming the top of the wall.

2 Tie a weight to a length of string and lower this through the hole in the wall plate. Tie the free end of the string to a stout 'draw' wire.

3 If the weight gets blocked on its way to the hole in the wall, use a long auger bit to drill through the noggin obstructing it.

4 Fish out the weighted string through the hole in the wall, using a piece of wire bent to form a hook. Now, pull through the draw wire.

5 Tie the draw wire to the cable you wish to run, then return to the hole in the wall's top plate, and use the string to pull up the draw wire.

6 Then use the draw wire to pull the length of cable through. Remember, do this smoothly and don't use force if there's an obstruction.

Ready Reference

TRICKS OF THE TRADE

Hollow internal partition wall

Drill a hole in the top or bottom plate, then drill another in the wall where the cable is to emerge. Drop a weighted piece of string through one of the holes and hook it out through the other. Use this to pull through a stout draw wire which is attached to the cable.

● if the weighted piece of string gets obstructed by a noggin or its way to the hole in the wall, use a long auger bit to drill through the noggin.

● don't pull the cable through with the weighted string – the string tends to snap

● never run cable down the cavity of an external wall– treat these as solid walls.

Under floors

Use a technique known as fishing:
● lift the floorboards at either end of the run
● thread stiff wire beneath the floor through one hole and hook it out of the other with another piece of wire
● use the longer piece of wire to pull the cable through.

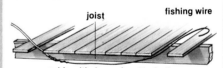

joist   fishing wire

cable with draw wire attached

cable pulled through

● if there's a gap beneath a ground floor you can 'fish' the cable diagonally across the room under the joist

● if the gap under the joists is large enough you can crawl in the space clipping the cable to the joists

● where the cable crosses the joists at right angles, run it through holes drilled 50mm (2in) below their top edges.

Over ceilings

If you can get above the ceiling into a loft, you can clip the cables to the joists. Otherwise you'll have to 'fish' the cable across (see above).

If you can't get above the ceiling and fishing doesn't work you'll have to surface-mount the cable.

INSTALLING CONVENIENCE CONTROLS

You can make your life more comfortable and your home that much more secure by installing a variety of special controls for your lighting and electrical appliances.

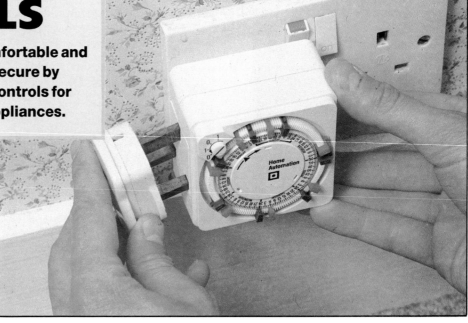

Special controls for electric appliances can be a real boon to the householder. They can make life much more comfortable by automatically switching appliances on and off, and more economic by preventing appliances from being left on to consume costly electricity. They can also help to make the home more secure by controlling lights, radios and curtains to give would-be burglars the impression that there's someone in.

But before you dash off to your local electrical supplies shop, pause for a moment's reflection. Are you being tempted by the sheer novelty of automatic controls? Remember, all automation is expensive, so it pays to take a slightly more hard-headed attitude towards making the decision. First of all, make sure that the equipment will actually do the job you have in mind. Read all the technical specifications carefully. You don't want to discover that your new dimmer light switch won't allow two-way switching or won't work on fluorescent lights. Secondly, do make sure that you know exactly what you're getting for your money. You may find out that the price quoted in the sales leaflet is just a basic 'starter kit' and that you'll have to spend more money to achieve the full performance suggested by the advertisement. Thirdly, consider whether it's actually worth automating a particular appliance; after all, many of the currently available devices perform only fairly menial tasks. Finally, remember that the development of home technology is advancing rapidly; buy now and you may well find that next year you can buy something that does more and does it cheaper.

Dimmer switches

Although dimmer switches offer no automatic form of control, they are considerably more versatile than the conventional rocker switch – allowing you greater flexibility in controlling the level of artificial lighting in the room where they are installed. They're usually used to control tungsten filament lights and spotlights. However, you can dim even a fluorescent lamp provided you have a special choke for the fitting. Various types of dimmer switches are available, ranging from those

with a simple rotary knob to those with a separate on/off switch. Touch dimmers are the most recent development.

Connecting a dimmer switch into your existing circuit is perfectly straightforward. Switch off at the mains and remove the fuse for the particular circuit you're working on; then you can switch the mains back on and have some light to work by. Unscrew the faceplate of your existing switch and pull it carefully away from the mounting box. This will give you enough room in which to disconnect the cable cores. Then simply connect up the cores to the dimmer switch according to the manufacturer's instructions and screw the faceplate to the box. If you want to put a dimmer into a two-way system then remember you can only replace one of the switches with a dimmer. Most one-gang dimmers will fit a standard plaster-depth or surface-mounted box, but some need a deeper box. Two-gang and multi-gang dimmers may need a double box.

Automatic light controls

The most basic automatic light switch is the time delay switch designed primarily for use on communal landings and stairwells. When you want light, all you do is switch on and leave the device to turn the light off again after a pre-set interval – usually anything from five to twenty minutes, depending on the model. Most versions allow you to adjust the timing to suit your needs. The most simple type works by means of a large spring-loaded button, while more sophisticated models use electronic timers and touch plate controls.

Time delay faders are a sort of cross between a dimmer and a time delay switch. They fade out the light gradually over a pre-set delay time and so are extremely handy for a child's bedroom, say. These are normally fitted with dual touch plate controls; the upper plate allows the switch to work like a conventional touch dimmer, the lower one triggers the dimming sequence. Time delay faders can be simply installed in the place of ordinary rocker switches, but, as a rule, they are not suitable for use with fluorescent lights.

Security switches

These switches are useful from a security point of view because lights are thereby turned on and off automatically to convince would-be burglars that you're at home. The basic switch incorporates a light-sensing device that will turn on the light at dusk and then off after a certain period of time (usually between two and ten hours). The faceplate carries a dial for selecting the time the light is on, and two switches, one to allow the switch to function as an ordinary on/off switch and the other to activate the light sensing device. It's not a good idea to fit this type of switch in unusually light or dark situations where the light-sensing device could get confused; avoid fixing it in a corner where there is little natural light or close to a window by a street light.

Photoelectric security switches don't, as a rule, incorporate on/off switches, so, if necessary, manual override will have to be provided separately. However, these switches are usually designed to be installed outside to control lights in exposed conditions. They

INSTALLING A DIMMER SWITCH

1 *Switch off at the mains and remove the lighting circuit fuse; then switch the power back on and unscrew the existing faceplate from its mounting box.*

2 *Disconnect the old switch. Before fitting the dimmer switch brush away any plaster or debris that's fallen into the mounting box.*

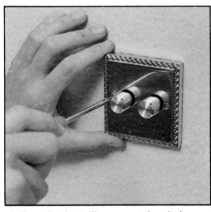

3 *Make the connections to the new switch following the manufacturer's instructions. You may have to remove covers to get access to the terminals.*

4 *If you're installing a metal switch, make sure the faceplate is earthed by linking it with the box earth terminal. Then screw the faceplate in place.*

USING A PLUG-IN DIMMER

1 *Plug-in dimmers can be easily moved, allowing you to dim any table lamps. They are not suitable for lamps below 40W or above 400W.*

2 *Simply plug the lamp into the dimmer socket. You'll then be able to control the brightness by moving the dial on the dimmer face.*

Ready Reference

INSTALLING DIMMER SWITCHES

Dimmer switches can easily replace one-way rocker switches and most two-way switches. However, in a two-way system only one switch need be replaced.

CONTROLLING THE LIGHT

There are three ways of switching lights controlled by a dimmer, depending on which model you fit;
● rotating an on/off knob
● flicking a separate rocker switch incorporated on the face plate
● tapping the touch plate.

MOUNTING BOXES

Most one-gang dimmer switches will fit into existing square plaster-depth (16mm/⅝in deep) mounting boxes (A), and have standard screw fixings.

Some dimmer switches will require deeper boxes – either 25mm (1in) or 35mm (1⅜in). If you're installing three – or four-gang switches, then you'll probably have to install rectangular mounting boxes (B). These are also available in various depths.

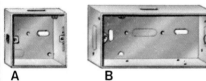

A   **B**

WATTAGE LIMITS

Dimmer switches operate between minimum and maximum wattage limits. Before buying one, check the light wattage of each lamp it will control. The minimum wattage is likely to be about 60W, so if you have a 40W lamp you won't be able to dim it successfully. On some switches the minimum can be as high as 120W, so a single 100W lamp would be too low.

The maximum wattage can be as low as 400W, which means that some switches would be unable to control a section of track lighting with, say, five 100W lamps.

DEALING WITH THE CORES

When replacing switches with dimmers, always follow the manufacturer's instructions. In particular
● take note of existing core connections
● apply the equivalent coloured insulation tape round cores with faded insulation so they'll be readily identifiable in the future
● don't separate cores that are joined together. Just fit them into the same terminal on the new dimmer.

INSTALLING A TIME-DELAY SWITCH

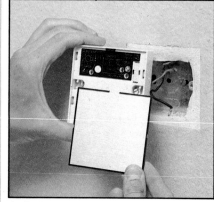

1 *Switch off at the mains and remove the existing switch. Take off the front cover of the switch to gain access to the terminal screws.*

2 *Connect the cores to the terminals as indicated on the switch. You can then fix the switch to the mounting box with the screws provided.*

3 *You can set the switch so the light will be switched off up to twenty minutes after being turned on. Use the special screwdriver to adjust the delay.*

4 *Finally, fit the touch plate back in position. Switch on at the mains and test the time setting. If necessary, adjust the setting again.*

FITTING A SECURITY SWITCH

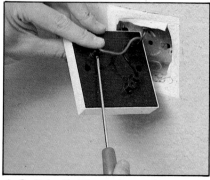

1 *Switch off at the mains and remove your old switch. Make the connections to the security switch and screw it to the mounting box.*

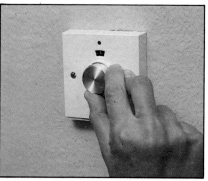

2 *You can programme the light switch to turn interior and exterior lights on or off automatically. Programmes can be easily cleared and overridden.*

can usually be mounted within plastic conduit systems and will switch outside lights on at dusk and off at dawn, so giving your home extra security when no one's in. And, of course, you'll have the lights on for you when you return from an evening out. Most exterior switches incorporate a designed time delay of 1 to 2 minutes so that car headlights won't cause the light to go off.

Automatic power control

Plug-in timers are merely a sort of sophisticated plug-in adaptor for ordinary power sockets. Once you have one in place, all you do is plug in whatever device you want the timer to control. This can be just about anything that can be powered from your home's ring circuit – standard lamps, radiators, blankets and radios. You programme the timer by using small pegs fixed in special holes on the dials or by moving small spring-loaded lugs; the timer will automatically turn the power on and off at these pre-set times.

The minimum period the power can be on for is thirty minutes, although you can control the timer to the nearest fifteen minutes. The on/off pegs are usually protected by a clear dust cover and spare pegs are normally provided with each timer so that more than one operation can be made in each cycle. Most basic versions will operate on a twenty-four hour cycle, although timers programmable for up to seven days are available. With these the setting intervals tend to be quite long – up to two hours in some cases. However, the timer with a longer cycle will obviously be more useful from a security point of view, since you can set it to turn lights on and off at different times each day.

Other control gear

Other devices on the market perform more specific tasks. An electric curtain controller, for example, will both open and close corded curtains provided the weight of pull on the cord required to do so is no greater than 8kg (17½lbs). The motor is controlled by a two-position switch and is simply plugged into the mains. As a safety precaution it will only operate for a period of five minutes before cutting out; that way any accidents in the event of a cord failure will be prevented.

Fan controllers are suitable for use with most electric extractor fans. They are basically specialised dimmer switches that allow you to vary the speed of the fan. They're normally fitted with a separate on/off switch and in some cases a switch for opening and closing the shutters found on very large fans. Other models also have reversing switches. Finally, immersion heater timers work in much the same way as plug-in timers, allowing a number of switching operations per day or per seven days.

FITTING A CURTAIN CONTROLLER

1 Gain access to your electric curtain controller by removing the two screws on top of the casing and then sliding it away from the housing.

2 You can only use the curtain controller with curtains that have endless cord. Feed the cord through the front slot and position it round the drive pulley.

3 Position the curtain controller where you want to fix it to the wall. The cord must not chafe on the housing. Drill and plug the wall and screw the box in place.

4 Slide the cover back onto the housing and fit the screws. Make sure the cords are in line with the top opening and there's no obstruction.

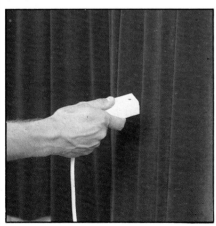

5 Plug in the power lead. You'll then be able to open and close your curtain by using the rocker switch that is already fitted to the switch cable.

6 If you find that the curtains don't close fully then you'll have to make adjustments to the pulley wheel using the small hexagon wrench provided.

PLUG-IN TIMERS

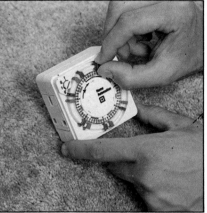

1 Programme the plug-in timer by first setting it to the correct day and time. Then slot in the nibs that will turn the appliance on and off.

2 Plug the timer in the nearest socket. You'll then be able to plug in the appliance. Finally, switch on both the appliance and the socket.

3 You can override the timer by turning the control knob anti-clockwise one position. Spare nibs for further programming are supplied with the timer.

FITTING DOOR BELLS

If you have difficulty hearing visitors when they knock on your front door, the solution is to install a new bell, buzzer or set of chimes. Should one prove inadequate, you can always connect up an extension bell as well, so your system is even more efficient.

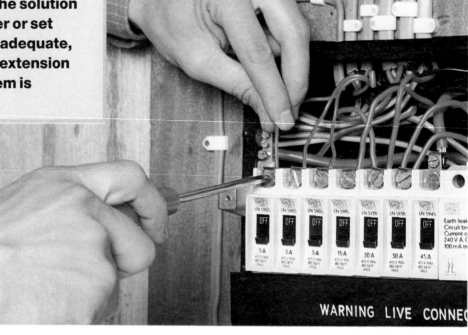

WARNING LIVE CONNEC

Imagine if someone was to knock on your front door while you were busy at the back of the house; the chances are you'd never hear them. Similarly, if you were in the garden and visitors called round, then the likelihood of them attracting your attention before they'd given up knocking on your door and gone home, is minimal. The obvious answer is to install a new bell, buzzer or set of chimes.

This needn't be a daunting job and in fact you'll find that even the most elaborate of the systems on the market is perfectly straightforward to install. Indeed, your most difficult task is likely to be deciding what sort of sound you want to announce the arrival of your visitors. The best thing to do is to visit an electrical shop where they're likely to have a display of what is available. Then all you have to do is listen to the various tones and decide which you like; but remember, whatever you install is likely to last for a long time, so you're going to have to pick a bell, buzzer or set of chimes which won't irritate you.

Making your choice

There are two principal types of electric bell, either of which you can install in your home. The most common is the trembler bell, which operates on what is called a make-and-break system. When an electric current is passed through the bell, the cores of an electromagnet are activated and they attract an arm, to which a striker and knob are attached; this then strikes a gong. At the same instant, the make-and-break contacts open, breaking the circuit and cutting off the current and causing the arm to return to its original position. When this happens, the circuit is reformed so the whole process is repeated – causing the arm to oscillate or 'tremble' to produce the familiar ringing of the bell – provided, of course, the bell push in the circuit is being depressed. The frequency of the trembling, and therefore the tone of the ring, can be altered simply by adjusting the contact screw. As soon as the finger is lifted off the bell push, the circuit is broken completely and the bell stops ringing. The big advantage of the trembler is that it will operate on both ordinary direct current (DC) from a battery or else on alternating current (AC)

CONNECTING BELLS TO BATTERIES

1 *If your bell has a separate battery you'll need two lengths of bell wire. The two floating cores should be joined and protected by insulating tape.*

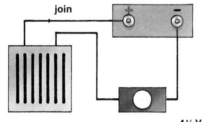

2 *Connecting two bells in parallel is one way of installing an extension bell. Remember to use identical bells, otherwise the system won't work.*

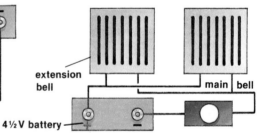

extension bell — main bell — 4½V battery

3 *Connecting two bells in series is better as there is no danger of one bell starving the other of power. But don't use two trembler bells together.*

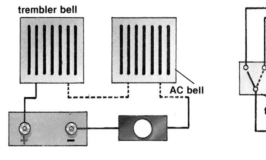

trembler bell — AC bell

4 *You can use an ordinary two-way switch as a changeover switch. That way you'll be able to select which bell you want working at a particular time.*

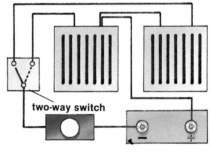

two-way switch

INSTALLING A BELL PUSH

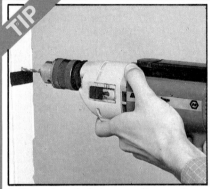

1 To make a hole in your door post, you'll probably have to drill through from both sides. Stick some tape right round the post to act as a guide.

2 Feed through the twin bell wire and check you have enough to make the connections. You can pull back the surplus after the push is fitted.

3 Connect the two cores to the two terminals on the bell push and then use a drill or bradawl to make pilot holes to fix the push to the post.

4 Finally use wood screws to fix the push securely in place. Bed the push on non-setting mastic if it will be exposed to rain.

Ready Reference

TIP: POSITIONING THE UNIT

Bear these points in mind when siting a bell or buzzer:
● a single bell or buzzer should be mounted in the hall, from where it will probably be heard throughout the house
● the kitchen is a good place for an extension bell, but it should be sited away from a source of steam as the mechanism could easily get damaged
● chimes with long tubes should be mounted where they won't get easily knocked.

POWERING AN EXTENSION BELL

If your extension bell is connected in series to the main one, twice the voltage will be required. You can provide this,
● with a more powerful battery
● by connecting two 4½V batteries in series.

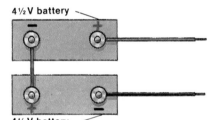

CHOOSING BELL PUSHES

A wide variety of bell pushes is available, including:
● illuminated pushes that can be used only when the circuit is powered by a transformer. This is because the bulb is continually alight, except when the push is used, and would quickly run down a battery
● small button pushes designed to take up as little room as possible on your door post
● pushes that have room for a name label. They should all be carefully positioned where they are easily accessible, clearly visible and not exposed to the weather.

MECHANICAL BELLS

As an alternative to electrical bells, you could choose a mechanical one. These work in one of three ways:
● by clockwork – they'll ring about 100 times before needing to be wound up
● by pulling a handle to cause a bell to rock on a pivot
● by pressure on a push that will make a mechanical chime sound.

Mechanical bells are usually mounted on the inner face of the front door and are extremely simple to fit.

---

from the mains, provided it comes via a low-voltage transformer.

An AC bell is similar in principle to the trembler bell, but has no make-and-break contact device. As a result it will only operate on AC current from the mains and must therefore be connected to a suitable transformer. It is the alternating pattern of the current itself that provides the required movement in the arm to make the bell ring.

A buzzer is basically an electric bell minus the striker and bell dome. That means that it's the arm hitting the electro-magnets that produces the buzzing noise. It, too, is made in DC versions for operation from a battery and in AC versions for use from the mains.

Chimes are more elaborate than simple bells and buzzers, and are, inevitably, more expensive. When the bell push is pressed, the current activates an electro-magnet, and a double-ended plunger is drawn across to strike one of the chime bars. When the bell push is released, it is sent back by the pressure of a spring to strike the second bar.

There is a wide range of models on the market and the most simple produces a two-note 'ding-dong' ring. Other models have special chimes playing more notes and some contain cassettes which produce familiar bars from popular tunes. Chimes can look rather ugly. This is because some models have long chime tubes that hang down underneath the casing. If you don't like the look of them, buy bar chimes which have all their apparatus concealed within the unit.

When choosing which type of bell, buzzer or chimes you want, it's well worth considering how it obtains its power, as well as what it sounds like. Where the power source is likely to be a mains transformer, either type of bell or buzzer may be used, but you'll probably find an AC bell or buzzer best. This is because

CONNECTING TO THE MAINS

1 *If you're going to connect your transformer to a spare fuseway, you'll have to fix it to the wall or back-board close to your consumer unit.*

2 *Run in the twin bell wire, fixing it to the wall with tacks or clips. Connect it to the secondary terminals that will provide the correct voltage.*

3 *Connect a length of 1.0mm^2 two-core and earth cable to the primary terminals. Ignore the earth core as most transformers don't need earthing.*

4 *Clip the cable to the wall and after switching off at the mains connect it to a spare 5A fuseway in the unit. Remember to label the fuseway.*

the middle, it's a good idea to mark the line of the intended hole on the post with a pencil or a length of tape. Provided your bell contains its battery, a single twin wire is all that's needed to link the bell and its push. This should run along as unobtrusive a route as possible and if you've got a picture rail in the hall you'll probably find it ideal to fix the wire on top. In fact the wire is so small that it's rarely noticed and can be kept in place with bell wire tacks. All you do is press the point between the two insulated cores of the bell wire and then knock it into the timber. If you don't want to go to that trouble, however, you could use self-adhesive bell wire.

You can then pass the wire through the hole drilled in the door post and, after removing the cover from the bell push, connect it to the two terminals. The wire is then drawn back through the hole so no excess wire remains on the outside of the door post, and the push can then be fixed to the door post. This is simply done by drilling a couple of pilot holes and then fixing it with wood screws; once it's fixed you can then replace the cover. The other end of the wire should then be connected to the bell terminals and, with the battery fitted, it'll be ready for use.

If, however, your battery has to be mounted separately, or else you're using a transformer, the circuitry is altered slightly. Only one of the cores from the push is connected to the bell itself and you have to run another length of bell wire from the spare bell terminal to the battery. Both cores of this second wire are then connected to the battery, while at the bell end the core which remains unconnected is joined, by means of a small connector, to the floating core running from the bell push.

Installing a transformer

The function of a transformer is to reduce the mains voltage so that it's safe to use with bells, buzzers and chimes. It's important to make sure that it is a bell transformer and is therefore designed specifically for this purpose.

The transformer will have two sets of terminals. One set is for the cable linking it to the 240V mains supply, while the others are low voltage and commonly have outputs of 3, 5 and 8 volts. You can also get transformers which have outputs of 4, 8 and 12 volts. Bells and buzzers usually require only 3 or 5 volts, while chimes are normally connected to the 8V terminals, although some models require 12V.

You can connect the transformer to the mains simply by plugging it into a spare socket, in which case the plug should have its 13A fuse replaced with a 3A one. You could also run a fused spur from the mains to the transformer – in which case you'd use a fused connection unit, also fitted with a 3A fuse.

Another way of obtaining mains power for your bell, buzzer or set of chimes is to connect

not only are they cheaper to buy, but with no make-and-break device there is the minimum of things that can go wrong: no contacts to corrode or burn and no adjusting screws to work loose and fall out.

Installing a bell

The simple circuit required for installing a bell is also suitable for the installation of a buzzer or a set of door chimes. You'll obviously require the new bell unit itself, a bell push, a length of twin bell wire, some tacks or insulated staples and a power source which will be either a 4½V battery or a special bell transformer. Bells, and all the necessary accessories and materials, are often available in kit form. You'll find that some bells have a special compartment in the unit for their battery; with others, the battery is housed separately. Remember, though, that circuit requirements are likely to vary between the

different models of bells, buzzers and chimes that are on the market. Before starting any installation, do make sure that you read all of the manufacturer's instructions very carefully.

The first thing to do is to fix the bell to the wall with woodscrews. It's best to fit it high up in the hall, where it'll be audible throughout the home, yet out of harm's way. If you're fixing into masonry, remember that you should drill and plug the holes before screwing the unit to the wall. You should then drill a hole about 6mm (¼in) in diameter in the front door post at the height of the bell push, so that the bell wire will be able to run straight through and into its back. Do make sure that this is at an easily accessible height for visitors, and that its position will be clearly visible. Unless you have a long drill bit, you might find that you'll have to drill in from both faces of the post. To help the two holes meet up with each other in

FITTING A CHIME UNIT

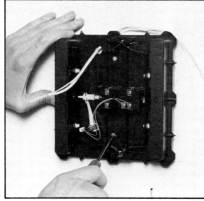

1 *Fix the bar chime unit high up on your hall wall. If you're fixing into masonry, you'll have to drill and plug the holes first.*

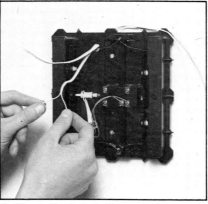

2 *Run in the twin bell wire and prepare the ends. Remember to read the maker's instructions carefully before making the connections.*

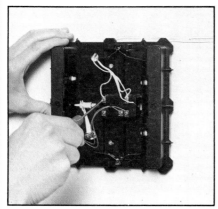

3 *Tack the wire to the wall, or if you're using self-adhesive wire make sure that it's pressed firmly in place. Then make the connections.*

4 *Finally, refit the cover of the chimes and, after switching on at the mains, check that your new system works efficiently.*

the transformer directly to the lighting circuit. This method should really only be used if you don't have a spare fuseway in your consumer unit or a free socket outlet, as it involves a bit of extra work. You'll have to break into the lighting circuit, and that means you'll have to lift the floorboards in the room above in order to gain access. Once you've done this and switched off at the mains, break into the circuit and fix a three-terminal junction box to a batten between two joists. Connect the cores of the lighting circuit cable to the junction box and then extend a branch cable from the box to the transformer. This cable should be 1.0mm² two-core and earth cable and will run to the primary terminals on the transformer. You can then connect the twin bell wire to the secondary terminals.

But probably the best way to obtain your mains power is to connect the transformer directly to a spare 5A fuseway in the con-

sumer unit. You should place the transformer close to the unit and run a short length of 1.0mm² two-core and earth cable to the spare 5A fuseway. On no account should you use bell wire for this section, as the cable will be carrying mains electricity which would overload it. For further details on selecting the correct cable or flex to connect to a spare fuseway see *Cable and Flex*. Once the bell wire has been connected to the two correct terminals on the other side of the transformer, the main switch can be turned on.

Installing an extension bell

There are times when your bell or buzzer can't be heard in the kitchen or garden. In that case the answer is to fit an extension bell. This is merely an extra bell or buzzer that is connected in parallel or in series to the main one (see diagram). If you are going to connect up the bells in parallel, then they

must be identical otherwise they won't work satisfactorily. In addition, the extension bell wire should not be too long, as this will result in erratic ringing.

It's probably better to connect the bells up in series. This is because the extra bell then becomes part of the whole circuit and the current must therefore pass through both bells. That means that there is no danger, as with parallel connection, of one bell 'starving' the other of current. However, if you're going to power the bells with a battery then you'll find that you can't successfully use two trembler bells in series. This is because the first bell would disrupt the current flow, and its subsequent irregular pattern would not allow the second one to work properly. The answer is to use an AC bell in conjunction with a trembler – that way there are no make-and-break contacts in the second bell – or else to modify a trembler bell by bridging the contacts with a piece of wire. In this case, the first bell will pass on identical current interruptions and so cause an identical trembling in the second bell.

An extension bell can also be connected to the terminals of door chimes, but it will ring only for the short time that the bell push is pressed by the caller. One way of avoiding this problem is to fit what is called a change-over switch. That way the caller is unlikely to hear the extension chimes and so depress the button longer.

Fitting a change-over switch

If you don't want both bells or chimes working at the same time, the answer is to fit a change-over switch. You can then have the main bell ringing when you are in the house, and the extension bell ringing when you're in the garden. The snag is, of course, that you must remember to switch the main bell back into the circuit when you come in from the garden; otherwise you'll be defeating the whole purpose of the switching arrangement. The correct switch to use is an ordinary two-way lighting switch. The twin wire from the bell push should be split, with one core going to the battery and the other going to the common terminal of the switch. From the L1 and L2 terminals of the switch, bell wire then runs to the main bell and the extension bell. For extra convenience, you could install a second bell push at the back door. If you already have a set of two-note chimes, then the front door push will give one note while the back door push will give the other; that way you'll know at which door the caller is. If, on the other hand, you already have a bell for the front door, then it's best to use a buzzer at the back so you can differentiate between them. Making the connections is not difficult, and as both pushes are unlikely to be used at the same moment both circuits can be connected to the same battery or transformer.

FLUORESCENT LIGHTING

Fluorescent lighting is glare-free and casts no hard, irritating shadows. It is therefore ideal for certain areas of the home, particularly the kitchen, bathroom, workroom and garage.

Many people have mixed feelings about fluorescent lights because of the nature or 'colour' of the light they emit. Admittedly they are not the best form of main lighting for living or dining areas as the light is harsh compared to ordinary tungsten filament light and doesn't give a relaxed atmosphere to the room. Nevertheless, they are ideal where good all-round lighting is required.

Fluorescent lighting can be fitted at any lighting point. However, an ordinary ceiling rose on a loop-in circuit will require some minor modification to the fixed wiring. This is not a difficult operation.

Types and uses

There are two basic types of fluorescent fitting – linear and circular – and both are made in a range of sizes. Circular tubes, in particular, are becoming more popular as they greatly improve the light output from a ceiling point and can be fitted flush to the ceiling and disguised with an attractive glass diffuser. The straight tubes likewise spread light evenly in a room, again often aided by a diffuser. In this case it's usually a corrugated or dimpled cover which is clipped over the fitting.

Fluorescent lights come in a variety of sizes; as a result they can be used for all sorts of purposes in kitchens, bathrooms, and in more specialised areas. For example, small tubes are ideal for concealed lighting in alcoves and can be hidden behind pelmets or baffles to highlight curtains drawn across a window. Sometimes they are used to feature cornices against the ceiling. There is also a type available which resembles a tungsten filament light bulb and can be used in an ordinary lampholder. And as the tubes last for 5,000 to 7,500 hours – about five year's average use – this more than compensates for the extra cost.

Installation and running costs

Fluorescent lights are more costly to install than a normal light, but because they are more efficient at turning electricity into light than a filament lamp they are cheaper to run. And they also have a longer life. In fact a 100W filament lamp will give light for ten hours for one unit of electricity (1 kilowatt/hour) while a 1500mm (5ft) tube will give four times as much light for the same cost over the same period.

The fluorescent fitting

There are two parts to a fluorescent fitting. The lamp itself is a long, thin glass tube, which is coated on the inside with a powder that fluoresces – gives off light – when the fitting is switched on. The tube contains argon gas, which is similar to neon, and a small amount of mercury, and at each end there is a tiny heater (electrode) which is coated in a special chemical. In some fittings there is more than one tube.

The other part of the fitting is the control gear. This is made up of several different components including a starter and 'choke' or 'ballast', and is responsible for starting up the light when it's switched on and controlling it when it's operating.

Most manufacturers sell an integral unit which incorporates both a tube and linear metal box designed to take the control gear. But they don't always have to be together. In fact, in some situations it's probably a good idea that they aren't. If you want to highlight some curtains, for example, you could conceal the tube behind a pelmet board or a baffle, holding it in place with spring clips about 150mm (6in) from the material. It should be connected to the control gear, which can be mounted on a solid surface nearby, using 0.5mm^2 (3 amp) or 0.75mm^2 (6 amp) flex. As the choke can get rather warm, the control gear should have some ventilation.

Given the positions where most fluorescents are used, it's unlikely you'll want to be able to control their brilliance. If you do you'll need to use a special dimmer and modify the fitting.

How the light works

In an ordinary tungsten bulb electricity flowing through the filament causes it to heat up to a white heat and so emit visible light. In a fluorescent tube there's no filament, but the electricity flowing between the two heater elements at each end causes the mercury vapour in the tube to emit ultra-violet (invisible) light. This is converted to visible light by the fluorescent powder on the inside of the tube.

In order to get an electric current to flow in the tube a high voltage is needed initially when the light is switched on. And it's the function of the choke and starter to provide this. At the same time the starter also has to heat up the elements. Once the light is operating, the starter switches itself off while the choke and power factor correction capacitor (PFCC) regulate the current flowing through the tube.

There are two types of starter. The thermal type has a tiny heating element which acts like a thermostat and turns off the current in the starter circuit when the elements are hot enough and current is flowing in the tube. The more common starter is the two-pin 'glow' type which doesn't have its own internal heating element.

Quick-start fittings

Some fittings have 'quick start' ballasts that don't need a starter, but a special tube is required with a metal strip running along its length, which is earthed at the lampholders at either end. When the light is switched on the current passes down the tube immediately – so there is no flick-flick effect or delay in the tube lighting. This type of fitting needs to be earthed. The manufacturers' catalogues usually contain details and circuit diagrams.

Colour range

Fluorescent tubes are manufactured to give off different types of light. In all there are 13 different colours to choose from. These range from the very cold white 'northlight' to the warmer yellow colours. Most of the fittings sold in retail lighting shops are supplied with a tube marked 'warm white' – a colour that isn't really warm when compared with the yellow light given out by an ordinary filament lamp. The tubes giving a yellow light are listed as 'de luxe warm white'.

Some fittings such as the very useful circular fluorescents with their diffusers and some of the 25/26mm slimline tubes are available in 'warm white' or the colder 'natural'. The very neat 15/16mm miniature tubes are available in three or four colours, but not in 'de luxe warm white'. 'Warm white' tubes are ideal for the kitchen, but they're not really acceptable for living rooms

Installing the fitting

You can install a fluorescent fitting almost anywhere instead of an existing tungsten filament lamp. If you want to connect the fitting to an existing lighting point, you'll first need to inspect the fitting or rose that's

MODIFYING LOOP-IN WIRING

1 *Before installing the four-terminal junction box, you have to fix a wooden batten between the joists near the lighting point.*

2 *Screw the junction box to the batten – it makes fixing the cores that much easier – and draw the cables into the ceiling void, then run them to the box.*

3 *Take earths to one terminal, red cores of the supply cables to another, black neutrals to a third and black switch core with red PVC to the fourth.*

4 *Lay a length of 1.0mm² two-core and earth cable from the lighting point to the junction box, strip back the sheathing and prepare the cores.*

5 *After you've sleeved the earth core and connected it to the earth terminal, take the red to the switch terminal and the black to the neutrals.*

6 *Follow the same procedure if you have to extend the lighting cable on an existing junction box system, and don't forget to screw on the cover.*

Ready Reference

FLUORESCENT LIGHT SIZES

Linear tubes range in length from 150mm (6in) to 2400mm (8ft). Tube diameters are
● 15mm (⅝in) – miniature
● 25mm (1in) – slimline
● 38mm (1½in) – standard
Light output varies from 4 to 125 watts.

Circular tubes are made in diameters of:
● 300mm (1ft) rated at 32 watts
● 400mm (1ft 4in) rated at 40 and 60 watts.

The most popular tube sizes for the home are 1200mm (4ft) with a light output of 40 watts and 1500mm (5ft) with light outputs of 65 and 80 watts. These are sold complete with their controls and usually a baffle or diffuser to disguise the tube. Apart from the tubes which give off 'white' light, others are available which give off pink, red, green, gold and blue light.

TYPES OF TUBE

Most fluorescent lights use the common bi-pin type of tube. There are two pins at each end which push into the sockets of the fitting to make the connection. The other type of tube is the bayonet type with a connection similar to that of an ordinary light bulb. It's now only found on 1500mm (5ft) 80W tubes.

A 40W tube 1200mm long will give adequate general lighting.

PARTS OF THE FITTING

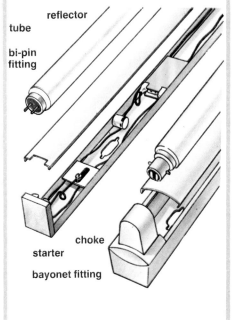

reflector
tube
bi-pin fitting
choke
starter
bayonet fitting

Ready Reference

FAULTS AND REMEDIES

Turn off the power at mains when carrying out repairs other than changing the tube itself.

FAULT Tube flickers and is reluctant to light, or tube glows at each end but fails to start.

Solution Faults could be due to malfunctioning starter; if so fit new one. Or it could be an ageing tube. Look for telltale signs of blackening at ends of tube; if present fit new tube of same size and type.

FAULT Tube glows at one end and flashes.

Solution Check tube connections. If pin holders damaged or bent, fit new holder.

FAULT Strong oily smell.

Solution Check the choke for signs of burning and replace it making sure you use the correct type to match the wattage of tube.

REPLACING A STARTER

A simple operation – locate the starter, push in and twist anti-clockwise to remove. Replace with a new one of the same type.

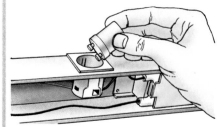

REPLACING A TUBE

With a bayonet-type fitting (1), push in and twist the tube against the spring-loaded lampholders. With a bi-pin tube (2), simply pull back one of the spring-loaded end brackets.

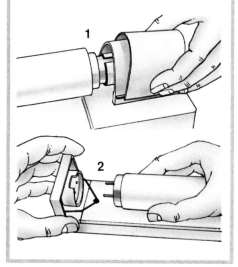

already there to see how the circuit is wired. If there is only one cable going into the rose or fitting on the fixed wiring side – ie, there's one black and one red insulated core and possibly an earth wire – then the circuit is wired on the junction box system. All you have to do when putting up the fluorescent light is to connect the cores to the relevant terminals in the fitting – black to the 'N' terminal, red to the 'L' terminal and the earth (which should be sleeved in green/yellow PVC) to the 'E' terminal.

However, if you've got loop-in wiring where there are two or more cables going into the fitting or rose, then some small modifications are necessary as there are no loop-in terminal facilities on a fluorescent fitting. All you have to do is to draw the cables back into the ceiling void or loft space and fit the cores to the relevant terminals of a four-terminal junction box. You then have to run a short piece of 1.0mm^2 two-core and earth flat PVC-sheathed cable from the junction box to the fluorescent light and connect it to the terminals.

If, as in many circuits, there is no earthing at the lighting point, it's necessary to run 1.5mm^2 green/yellow PVC-insulated cable from the fluorescent fitting back to the earthing terminal block in the consumer unit.

CONNECTING THE FITTING

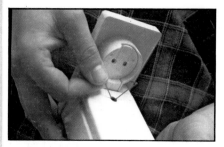

1 *Remove the diffuser and tube from the fitting and take off the backplate cover by undoing the retaining screws and prising out the spring clips.*

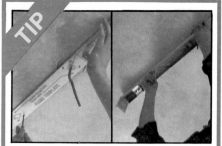

2 *Use the template supplied with the fitting – or the backplate itself – to test that the fixing holes are sound; then screw the fitting into position.*

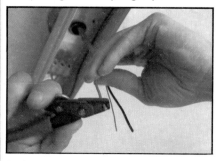

3 *If you've had to lay in a new cable, strip back the sheathing and prepare the cores. Don't forget, there should be a rubber grommet round the cable entry.*

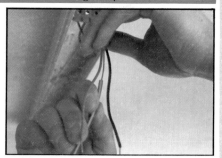

4 *Before connecting up the cores, you need to slip a length of green/yellow PVC sleeving over the earth wire so there is no exposed wire in the fitting.*

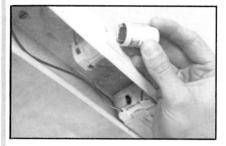

7 *Push the starter into its socket, which you'll find on the outside of the backplate. You have to twist it clockwise to secure it in position.*

8 *Replace the cover of the backplate and refit the spring clips. The tube is inserted in the holders at each end, which spring outwards for easy fitting.*

HOME PLUMBING

PART 4

HOME PLUMBING

TYPES OF PIPEWORK

Lead and iron are no longer used as plumbing materials, having been replaced by copper or stainless steel. Now plastic pipework is revolutionising domestic plumbing.

Virtually all **soil pipes** are now made from UPVC (1), which can be joined together using solvent welds or ring seals. Likewise, **overflow pipes** (2) are also made from UPVC, and lengths of these are connected with push-fit joins.

Waste pipes, made of UPVC and ABS plastic, are used for taking water away from baths, basins and sinks (3). Depending on the system they can be joined either by solvent welding or push-fit connections.

Plastic can also be used for water supply pipes. **Polybutylene pipes** (4) can take hot and cold water, the pipes being joined by compression fittings or special push-fit connectors. Similarly, **CPVC pipe** (5) can be used for hot and cold runs, but this is joined with solvent welds.

Black **polythene pipe** (6), the first plastic pipe to be used generally in domestic plumbing, is only suitable for cold water supplies, and consequently is mainly employed for garden and other outside water services.

Rainwater downpipes (7) are made from UPVC and have either circular or square profiles.

Half-hard temper **copper pipe** (8) is used for hot and cold distribution and central heating pipes, being easy to bend and join. **Stainless steel** (9) has also been used, mainly because it can be joined to copper and galvanised steel without causing electrolytic action.

Flexible copper pipe (10), which can be bent simply in the hands, is ideal for making the awkward connections between tap tails and the supply pipes without having to alter the existing runs.

UNDERSTANDING WATER SUPPLY

Each one of us uses about 160 litres (35 gallons) of water a day, and takes it for granted. Only in a long spell of dry weather comes an awareness that we should use it carefully. Our use is controlled by the supply system – this is how it works.

In the last 50 years the consumption of water has almost doubled. Rising standards of living have given rise to increased consumption, and a greater awareness of the need for hygiene has also played a large role in increasing the demand. Faced with this high demand, supply sources have been hard pressed to keep up.

Where it comes from

Water is supplied by the local water authority (or the 'Undertaking' as it is known in the plumbing trade). After falling as rain it is collected in reservoirs which are fed by streams and rivers, or is pumped from underground wells. Water varies a lot in its chemical makeup since it picks up minerals and gases as it flows. If it picks up calcium, magnesium and sodium salts it will be 'hard' – the menace of pipe systems. Before being distributed it is usually filtered through sand and pebble beds to remove solids and organisms, and may have chlorine added to it to ensure that it is 'potable' – drinkable. Fluoride is also sometimes added for the protection of teeth.

Distribution is carried out by a network of pipes starting with 'trunk mains' which may be as much as 610mm (24in) in diameter. These split into mains and sub-mains which run underneath streets and side streets. It is these sub-mains which are tapped by individual houses for their supply.

The house system may be 'direct' in which all cold water supplies are piped direct from the rising main, with the cistern only being used to supply the hot water tank. Or it may be an 'indirect' system in which all cold-water supplies are taken from the cistern, with the exception of a direct supply to the kitchen sink for drinking purposes.

For water to flow through the trunk mains – and eventually into your house – it must be under a certain amount of pressure. This pressure is assisted by pumps but it is vital that somewhere in the mains system the water should reach a height in a reservoir or water tower, higher than any domestic system it has to supply. The vertical distance through which the water 'falls' is known as the 'pressure head' and without it our cisterns would never fill up without a lot of expensive additional pumping. The storage cistern also provides a pressure head inside the house, which is why it's preferable to have it in the roof space.

The house system

The sub-main underneath the road is tapped by the 'communication pipe' which ends at the authority's stop-valve. This is usually situated under the pavement about 300mm (1ft) outside the boundary of your property. The stop-valve is located at the bottom of a vertical 'guard' pipe – about 1 metre (39in) deep – which is covered at the surface by a hinged metal cover. It should only be operated by the water authority and requires a special key to turn it. But in a real emergency you may be able to turn it yourself. In old houses it may be the only way of turning off the water supply. After this stop-valve the water enters the service pipe and from then on all pipes become your responsibility.

The service pipe continues under the wall of the property at a depth of at least 750mm (2ft 6in) to protect it from frost – though some water authorities insist that it should be 900mm (3ft) deep. As it travels under the house wall or foundation it usually goes through an earthenware pipe to protect it

5

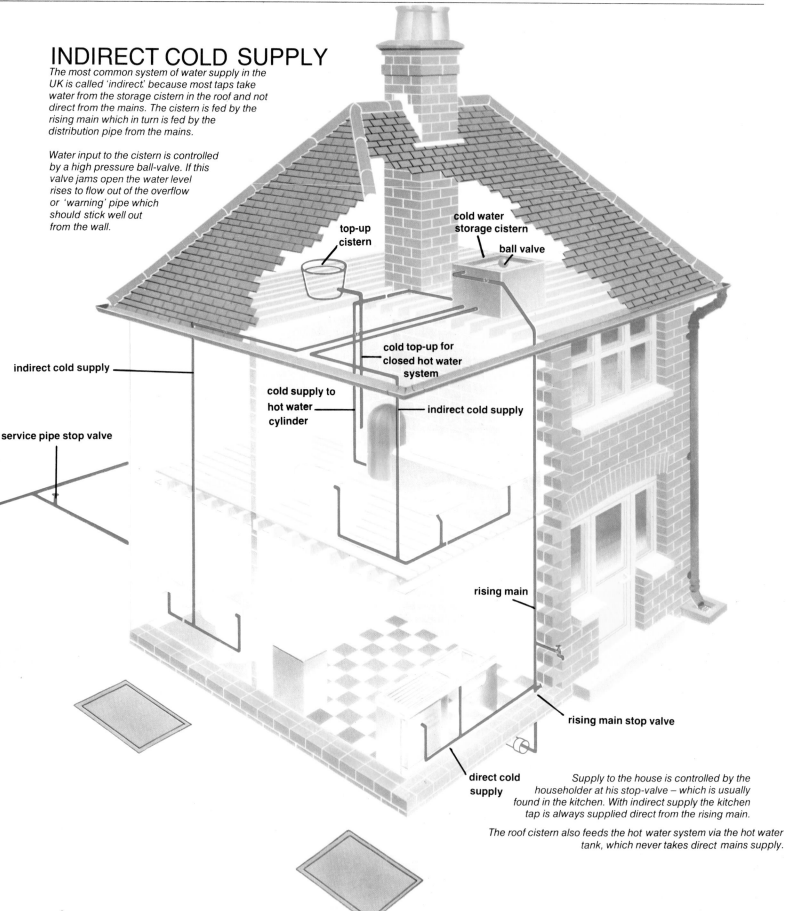

INDIRECT COLD SUPPLY

The most common system of water supply in the UK is called 'indirect' because most taps take water from the storage cistern in the roof and not direct from the mains. The cistern is fed by the rising main which in turn is fed by the distribution pipe from the mains.

Water input to the cistern is controlled by a high pressure ball-valve. If this valve jams open the water level rises to flow out of the overflow or 'warning' pipe which should stick well out from the wall.

top-up cistern

cold water storage cistern

ball valve

cold top-up for closed hot water system

indirect cold supply

cold supply to hot water cylinder

indirect cold supply

service pipe stop valve

rising main

rising main stop valve

direct cold supply

Supply to the house is controlled by the householder at his stop-valve – which is usually found in the kitchen. With indirect supply the kitchen tap is always supplied direct from the rising main.

The roof cistern also feeds the hot water system via the hot water tank, which never takes direct mains supply.

6

from possible settlement which might cause it to fracture. To prevent any risk of freezing in cold weather the service pipe should not emerge above ground level until it is at least 600mm (2ft) inside the inside wall surface.

Up to about 40 years ago, service pipes were usually made of lead (in fact the word plumbing originally stemmed from the Latin word for lead – *plumbum)*. Today copper and polythene are used instead. The latter is particularly good as it is a poor conductor of heat and is less prone to freezing and fracture.

The service pipe

The service pipe continues under the wall near the kitchen sink, which means that it is often attached to the inner face of the outside wall. This is contrary to the recommendation that it should be attached to an inside wall, and so such a pipe should be lagged with insulation material. The pipe should also be insulated if it comes through any sub-ground floor cavity where it would be subjected to the icy blasts of winter from under-floor ventilation. Again these precautions are both intended to minimise the risk of frost damage.

When the service pipe rises above the ground floor it is called the 'rising main' and it eventually terminates in the supply cistern, which is usually in the roof cavity. The householder's main stop-valve is usually found on the rising main a little way above floor level. This is the most important 'tap' in the house. In any plumbing emergency – when bursts or leaks occur, for example, your first action should be to turn this tap off, thus isolating the house system from the mains water supply. The stop-valve should always be turned off when you go away if the house is going to be empty. In old houses the location of the stop-valve may vary considerably, it may be in the cellar, under the stairs, or even under a cover beneath the front path – or it may not exist at all, in which case the authority's stop-valve is the only control.

Branch supply pipes

At least one 'branch' supply pipe leaves the rising main close above the stop-valve and drain tap – this is to the tap over the kitchen sink. This tap must be supplied direct from the main supply as it is supposed to provide all drinking and cooking water. Water which has been in a storage cistern is no longer considered drinkable, sometimes termed 'potable', as it may be slightly contaminated by debris in the storage cistern.

Other branches may be taken at this point to an outside tap, or to a washing machine or dishwasher.

The rising main continues upwards and while its ultimate destination is the cold water storage cistern the pipework in between will vary from house to house, depending on

OTHER SYSTEMS

Other systems
There are other sorts of supply systems both for hot and cold water – and many variations. Systems reflect the design of buildings and the regulations.

Direct cold supply
The direct cold water system takes water direct from the main to all cold water taps. A roof storage cistern is still used but only as a supply reservoir for the hot water tank. Not only the main cistern but also all WC cisterns must have high pressure valves. The indirect system has the advantage of relieving the piping of high pressures and providing a temporary reserve in periods of drought when supplies may be restricted.

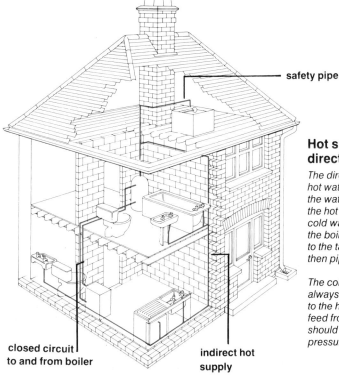

indirect cold supply

direct cold supply

rising main

safety pipe

closed circuit to and from boiler

indirect hot supply

Hot supply from direct tank

The direct or 'open' system of hot water supply is based on the water being supplied to the hot water tank from the cold water cistern, passed to the boiler for heating, returned to the tank for storage and then piped to the supply taps.

The cold water cistern is always used to supply water to the hot water tank. Direct feed from the mains supply should never be used as the pressure would be too great.

INDIRECT HOT WATER SUPPLY

In an indirect or 'closed' hot water system a closed pipe runs from the boiler, through a heat exchanger in the hot water tank and back to the boiler again. This closed system contains water which never comes into contact with the hot water used by the household. The closed circuit between boiler and hot water cylinder loses water very slowly, and is topped up automatically by water from a small reservoir cistern in the loft. A safety pipe returns over-heated water to this or the main cistern.

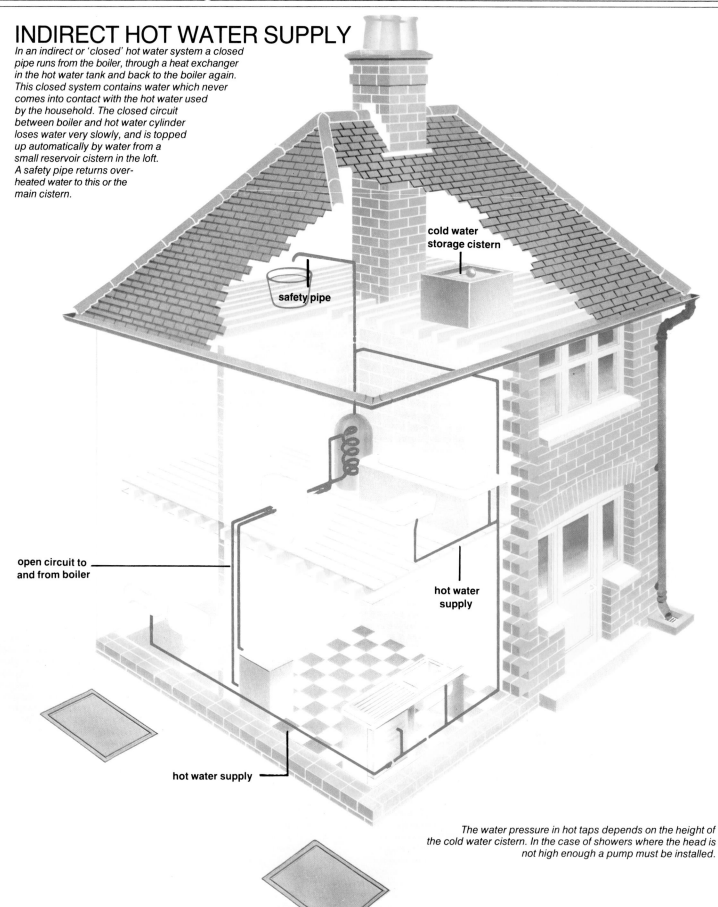

cold water storage cistern

safety pipe

open circuit to and from boiler

hot water supply

hot water supply

The water pressure in hot taps depends on the height of the cold water cistern. In the case of showers where the head is not high enough a pump must be installed.

whether a direct' or 'indirect' system has been installed.

In many areas indirect systems must be installed in new buildings, yet in Western Europe direct systems are the rule. Indirect systems have been encouraged because of the difficulty in maintaining constant mains pressure particularly at times of peak demand. Routing of most supplies through the storage cistern evens out fluctuations, and it also rules out the risk of 'back siphonage' whereby dirty water could be sucked back into the mains supply – though this rarely occurs. The 1976 drought in the UK provided good reason for indirect systems, since each house had an emergency supply in the storage cistern if the mains water had to be shut off.

Cisterns

The 'tank' in your loft or attic is in fact a 'cistern'. Cisterns are not sealed – though they should be covered – and so are subject to atmospheric pressure. Tanks are completely sealed – as with a hot water storage tank – and are not subject to atmospheric pressure.

Cold water cisterns ,have traditionally been made of galvanised mild steel and it is quite likely that you will find one like this in your loft. They are still available, but are not usually installed in new houses. Other materials used have been asbestos, cement, copper and glass fibre, but today the most common material is plastic, of which glass fibre reinforced polyester (GRP), polythene and polypropylene are the most common varieties.

The advantages plastics have over all other cistern materials are their lightness in weight, resistance to corrosion and flexibility. Galvanised steel is heavy and liable to corrode, while asbestos and cement are not only heavy but can become porous and are prone to accidental damage. Don't forget the capacity of a typical cistern is 227 litres (50 gallons), and this water alone weighs nearly 0.25 tonne (¼ ton), so all cisterns must be fully supported on the joists. With rigid materials such as steel the cistern can rest across the joists, but with plastic and glass fibre a platform should be installed to support the whole area of the bottom, otherwise the material may develop local weaknesses.

Cisterns should be covered to prevent any contamination of the water. Where the underside of the roof is exposed dust and dirt are liable to fall in. The top and sides should also be insulated to minimise the risk of freezing. The bottom is left uncovered to allow rising warm air from rooms below to keep the water above freezing point, and so you shouldn't insulate the roof space under the cistern.

Cisterns were often installed before the roof was put on and if you want to replace yours, perhaps because it's made of steel and is corroding, you may not be able to get it through the trap door. While it is sometimes suggested that a cistern should be cut up to get it out this is in fact a very heavy and arduous job in such a confined space and it would be better to manoeuvre it to one side and leave it in the loft, installing a new cistern alongside. Modern plastic cisterns can literally be folded up so they can be passed through small loft hatches.

Pipes and taps

Water leaves the storage cistern in distribution pipes which are usually 22mm (¾in) or 15mm (½in) in diameter. In a direct system, supply from the cistern will usually only be to the hot water tank, and in an indirect system this link must also be direct – but other distribution pipes are used with branches to supply the other appliances – basins, baths and WC cisterns. Distribution pipes usually end in taps but in the case of a WC a low pressure ball-valve controls the flow.

The WC in an indirect system has a low pressure ball-valve because when the water leaves the storage cistern it is no longer at mains pressure but at normal atmospheric pressure which is pressing down on the surface of the stored water. This means that the higher up the house a tap or other outlet is situated the lower will be the water pressure. In practice this means that you can't have a tap in an indirect system which is above the level of its distribution outlet from the cistern. Showers are particularly affected by this difference of pressure, and if there is not sufficient 'head' to 'drive' the shower a special pump may have to be installed.

Cold water supplied to the hot water tank is heated in two different ways again called indirect and direct systems – or, respectively, closed and open. In the latter the cold water is circulated through the boiler, where it is heated, and returned to the tank from where it flows to tapped outlets. In the indirect system the cold water supplied never actually goes to the boiler, instead it is heated in the tank by a coiled pipe or jacket containing hot water which is continuously circulating through the boiler. In either case a pump often helps the water flow through the boiler, and supplementary or alternative heat may come from an immersion heater. If there is no boiler but only an immersion heater in the tank the system is essentially direct with the heating of the water taking place in the tank rather than in the boiler.

Draining the system

Just above the rising main stop-valve should be a drain cock. With the stop-valve turned off the drain cock can be used to drain part of the cold water system when repairs are necessary – the hot water system has its own drain cock.

Ready Reference

PIPE SIZES AND THEIR USES

Distribution pipes
● 22mm (¾in) pipe – water supply to bath and hot water cylinder
● 15m (½in) pipe – WC, basin, bidet and shower supplies
● 28mm (1in) pipe – for use with multiple appliances, but usually unnecessary.

Warning pipes (Overflows)
● these must have a diameter greater than that of the inlet pipe to prevent cold water cisterns and WC cisterns from overflowing.

CONNECTIONS AT COLD WATER CISTERN

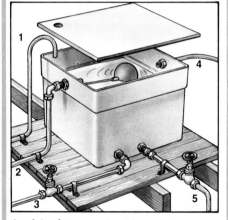

1 safety pipe   **3 cold supply to taps**
2 rising main   **4 overflow**
           5 cold supply to hot water tank

DRAINING THE SYSTEM

To drain the system from the mains stop-valve to cistern, turn off the stop-valve and attach one end of the hose to the drain cock, which should be just above the stop-valve, and run the other end to a drain. Then open the drain cock.
Drain remainder of system by turning off

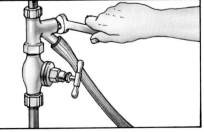

mains supply and opening cold water taps. The hot water system has its own drain cock, usually found close to the boiler.

WASTE WATER SYSTEMS

A waste water system must be able to dispose of used water from the kitchen and bathroom efficiently and hygienically, and some also have to cater for rainwater falling on the roof. Here's how it's done.

The supply of hot and cold water to the taps in your house is really only half the domestic plumbing story. You also need a waste system to remove what you've used or don't want. And besides coping with the dirty water from the bath, basin and sink and the waste from the WC, the system also has to deal with the rainwater which falls on the roof.

The drainage system therefore has to be efficient and durable, and for obvious reasons of hygiene, self-cleansing. Waste matter mustn't be allowed to remain in the pipes and if blockages occur it should be possible to remove them easily.

How the drainage system works

There are several domestic drainage systems but each of them can be broken down into five separate sections. When waste water leaves an appliance of any sort, it will go immediately through a 'waste trap' – a 180° bend containing a water seal which fills the trap whenever the waste pipe empties. This keeps drain smells out of the room and prevents insects and the like from entering the home. With WCs it also makes self-cleansing easier. WC traps are cast as an integral part of the WC pan, but on other appliances they are separate, and are attached to the outlet pipe by a large retaining nut.

From the trap, waste water enters a branch pipe which leads to the main vertical drainage 'stack'. This takes it below ground level to the first underground section of the drainage system where it flows through at least one inspection chamber (covered with a manhole cover) and into the public sewer, which is usually situated underneath the road. The sewer is provided by the public health authority and it is their responsibility to remove all waste running into it.

Often rainwater from the roof is fed into the drainage system to flow into the public sewer. But some authorities provide a separate street drain for it or insist on the provision of soakaways (pits filled with rubble and gravel which allow the water to soak into the surrounding earth) near the house. Tanks and cisterns rarely overflow, but when they do they discharge clean water, so it's not necessary for the overflow pipes to be located over a drain.

The water can fall directly onto the ground.

The cost of laying public sewers in rural areas means that the waste from many houses in these parts flows into a cess pool or septic tank. These are specially constructed pits for storing effluent (and in the case of a septic tank, for breaking it down into harmless matter). Both of these require periodic pumping out, cess pools much more often as they store all the waste. If you're buying a house with one of these systems, check how often this has to be done, who does it and how much you may have to pay.

How it all began

Proper plumbing systems have only been around for about 100 years. The large urban expansion which took place during the Industrial Revolution lead to squalid housing conditions, and disease was rife. Eventually, enclosed sewers were introduced along with piped water supplies and pottery WC pans. By the 1870s many homes were equipped with a basin, a WC and a sink; but an acute shortage of qualified plumbers lead to ridiculous installations which often produced as great a health threat as before. The London County Council took the lead in sorting things out by laying out a set of rules in 1900, establishing the 'two-pipe' system – one stack for waste water from basins and sinks, another for 'soil water' from WCs.

The amount of pipework needed with the two-pipe system, and the increased siphonage problems on tall buildings, led to the introduction of the 'one-pipe' system. This system was the forerunner of the modern 'single stack' system and abandoned the distinction between the soil and the waste pipe stacks. It was only used extensively on multi-storey buildings.

On the one-pipe system all discharges flowed into a single stack which had an open-ended outlet at roof level. All traps had deep seals and each branch pipe was also connected to a vent pipe which rose to eaves level.

The single stack system was developed in the UK in the late 1940s to overcome the drawbacks and complications of the two-pipe systems, and to simplify the installation – everyone must be familiar with the untidy cluster of pipes on the outside walls of houses with these systems.

The advent of light plastic piping helped in this development, as it made the production of accurate mouldings easier, and cut down the installation time because plastic was quicker to join than the old metal piping.

The single stack system

This consists of a single waste stack into which all the branch pipes discharge. However, ground floor waste doesn't have to go

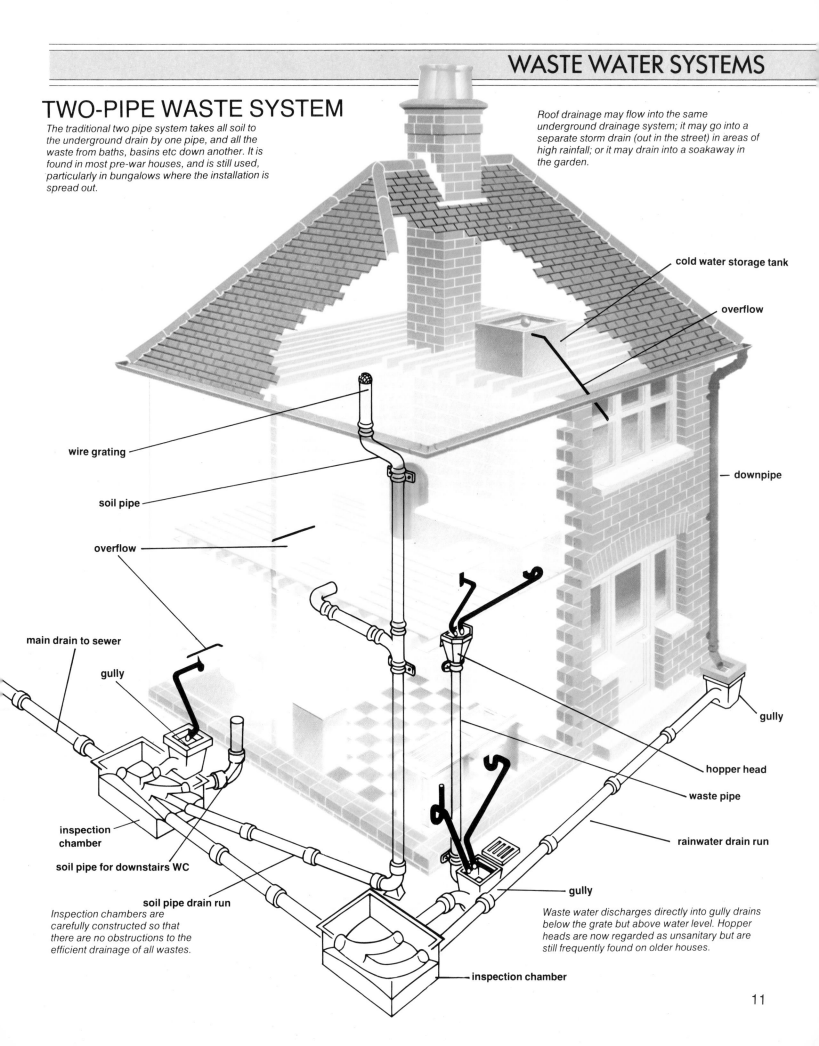

SINGLE STACK WASTE SYSTEM

In most modern systems it is preferable to install a single stack system which involves less pipework provided that sources of waste are not too far from the stack itself.

In a single stack system the waste doesn't all have to go down the same stack – rainwater doesn't in any case. Ground floor waste and soil outlets can go direct into the underground drain. Waste outlets must discharge into trapped gullies. This arrangement is sometimes necessary where pipe runs get too long for the proper functioning of the single stack system or where the layout of appliances makes direct access to the drain more sensible.

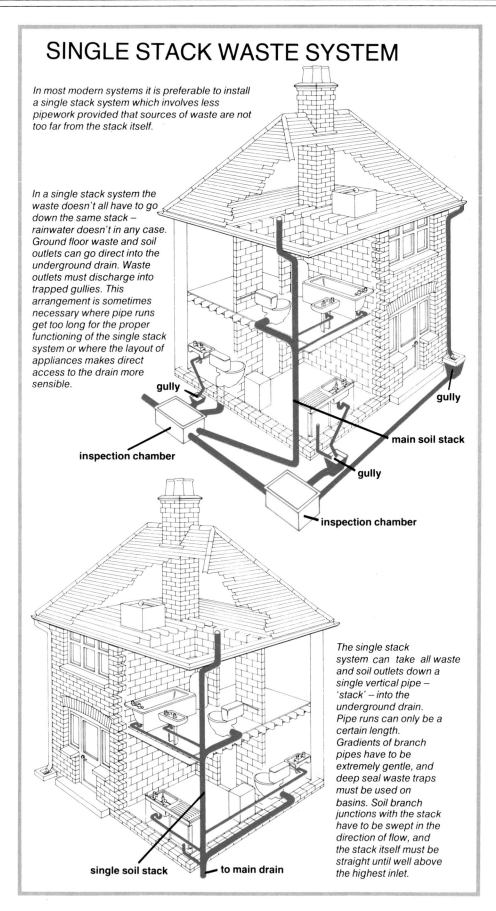

gully

inspection chamber

gully

main soil stack

gully

inspection chamber

The single stack system can take all waste and soil outlets down a single vertical pipe – 'stack' – into the underground drain. Pipe runs can only be a certain length. Gradients of branch pipes have to be extremely gentle, and deep seal waste traps must be used on basins. Soil branch junctions with the stack have to be swept in the direction of flow, and the stack itself must be straight until well above the highest inlet.

single soil stack   **to main drain**

into the stack. Sink waste water may flow into a trapped gully and ground-floor WCs may be connected directly into the underground drain. This avoids any risk that a blockage at the base of the stack (where it bends to join the underground drain) could lead to waste water being forced back along the waste pipes to ground-floor appliances.

In appearance the single-stack system is the simplest waste system of all and the most economical to install. As a result it is incorporated in the majority of new houses. But because the branches have to be comparatively short, the system is less useful in bungalows where appliances are likely to be spread out. Usually all the pipework is sited indoors, which means a neater appearance for the house exterior; it also reduces the possibility of frost damage. All you'll see of the system is a tell-tale vent pipe poking up through the roof.

In order to make the system work properly a number of technical regulations have to be taken into account when it's being installed. These relate to the length, diameter, bend radii and angles of bend of the branch pipes, the use of P-traps and S-traps on waste pipes other than WCs (see *Traps for each appliance*), the positioning of the stack connectors, and the dimensions of the stack itself. While the system may look simple, considerable research has been done to ensure that problems of siphonage aren't likely to occur.

The two-pipe system
The principles of the two-pipe system were based on a belief that all kinds of disease were caused by the 'bad air' in drains, and the system aimed to keep this out of homes. The basic principle was that the 'soil' discharge from WCs went directly down one stack into the underground drain. All other discharges, termed 'waste', went down another stack which led into a trapped gully (a cast drain incorporating a water trap) at ground level and from there joined the soil discharge under-ground. Sometimes waste had to fall into a channel at ground level before running into the drain.

All waste and soil pipework had to be fixed to the outside of the building. The soil pipe was continued upwards to eaves level where it terminated open-ended in a wire cover to keep nesting birds from causing a blockage. This allowed free passage of air from the underground drain.

When the two-pipe system came into existence, most homes only had an outside WC (quite often shared) and a kitchen sink, so discharge was entirely at ground level, but when upstairs bathrooms became popular waste was directed into hoppers attached to stand-pipes, which caused new problems. Hoppers were not self-cleansing and soapy water drying on the inside could start to smell; draughts could also blow up the pipe to the hopper, bringing smells from the drain at the bottom. This led to some authorities banning hoppers and insisting on discharge direct into another stack which meant installing an eaves-level vent as with the soil stack.

On buildings over two storeys high this created another problem known as 'induced siphonage'. When water flowing down the waste stack from one outlet passed another outlet where it joined the stack, it could cause a partial vacuum in the second pipe which could suck out the contents of the water trap. To cure this problem the upper part of each trap had to be connected to a branch vent pipe which either connected to a separate vertical stack to eaves level, or joined the vented waste stack at least 900mm (3ft) above the level of the highest waste connection. If you live in a tall house you may have this system, and any repairs to vent pipes should follow the existing system. The alternative is to take out the entire system and replace it with a single stack arrangement.

Traps for each appliance

The traditional trap was a simple U-shaped bend attached to a horizontal branch outlet – today called a 'P' trap. If the branch outlet is vertical this trap bends round again into a double 'U' or 'S' outlet. In systems with lead pipes, the traps were often formed from lengths of pipe, while with modern plastic waste systems the traps are separate and easily detachable. The plastic bottle trap, which performs the same function, is also now widely used, and this is more compact and neater in appearance.

The depth of the water-filled part of the trap is known as the 'depth of seal'. Shallow traps have a seal depth of around 50mm (2in), 38mm (1½in) or 19mm (¾in), while 'deep-seal' traps have a 75mm (3in) seal.

Lead traps usually allow access for clearing blockages, and this is obtained by unscrewing an access cap or 'eye'. Modern plastic traps are connected by screwed collars at both ends and can be completely removed for cleaning if blocked. The lower part of bottle traps likewise completely unscrews. Adjustable plastic traps are available for fixing to existing pipework where access is difficult and special adaptors are used to link to copper and iron pipes.

Traps must remain filled with water and it is against the bye-laws if they don't. This is the most important and lasting principle handed down from the waste disposal thinking of the last century.

The water seal can be lost from traps for lots of reasons. Siphonage is the worst problem and where it occurs it's usually due to a badly designed system. Simply, if the air pressure beyond the trap is slightly less than the normal atmospheric pressure acting on the surface of the water in the trap, the water will drain away. This is more likely with 'S' traps than 'P' traps, and with shallow rather than deep traps. The problem of siphonage led to the introduction of venting systems and dictated the dimensions in the single stack system (and also excluded the use of 'S' traps).

Overflow pipes

There are two sorts of overflow pipes – those which are connected to storage cisterns and WC cisterns, and those which are attached to or form a part of appliances such as basins and baths. They are known in the trade as warning pipes. Both sorts should be fitted to avoid the risk of overflows damaging your home. This may be caused when you forget to turn off the bath, or by mechanical failure when the ball-valve on the water storage tank jams open.

In sinks, basins and baths the overflow must discharge into the branch waste pipe between the trap and the appliance, or into the trap above the water level of the seal, and must be able to cope with the flow of water from one tap turned full on.

Sink and basin overflows are usually built into the design of the appliance, while those for baths are supplied as part of the plumbing and connect to a slot in the waste outlet casting.

Overflows from tanks and cisterns consist of a length of pipe of a minimum 22mm (⅞in) internal diameter, capable of discharging water as quickly as any incoming flow. They usually emerge through the outside wall and stick out far enough to avoid any water flow sluicing down the wall surface, which could be a potential source of damp.

Pipe and trap materials

All waste and soil pipes are today mainly manufactured in plastic. Branch pipes were made of lead or copper, stack pipes of cast iron, traps of lead or brass and underground pipes of vitrified clay. Only the latter still predominantly utilize the traditional material.

Your legal position

Drainage regulations fall under the Public Health Acts as well as the Building Regulations, so it's important to know where you stand. The householder is responsible for the entire drainage system until it enters the public sewer – even though this is usually beyond the boundary of the property. While blockages beyond the lowest inspection chamber are rare, any clearance work can be very expensive – particularly if you use a '24-hour' plumbing service. The public sewer is provided by the public health authority and is their responsibility.

If your house was built as one of a group of houses, then it's quite possible that you'll have shared drainage facilities. This means there is one drainage pipe collecting the waste of several homes before it discharges into the public sewer. The system was adopted because it saved installation costs. If your house was built before 1937, it's still the responsibility of the local authorities to cleanse the shared drainage runs, although you're responsible for clearing blockages and for maintenance. But if you live in a post-1937 house then the responsibility for the shared drains rests collectively on all the owners concerned and if a blockage is caused by someone else you will have to pay a proportion of the bill. It is therefore important when moving house to check out the exact position. If this is difficult to ascertain, try the Environmental Health Officer for advice; he should also be consulted if you want to change the system.

PLASTIC WASTE TRAPS

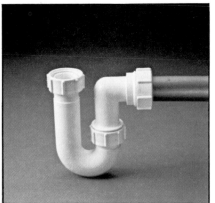
The modern U-bend *is made from one of several plastic materials.*

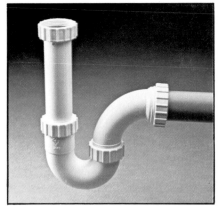
A U-bend with telescopic extension *can be adjusted to existing appliances.*

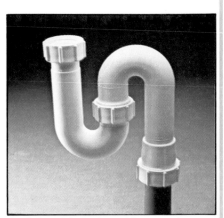
An S-bend *is designed for use where the outlet is vertical.*

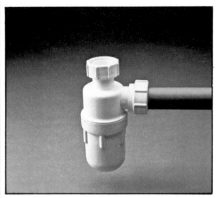
A bottle trap *gives a neater appearance, but is less efficient.*

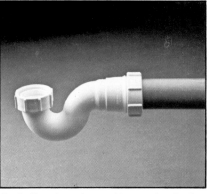
A shallow trap *is used beneath a bath or shower where space is crucial.*

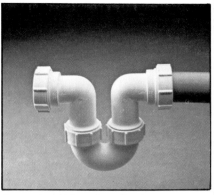
A running U-trap *handles two or more untrapped appliances piped together.*

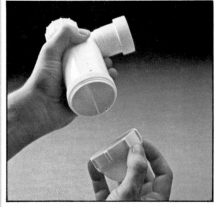
A dip partition bottle trap *has a base which unscrews.*

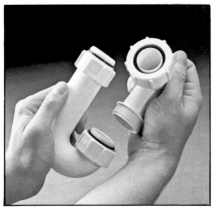
All modern traps come apart for easy cleaning and installation.

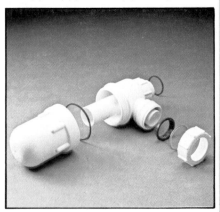
A dip tube trap taken apart to show the O rings and washers.

DRAINING PLUMBING SYSTEMS

When you are carrying out repairs or alterations to your plumbing or wet central heating system, you will usually have to drain water from the parts you are working on. Here's what you'll have to do.

Virtually all major and many minor plumbing operations demand the partial or total drainage of either the domestic hot or cold water supply. If you have a 'wet' central heating system you'll also have to drain that before carrying out repairs or alterations. Before attempting this – long before the need for drainage arises, in fact – you should make yourself thoroughly familiar with the design and layout of these systems in your home. Here are some questions to which you should know the answers:

● Are all cold water draw-off points supplied direct from the rising main, or are the bathroom cold taps and the WC cistern supplied with water from a main cold water storage cistern (probably situated in the roof space)?
● Is the hot water system 'direct' or 'indirect' (see pages 9 to 13)?
● If the system is direct, is the domestic hot water heated solely by means of an electric immersion heater, solely by means of a domestic boiler (gas, oil or solid fuel), or are both means of heating available?
● If hot water is provided solely by means of an immersion heater, is there a drain-valve at the base of the cold supply pipe from the storage cistern to the hot water cylinder?
● If hot water is provided by means of a boiler, is there a drain-valve on the pipework beside the boiler, or possibly incorporated into the boiler itself?
● If the system is indirect, is it a conventional indirect system (indicated by the presence of a small feed-and-expansion tank in the roof space, feeding the primary circuit) or is it a self-priming indirect system such as the Primatic?
● Is there a 'wet' central heating system provided in conjunction with hot water supply?
● Where is the main stop-valve, and are there any other stop-valves or gate-valves fitted into distribution or circulating pipes in the system?
● Are there drain-valves at low points in the central heating circuit?

Draining down for simple repairs

Once you are thoroughly familiar with the contents and layout of your own plumbing and central heating systems, you will be able to work out for yourself how much draining-down will be necessary before you undertake any particular item of maintenance or any particular project. If, for instance, you wish to rewasher the cold tap over the kitchen sink (this is supplied direct from the rising main) or to tee into the rising main to provide a garden water supply, all that you need to do is to turn off the main stop-valve and to turn on the kitchen cold tap until water ceases to flow from it. You will then have drained the rising main to the level of the cold tap. In many modern homes a drain-valve is provided immediately above the main stop-valve to permit the rising main to be completely drained.

Rather more drainage is necessary when you wish to renew the washer on a hot tap, or on a cold tap supplied from a storage cistern, or to renew a ball-valve in a WC cistern that is supplied with water from a storage cistern. First of all, see if there are any stop-valves or gate-valves on the distribution pipes leading to the particular tap or ball-valve. There could be gate-valves on the main hot and cold distribution pipes just below the level of the main cold water storage cistern. There could even be a mini-stop-valve on the distribution pipe immediately before its connection to the tail of the tap or ball-valve.

In either of these circumstances you're in luck!. All you have to do is to turn off the appropriate gate-valve or mini-stop-valve and then to turn on the tap or flush the lavatory cistern. You can then carry out the necessary repairs.

Avoiding unnecessary drainage

The chances are, though, that the main stop-valve will be the only one in the system, and that you'll have to contemplate draining the main cold water storage cistern and the appropriate distribution pipes before you can get on with your task, by turning off the main stop-valve and draining the cistern and pipes from the taps supplied by the cistern. This, however, will mean that the whole of the plumbing system is out of action for as long as it takes you to complete the job. It is generally better to go up into the roof space and lay a slat of wood across the top of the cold water storage cistern. You can then tie the float arm of the ball-valve up to it, so that water cannot flow into the cistern. Then drain the cistern by opening the bathroom taps. In this way the cold tap over the sink will not be put out of action.

Here's another useful money-saving tip: even if you are draining down to rewasher a hot tap, there is no need to run to waste all that hot water stored in the hot water cylinder, *provided that your bathroom cold taps are supplied from the cold water storage cistern.* Having tied up the ball-valve, run the bathroom *cold* taps until they cease to flow and only then turn on the hot tap you want to work on. Because the hot water distribution pipe is taken from above the hot water storage cylinder, only a little hot water – from the pipe itself – will flow away to waste and the cylinder will remain full of hot water.

For the same reason, unless you expect to have the hot water system out of action for a

WHERE TO DRAIN THE SYSTEM

On a well-designed plumbing system you should find that drain-valves have been installed at several points, so that partial draining-down is possible.

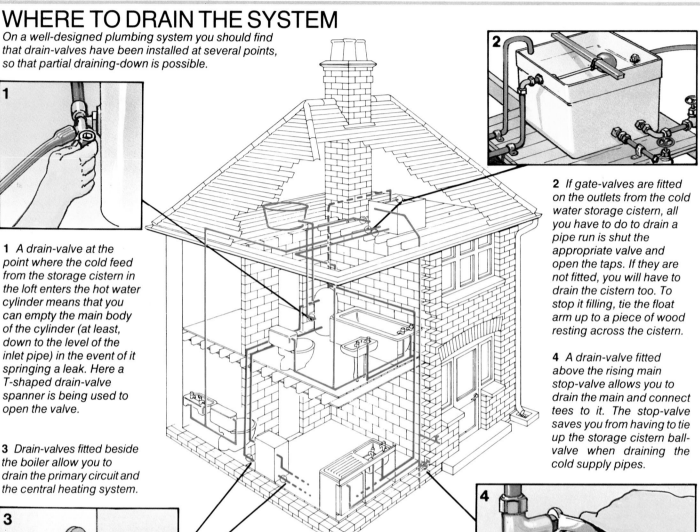

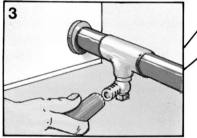

1 A drain-valve at the point where the cold feed from the storage cistern in the loft enters the hot water cylinder means that you can empty the main body of the cylinder (at least, down to the level of the inlet pipe) in the event of it springing a leak. Here a T-shaped drain-valve spanner is being used to open the valve.

3 Drain-valves fitted beside the boiler allow you to drain the primary circuit and the central heating system.

2 If gate-valves are fitted on the outlets from the cold water storage cistern, all you have to do to drain a pipe run is shut the appropriate valve and open the taps. If they are not fitted, you will have to drain the cistern too. To stop it filling, tie the float arm up to a piece of wood resting across the cistern.

4 A drain-valve fitted above the rising main stop-valve allows you to drain the main and connect tees to it. The stop-valve saves you from having to tie up the storage cistern ball-valve when draining the cold supply pipes.

Action checklist

Which part of the system you drain, and how you go about it, depends on the job you're doing. Here's a brief checklist of the sequence of operations in each case.

Job: to rewasher/replace kitchen cold tap, tee off rising main for new supply pipe;
● turn off rising main stop-valve and drain rising main via drain-valve
● if no drain-valve fitted, open kitchen cold tap to drain main down to level of tee to kitchen sink.

Job: to rewasher/replace other cold tap, renew WC ball-valve, extend cold supply;
● if gate-valve fitted to outlet at cold cistern, close valve and open lowest appropriate cold tap; otherwise
● tie up arm of cold cistern ball-valve and drain cistern by opening cold taps.

Job: to rewasher/replace hot tap, extend existing hot supply;
● close gate-valve on outlet at cistern or tie up cistern ball-valve
● open <u>cold</u> tap until flow stops
● <u>only then</u> open hot tap.

Job: to replace hot cylinder;
● close gate-valve or tie up ball-valve arm
● turn off boiler or immersion heater
● empty cylinder via cylinder drain-valve
● close gate-valve on outlet from feed/expansion tank, or tie up ball-valve
● drain primary circuit via drain-valve at boiler.

Job: to replace cold cistern;
● close rising main stop-valve
● drain cistern by opening cold taps (hot water will still run from cylinder).

Job: to replace boiler;
● on **direct systems,** turn off boiler or immersion heater and also heating system
● close rising main stop-valve
● open all taps, and drain boiler from drain-valve nearby
● on **indirect systems,** turn off boiler
● close feed/expansion tank gate-valve
● drain primary and central heating systems from drain-valves at boiler.

prolonged period there is no need to switch off the immersion heater or to let out the boiler when carrying out a maintenance operation on the bathroom hot tap.

Problems with air locks

If your hot and cold water distribution systems are properly designed – with 'horizontal' runs of pipe actually having a slight fall away from the storage cistern or the vent pipe to permit air to escape – then the system should fill up with little or no trouble when you untie the ball-valve and permit water to flow into the cistern again. Should an air-lock prevent complete filling, try connecting one end of a length of hose to the cold tap over the kitchen sink and the other end to one of the taps giving trouble. Turn on first the tap giving trouble and then the one over the kitchen sink. Mains pressure from this cold tap should blow the air bubble out of the system.

Draining the whole system

Very occasionally – perhaps because of a major reconstruction of the system or because of that most traumatic of all plumbing emergencies, a leaking boiler – it may be necessary to drain the whole system. Let's assume, first of all, that you have either a direct hot water system or a self-priming indirect one.

Switch off the immersion heater and let out or switch off the boiler. Turn off the central heating system if this is operated from the self-priming cylinder. Close the main stop-valve and open up every tap in the house – hot as well as cold. Connect one end of a length of hose to the drain-valve beside the boiler or, if the cylinder is heated by an immersion heater only, at the base of the cold supply pipe entering the cylinder, and take the other end of the hose to an outside gully. Open up the drain-valve and allow the system to drain.

If you have an indirect system you should again turn off the boiler and central heating system. Then close the gate-valve leading from the feed-and-expansion tank, or tie up it's ball-valve, and drain the system from the boiler drain-valves.

How you proceed depends upon the reason for which you have carried out the draining-down. Your aim should be to get as much of the plumbing system as possible back into operation quickly.

Restoring partial supplies

The first step is to go up into the roof space and tie up the ball-valve on the main storage cistern as already described. Open up the main stop-valve and water supply will be restored to the cold tap over the kitchen sink.

It should also be possible to restore the bathroom cold water supplies. Trace the distribution pipe that takes water from the cold water storage cistern to the hot water cylinder.

COPING WITH AIRLOCKS

Clear supply-pipe airlocks by linking the affected tap to the kitchen cold tap with hose secured by worm-drive clips. Open the affected tap first, then the kitchen tap.

Avoid airlocks in primary or heating circuits by filling them upwards via a hose linking the kitchen cold tap and the boiler drain-valve. Close vents as radiators fill.

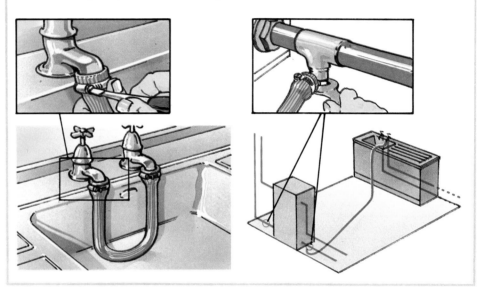

Find a cork of the correct size, lean into the cistern and push it into the pipe's inlet. Before doing so, it is a good idea to screw a substantial woodscrew part of the way into the cork to facilitate removal. You can then untie the ball-valve and allow the cistern to refill; no water will flow to the hot cylinder.

Draining heating systems

If you have a conventional indirect hot water system – perhaps installed in conjunction with a central heating system – you can drain the primary circuit, together with the radiator circuit if there is one, without draining the water from the outer part of the storage cylinder. Because of the increased risk of corrosion that arises from water and air coming into contact with steel surfaces, a radiator circuit should be drained only when absolutely essential. When this has to be done – to add additional radiators, perhaps – you should tie up the ball-valve serving the feed-and-expansion tank and drain from both the drain-valve beside the boiler and from any drain-valves provided at low points of the system. You must, of course, let out or switch off the boiler before attempting this.

When refilling the primary circuit (or when refilling a direct system with boiler) it may help to prevent the formation of air-locks if you connect one end of your garden hose to the boiler drain-valve and the other end to the cold tap over the kitchen sink. Open them both up and the system will fill upwards, with air being driven out in front of the rising water. As the central heating circuit refills,

open up all the radiator vents – and any other air vents that there may be in the system – and leave them open until water begins to flow through them. It is a good idea, when refilling a central heating system, to introduce a reliable corrosion-proofer into the feed-and-expansion tank to prevent future internal corrosion, but you can do this only if you fill the system from the top, not from the bottom.

Winter precautions

One final point: if you are leaving your home empty during the winter months, you should drain the main cold water storage cistern and, if you have a direct hot water system and will be away for more than two or three days, you should drain the hot cylinder, the boiler and its circulation pipes as well. Human memory is fallible. Having done so, leave a conspicuous notice on the boiler and by the immersion heater switch saying 'SYSTEM DRAINED – DO NOT LIGHT BOILER OR SWITCH ON HEATER UNTIL IT HAS BEEN REFILLED'.

Because of the risk of corrosion already referred to, the primary circuit and any central heating system connected to it should not be drained in these circumstances. If you have a central heating system that is capable of automatic control, leave it switched on under the control of a frost-stat. This is a thermostatic control, usually positioned in a garage or in the roof space, that will bring the heating into operation when a predetermined, near-freezing-point temperature, is reached.

INSTALLING A SINK UNIT

The sink is a highly important item of kitchen equipment, and replacing an old model is usually one of the first priorities for anyone modernising their kitchen. In this article we consider the range available and how to fit them.

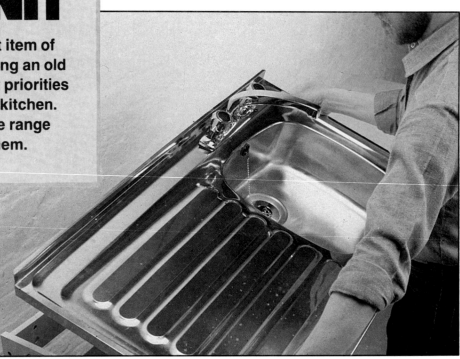

If your house was built in the 1930s or 1940s, and the kitchen has never been modernised, the chances are that it contains the original deep white glazed stoneware 'Belfast pattern' sink, supported by heavy cast-iron brackets built into the wall. It will incorporate a weir overflow and will probably have a detachable wooden draining board. A deep sink of this kind was regarded as the height of domestic luxury in the pre-war and early post-war years. An even older property might have a shallow yellow 'London pattern' sink, probably supported by brick pillars. In either case the water will very likely come from brass bib-taps (taps with horizontal inlets) projecting from a tiled splash-back fixed to the wall behind the sink. Old London pattern sinks were sometimes installed with an untrapped waste that passed through the kitchen wall to discharge over an outside gully drain. More recent sinks would have a lead or brass U-trap screwed to the waste outlet from which a branch waste pipe would discharge over the gully.

Sink units
Because these old stoneware sinks were certain death to crockery dropped into them, and looked increasingly dated, they were gradually replaced by sink units with one-piece sink tops. The sink tops were made of enamelled pressed steel or stainless steel, and the units into which they were fixed became the starting point for complete kitchen ranges incorporating continuous work surfaces. The early enamelled pressed steel sink tops had the disadvantage that the enamel was vulnerable to accidental damage. Dropping any hard object onto them could easily chip or crack the enamel. The stainless steel sink therefore became the most important innovation.

Taps and traps
It was usual, when replacing an old stoneware sink with a stainless steel or an enamelled pressed-steel sink, to get rid of the old bib-taps projecting from the wall, and to replace them with chromium-plated brass pillar taps or a mixer fitted into the holes provided at the back of the sink and connected to the hot and cold water distribution pipes concealed within the unit.

Early sinks of this kind were provided with traps, also concealed within the unit. The trap might still be of brass with a copper waste pipe, but plastic was soon introduced, connected to a plastic waste pipe by means of ring-seal push-fit connectors. Bottle traps, as distinct from the traditional U-traps, became increasingly popular. They were neater in appearance, space saving and easy to dismantle in case of a blockage, although their discharge rate was not as great. Modern ground floor sinks often still discharge over a yard gully, but the waste pipe outlet should be taken to below the gully grid either through a slotted grid or by the use of a back or side-inlet gully.

Overflows
Early sink tops had a built-in overflow consisting of a unit welded to the back of the sink. But these inevitably leaked after a time, and nowadays they have been replaced by a flexible overflow pipe. This is like the overflow pipe from a bath which is taken from the sink's overflow outlet to connect, by means of a sleeve or 'banjo' fitting, to the slotted waste pipe, before its connection to the trap. Householders who possess a sink of the older pattern with a leaking built-in overflow, will find that if the sink is dismounted and turned upside down, the overflow unit can be sawn off and replaced with one of the more modern waste and overflow fittings. But, of course, it may be better to replace the the sink.

New developments
Nowadays, there is no question of being restricted to a single sink with either right or left-hand drainer. Double sinks, one for washing the crockery and cutlery and the other for a hot rinse before air drying, have become more and more popular. The two sinks may be of equal size, around 450mm (18in) in width, or one may be smaller than the other for use in food preparation. A second sink like this might be only 240mm (10in) in width. There are also sinks with double drainers, though these are rather less in demand as they take up a lot of space; they are usually around 2m (6ft 6in) long. Overall sizes of rectangular sinks and drainer units range from about 900mm (3ft) to 1500mm (5ft) in length, and usually measure 500 or 600mm (20 to 24in) deep, to fit metric base units. Some sink tops are still available in the 21in (533mm) size to match old imperial base units. There are also many intermediate sizes, and bowl depths may range between 130 and 180mm (5 and 7in).

Early glass-reinforced plastic sink tops and drainers proved to be a complete disaster. They were incapable of standing up to the very heavy use to which sinks are subjected, their colours faded and they cracked, and crazed. Considerable advances have since been made, and modern plastic sinks and sink tops seem well able to stand up to everything that is required of them.

Ceramic sinks are making a come back, though they are very different from the old Belfast and London pattern sinks. Modern ranges include tough inset sinks and tops in an attractive range of colours. There are inset round bowls 450mm (18in) in diameter with an accompanying but separate round drainer 380mm (15in) in diameter. Then there is a conventional rectangular double sink and drainer – all of ceramic ware – in an overall size of 1125 x 505mm (45 x 20in). There is also a conventional rectangular single sink and drainer and round double sinks and drainer in one unit. A feature of these new ceramic units is their extreme toughness.

The waste and overflow of the new ceramic sinks are arranged in exactly the same way as those of the old Belfast models. A built-in overflow connects to the slot in a slotted waste outlet that is bedded on mastic in the outlet hole. Stainless steel sinks are provided with the flexible overflow already referred to, which connects to the slotted waste below the sink but above the trap. Double sinks have only one trap. This is fitted into the outlet of the sink nearest to the drain outlet, the waste from the other sink being connected to it above the level of the single trap.

Mixers
Individual sink pillar taps are still freely available, but the choice nowadays is more likely to be a sink mixer. A mixer with a swivel spout is an essential where a double sink is installed.

Sink mixers differ from bath and basin mixers in one important respect. The latter are simply two taps with a single spout. The hot and cold streams of water mix within the body of the mixer unit. Sink mixers have separate channels for the hot and cold streams of water which mix in the air as they leave the spout. The reason for this is that the cold water supply to the kitchen sink (the household's supply of water for drinking and cooking) comes direct from the rising main. The hot supply usually comes from a cylinder storage hot water system, fed with water from a main cold water storage cistern. It is illegal to mix, in one fitting, water from the main and water from a storage cistern.

Everybody is familiar with the conventional sink mixer, made of chromium-plated brass with 'shrouded' cross-top handles of plastic and a long swivel spout. Nowadays, though, there are some exciting new designs available. With some the mixer unit is fitted into just one hole at the back of the sink. The other hole may be blanked off or may be used to accommodate a rinsing brush, supplied with hot water by a flexible tube connected to the hot water supply pipe.

Putting in the sink top
When you come to install your new sink it's a good idea to make the first job fitting the taps or mixer, waste and overflow to it. This will avoid unnecessary interruption to the rest of the plumbing services. Start by putting in the combined waste and overflow unit, then attach the taps or mixer. If the sink is made of stainless steel the shanks of the taps will protrude through the holes so you won't be able to screw up the back-nuts tight. Use 'top hat' washers or spacers to accommodate the shanks.

When the sink is in position the tap tails will usually be fairly inaccessible, so it may be a

good idea to attach purpose-made extension pieces to bring them to a level below the sink basin where they will be accessible.

When you've got the new sink top ready, you'll have to turn off the main stop-valve and drain the hot and cold water pipes which supply the existing sink. Then you can disconnect the waste outlet, and use a cold chisel and hammer to chip away any seal between the back of the sink and the wall. You can remove the old sink (remember, it's going to be very heavy) and saw off the heavy cantilevered brackets that supported the old sink flush with the wall.

The hot and cold water supply pipes to the bib-taps over the old sink will probably be chased (inset) into the wall, so you'll have to unscrew and remove the old taps, excavate the pipes from the wall and pull them forward so that they can be connected to the tails of new taps.

With the new sink unit in position, the next job is to cut the water supply pipes to the correct length to connect to the tails of the taps. The sink top simply rests on the sink unit, so the tails of the taps can now be connected to the water supply pipes. If the trap of the old sink will connect to the new waste it can be reused.

THE PLUMBING CONNECTIONS

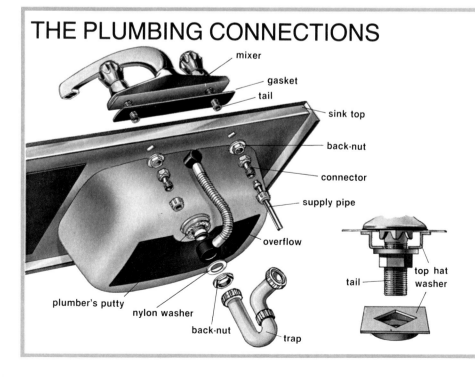

mixer
gasket
tail
sink top
back-nut
connector
supply pipe
overflow
plumber's putty
nylon washer
back-nut
trap
tail
top hat washer

INSTALLING A SINK TOP

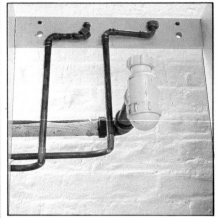

1 Take out your old sink top and check that the existing plumbing connections are undamaged. Replace as necessary.

2 Place your new sink top downwards on the floor. Take the waste outlet and press plumber's putty around the top of the screw.

3 Press the outlet firmly into position in the sink outlet aperture, at the same time squeezing out excess putty. Then put on the plastic washer.

6 Place the outlet collar of the banjo unit firmly on top of the plastic washer and support it with one hand before putting on the back-nut.

7 Put on the back-nut and screw it up tightly against the banjo unit collar, making sure it runs straight towards the sink outlet hole.

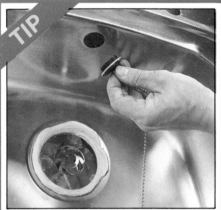

TIP

8 Screw up the overflow rose to the banjo unit overflow pipe. To help get it tight, hold the back of the outlet with a pair of pliers.

11 Take the mixer unit and ensure that the rubber gasket has no grit on it; then place the inlet tails into the holes and press the unit into position.

12 Screw on the inlet tail back-nuts and tighten them, making sure the gasket remains flat. You don't need to use any plumber's putty.

13 When the outlet and mixer installation is complete, lift the sink top into its correct position and screw it to the kitchen unit.

4 *With the plastic washer pushed firmly home, take a roll of PTFE tape and run it around the thread right up to the end of the outlet.*

5 *Before putting on the banjo unit run a thick film of pipe-jointing compound around the uppermost surface of the plastic washer.*

9 *Run a knife around the edge of the plumber's putty squeezed out from around the outlet flange. Be careful not to score the metal.*

10 *Peel away the surplus putty and check that the outlet flange is tightly held into the sink. If not, tighten the back-nut further.*

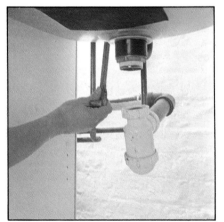

14 *Attach the inlet pipes to the mixer tails and tighten the nuts with a crowsfoot spanner, which helps you reach them.*

15 *Check that the old trap is clear and screw it up tightly to the outlet pipe; then turn on the taps to check that there are no leaks.*

Ready Reference

SINK DESIGNS

Sink designs come in several different variations particularly in the inset range. Think carefully about what you use your sink for, and what space you have available before deciding on size and design.

TYPICAL SINK SIZES

S=single, D=double, Si=sink, Dr=drainer

	Tops	Inset
SDrSSi	42x31in	37x19in
	1000x500mm	940x485mm
	1000x600mm	
	1200x600mm	
DDrSSi	63x21in	55x19in
	1500x500mm	1395x485mm
	1500x600mm	
SDrDSi	63x21in	55x19in
	1500x600mm	1395x485mm
DDrDSi	84x21in	74x19in
	2000x600mm	1850x485mm

TYPICAL DESIGNS

If you don't have a dishwasher a double bowl is useful – one for washing and one for rinsing.

double bowl

A double drainer will give you a greater working area at the sink but will cut down on the remainder of your work surface.

double drainer

If you're short of space you may dispense with the drainer altogether and use an inset bowl only. There are also units with small subsidiary bowls specially incorporated to house a waste disposal unit. These may also be supplied with trays which fit in or over the bowl, facilitating such tasks as salad preparation.

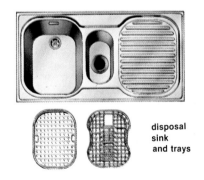

disposal sink and trays

INSTALLING AN INSET SINK

If you're fitting a new kitchen, or modernising an old one, one job you'll almost certainly have to carry out is to install an inset sink into a worktop.

Not so long ago, an assortment of cupboards, work surfaces and a kitchen sink unit formed the framework of the average kitchen. It was not a particularly efficient arrangement, but because few appliances had to be fitted in it didn't matter too much if a little space was wasted. However, as more and more homes acquired washing machines, tumble dryers, refrigerators and the like, some way had to be found of fitting these appliances into what was often a relatively small area.

What resulted from this was the 'integral' kitchen which housed all this equipment under roomy and well-lit worktops. And hand in hand with this development went the introduction of the inset sink.

The old enamelled and stainless steel sit-on sinks, with their single or double drainers, completely covered their base units. From a functional point of view they were ideal because the one-piece top meant that it was virtually impossible for water to seep into the cupboard below. Yet the kitchen sink remained a conspicuous, and somewhat unattractive, feature, divorced from other kitchen surfaces. And because of the space it took up, the unit was restricted to only one or two positions in the room. Consequently, many kitchens had to be planned around it, which naturally limited the ways in which they could be made more labour-saving and pleasant to work in.

However, once the move to creating uninterrupted work surfaces took hold, the benefits of installing a 'built-into-the-worktop' sink became readily apparent. For the first time it meant that a sink could be fitted into an overall design, which could still retain a clean, streamlined look. It didn't have to be fitted directly over a base unit, which gave far more flexibility as to where it could be positioned. However, there still had to be sufficient clearance under the worktop to take the bowl, and the plumbing supply and waste runs still had to make sense.

In fact, the idea for inset sinks stemmed from bathroom and bedroom vanity units, where a washbasin was let into the surface of a small cupboard. The surrounding melamine-finished surface was easy to clean and provided a standing area for bottles, cosmetics and the like. It was only a matter of time before the idea was adopted in the kitchen.

Choosing an inset sink

Whether you're revamping your kitchen, or just modernising the existing sink, there are a number of points to take into account before buying a new inset model.

The first is to decide what exactly the sink has to handle, because this will give you a fair guide as to the size you'll need, and whether two bowls would be better instead of just one. Indeed, there are a number of advantages in installing two or even two-and-a-half bowls (the 'half' being specifically for cutlery) not the least being that you'll still have access to the taps even if one bowl is occupied. And the amount of extra plumbing you'll have to carry out is quite small. All it entails is slightly extending the waste run. If you install a mixer tap with a swivel spout this can be used to fill both bowls so there's no additional work on the water supply side.

As with sit-on sinks, there is a wide range of bowl/drainer combinations. There are also individual round bowls which don't have an attached drainer, although there are separate drainers available that you have to let into the worktop nearby.

Round bowls do look attractive and they are increasing in popularity, but they have a couple of disadvantages. They tend to be shallower than the traditional rectangular shape – generally, the deeper the bowl the better – and their shape sometimes makes it awkward to submerge large pans and grill trays when they're being washed.

Which material to go for?

The other main consideration when choosing a sink is the material it's made of. Nowadays there is a far wider choice than ever before.

Stainless steel has retained its popularity, principally because it is relatively cheap and there is a wide range of styles available. Yet while it is heat-resistant and hard wearing, it can suffer at the hands of scourers and abrasive cleaners which leave minute surface scratches. You may also find this material somewhat clinical in appearance. However, if you do there are alternatives.

Don't shy away from plastic, for example. Admittedly the early glass-reinforced plastic tops proved to be a disaster: they simply weren't sturdy enough to cope with the use – and misuse – a kitchen sink is subjected to. But the ones on sale now are vastly different. These are made of impact-resistant modified polycarbonate in a range of attractive colours that extend right through the material. You can buy double as well as single sinks with round or rectangular bowls. As far as temperature resistance is concerned these sinks are very tough, and to prove it they are put through some remarkably nasty tests. One manufacturer, for example, has tested such sinks in hot water at up to 95°C for 40 days, in boiling water at five different levels of water hardness for 50 hours and by placing hot

THE PLUMBING CONNECTIONS

Right: Each bowl outlet should be connected to a 75mm (3in) deep seal P- or S-trap which is linked to 38mm (1½in) UPVC waste pipe. The overflows should connect to the outlets above the traps. You may have to move the supply pipes away from the wall so they can reach the tap positions.

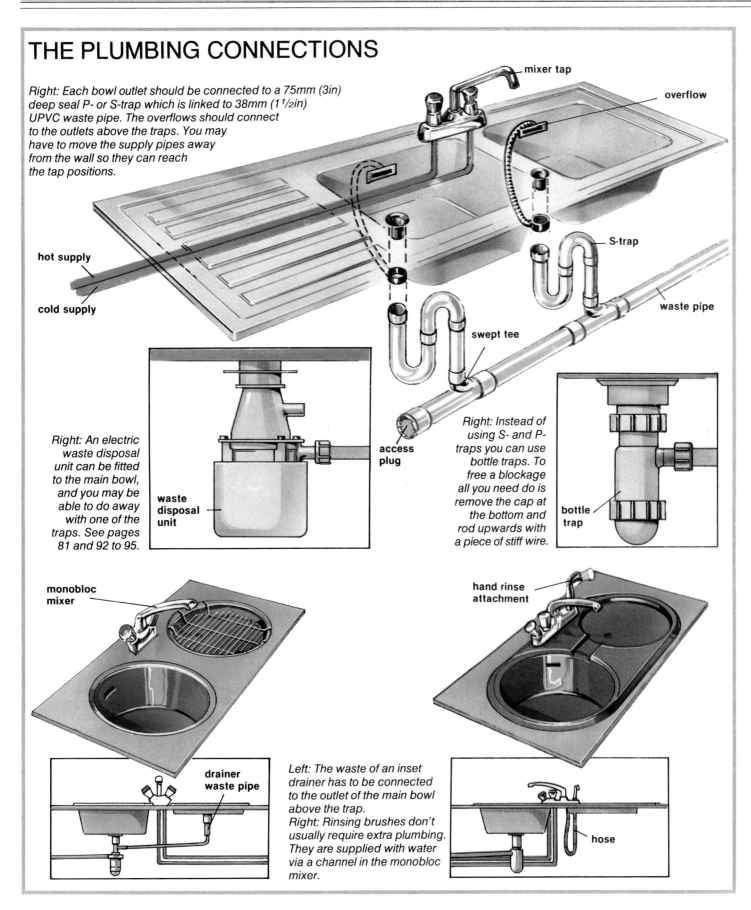

mixer tap

overflow

S-trap

hot supply

cold supply

waste pipe

swept tee

access plug

waste disposal unit

Right: An electric waste disposal unit can be fitted to the main bowl, and you may be able to do away with one of the traps. See pages 81 and 92 to 95.

Right: Instead of using S- and P- traps you can use bottle traps. To free a blockage all you need do is remove the cap at the bottom and rod upwards with a piece of stiff wire.

bottle trap

monobloc mixer

hand rinse attachment

drainer waste pipe

Left: The waste of an inset drainer has to be connected to the outlet of the main bowl above the trap.
Right: Rinsing brushes don't usually require extra plumbing. They are supplied with water via a channel in the monobloc mixer.

hose

INSTALLING AN INSET SINK

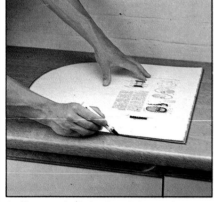

1 *If space is limited and the worktop is fixed in position, check underneath that there is clearance for the bowls and then mark round the template.*

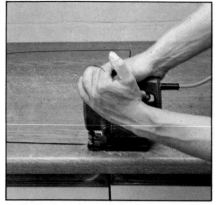

2 *Drill a hole through the worktop on the waste side of the cut-out. Insert the jigsaw and cut out the hole, supporting the waste on the underside.*

3 *Test fit the sink in the hole, wriggling it a little to get it to drop down flush with the top. If it sticks, file back the area where it catches.*

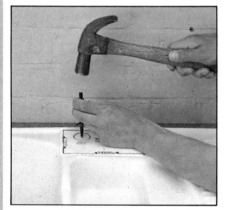

6 *If the sink doesn't have a tap hole punched, place the special template over the knockout and gently use a hammer and punch to make one.*

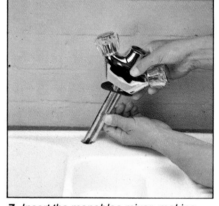

7 *Insert the monobloc mixer, making sure that it sits on a rubber gasket. Then use a spanner to tighten the back-nut underneath the sink.*

8 *Make up the outlets for the main and half bowls and the overflow. Some outlets are bedded on plumber's putty while others sit on special plastic washers.*

saucepans on them for short periods at temperatures up to 180°C. No domestic sink is likely to experience anything like that amount of misuse; even so the sinks weathered the punishment.

Ceramic sinks are once more on the market and are becoming increasingly popular. Again, they are very different from their early counterparts, but one thing hasn't changed. They spell certain death to any piece of crockery dropped into them. It's a point that should perhaps be borne in mind when choosing a sink top. Having said this, these sinks are available in an attractive range of colours (you can even get a mixer tap to match), and as with plastic and stainless steel models some versions have integral drainers. Once installed these sinks are highly resistant to being damaged. However, if you do plump for a ceramic sink and you want to install a waste disposal unit check

that the two are compatible, because it's impossible to widen the outlet as you can do with a stainless steel top.

Choosing the taps
Apart from all the other considerations it's important to choose an inset sink with the taps in mind.

If you go for a two or two-and-a-half bowl top then you're going to need some form of swivel mixer. Some sinks will only take a monobloc mixer because there is only one access hole for the hot and cold supply pipes. Others take conventional mixers. Alternatively, you could use separate pillar taps.

Some sink tops are reversible, in that depending on which way round you fit them they can have a left-hand or right-hand drainer. Obviously you can't have tap holes on both sides of the bowl, so to get round the problem usually there are knockouts in the

potential tap sites and you just remove those you want to use.

Sometimes no provision is made for taps. In this case you'll have to install bib taps coming out of the wall or drill holes through the worktop itself and fit the taps to these.

How to install an inset sink
Installing an inset sink presents no special difficulties. As with conventional sinks, and indeed most other plumbing fittings, it's best to carry out as much work as possible before putting the worktop in position. But if the worktop is fixed, rather than remove it work in situ instead. First, fit the taps. With a mixer you'll need a flat washer between the base and the sink top. And for a plastic or stainless steel sink, you'll probably need to use top hat or spacer washers over the tap tails to accommodate the protruding shanks before screwing on the back-nuts.

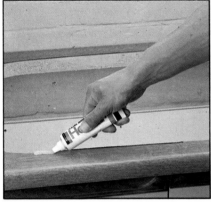

4 *Some sinks are bedded on a rubber or plastic seal. If not, run silicone rubber or non-setting mastic round the edge of the hole before fitting the sink.*

5 *Lower the inset sink into the hole and then fasten it in position underneath using the clips provided. Clean away any sealant that oozes from the edges.*

9 *Use tap connectors and special reducers to connect the 15mm (1/2in) hot and cold supply runs to the tap tails, which on this model are slightly narrower.*

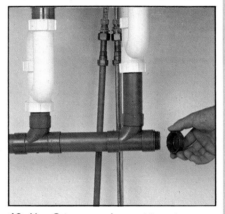

10 *Use S-traps and swept tees to connect the 38mm (1 1/2in) wastes to a common waste run. An inspection eye at the end of the run aids blockage removal.*

The tap tails will be difficult to get to once the sink is in position, particularly if the unit you are fitting over has a back to it. Therefore it's best to fit a small run of pipe, or lengths of corrugated flexible pipe, to each of the tap tails at this stage.

The waste and overflow unit is usually supplied with the sink. Don't forget to bed the outlet on a layer of mastic, and as you tighten up the back-nut make sure the slot in the shank points in the direction of the over-flow. Next, screw the overflow to the outlet point at the top of the sink bowl and then slip the 'banjo' connector at the other end of the flexible hose over the slotted waste. This is held in place by another back-nut.

As far as marking out the work surface is concerned, most sink manufacturers supply a template indicating the area of worktop to be removed. Needless to say this must be done with care and accuracy, and for this reason it's best to work on the top surface and not the underside so there's no risk of getting the sink in the wrong place.

Drill a hole through the waste side of the cut-out and then use a jigsaw to cut the hole. You can then fit the retaining brackets or rim round the underside edge. The fixing clips on the sink are secured to these when it's set in its final position.

Usually, inset sinks are provided with a rubber seal or gasket so that when fitted there's a watertight seal between the bowl and drainer and the worktop. If there isn't one, run a continuous bead of non-setting mastic round the perimeter and bed the top firmly onto this.

Once you've lowered the sink into position and clipped it in place all that then remains is to set the worktop in position on top of the unit and to connect the waste pipe and the hot and cold supply runs.

Ready Reference

CHECK UNDERSURFACE CLEARANCE

You've got considerable flexibility as to where you position an inset sink – it need not necessarily be directly over a base unit. But wherever you propose to site it make sure there is sufficient depth under the worktop to accommodate the bowls.

WHICH SINK TO CHOOSE

Inset sinks can have one, two or two and a half bowls. Some incorporate drainers, but with individual bowls separate drainers have to be installed alongside.

Many inset sinks are made of stainless steel, but if you choose a plastic or ceramic sink you have the added option of a wide range of colours.

TIP: CARE WITH HOT PANS

Whatever material your sink is made of it will withstand all likely treatment. If you've a plastic sink it's advisable not to put frying pans that have just been used for frying hot meat, dry cooked foods and hot oil directly in the sink. First allow the pan to cool briefly.

TIP: FITTING A WASTE DISPOSER

If you're installing a ceramic sink and you also want a waste disposal unit, make sure the outlet of the sink is compatible with the inlet on the disposer. Ceramic sinks can't be cut, so the two must match exactly.

BOWL ACCESSORIES

There are various accessories you can fit over the bowl of the sink such as a draining tray (A) and a chopping board (B). Ideally, use the chopping board over the sink with a waste disposer so that any vegetable matter can be hygienically flushed away.

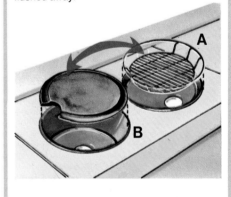

PLUMBING IN KITCHEN APPLIANCES

Washing machines and dishwashers can be a great boon in the house. They are best plumbed into a water supply and the waste outlet, otherwise you'll find they don't save as much time as they should.

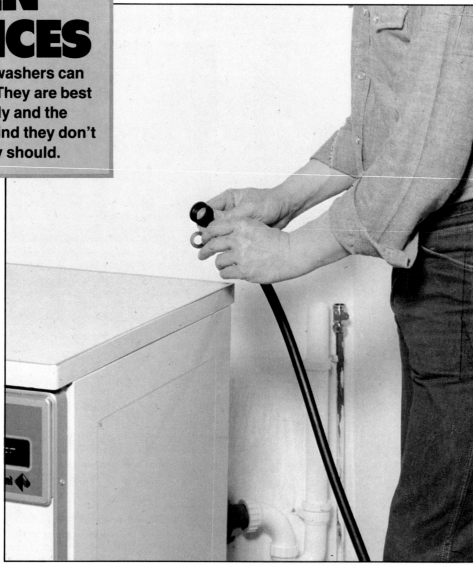

These days you'll probably opt for an automatic washing machine that fills and empties itself according to a pre-set programme, and so can be left unattended. There is a choice between top loaders and front loaders, although the latter are by far the more common. Obviously top loaders can't fit under a work surface, but drum-type top loaders tend to be narrower and this may suit your particular space requirements.

Dishwashers are almost always automatic, except for some small, cheaper sink-top models. They, too, are available as top or front loaders, though again front loaders are by far the more popular. They are also easier to load and unload, as with top loaders it's easy for crockery and cutlery to slip to the bottom of the machines.

Washing machines have become almost a necessity in busy family homes, especially where there are young children. Dishwashers are far less common, but sales are developing rapidly as more and more people wake up to their advantages. It's a simple matter to stack a dishwasher with dirty crockery direct from the meal table and then turn it on before going to bed at night. Again, for a family the labour saving is considerable.

Some washing machines don't have to be plumbed in. The inlets can be attached to the kitchen taps when the sink isn't being used, and the outlet can be hooked over the edge of the sink. The same goes for dishwashers, which usually require only a cold water feed. But to keep things really neat and tidy as well as more practical, it is best to create permanent connections for both the water supply and the waste outlet. In most kitchens this should be a fairly easy task, provided you have room for the machines in the first place.

As far as the capacities of washing machines and dishwashers go, you don't really have much choice. Washing machines have a capacity of about 4-5kg (9-11lb) and dishwashers will function quite happily provided you stack them up within the obvious tray limitations. It's important to follow the manufacturers' instructions for day-to-day maintenance. Many washing machines need their outlet filter cleaned regularly, as

do dishwashers. They may also need regular doses of salts, not to mention rinse aids.

Water supply

There are a number of ways in which you can arrange the water supply. One of them is sure to suit your plumbing system or the layout of your kitchen or utility room. A washing machine may need a hot and cold supply; dishwashers and some cheaper washing machines need only a cold supply.

Let's first consider the conventional means of plumbing in – the means that a professional plumber would almost certainly adopt if you called him in to do the job for you. It is likely to be most satisfactory where the machine is to be positioned in the immediate vicinity of the kitchen sink and the 15mm (½in) hot and cold supply pipes to the sink taps are readily accessible and in close proximity to each other.

The technique is to cut into these two pipes

at a convenient level, after cutting off the water supply and draining the pipes, and to insert into them 15mm compression tees. From the outlets of the tees lengths of 15mm (½in) copper tube are run to terminate, against the wall, in a position immediately adjacent to the machine. Onto the ends of these lengths of pipe are fitted purpose-made stop-cocks. These are usually provided with back-plates that can be screwed to the wall after it has been drilled and plugged. The outlets of the stop-cocks are designed for connection to the machine's inlet hose or hoses.

As an alternative, which is best used where the hot and cold water pipes in the kitchen are in close proximity to the position of the machine, you can use a special patent valve. This is a 'tee' with a valve outlet designed for direct connection to the washing machine hose. There are compression joints at each end of the tee and the valve is particularly

PLUMBING IN A WASHING MACHINE

Plumbing in a washing machine shouldn't present too many problems. Normally it's sited next to an existing sink, so you'll know that the water supply pipes and drainage facilities are close at hand.

Most machines are run off separate 15mm (½in) hot and cold supplies (1 & 2) taken from tees (3) inserted in the pipe runs to the sink. You should also insert some form of stop-valve (4) into the pipes so the machine can be isolated for repairs. You'll have to use female/male connections (5) to join the copper pipes to the machine's rubber inlet hoses (6).

When the water has been used, it's fed into a rubber drain hose (7) which should be loosely inserted into the top of the stand-pipe (8). This in turn connects to a 75mm (3in) trap and from here the waste water is taken in 38mm (1½in) pipe to discharge in the gully outside below the grille.

Dealing with single-stack drainage

From the trap at the bottom of the stand-pipe (11) the waste water is conducted to the main drainage stack (12) where the pipe is connected via a fitting known as a strap boss(13).

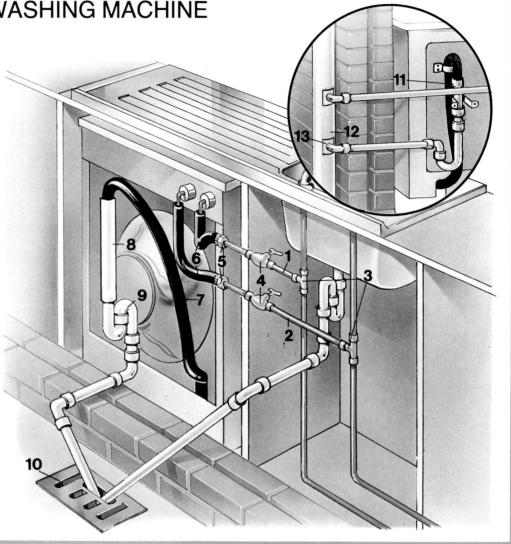

easily fitted because there is no tube-stop in one of these joints. This cuts out the difficult business of 'springing' the cut ends of the pipe into the tee.

Then there are valves which can be connected without cutting a section out of the water supply pipes. With one such valve the pipe is drained and is then drilled with a 8mm (⁵⁄₁₆in) bit. A back-plate is then fitted to the wall behind it and a front-plate, with a short projecting pipe and a rubber seal that fits into the hole in the pipe, is clamped to it. The washing machine valve then screws into this front-plate.

Yet another valve is self-tapping and screws its own hole in the water pipe. This, so the makers claim, can be done without cutting off the water supply and draining the pipe.

A valve which depends upon drilling the water supply pipe will not permit the same flow of water as one in which the pipe is cut and a tee inserted. It must be said, though,

that this seems to make very little difference in practice, but obviously in the former case the tightening of the connection must be more than sufficient for it to work properly.

Putting in drainage

The simplest method is undoubtedly to hook the machine's outlet hose over the rim of the kitchen or utility room sink when required. However, this method isn't always convenient and is certainly untidy. An alternative is to provide an open-ended stand-pipe fixed to the kitchen wall into which the outlet hose of the machine can be permanently hooked. The open end of the stand-pipe should be at least 600mm (24in) above floor level and should have an internal diameter of at least 35mm (1³⁄₈in). A deep seal (75mm/3in) trap should be provided at its base and a branch waste pipe taken from its outlet to an exterior gully, if on the ground floor, or to the main soil and waste stack of a single stack

system if on an upper floor. As with all connections to a single soil and waste stack this should be done only under the supervision of the district or borough council's Building Control Officer. Manufacturers of plastic drainage systems include suitable drainage stand-pipes and accessories in their range of equipment (the trap and pipe being sold as one unit).

It is sometimes possible to deal with washing machine or dishwasher drainage by taking the waste pipe to connect directly to the trap of the kitchen sink and this course of action may be suggested at DIY centres and by builders' merchants staff. But it must be stressed that this is not recommended by the manufacturers of washing machines, who consider that it involves a considerable risk of back-siphonage. This could lead to waste water from the sink siphoning back into the machine. In the case of a washing machine this could mean considerable problems.

PLUMBING IN A DISHWASHER

1 Start by working out how to run the waste outlet. This will often mean making a hole in the wall using a club hammer and cold chisel.

2 Measure up the run on the inside, then cut a suitable length of 38mm (1½in) PVC plastic waste pipe and push it through the hole you have made.

3 Make up the outside pipe run dry, to ensure it all fits, then solvent weld it. It's useful to put in an inspection elbow in case of blockages.

6 Carry on assembling the run on the inside using standard waste pipe fittings. Try to keep the run close to the wall for a neat appearance.

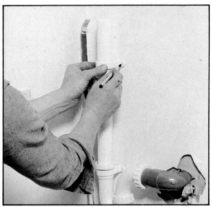

7 Take the trap and stand-pipe, which you can buy as a standard fitting or make up yourself, and mark the bracket positions on the wall.

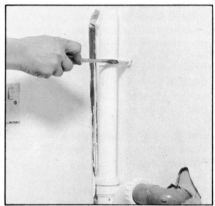

8 Drill and plug the wall, and fix the stand-pipe in position. Make sure that it is fully supported and vertical and the trap is screwed tight.

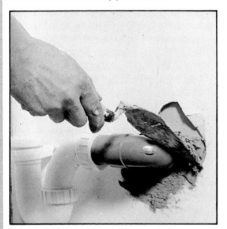

11 Make good the damage to the wall both on the inside and out; the plastic pipe will be held firmly in place by the mortar and plaster.

12 You can now move the machine into position and connect it up. The inlet hose has a female screwed connector, which must have a washer in it.

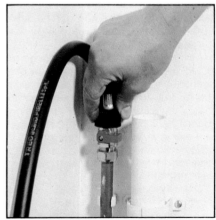

13 With the washer in place, screw up the connector to the tap on the inlet pipe; it's enough to hand-tighten this connection.

4 *If the run terminates in a gully drain, then make sure that you fit the pipe so that the end is situated below the level of the water.*

5 *When you have completed the outside waste run, replace the grid. Cut away as much of it as necessary to fit round the pipe, using a hacksaw.*

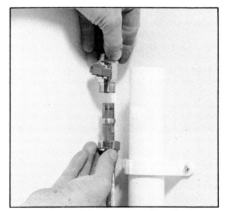

9 *Run the cold water supply using 15mm (¹/₂in) pipe via a tee cut into tne domestic cold supply, and attach a running tap to the end.*

10 *Secure the supply pipe to the wall using pipe brackets, then go back and make sure that all your connections are sound.*

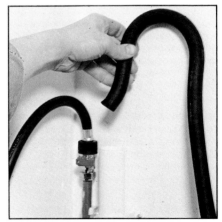

14 *Take the outlet hose from the machine and place it in the top of the stand-pipe.You should not attempt to make the connection airtight.*

15 *Move the machine exactly into position and check that it is level; if not, adjust the feet. Then turn on the water and test the machine.*

Ready Reference

INSTALLATION CHECKLIST

When installing a washing machine or dishwasher, remember that:
- it's usual to take the water supply from the domestic cold water system; if you want to use the mains you may need a pressure reducer, so check with the manufacturer's literature
- if the machine takes a hot and cold supply you will have to ensure that there is sufficient pressure in the hot supply and that this is the same as that from the cold
- to operate at maximum efficiency, the machine should stand on a level surface and this should be firm; washing machines in particular are extremely heavy when full of water.

BATHROOM REGULATIONS

If you want to put your washing machine in the bathroom then there are electrical rules that must be obeyed:
- it must be permanently wired in
- you must not be able to touch the controls when you're in the bath or shower.

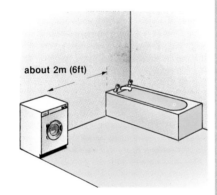

TIP: CHECK DIMENSIONS

If the machine is going to be put between existing units or under a work surface you'll have to measure up carefully before you buy. Make sure there is enough space behind for the plumbing work.

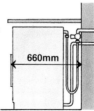

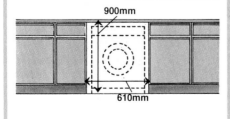

PLUMBING IN A BATH

Replacing a bath may seem to be an ambitious do-it-yourself project but it is well within the capabilities of the determined home handyman prepared to tackle the job carefully and logically. Here is what is involved.

As with many other plumbing projects the most difficult part is likely to be the removal of the old fitting rather than the installation of the new one.

The old bath will almost certainly be made of enamelled cast iron. The once-white enamel may be discoloured and wearing away, and may even reveal rusting bare metal underneath. Green or brown coloured stains beneath the taps indicate a long-neglected need for rewashering. The taps may look out of date and have worn chromium plating. The finish of the bath may be old and unattractive and the bath itself not panelled in.

Checking it out

First have a look at the existing bath. If there are side or end panels, strip them off and examine, with the aid of an electric torch, the water supply pipes and the waste and the overflow arrangements in the cramped and badly lit space between the foot of the bath and the wall. You will see that the water supply pipes connect the threaded tails of the taps by means of brass 'swivel tap connectors' or 'cap and lining joints'.

Check whether the water supply pipes are made of copper or lead by scraping their surface with the blade of a pocket knife. If this reveals the characteristic grey sheen of lead you should think of replacing the piping. If you *do* want to retain the lead piping you will have to call in a qualified plumber – it's not an easy task. If the pipes are of copper you should be able to tackle the entire project without professional aid.

The overflow from a modern bath is taken, by means of a flexible pipe, to the waste trap. In the past, the overflow pipe often simply led through the external wall, and was the source of incurable bathroom draughts. If your bath's overflow is like this, you'll have to cut it off flush with the wall.

If the bath has adjustable feet, apply some penetrating oil to the screws. Once they begin to move, lowering the level of the bath before you attempt to remove it can help to prevent damage to the wall tiling.

The alternatives

It is possible to replace your cast iron bath with a new one made of the same material, but more modern in styling. However, these baths are expensive and very heavy indeed. Carrying one into the bathroom and fitting it requires considerable strength (you'd need at least one strong helper) as well as care. There are other snags about enamelled cast iron baths. They normally have a slippery base that can make them dangerous to use – particularly by the very young and the elderly, though some are available with a non-slip surface. Furthermore, the material of which they are made rapidly conducts the heat away from the water and while this didn't matter too much in the days when energy was plentiful and cheap, large amounts of hot water cost rather more today.

One economical alternative is an enamelled pressed steel bath. This is lighter and cheaper than enamelled cast iron but can be more easily damaged in storage or installation.

For do-it-yourself installation a plastic bath is the obvious choice. These are made of acrylic plastic sheet, sometimes reinforced with glass fibre. They are available in a number of attractive colours and, as the colour extends right through the material of which they are made, any surface scratches can be easily polished out. They are light in weight and one

man can quite easily carry one upstairs for installation. The plastic of which they are made is a poor conductor of heat which means that they are both comfortable and economical to use. Many of them have a non-slip base to make them safe.

But plastic baths do have their snags. They are easily damaged by extreme heat. You should be beware of using a blow torch in proximity to one and a lighted cigarette should never be rested, even momentarily, on the rim. A fault of early plastic baths was their tendency to creak and sag when filled with hot water and, sometimes, when you got into them. This has now been overcome by the manufacturers who provide substantial frames or cradles for support; but these frames must be assembled and fixed exactly as recommended. Some come already attached to the bath.

A combined plastic waste and overflow assembly is likely to be the choice nowadays for any bath, and is obligatory with a plastic bath. If a rigid metal trap is used with a plastic bath, the material of the bath could be damaged as hot water causes unequal expansion.

You obviously won't want to re-use the old bath taps and will probably opt for either individual modern ¾in bath pillar taps or a bath mixer. A mixer should be chosen only if the cold water supply is taken from the same cold

REPOSITIONING A BATH

In many bathrooms, a new bath simply takes the place of an existing one; there's no room for manoeuvre. But in some cases moving the bath to another position in the room can lead to a more practical arrangement and better use of the available space. In this bathroom the new bath was installed at the other side of the room, so that the space it had formerly occupied could house a shower cubicle and a WC. Moving the bath to this position involved extending the existing hot and cold water supply pipes, but brought it nearer the soil stack on the outside wall and meant that the waste pipe was short and simple to connect up outside.

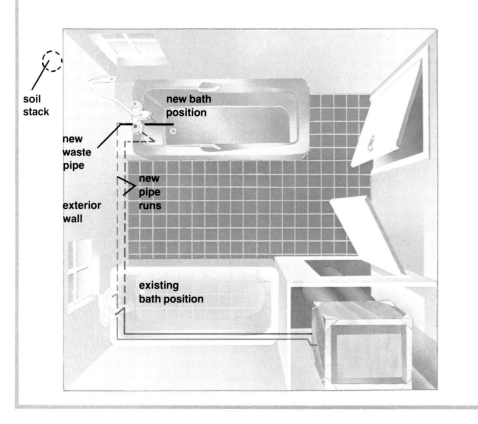

soil stack

new waste pipe

exterior wall

new bath position

new pipe runs

existing bath position

Ready Reference

EQUIPMENT ROUND-UP
To replace a bath, you're likely to need the following tools:
● crowsfoot wrench
● adjustable spanner
● adjustable wrench
● hacksaw (possibly)
● spirit level

You'll also need:
● new bath — measure up carefully before you buy it to make sure it fits. It should come complete with supports, carcase and side panels, otherwise you'll need these as well
● new overflow connection, waste outlet and PVC trap
● taps/mixer and new inlet pipe if you are replacing them
● plumber's putty

KNOW YOUR BATH

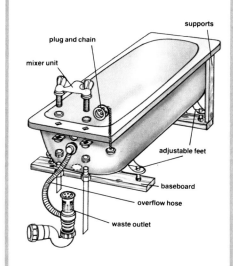

supports

plug and chain

mixer unit

adjustable feet

baseboard

overflow hose

waste outlet

THE SPACE YOU NEED
You need a minimum amount of space around a bath (below) and also a minimum ceiling height above it (right).

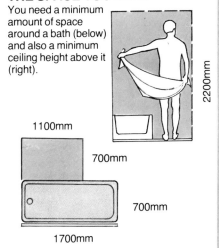

2200mm

1100mm

700mm

700mm

1700mm

water storage cistern that supplies the hot water system. It should not be used where the cold water supply to the bathroom comes directly from the mains supply.

How to proceed
To avoid too long a disruption of the domestic hot and cold water supplies you can fit the taps, waste and trap into the new bath before removing the old one.

Slip a flat plastic washer over the tail of each tap and insert the tails through the holes provided for them. A mixer usually has one large flat washer or gasket with two holes — one for each tap tail. Beneath the rim of the bath, slip 'top hat' or 'spacer' washers over the tails to accommodate the protruding shanks of the taps. Screw on the back-nuts and tighten them. For details, see pages 57 to 59.

Bed the waste flange onto plumber's putty or non-setting mastic, secure the back-nut

and connect up the trap. Then connect up the overflow pipe.

Removing the old bath may well be the most difficult part of the procedure. Turn off the hot and cold water supplies and drain the distribution pipes from the bath taps. If you haven't done so already, remove the bath panel to give access to the plumbing at the foot of the bath. You can try to unscrew the back-nuts holding the taps in position, but it's generally easier to undo the nuts that connect the distribution pipes to the tails of the taps. In order to reach the one nearest the wall you may have to dismantle the overflow, either by unscrewing it or, if it is taken through the wall, by cutting it off flush with the wall. Then undo the waste connection.

The bath is now disconnected from the water supply pipes and from the branch waste pipe and can be pulled away from the wall. Unless you particularly want to save the old bath and have some strong helpers, do not attempt to remove it from the room or the house in one piece. It is very heavy. The best course of action is to break it into manageable pieces. Drape an old blanket over it to prevent flying chips of enamel and wear goggles to protect the eyes. Then, with a club hammer, break the bath up into pieces that you can easily carry away.

Place the new plastic bath in position and assemble the cradle or other support exactly as recommended by the manufacturer. It is most unlikely that the tails of the new taps will coincide with the position of the tap connectors of the old distribution pipes. If they don't, the easiest way of making the connections is by means of bendable copper pipe. This is corrugated copper tubing – easily bent by hand. It is obtainable in 15mm and 22mm sizes and either with two plain ends for connection to soldered capillary or compression joints, or with one plain end and a swivel tap connector at the other. For this particular job two lengths of 22mm corrugated copper pipe will be required, each with one end plain and one end fitted with a swivel tap connector.

Offer the corrugated pipe lengths up to the tap tails and cut back the distribution pipes to the length required for connection to the plain ends. Leave these pipes slightly too long rather than too short. The corrugated pipe can be bent to accommodate a little extra length. Now connect the plain ends to the cut distribution pipes using either soldered capillary or Type 'A' compression couplings.

The chances are that the distribution pipes will be ¾in imperial size. If you use compression fittings an adaptor — probably simply a larger olive — will be needed for connection to a 22mm coupling. If you use soldered capillary fittings, special ¾in to 22mm couplings must be used. Remember to keep the blowtorch flame well away from the plastic of the bath. Connect up the swivel tap connectors of the corrugated pipe and the overflow of the bath. Do this in a logical order. First connect the tap connector to the further tap. A fibre washer inside the nut of the tap connector will ensure a watertight joint. Then connect up the flexible overflow pipe of the combined waste-and-overflow fitting to the bath's overflow outlet. Finally connect the nearer tap to the nearer tap connector.

If you have installed new pipework then you can install the entire trap, waste and water supply pipe spurs before moving the bath into position. Whatever you have decided upon, finish making all the connections, then re-instate the water supply and check for leaks.

The level of the positioned bath should now be checked using a spirit level, and adjustments made (you'll need a spanner to set the adjustable feet). When all is level, fit the side and end panels in position and the job is finished.

TAKING OUT THE OLD BATH

1 Think about how you're going to get the old bath out before you begin. The connections are likely to be inaccessible, old and corroded.

2 Start by trying to detach the waste trap using an adjustable wrench and, if necessary, penetrating oil.

3 Undo the back-nuts underneath the taps or mixer. These are likely to be more difficult to undo than the trap; use a crowsfoot wrench.

4 If the back-nuts won't undo you may have to detach the supply pipes at another joint. Use an adjustable spanner to undo the nut.

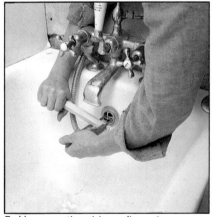

5 Unscrew the old overflow pipe. Alternatively you can simply saw off both supply and overflow pipes — but you'll need to install new ones.

6 When the bath is free, drag it out of position. You'll need at least one other person to help you get a cast iron bath out unless you break it up first.

ATTACHING THE NEW FITTINGS

1 *Start to assemble the new plumbing. Wind PTFE tape around the screw thread of the waste outlet and spread some plumber's putty underneath the rim.*

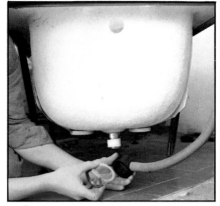

2 *Put the waste outlet in position and make sure that it is firmly seated. These days the overflow will be made of plastic and connects to the waste outlet.*

3 *Attach the overflow to the outlet with a locking nut and a plastic O ring, which is inserted between them. Screw up the nut and tighten gently.*

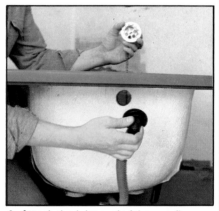

4 *Attach the inlet end of the overflow which will have the plug and chain attached to it. Screw it into the pipe connector and tighten it up.*

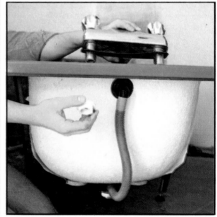

5 *Take the mixer and check that the rubber gasket is in position between the unit and the bath, and also that it is clean and free from bits of grit.*

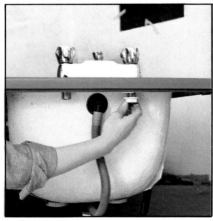

6 *Screw the back-nuts up onto the trap and tighten them. Insert a flat plastic washer or top hat washer between the nut and the bath.*

Ready Reference

BATH TYPES

Most baths sold today have outside dimensions of about 1675mm (66in) long, 750mm (30in) wide, and 550mm (21in) high. Shorter baths are available for particularly small bathrooms and these are roughly 1525mm (60in) and 1375mm (54in) long. Other baths may be up to 1825mm (72in) long and 1100mm (43in) wide. They also come in different bottom mouldings to make them safe and often have handles to help the less active get in and out. Although most are basically rectangular inside and out some are oval-shaped and designed to fit into corners. There are also special baths for the disabled which are much shorter and formed in the shape of a seat.

Plain traditional rectangular

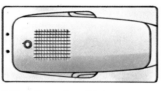

Off-rectangular with handles

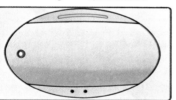

Large oval with side plumbing

Corner bath

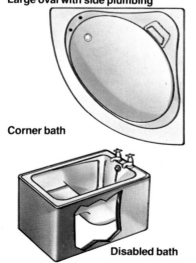

Disabled bath

INSTALLING THE NEW BATH

1 If you have installed new pipework, you should attach inlet spurs to the taps before you have to install the bath in its final position.

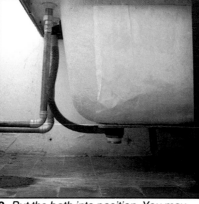

2 Put the bath into position. You may want to stand it away from the wall at the front end so that you can build in a shelf. Connect the inlet pipes.

3 Fit the waste trap and attach it to the waste pipe. When all the pipework is connected up, turn on the water and check for leaks.

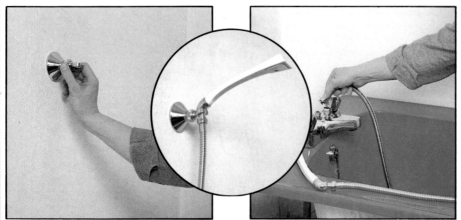

4 When installing a mixer with a shower attachment, fix the shower head bracket to the wall and fit the shower head into the bracket (inset).

5 Attach the outlet end of the flexible shower hose to central outlet on the mixer unit. It should plug in and click into position with a slight turn.

TIP

6 Check that the bath is level both lengthways and widthways with a spirit level. Adjust the screwed-on feet to get the level right.

7 Fix the bath panels in position by screwing them to the wooden carcase which surrounds the bath and is supplied by the manufacturer.

8 Screw the panels on carefully. They will usually be made of moulded high impact polystyrene which is easily chipped around the screw holes.

9 When all the bath work is complete you will have to make good the décor. If possible tile around the bath and box in the pipework.

REPLACING A WASHBASIN

Replacing a washbasin is fairly straightforward. It's a job you'll have to undertake if the basin is cracked – but you may also want to change the basin if you're redesigning your bathroom and adding some up-to-date fittings.

A part from replacing a cracked basin, which you should do immediately, the most common time to install a new basin is when you're improving a bathroom or decorating a separate WC. The chances are that the basin you'll be removing will be one of the older ceramic types, wall-hung, a pedestal model or built into a vanity unit.

The main advantage of a wall-hung basin is that it doesn't take up any floor space and because of this it is very useful in a small bathroom, WC or cloakroom. You can also set the basin at a comfortable height, unlike a pedestal basin the height of which is fixed by the height of the pedestal. However, it's usual to fit a wall-hung basin with the rim 800mm (32in) above the floor.

Vanity units are now increasing in popularity. In fact they're the descendents of the Edwardian wash-stand, with its marble top, bowl and large water jug. The unit is simply a storage cupboard with a ceramic, enamelled pressed steel or plastic basin set flush in the top. The advantage of vanity units is that you have a counter surface round the basin on which to stand toiletries. There is rarely, if ever, sufficient room for these items behind or above conventional wall-hung or pedestal basins. Usually the top has some form of plastic covering or can be tiled for easy cleaning.

Fittings for basins

It's a good idea to choose the taps and waste fittings at the same time you select the basin, so everything matches. You could perhaps re-use the taps from the old basin, but it's doubtful if these will be in keeping with the design of the new appliance. As an alternative to shrouded head or pillar taps, you could fit a mixer, provided the holes at the back of the basin are suitably spaced to take the tap tails. But remember that because of the design of most basin mixers, you shouldn't use them if the cold water supply is directly from the mains.

Ceramic basins normally have a built-in overflow channel which in most appliances connects into the main outlet above the trap. So if you accidentally let the basin overfill you reduce the risk of water spillage.

PUTTING IN A NEW BASIN

You should have little trouble installing a new washbasin in the same place as the old one. It's also a good opportunity to check the pipe runs. If they're made of lead it's a good idea to replace them.

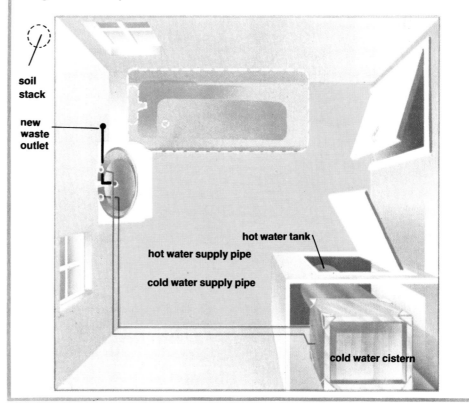

soil stack

new waste outlet

hot water tank

hot water supply pipe

cold water supply pipe

cold water cistern

Vanity unit basins are usually sold complete with a waste and overflow unit which resembles that of a modern stainless steel sink. A flexible tube connects the overflow outlet of the basin with a sleeve or 'banjo' unit which fits tightly round a slotted waste fitting.

With both types of basin the flange of the waste outlet has to be bedded into the hole provided for it in the basin on a layer of plumber's putty. The thread of the screwed waste must also be smeared with jointing compound to ensure a watertight seal where the 'banjo' connects to it.

Traps

The outlet of the waste must, of course, connect to a trap and branch waste pipe. At one time it was the practice to use 'shallow seal' traps with a 50mm (2in) depth of seal for two-pipe drainage systems, and 'deep seal' traps with a 75mm (3in) depth of seal for single stack systems. Today, however, deep seal traps are always fitted.

Of course, the modern bottle trap is one of the most common types used. It's neater looking and requires less space than a traditional U-trap. Where it's concealed behind a pedestal or in a vanity unit you can use one made of plastic, but there are chromium-plated and brass types if you have a wall-hung basin where trap and waste will be clearly visible. The one drawback with bottle traps is that they discharge water more slowly than a U-trap. You can now also buy traps with telescopic inlets that make it easy to provide a push-fit connection to an existing copper or plastic branch waste pipe (see page 18).

Connecting up the water supply

It's unlikely that you'll be able to take out the old basin and install a new one without making some modification to the pipework. It's almost certain that the tap holes will be in a different position. To complicate matters further, taps are now made with shorter tails so you'll probably have to extend the supply pipes by a short length.

If you're installing new supply pipes, how you run them will depend on the type of basin you're putting in. With a wall-hung basin or the pedestal type, the hot and cold pipes are usually run neatly together up the back wall and then bent round to the tap tails. But as a vanity unit will conceal the plumbing there's no need to run the pipes together.

You might find it difficult to bend the required angles, so an easy way round the problem is to use flexible corrugated copper pipe which you can bend by hand to the shape you need. You can buy the pipe with a swivel tap connector at one end and a plain connector, on which you can use capillary or

FITTING A VANITY UNIT

1 Cut a hole in the vanity unit with the help of the template provided or, if the hole is precut, check the measurement against that of the sink.

2 Prop the basin up while you install the mixer unit. Start with the outlet spout which is fixed with a brass nut and packing washers.

5 Now complete the tap heads by first sliding on the flange which covers up the securing nut; next put on the headwork and tighten the retaining nut.

6 Finish off the tap assembly by fitting the coloured markers into place (red for hot is usually on the left), and gently pressing home the chrome cap.

TIP

9 Before you put the basin into its final position put a strip of mastic around the opening in the vanity unit to ensure a watertight seal.

10 Press the basin gently into position and fix it to the underside of the top of the vanity unit. Attach the waste plug to its keeper.

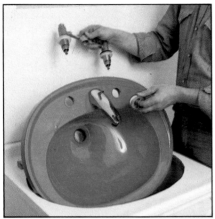

3 *Now take the water inlet assembly and check that the hot and cold spur pipes are the right length so that the tap sub-assemblies are correctly positioned.*

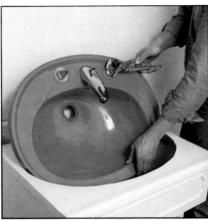

4 *Fix the assembly in position with the brass nuts supplied by the manufacturer. Make sure that all the washers are included otherwise the fitting won't be secure.*

7 *Now insert the waste outlet. Make sure the rubber flange is fitted properly and seats comfortably into the basin surround.*

8 *Turn the basin over; secure the outlet and the pop-up waste control rods. These may need shortening depending on clearance inside the vanity unit.*

11 *Now fix the inlet pipes to the two mixer connections and screw on the waste trap. Take the doors off the vanity unit to make access easier.*

12 *Turn the water back on and check for leaks. Check the pop-up waste system works, then put the doors of the vanity unit back on.*

Ready Reference

BASIN SIZES

On basins, the dimension from side to side is specified as the length, and that from back to front as the width.

Most standard sized basins are between 550 and 700mm (22 and 28in) long, and 450 to 500mm (18 to 20in) wide.

BASIN COMPONENTS

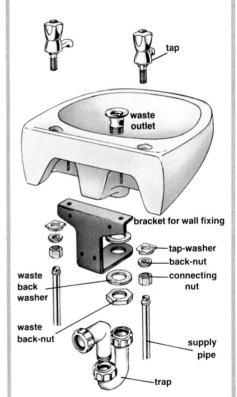

tap

waste outlet

bracket for wall fixing

tap-washer

back-nut

connecting nut

waste back washer

waste back-nut

supply pipe

trap

THE SPACE YOU'LL NEED

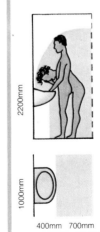

2200mm

1000mm

400mm   700mm

Think about the space around your basin particularly if you are installing a new one. You not only need elbow room when you are bending over it, such as when you are washing your hair, but also room in front to stand back – especially if you put a mirror above it. Here are the recommended dimensions for the area around your basin.

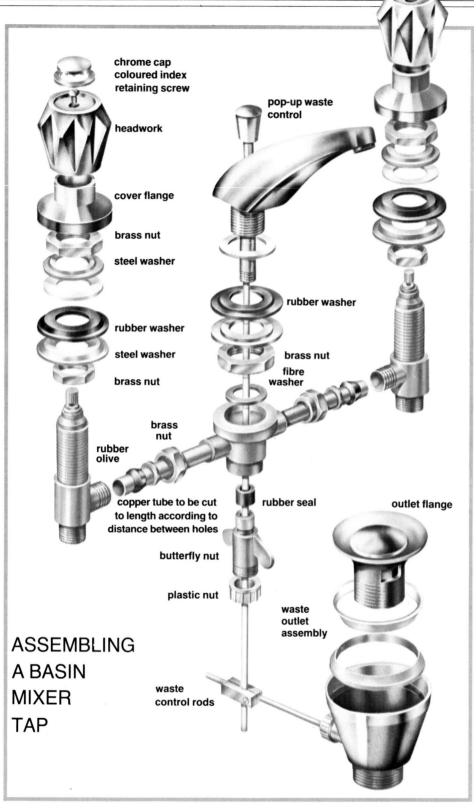

chrome cap
coloured index
retaining screw

headwork

cover flange

brass nut

steel washer

pop-up waste control

rubber washer

rubber washer

steel washer

brass nut

brass nut

fibre washer

brass nut

rubber olive

copper tube to be cut to length according to distance between holes

rubber seal

outlet flange

butterfly nut

plastic nut

waste outlet assembly

ASSEMBLING A BASIN MIXER TAP

waste control rods

When fitting the taps all you have to do is to remove the back-nuts and slip flat plastic washers over the tails (if they aren't there already). The taps can then be positioned in the holes in the basin. When this has been done more plastic washers (or top hat washers) have to be slipped over the tails before the back-nuts are replaced. It's important not to overtighten these as it's quite easy to damage a ceramic basin.

Because some vanity unit basins are made of a thinner material, you may find that the shanks of the taps fitted into them will protrude below the under-surface of the basin. The result is that when the back-nut is fully tightened, it still isn't tight against the underside of the basin. To get round the problem you have to fit a top hat washer over the shank so the back-nut can be screwed up against it.

Mixers usually have one large washer or gasket between the base of the mixer and the top of the basin and you fix them in exactly the same way.

When you've fitted the taps you can then fit the waste. With a ceramic basin you'll have to use a slotted waste to enable water from the overlfow to escape into the drainage pipe. Getting this in place means first removing the back-nut so you can slip it through the outlet hole in the basin – which itself should be coated with a generous layer of plumber's putty. It's essential to make sure that the slot in the waste fitting coincides with the outlet of the basin's built-in overflow. You'll then have to smear jointing compound on the protruding screw thread of the tail, slip on a plastic washer and replace and tighten the back-nut. As you do this the waste flange will probably try to turn on its seating, but you can prevent this by holding the grid with pliers as you tighten the back-nut.

Finally, any excess putty that is squeezed out as the flange is tightened against the basin should be wiped away.

A vanity unit will probably be supplied with a combined waste and overflow unit. This is a flexible hose that has to be fitted (unlike a ceramic basin, where it's an integral part of the appliance). The slotted waste is bedded in exactly the same way as a waste on a ceramic basin. You then have to fit one end of the overflow to the basin outlet and slip the 'banjo' outlet on the other end over the tail of the waste to cover the slot. It's held in position by a washer and back-nut.

Fitting the basin

Once the taps and waste have been fixed in position on the new basin, you should be ready to remove the old basin and fit the new one in its place. First you need to cut off the water supply to the basin, either by turning off the main stop-valve (or any gate valve on

compression fittings at the other. If you're using ordinary copper pipe, the easiest way to start is by bending the pipe to the correct angle first, and then cutting the pipe to the right length at each end afterwards. See pages 25 to 27.

Preparing the basin

Before you fix the basin in position, you'll need to fit the taps (or mixer) and the waste. It's much easier to do this at this stage than later when the basin is against the wall because you will have more room to manoeuvre in.

the distribution pipes) or by tying up the ball-valve supplying the main cold water storage cistern. Then open the taps and leave them until the water ceases to flow. If the existing basin is a pedestal model you'll have to remove the pedestal which may be screwed to the floor. Take off the nut that connects the basin trap to the threaded waste outlet and unscrew the nuts that connect the water supply pipes to the tails of the taps. These will either be swivel tap connectors or cap and lining joints. You'll need to be able to lift the basin clear and then remove the brackets or hangers on which it rests.

You'll probably need some help when installing the new basin as it's much easier to mark the fixing holes if someone else is holding the basin against the wall. With a pedestal basin, the pedestal will determine the level of the basin. The same applies with a vanity unit. But if the basin is set on hangers or brackets, you can adjust the height for convenience.

Once the fixing holes have been drilled and plugged, the basin can be screwed into position and you can deal with the plumbing. Before you make the connections to the water supply pipes you may have to cut or lengthen them to meet the tap tails. If you need to lengthen them you'll find it easier to use corrugated copper pipe. The actual connection between pipe and tail is made with a swivel tap connector – a form of compression fitting.

Finally you have to connect the trap. You may be able to re-use the old one, but it's more likely you'll want to fit a new one. And if its position doesn't coincide with the old one, you can use a bottle trap with an adjustable telescopic inlet.

FITTING A PEDESTAL BASIN

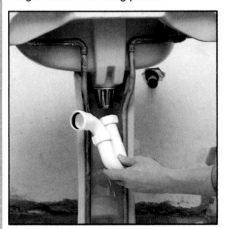

1 Stand the basin on the pedestal to check the height of the water supply pipe runs and the outlet. Measure the height of the wall fixing points.

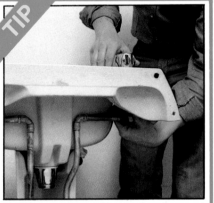

2 When you're making up the pipe run to connect to the tap tails, plan it so the pipes are neatly concealed within the body of the pedestal.

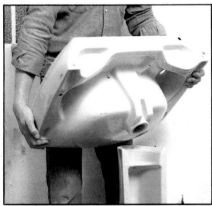

3 Line up the piped waste outlet and fix the trap to the basin outlet. A telescopic trap may be useful here to adjust for a varying level.

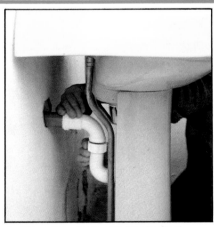

4 Move the whole unit into its final position, screw the basin to the wall, connect the waste trap to the outlet, and connect up the supply pipes.

REPLACING YOUR WC

Replacing your WC need not be a frightening prospect provided you follow a few basic rules. It also gives you the opportunity to install a quieter and more efficient piece of equipment.

There are several reasons why you may wish to remove and replace your WC suite. The existing pan may be cracked, in which case replacement must not be delayed, and no attempt should be made to repair it. Or the porcelain may be crazed making it unsightly, and difficult to keep clean. Most likely, however, the reason will be that your existing WC is simply old fashioned and due for replacement as part of an overall improvement plan.

Pan or cistern?
If it's just the pan you find fault with then that's all you need to replace. Colours for sanitary-ware, as WCs are usually called by the manufacturers, are fairly standardised, and you should have no difficulty in obtaining a pan to match the existing cistern.

If, on the other hand, you want to convert an old-fashioned lavatory suite with a high-level cistern, it may be possible to replace only the flushing cistern and flush pipe (or 'flush bend' as it is often called) with a low level one, while keeping the existing pan.

However, in order to accommodate the flushing cistern, the pans of low level suites are usually positioned 25 to 50mm (1 to 2in) further from the wall behind the suite than are those of high level ones. If you overlook this point you are likely to find that the seat and cover of the pan cannot be raised properly when the new cistern is fitted.

Slim-line cisterns
In recent years manufacturers have developed slim-line flushing cisterns or 'flush panels' only about 115mm (4¼in) deep. These can, in most cases, be used to convert a WC from high level to low level operation without moving the pan. With such a cistern the flushing inlet to the pan can be as little as 130mm (5¼in) from the wall behind, instead of the 200 to 230 (8 to 9in) required by an ordinary low level cistern. To make room for the full 9 litres (2 gal) of water needed for an adequate flush, these slimline cisterns are rather wider from side to side than conventional ones. So make sure that there is sufficient unobstructed width of wall behind the suite to accommodate it.

PLANNING THE MOVE
The biggest problem concerns the position of the soil stack. In this bathroom the old soil pipe was disconnected, and a new soil pipe run was installed on the outside of the bathroom wall to link the new WC to the existing soil stack. This was much neater than running the new pipe inside the bathroom, where it would have had to be boxed in.

The other alteration to existing pipework involved cutting the cold feed to the cistern part-way along its run, and re-connecting it to the new cistern.

exterior wall — **new soil pipe** — **soil stack position**

new WC

existing WC

cold feed to cistern

new bath position

Siphonic suites

Close-coupled lavatory suites, in which the pan and cistern form one unit without even the short flush bend of a low level cistern, are neater in appearance than the other kinds. They are particularly silent and effective where they are flushed and cleansed by siphonic action, as distinct from the 'wash down' action in which flushing simply releases the full contents of the cistern into the pan, and the weight of water carries away its contents. They also provide a larger water surface area than older pans, an important factor in maintaining the cleanliness of the pan.

There are two kinds of siphonic suite, single-trap and double-trap. The single-trap pattern is the simpler and cheaper. The outlet is first constricted and then widened to connect to the branch drain or soil pipe. When the suite is flushed, water completely fills the restricted section of the outlet and passes on, taking air with it, to create a partial vacuum. Atmospheric pressure then pushes the contents of the pan into the drain. The siphonic action is broken, often with a gurgle, as air passes under the bend of the trap.

With a double-trap siphonic suite a specially designed air pipe or 'pressure reducer' connects the air space between the two traps to the channel through which the flushing water passes. As this water flows past the pressure reducer it sucks up air from the space between the two traps, in the same way that the wind passing over the top of a chimney sucks up air from a room below. It's this that creates the partial vacuum on which siphonic action depends. Where a double-trap siphonic suite is working properly, you'll see the water level in the pan fall before the 'flush' water flows in. Although more expensive than other kinds, these suites are valuable where, as in an entrance lobby cloakroom for instance, silent operation is a prime consideration.

Just as low level WC suites normally project further from the wall behind them than high level ones, close-coupled suites project further than either. Don't forget this when considering the provision of such a suite in a small bathroom or cloakroom. You may have to change the position of the washbasin and this, in turn, could obstruct the door.

Pan fixings

Moving an existing WC pan isn't always easy. It's likely to depend largely upon whether it is installed upstairs or on the ground floor. Upstairs WCs usually have a P-trap outlet, which is almost horizontal and is connected to a branch soil pipe by means of a putty or mortar joint. This can easily be broken with a club hammer and cold chisel

once you have disconnected the pan from the floor.

Downstairs WCs usually have their bases firmly cemented to a solid floor and usually have an S-trap outlet which is vertical. This connects via a cement joint to an earthenware drain socket protruding above floor level. To remove such a pan it's necessary to break the outlet. Use a cold chisel to detach the front part of the pan from the floor, then use a cold chisel and hammer again to clear the pan outlet and the joining material from the drain socket.

Nowadays it is usual to connect both ground floor and upstairs WCs to the soil pipe using a flexible joint, usually a patent plastic push-fit joint with a spigot that is inserted into the drain and a 'finned' socket that fits over the WC pan outlet.

Such patent joins are nowadays manufactured in a range that covers virtually any WC installation. Not only are they easy to use but they help reduce the noise of a flushing lavatory. It's not considered to be good practice today to cement the base of a WC to a solid floor, as the setting of the cement can create stresses resulting in a cracked pan. It is best to remove every trace of cement from the floor and, having achieved a dead-level base, to secure the WC pan with screws driven into plugs pushed into holes drilled in the floor.

How to start

After you have turned off the water supply and flushed the cistern to empty it, the next step is to disconnect the cistern's water supply, overflow and outlet pipes. So begin by unscrewing the cap-nut connecting the water-supply pipe to the cistern's ball-valve inlet. Then undo the back-nut retaining the cistern's overflow or warning pipe. Finally undo the large nut which secures the threaded outlet of the cistern to the flush pipe. It should now be possible to lift the old cistern off its supporting bracket or brackets.

If the WC suite is a very old one and screwed to a timber floor, unscrew and remove the pan's fixing screws. Then, taking the pan in both hands, pull it from side to side and away from the wall. If the connection to the soil pipe is made with a mastic or putty joint, the pan outlet should come easily out of its socket (which will have to be cleaned of all jointing material before the new unit is fitted). If a rigid cement joint has been used then there's usually no alternative but to use a bit of force. This means deliberately breaking the pan outlet, just behind the trap and above the pipe socket, with a club hammer. You can then prise the front part of the pan away from the floor using a cold chisel and hammer. This will separate the pan outlet from the pipe. At this point it's a

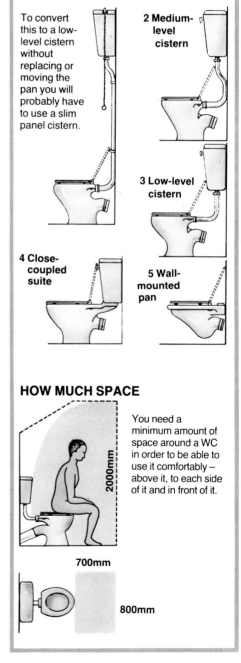

Ready Reference

PAN AND CISTERN POSITIONS

There are various WC suite arrangements you're likely to come across. The position of the pan in relation to the cistern is crucial, and if you're changing one without the other you must measure up carefully, to ensure that major changes of position can be avoided.

1 High level cistern

To convert this to a low-level cistern without replacing or moving the pan you will probably have to use a slim panel cistern.

2 Medium-level cistern

3 Low-level cistern

4 Close-coupled suite

5 Wall-mounted pan

HOW MUCH SPACE

2000mm

700mm

800mm

You need a minimum amount of space around a WC in order to be able to use it comfortably – above it, to each side of it and in front of it.

REMOVING THE OLD PAN

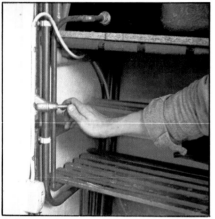

1 Locate the water pipe which supplies the WC cistern and completely shut off the stop valve which controls it. If no valve exists, block the cistern outlet.

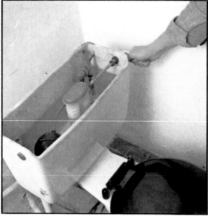

2 Lift the top off the cistern and then press the flush handle to empty it. No more fresh water should flow in as the ball float falls.

3 Disconnect the overflow pipe. If it is made of lead you should replace it with a PVC pipe run. Saw it off if you are repositioning the WC elsewhere.

4 Disconnect the supply pipe in the same way as the overflow. If you are replacing the piping altogether, you can cut through it with a hacksaw.

5 Disconnect the cistern from the pan. A close-coupled one is lifted off; with other suites you may have to disconnect the flush pipe between cistern and pan.

6 Unscrew the pan from the floor, and then use a hammer and cold chisel to break the joint between the pan and the outlet, tapping gently but firmly.

7 When you have fractured the joint, ease the pan away from the pipe. Even if it is bedded on mortar it should come away easily. Chip away the old mortar.

8 Dispose of the pan and extract any loose bits of debris from the socket. Stuff newspaper into the opening to stop bits falling into the soil pipe.

9 If you are going to use the pipe again clean it out carefully, ready to be connected up to the new WC pan with a proprietary connector.

INSTALLING THE NEW PAN

1 Offer up the pan to the outlet (note that here a new PVC soil pipe has been installed). When it fits snugly, mark down the positions for the fixing screws.

2 Drill the holes and reposition the pan and cistern. Fit the pan outlet into the white push-fit adaptor so that it is firmly in position.

3 Secure the cistern to the wall with screws and plugs. Then attach the new overflow pipe, finally tightening up the lock-nut with an adjustable spanner.

4 Assemble the internal flushing mechanism, see Ready Reference. Attach the water supply pipe and the flushing handle.

5 Fit the seat assembly, making sure that the gaskets are correctly in place between the seat and the pan; screw up the nuts tightly.

6 Restore the water supply. Check that the cistern fills to the correct level and adjust the ball-valve if it does not. Finally flush to fill the pan trap.

Ready Reference

CISTERN MECHANISMS

There are two sorts of flushing mechanism the bell type in well-bottom cisterns and the piston type found otherwise. The latter is by far the more popular today.

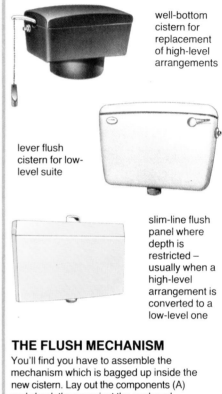

well-bottom cistern for replacement of high-level arrangements

lever flush cistern for low-level suite

slim-line flush panel where depth is restricted – usually when a high-level arrangement is converted to a low-level one

THE FLUSH MECHANISM

You'll find you have to assemble the mechanism which is bagged up inside the new cistern. Lay out the components (A) and check them against the enclosed instruction leaflet before assembling them correctly (B).

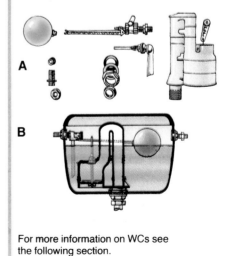

For more information on WCs see the following section.

THREE TYPES OF WC

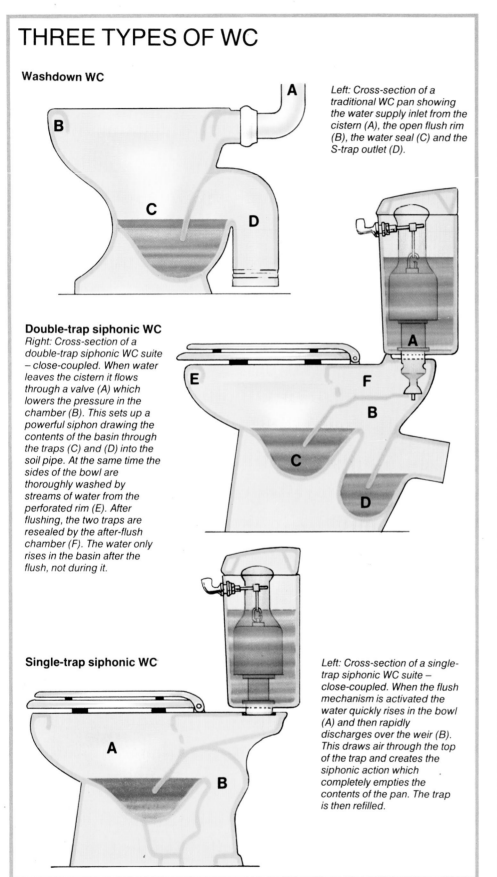

Washdown WC

Left: Cross-section of a traditional WC pan showing the water supply inlet from the cistern (A), the open flush rim (B), the water seal (C) and the S-trap outlet (D).

Double-trap siphonic WC
Right: Cross-section of a double-trap siphonic WC suite – close-coupled. When water leaves the cistern it flows through a valve (A) which lowers the pressure in the chamber (B). This sets up a powerful siphon drawing the contents of the basin through the traps (C) and (D) into the soil pipe. At the same time the sides of the bowl are thoroughly washed by streams of water from the perforated rim (E). After flushing, the two traps are resealed by the after-flush chamber (F). The water only rises in the basin after the flush, not during it.

Single-trap siphonic WC

Left: Cross-section of a single-trap siphonic WC suite – close-coupled. When the flush mechanism is activated the water quickly rises in the bowl (A) and then rapidly discharges over the weir (B). This draws air through the top of the trap and creates the siphonic action which completely empties the contents of the pan. The trap is then refilled.

good idea to stuff a bundle of rags or screwed-up newspaper into the drain socket to prevent any debris getting into the soil pipe. Next attack the socket to remove the remains of the pan's outlet. For this, use a small cold chisel and hammer but do it carefully to avoid damaging the drain socket itself – this will be used again. It's best to keep the point of the chisel pointing towards the centre of the pipe. Try to break it right down to the shoulder of the socket at one point and the rest will then come out fairly easily. Repeat the chipping process to remove all the old jointing material. Remove the bundle of rags or newspaper with the fragments of pipe and jointing material. Then with your cold chisel, remove every trace of the cement base that secured the old pan to the floor.

Installing the new pan
Don't set the pan on a cement base – just use screws and plugs to fix it to the floor. But first you've got to get the connection to the pipe socket right. Start by positioning the patent push-fit joint in the pipe end. Then offer up the new pan to the patent push-fit socket and move the pan around until it fits snugly. To fix the pan, mark the screw positions on the floor by tapping a nail through the screw-holes, and draw round the base on the floor so that you can replace it in exactly the same position. Drill holes in the floor at the points marked and finally fit the screws. If it's a solid floor, of course, it's essential to use plastic or fibre plugs in the screw holes.

For fixing the pan, it's advisable to use brass non-corroding screws with a lead washer slipped over each one so you won't crack the pan as you tighten the screws. Screw the pan down, checking that it is exactly horizontal with the aid of a spirit level laid across the top of the bowl. If it is not dead-level, pack the lower side with thin wood or plastic strips. The latter are more suitable because thin wood rots too easily. Finally check that the outlet of the pan is firmly pushed into the connector and that you've followed any specific fitting instructions from the manufacturer.

Fitting the cistern
Fix the new cistern to the wall at the level above the pan recommended by the manufacturer. In the case of a separate cistern, secure the upper end of the flush pipe to the cistern, usually by means of a large nut, and the lower end to the pan's flushing horn with a rubber cone connector. With a close-coupled suite, follow the manufacturer's instructions. You will now quite likely have to extend or cut back the water supply pipe to connect it to the new cistern. Complete the job by cutting and fitting a new overflow.

INSTALLING A SHOWER

Showers have become a part of the modern home, whether fitted over the bath or in a separate cubicle. They save time, space and energy and are quite easy to install once the design is right.

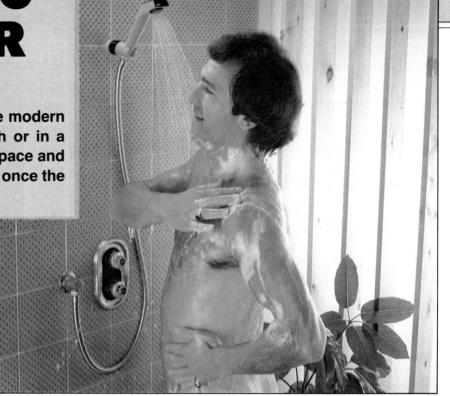

It is possible for four or five members of a family to have showers in the same time – and with the same amount of hot water – that would be needed for just one of them to have a bath. Showers, if properly installed, are safer for use by the elderly and the very young than a sit-down bath and need less cleaning. They are also more hygienic to use than a bath, as the bather isn't sitting in his own soapy and dirty water, and can rinse thoroughly in fresh water.

Where a shower is provided in its own cubicle, as distinct from over a bath, it takes up very little extra space. One can be provided in any space which is at least 900mm (36in) square, and can be put in a variety of locations such as a bedroom, on a landing, in a lobby or even in the cupboard under the stairs.

Yet shower installation can all too often prove to be a disappointment. Poorly designed systems may provide only a trickle of water at the sprinkler, or may run icy cold until the cold tap is almost turned off, and will then run scalding hot.

So, although it is possible to provide a shower in virtually any household, it is important that you match the shower equipment and your existing hot and cold water systems. If you have a cylinder storage hot water system, which is by far the commonest kind of hot water supply to be found in British homes, a conventional shower connected to the household's hot and cold water supplies is likely to be the most satisfactory and the easiest to install. But the hot and cold water systems must comply with certain quite definite design requirements if the shower is to operate safely and satisfactorily.

Pressure

The most important requirement is that the hot and cold supply pipes to the shower must be under equal water pressure. With a cylinder storage hot water system, whether direct or indirect (described on pages 9 to 13), hot water pressure comes from the main cold water storage cistern supplying the cylinder with water. The cold water supply to the shower must therefore also come from

this cistern (or perhaps from a separate cistern at the same level); it must not be taken direct from the cold water main. It is, in fact, illegal to mix, in any plumbing appliance, water which comes direct from the main and water coming from a storage cistern. However, quite apart from the question of legality, it is impossible to mix streams of water satisfactorily under such differing pressures. The shower will inevitably run either very hot or very cold, depending on which stream is the high-pressure one.

The cold water storage cistern must also be high enough above the shower sprinkler to provide a satisfactory operating pressure. Best results will be obtained if the base of the cold water storage cistern is 1.5m (5ft) or more above the sprinkler. However, provided that pipe runs are short and have only slight changes of direction, a reasonable shower can be obtained when the vertical distance between the base of the cistern and the shower sprinkler is as little as 1m (39in). The level of the hot water storage tank in relation to the shower doesn't matter in the least. It can be above, below or at the same level as the shower. It is the level of the cold water storage cistern that matters.

There is yet another design requirement for conventional shower installation which sometimes applies. This is that the cold water supply to the shower should be a separate 15mm (½in) branch direct from the cold water storage cistern, and not taken from the main bathroom distribution pipe. This is a safety precaution. If the cold supply were

taken as a branch from a main distribution pipe, then flushing a lavatory cistern would reduce the pressure on the cold side of the shower causing it to run dangerously hot. For the same reason it is best for the hot supply to be taken direct from the vent pipe immediately above the hot water storage cylinder and not as a branch from another distribution pipe, though this is rather less important. A reduction in the hot water pressure would result in the shower running cold. This would be highly unpleasant, although not dangerous.

Mixers

Showers must have some kind of mixing valve to mix the streams of hot and cold water and thus to produce a shower at the required temperature. The two handles of the bath taps provide the very simplest mixing valve, and push-on shower attachments can be cheaply obtained. Opening the bath taps then mixes the two streams of water and diverts them upwards to a wall-hung shower rose. These very simple attachments work quite satisfactorily – provided that the design requirements already referred to are met. However, it isn't always easy to adjust the tap handles to provide water at exactly the temperature required.

A bath/shower mixer provides a slightly more sophisticated alternative operating on the same principle. With one of these, the tap handles are adjusted until water is flowing through the mixer spout into the bath at the required temperature. The water is then

CHOOSING THE RIGHT SHOWER TYPE

The type of shower you can install depends on the sort of water supply you have in your home. This chart will help you make the right selection.

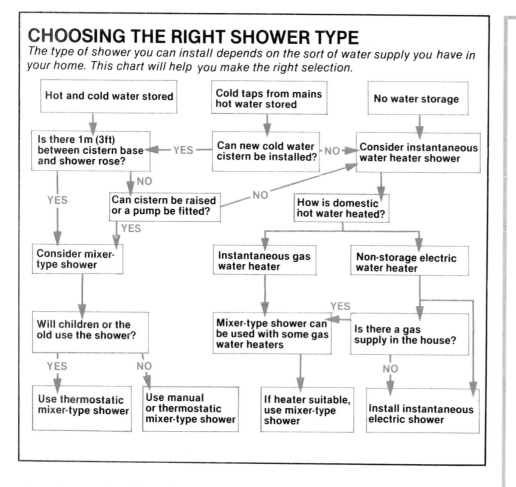

Ready Reference

WHY HAVE A SHOWER?

Showers have many advantages over baths:
● they are hygienic as you don't sit in dirty, soapy water and you get continually rinsed
● they are pleasant to use. Standing under jets of water can be immensely stimulating, especially first thing in the morning
● they use a lot less water per 'wash' than a bath, which saves energy and is also an advantage where water softeners are in use
● economy of hot water usage means that at peak traffic times there is more water to go round
● showers take less time, they don't have to be 'run', and users can't lay back and bask, monopolizing the bathroom
● easy temperature adjustment of a shower gives greater comfort for the user and lessens the risk of catching cold in a cold bathroom.

SHOWER LOCATION

You don't have to install a shower over a bath or even in the bathroom. A bedroom is one alternative site, but landings and utility rooms are another possibility. Provided a supply of water is available, the pressure head satisfactory, and the disposal of waste water possible, a shower can provide a compact and very useful house improvement in many parts of the home.

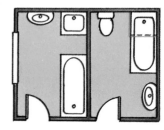

In a bathroom a shower will usually go over a bath, which is the easiest and most popular position. In a larger bathroom a cubicle is a good idea.

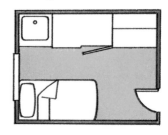

In a bedroom a shower can be easily fitted at the end of built-in wardrobes.

---

diverted up to the head by turning a valve.

Then there are manual shower mixers. These are standard equipment in independent shower cubicles and may also be used over a bath. With a manual mixer the hot and cold streams of water are mixed in a single valve. Temperature, and sometimes flow control, are obtained by turning large knurled control knobs.

Finally, there are thermostatic shower mixing valves. These may resemble manual mixers in appearance but are designed to accommodate small pressure fluctuations in either the hot or cold water supplies to the shower. They are thus very useful safety devices. But thermostatic valves cannot, even if it were legal, compensate for the very great difference of pressure between mains supply and a supply from a cold water storage cistern. Nor can they add pressure to either the hot or cold supply. If pressure falls on one side of the valve the thermostatic device will reduce flow on the other side to match it.

Thermostatic valves are more expensive but they eliminate the need to take an independent cold water supply pipe from the storage cistern to the shower and can possibly reduce the total cost of installation.

Where a shower is provided over an existing bath, steps must be taken to protect the bathroom floor from splashed water. A plastic shower curtain provides the cheapest means of doing this but a folding, glass shower screen has a much more attractive appearance and is more effective.

Electric showers

You can run your shower independently of the existing domestic hot water system by fitting an instantaneously heated electric one. There are a number of these on the market nowadays. They need only to be connected to the rising main and to a suitable source of electricity to provide an 'instant shower'. You'll find more information about these on pages 115 to 119.

Installing a bath/shower mixer

To install a shower above a bath, first disconnect the water supply, and drain the cistern (see pages 49 to 51). Remove the bath panel, if there is one, and disconnect the tap tails from the supply pipes. Then unscrew and remove the tap back-nuts and take the taps off.

You can now fix the new mixer in place (see pages 106 to 110). Finally, decide on the position for the shower spray bracket and fix it in place.

HOW TO ADAPT YOUR SYSTEM

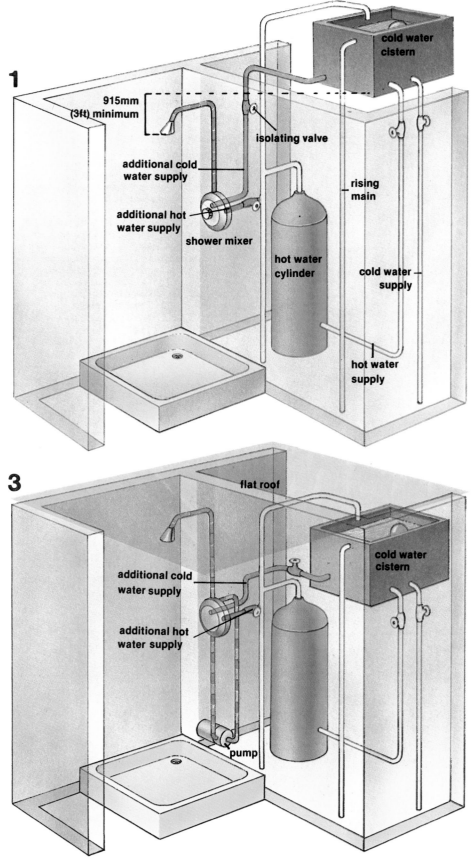

1 : Just add pipework

◁ *The most common domestic plumbing system has a cold water cistern in the loft which feeds a hot water tank. In this case you must check that the vertical distance from the bottom of the cold cistern to the shower outlet head is at least 915mm (3ft). To install a shower you must take a 15mm cold water supply direct from the cistern to the cold inlet of the mixer, and a 15mm (1/2in) hot water supply from the draw-off pipe, which emerges from the hot water tank, to the hot water inlet of the mixer.*

2 : Raise the cistern

▷ *In many older houses the cold water cistern may be in the airing cupboard immediately above the hot water tank, or in another position but still beneath ceiling height. This will usually mean that there is insufficient pressure for a mixer-type shower on the same floor. To get round this problem the cistern can be raised into the loft by extending the pipework upwards. Moving an old galvanised cistern will be rather arduous so this is a good opportunity to replace it with a modern plastic one, (see pages 156 to 159).*

3 : Install a pump

◁ *In some homes which have flat roofs it is impossible to raise the cistern indoors to provide a sufficient pressure head for a shower on the same floor. While you could consider putting the cistern on top of the roof this would involve providing extensive insulation and is an unsatisfactory solution. Pump-assisted mixer showers are available which will artificially increase the pressure head when the shower is turned on and these are fairly simple to install. As they are electrically operated they should be situated outside the bathroom area.*

4 : Add a new cistern

▷ *Many modern houses have combination hot and cold water storage units which are supplied and installed as one unit. They have a disadvantage in that cold water capacity is about one-third of the hot water cylinder and would provide an insufficient supply for a shower. This problem can be overcome by installing a pump and a supplementary cold water storage cistern. To ensure similar hot and cold pressures at the shower the supplementary cistern must be at a comparable level with the combination unit's cold water storage.*

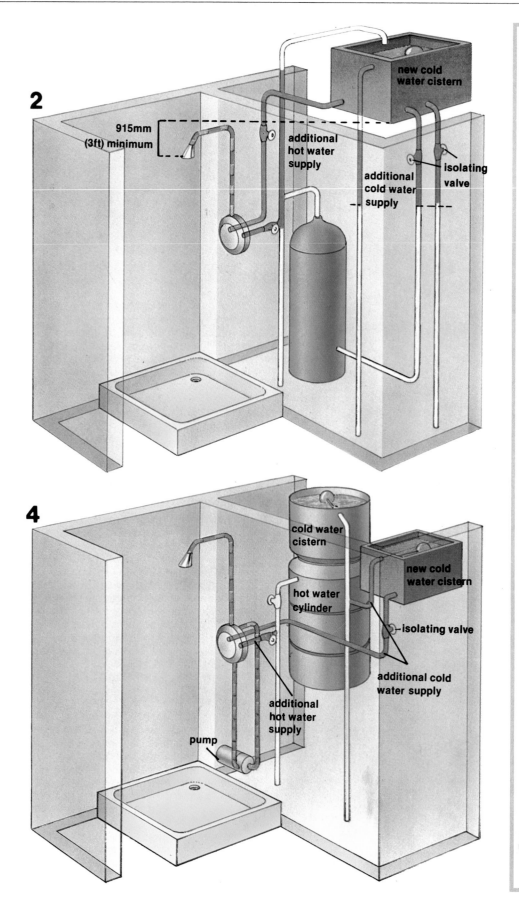

2

915mm (3ft) minimum

additional hot water supply

new cold water cistern

additional cold water supply

isolating valve

4

cold water cistern

hot water cylinder

new cold water cistern

isolating valve

additional cold water supply

additional hot water supply

pump

Ready Reference

TYPES OF SHOWER

There are two basic types of shower:
● those attached to a mixer on a bath
● those independent of the bath, discharging over their own bases, in their own cubicles.

Bath showers may be attached to a mixer head on which you have to adjust both taps, or they may simply fit over the tap outlets. The shower head in either case is detachable and may be mounted at whatever height you require.

Independent showers have fixed position heads or are adjustable. They may have a single control mixer, or a dual control which means that you can adjust the flow as well as the temperature. Thermostatic mixing valves are also available which can cope with small pressure fluctuations in the hot and cold water supply. These only reduce pressure on one side of the valve if that on the other side falls; they cannot increase the pressure unless they have already decreased it.

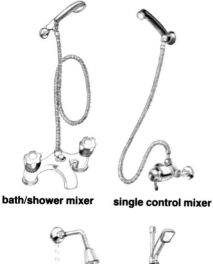

bath/shower mixer   **single control mixer**

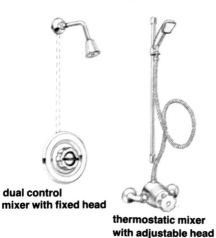

dual control mixer with fixed head

thermostatic mixer with adjustable head

PLUMBING IN AN ELECTRIC SHOWER

If you would like to install a shower but think you can't because there's insufficient water pressure, you might like to consider an instantaneous electric shower. It's connected directly to the mains cold water supply, so you are guaranteed a good jet of water. And as you heat only the water you use, it's very economical to run.

U ntil quite recently a properly functioning shower was all but an impossibility in many homes. Either it lacked the cylinder storage hot water system needed to supply a conventional shower, or the system that existed wouldn't permit a successful shower installation. For example, the main cold water storage cistern might have had insufficient capacity to supply the cold side of the shower mixer as well as feeding the hot water storage cylinder, or it may have been situated at too low a level to give adequate pressure at the shower rose. (For more information about the theory of shower design see previous section.)

The increasing popularity of showers has led to two new developments: the electric shower pump which increases pressure at the shower rose where this is inadequate; and the instantaneous electric shower.

Going back to geysers

There is nothing particularly new about appliances which heat water 'instantaneously' as it flows through them. The Edwardian geyser, installed over the bath in many a turn-of-the century middle-class home, was an early example. The modern single-point or multi-point instantaneous gas water heater – which can provide hot water for the whole house – is its direct descendant. Instantaneous water heaters were designed for connection directly to the rising main so they could operate under mains pressure. They needed no cold water storage cistern or storage cylinder and they had the advantage that heat energy was expended only to heat water that was actually to be used at that time.

However, until a couple of decades ago, the only instantaneous water heating appliances that were available were – like the early geysers – gas-operated. It just wasn't possible to devise an electric appliance that could 'instantaneously' heat a sufficiently large volume of water to fill a sit-down bath, a sink or even a wash basin. It still isn't. But

manufacturers have now produced electric water heaters powerful enough to provide a steady flow of hot water for spray hand-washing over a washbasin in a WC compartment and for the provision of a shower. In neither case is very hot water needed in large volumes.

An instantaneous electric water heater is a relatively compact appliance that needs only to be connected – by means of a 15mm (½in) branch water supply pipe – to the main supply, and to a suitable supply of electricity. It is normally operated by a flow-switch which ensures that electricity is switched on only when water is flowing through the appliance. As it does so, it passes over powerful electrical heating elements.

Temperature control was originally obtained solely by controlling the volume of water flowing through the heater. Opening up the tap or control valve produced a heavy flow of cool water. As the control valve was closed down and the flow diminished, warmer and warmer water was obtained from the shower spray.

The crude, early models were something of a disaster and were frowned on by water authorities and electricity boards. They rarely provided a satisfactory shower. The flow was markedly less than that from a conventional, cylinder-supplied shower. Flushing the WC or opening up any other tap in the house would reduce the pressure of the water entering the heater, so reducing the flow and raising the water temperature from the shower spray. Such unpredictable temperature changes could cause serious scalding to an unsuspecting user. Other problems arose from the hard water scale that tended to form on the heating elements.

Instantaneous showers today

However, an unhappy experience a decade or so ago with one of the early instantaneous electric showers need not deter you from having a modern one installed today. There have been some tremendous advances in design and construction and you can be confident that a modern model will work

WHAT'S INSIDE THE CASING

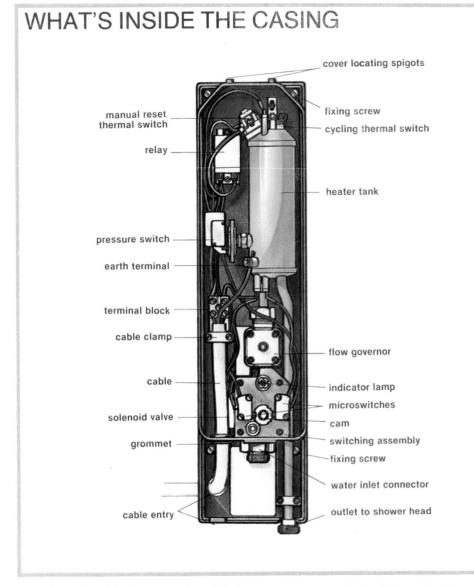

cover locating spigots

manual reset thermal switch

fixing screw

cycling thermal switch

relay

heater tank

pressure switch

earth terminal

terminal block

cable clamp

flow governor

cable

indicator lamp

microswitches

solenoid valve

cam

grommet

switching assembly

fixing screw

water inlet connector

cable entry

outlet to shower head

properly provided that it is properly installed according to the manufacturer's instructions.

Most instantaneous showers must be supplied with water at a minimum pressure of 1.05kg per sq cm (15lb per sq in). They are intended for connection direct to the mains supply, though they can be supplied by a cistern if it is at least 10.75m (35ft) above the level of the shower spray. In most cases mains water pressure will be adequate, but those who live in an area where mains pressure is low should check the actual pressure with their local water authority before incurring the expense of installation.

Modern electric showers usually have an electrical loading of 6kW to 7kW and it is often possible, for the sake of economy, to switch to a low setting of 3kW or 4kW during the summer months. Choose a model that incorporates a temperature stabiliser. This is an anti-scald device that maintains the water

temperature at the level chosen by the user of the shower, despite any fluctuations in pressure which may result from water being drawn off from taps or by flushing the W.C. Should there be a drop in pressure beyond the capacity of the stabiliser, a safety sensor turns the shower off completely.

When choosing your instantaneous electric shower, look for evidence that it has been approved by such national safety committees as the B.E.A.B., the National Water Council and the A.N.T. (Assessment of Techniques) Committee of the Institute of Electrical Engineers.

Fitting a shower

Although instantaneous electric showers can be fitted over a sit-down bath, they are usually installed in a separate shower cubicle which may be in a bathroom, in a bedroom or even on a landing. The shower tray must

have a trapped outlet and the branch waste pipe can discharge by the same route as basin or bath wastes (see WASTE WATER SYSTEMS, pages 14 to 18).

Plumbing connections should be straight-forward. It's best to connect the supply pipe to the shower heater first and then work backwards to the main supply, making this connection last of all. In this way you will interrupt the supply to the rest of the house as little as possible.

The connection to the shower may be a simple compression coupling (described on pages 20 to 24) or it may have a screwed male thread. In which case you'll need a compression fitting with a coupling at one end and a female screwed connector at the other. To connect into the rising main you should use a compression tee (as described on pages 28 to 32).

Obtaining the power

Instantaneous showers get their power from a separate radial circuit taken from the consumer unit. As most models of shower have a loading of either 6 or 7kW they can be supplied safely by a circuit that has a current rating of 30A and is run in 6mm² two-core and earth cable. Recently, however, an 8kW shower has been introduced on the market by some manufacturers. This shouldn't pose extra problems for anyone intending to install it: provided the radial circuit originates at either a cartridge fuse or MCB – which both have the effect of uprating the circuit by one third – then a 30A circuit will be adequate. Should you decide to install one of these larger showers then it's still probably a good idea to check their requirements with the makers beforehand.

Showers should be controlled by a 30A double-pole cord-operated switch. From this a length of 6mm² two-core and earth cable will run to the shower unit. There is one type that requires a slightly different method of connecting up. If you're going to fit a shower that has a control unit already connected to a length of three-core flex then you'll have to fix a flex outlet unit on the wall near the shower unit so you can connect the flex into the circuit.

Fitting the switch

Ceiling switches can either be surface or flush mounted. If you're going to surface mount one, you'll have to pierce a hole in the ceiling so the cables can be drawn through into a plastic mounting box. Before fixing this in position with No 8 wood screws, you should knock a thin section of plastic from the base to align with the hole in the ceiling. Ideally the box should be fitted against a joist, but if there isn't one suitably placed, you'll have to fix a support batten between the joists made from 75 x 25mm (3 x 1in) timber with a hole drilled in it big enough to let two lengths of

INSTALLING THE SHOWER UNIT

1 First take the shower spray support assembly and fix it to the wall. It is important to follow the manufacturer's recommendations as to height.

2 Remove the control knobs and any other fittings from the shower unit to enable the faceplate to be taken off before further installation takes place.

3 Carefully position the unit on the shower cubicle wall and mark the screw fitting holes, water and power channels; drill out the fixing holes.

4 Using a hole saw attachment for your drill, cut holes in the cubicle wall for the water and power supplies, then fix the unit to the wall.

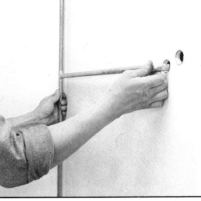

5 Make a tee junction with the main, and run a length of pipe to the water access; then add an elbow and length of pipe to go through the wall.

6 Use a swivel tap connector to attach the cold water feed to the unit; this is linked to the inlet pipe by a soldered capillary joint.

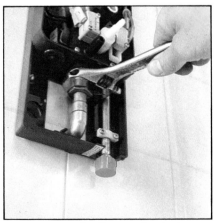

7 Make sure the fibre washer in the connector is in place; then screw it up and tighten. Don't use any sealant on the nylon inlet.

8 Attach the shower hose to the screwed outlet, making sure that the rubber washer is in place. Then make the electrical connections (page 118).

9 Turn on the water supply and also the electricity to make sure that the unit works. Finally, replace the cover and control knobs.

6mm² cable pass through. When you're feeding the cables into the mounting box, it's a good idea to write 'mains' on the end of the circuit cable and 'shower' on the end of the shower feed cable. This could be surface mounted on the ceiling and wall, but it's neater to conceal it in the ceiling void and chase it into the wall, running it in plastic conduit.

You can now strip back the insulation and make the connections. The mains cable should go to the 'supply' side of the switch, with the red core going to the terminal marked L and the black to the one marked N, and the shower cable to the equivalent terminals on the 'load' side. Remember to sleeve the earth cores in green/yellow PVC and connect them to the earth terminal in the switch. Place the six cores neatly in the box and screw the switch to it.

If you're going to flush-mount the switch you'll have to mark the size of the mounting box on the ceiling and, using a pad saw, carefully cut out an equivalent size hole. Then cut a piece of timber to fit between the joists, lay it across the hole and mark the square on it. Knock out a blank from the base of the metal box and drill a hole in the corresponding spot in the timber. Then screw the box to the timber and fix the timber to the joists at a height above the ceiling that allows the box edge to sit flush with the ceiling surface. This can be checked by holding a straight edge across the hole in the ceiling. You should then thread in the two marked cables and make the connections. If you want to fix the switch at a point where there is a joist you can always cut away a section of it. This is best done by using a drill fitted with a 25mm (1in) wood bit to remove most of the wood and then chiselling the remainder away. That way you won't need access to the ceiling void as long as you can 'fish' the cable across the ceiling using a length of stiff wire.

Connecting into the shower

The cable to the shower can be run down the wall on the surface, using plastic cable clips or mini-trunking, or buried in a chase chopped in the plaster. The cover of the control unit must be removed to allow you access to the terminal block, but do read fully the manufacturer's instructions before going any further. Thread in the cable and strip off some of the sheathing and insulation before connecting the red core to the L terminal and the black to the N terminal. Before connecting the earth core to the earth terminal make sure you've sleeved it in green/yellow PVC. If the unit has a cable clamp, fix the cable in it, double checking that it's the whole, sheathed cable that is held by it and not just individual cores. This is very important as it serves to protect the con-

CONNECTING THE POWER

1 After fixing the shower unit to the bathroom wall and making the connection from the rising main, thread in the circuit cable.

2 Feed the cable up the unit and strip it before connecting the red and black cores to the L and N terminals respectively.

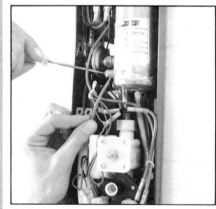

3 Remember to sleeve the bare earth core in green/yellow PVC before feeding it into the earth terminal and connecting it up.

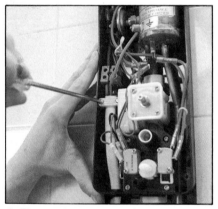

4 Then make sure that the clamp plate will bear down on the cable sheathing before tightening it up to protect all the connections.

nections. Finally, refit the unit cover, finish off the radial circuit connections at the consumer unit, switch on at the mains and test the shower.

Fitting a flex outlet plate

You'll have to use a flex outlet plate only if there is already a flex connected to the shower unit. This can be fitted on either a one-gang moulded plastic box for surface mounting, or else in a 35mm (1½in) metal box for flush mounting, in which case you'll have to chop a hole. After fixing one or other of the boxes to the wall, run the cable into it through a knockout hole, which, in the case of the metal box, should be fitted with a grommet. The unit has three banks of terminals with two terminal screws per bank and you should connect the green/yellow sleeved earth core to a terminal of the non-shielded bank marked 'E'. Then connect the red insulated core to a terminal of one of the

shielded banks and the black to a terminal of the other bank.

Prepare the end of the flex by stripping off approximately 12mm (½in) of insulation from the end of each core. Remember to thread the flex through the hole in the unit's cover before you connect the flex to the unit as you won't be able to fit it after you've made the connections. Then connect the earth core, which should be already sleeved in green and yellow PVC, to the other terminal in the 'E' bank, the brown core to the bank containing the red core and the blue core to the bank containing the black circuit core. Tighten the cord clamp, again making sure that it's the flex sheath that it grips and not the unsheathed cores as this protects the connections. Lay the six cores neatly in the box and fix the unit to the box with the two screws supplied. You can then switch on the power and test the shower.

THE ELECTRICAL CONNECTIONS

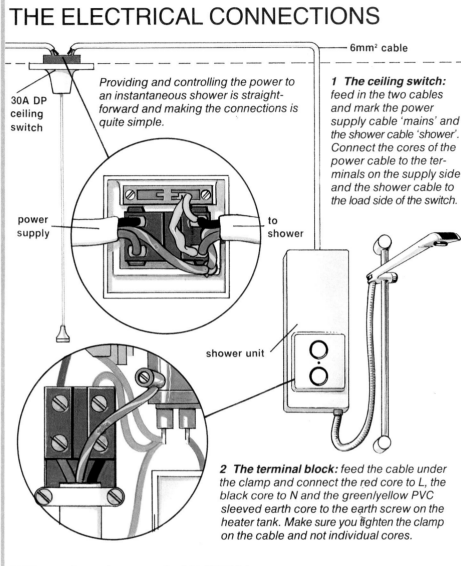

Providing and controlling the power to an instantaneous shower is straightforward and making the connections is quite simple.

1 The ceiling switch: *feed in the two cables and mark the power supply cable 'mains' and the shower cable 'shower'. Connect the cores of the power cable to the terminals on the supply side and the shower cable to the load side of the switch.*

6mm² cable

30A DP ceiling switch

power supply

to shower

shower unit

2 The terminal block: *feed the cable under the clamp and connect the red core to L, the black core to N and the green/yellow PVC sleeved earth core to the earth screw on the heater tank. Make sure you tighten the clamp on the cable and not individual cores.*

FITTING A CEILING SWITCH

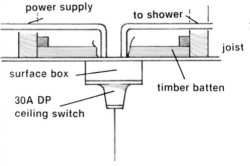

power supply

to shower

joist

surface box

30A DP ceiling switch

timber batten

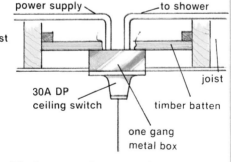

power supply

to shower

joist

30A DP ceiling switch

timber batten

joist

one gang metal box

Surface mounted: *try to mount the switch on a joist. If you can't, fit a timber batten. Drill holes in the batten and ceiling to admit the cables and remove a knockout from the base of the box. Fix the box to the ceiling and make the connections.*

Flush mounted: *use a pad saw to cut a hole in the ceiling for the mounting box. Fix the box to a batten between the joists and set the batten so the box is flush with the ceiling. Feed the cables through and make the connections.*

Ready Reference

PLUMBING REQUIREMENTS

The shower unit should be connected directly to the cold water mains supply. If this isn't possible, a storage tank may be used to supply the unit; but it must be about 10.75m (35ft) above the shower spray head.

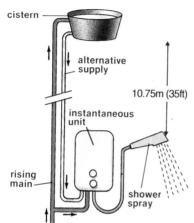

cistern

alternative supply

10.75m (35ft)

instantaneous unit

rising main

shower spray

USING THE SHOWER

After turning on the unit, you'll have to wait a short while so the water retained in the heater tank and shower fittings from the last shower is drawn off. The water temperature is controlled by the rate of flow through the heater – the slower the flow rate, the higher the temperature, and vice versa. Because the cold water supply is likely to be comparatively colder in the winter than in summer, this means in winter you may have to put up with a slower flow rate in order to get the required temperature.

ELECTRICAL CONNECTION

When you're wiring up an instantaneous shower, you must ensure that:
● it is permanently connected to its own separate 30A power supply, and is properly earthed
● it is controlled by a 30A double-pole cord-operated switch mounted on the ceiling. An ordinary ceiling light switch is not suitable.

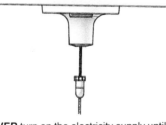

NEVER turn on the electricity supply until all the plumbing has been completed, including mounting the handset and hose, and the power supply and earthing connections are made.

CONNECTING SHOWER FITTINGS

Before you get to grips with installing a new shower cubicle, you ought to select the type of control fitting you're going to use. Your choice may affect the way you organise the plumbing.

Once you've decided where you're going to site your shower – over a bath or in a separate cubicle – you'll have to determine what type of fitting you're going to use to run it. In order for the shower to work effectively, you need to be able to control the rate of flow of water and also, more importantly, it's temperature. There's nothing worse than standing under a stuttering supply of water that's hot one minute and cold the next. So it's the job of the shower fitting to provide this control fast and effectively.

Some fittings work by having individual taps to control the hot and cold water supplies, while the more sophisticated types have a simple valve or a mixer. How they are connected up to the water supply depends primarily on their design. For example, instantaneous showers (see the previous section) need only to be connected to the mains cold water supply, as they heat all the hot water required just before it comes out of the shower rose. A hot water supply is therefore unnecessary. But for all other showers, the temperature of the water is controlled by mixing together separate supplies of hot and cold water which may also be at different pressures.

The simplest fittings

Before proper showers over a bath and separate shower cubicles became popular, it was quite common to find a rather makeshift device being used to supply a spray of water. This consisted of a length of rubber hose with a rose attached at one end and two connectors fitted at the other which slipped over the hot and cold taps on the bath. By adjusting these taps you could regulate the flow and temperature of the water. In fact the principle of this very basic mixing valve was used in early shower cubicles. Gate valves on the hot and cold distribution pipes were used to control the flow, and the two supplies were mixed at a 'tee' in the pipework before being fed in a single pipe to an overhead shower rose.

Mixer taps

An improvement on this very simple arrangement, as far as showers over baths are con-

cerned, is the bath/shower mixer. This resembles an ordinary mixer tap on a bath, except that a flexible metal hose rises from the centre of the mixer to a spray head which can be fixed at varying heights on the wall above the bath. Again the water is mixed by adjusting the hot and cold taps, and at this stage it will be coming out of the spout of the tap. When the required temperature has been reached you pull up a lever on the body of the tap and this diverts the water upwards to the spray head.

Nowadays, showers in cubicles normally have what's known as a manual mixing valve. This has two inlets, one for the hot and another for the cold supply; but the temperature is regulated by turning just one mixer knob. The flow may also be adjusted by turning another knob which is set round the outside of the temperature control. In this way you can control the water more quickly and positively than you could do if you had to adjust two separate taps (which tends to be a bit of a juggling act).

Shower mixers are constantly being improved so that they are more convenient and safer to use. With one modern manual mixing valve, for example, the temperature of the water is controlled by turning a knurled knob, not unlike the handle of a tap. And the flow and on/off control is worked by pushing in or pulling out this knob. You can therefore control the flow and temperature of the water

in one movement. Another advantage of this kind of control is that the shower can be stopped instantly if the pressure on the cold side falls (as a result of a toilet being flushed or cold water being drawn off elsewhere in the house, for example). If this happened the shower would suddenly run very hot, but by flicking the control knob downwards the flow ceases. It's not so serious if the pressure falls on the hot side, because the shower would just run cold. But again, to prevent discomfort the flow can be stopped quickly by flicking the control knob.

However, prevention is better than cure and there are ways of organising the plumbing so that this problem can't arise. To alleviate the danger it's best to run the 15mm (½in) cold water supply pipe to the shower direct from the cold water storage cistern and not as a branch from the 22mm (¾in) distribution pipe to the bathroom. This will supply a continuous volume of cold water provided the cistern is working properly.

Thermostatic valves

Of course it may mean too much of an upheaval to lay in a new pipe run, but instead you could install a special thermostatic mixing valve. This enables you to pre-set the temperature of the shower water and this will remain constant despite fluctuations of pressure in the hot and cold supplies. And apart from this, thermostatic mixers provide

INSTALLING A FIXED ROSE

1 To mount the wall fixing, thread one end of the double-ended screw supplied into the hole in the base of the casting.

2 With the flange in place, screw the fitting into the shower wall using a pre-drilled fixing hole. The inlet hole must point downwards.

3 Screw the outlet rose onto the outlet pipe by removing the rose and inserting an Allen key into the recess you will find inside.

4 Attach the outlet fitting to the wall fixing, by tightening the fixing nut on the rose so it crushes the olive. But don't chip the chrome.

5 Make sure that the outlet rose swivels firmly but freely on its ball bearing, and that it emerges at right angles to the wall.

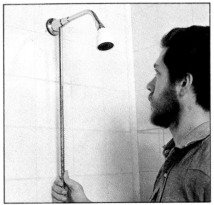

6 Screw the supply pipe into the outlet supply until it is tight against the washer, and check that it is truly vertical.

7 Attach the supply pipe to the thermostatic control unit and mark the position of the supply pipe holes on the shower wall.

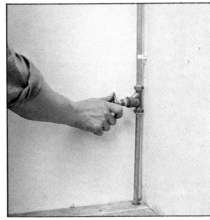

8 Turn off the water supplies via stop-valves, if fitted, and tee off the supply pipes to feed the hot and cold inlets of the shower mixer.

9 Drill holes in the shower wall so that the supply pipes can be fed through from behind and connected up to the shower mixer.

INSTALLING AN ADJUSTABLE ROSE

1 Fit the two wall fixing brackets to the end of the runner, and align them both so that they are pointing in the same direction.

2 Mark the positions for the fixing screws on the shower wall, drill the holes and then proceed to screw on the uppermost bracket.

3 Slide on the movable rose support and fix the lower bracket to the wall. Cover the screw entry holes with plastic caps.

4 Take the one-piece shower head and rose and screw on the flexible hose, making sure that the fibre washer is correctly placed.

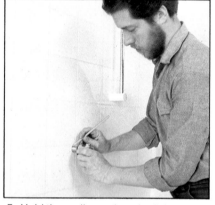

5 Hold the wall supply point fixing in place and mark the wall for drilling. Drill the hole, making sure you don't damage the tiled surround.

6 Insert the fixing and screw it up tight. Then take your chosen mixer, drill its fixing holes and plumb in the supply pipes.

just that extra margin of safety and assurance against discomfort.

Before buying a thermostatic mixing valve, it's important that you recognise its limitations as well as its advantages. These valves can deal with relatively minor fluctuations in pressure that can result from water being drawn off from one or other of the supply pipes. They can't accommodate the great differences in pressure between a hot water supply under pressure from a storage cylinder and a cold supply taken direct from the main (in any case, you should never arrange your shower plumbing in this way). Some thermostatic valves even require a greater working 'hydraulic head' (the vertical distance between the cold water cistern and the shower rose) than the 1m (3ft) minimum that is usual for manual mixers. So it's a good idea to check on these points and on the 'head' available before you buy one of them.

Shower pumps

An inadequate 'head' is, of course, one of the commonest reasons why a shower won't work properly. Although the minimum distance between the base of the cold water cistern and the shower rose must be 1m (3ft), for best results this distance ought to be 1.5m (5ft) or more.

However, all is not lost if you can't get this head because you can install a shower pump. They're expensive but they can make the difference between a stimulating shower and a miserable, low-pressure trickle, which isn't much good to anyone.

Different types of pump are controlled in different ways. Some have manual switches which are controlled by a pull-cord. In this case the pump is only switched on after the water has begun to flow, and is turned off before it has been stopped. Other pumps are operated automatically when the water is

turned on at the shower by the movement of water in the pipes.

You can install a simple pump between the mixer and the shower rose outlet, but you may find it difficult to conceal. On the other hand, automatic pumps must be connected into the water supply before it reaches the mixer, so it's easier to choose a convenient site where the pump can be hidden from view or disguised.

Shower pumps need quite a lot of plumbing in, and if you're not careful about planning you may end up with a lot of exposed pipework. It's also worth remembering that when you wire up the electricity supply you have to connect the pump to a fused connection unit with a double-pole switch. And if the pump is situated inside the bathroom it must be protected from steam and water (except in the case of units specially designed to be inside the shower cubicle).

THREE TYPES OF SHOWER

There are several types of shower mixer available on the market. They fall into two types – those which simply mix the hot and cold flows, and those which make an effort to provide the mixed flows at a constant, pre-set, temperature. All of them are usually finished in chrome and the controls are made of a strong plastic which will resist most knocks and blows.

Surface-mounted mixer
Left: This is a surface-mounted mixer control with separate supply pipes emerging through the wall to supply the control which provides power over flow and temperature.

Built-in mixer
Right: This built-in control is supplied from behind the shower wall so that the supply pipes are hidden. These fittings are also available in a gold finish.

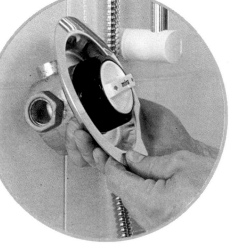

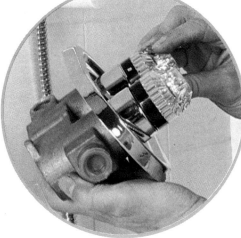

Thermostatic mixer
Left: This thermostatic mixer is also supplied from behind and provides two separate controls – one for pre-setting the temperature, and one for adjusting the flow of the water once the user is inside the shower.

Ready Reference

TYPES OF SUPPLY

Here is a summary of the various types of shower supply you could choose:

Rear supply – surface mounting
Both hot and cold supplies come through the wall behind the mixer, which is surface mounted on the cubicle wall.

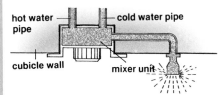

Surface supply – surface mixing
The hot and cold supplies come independently through the shower wall and can be seen entering the surface-mounted mixing unit.

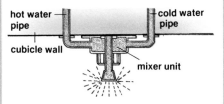

Surface supply – thermostatic mixing
Water supplies come through the wall into the surface-mounted unit, and then are regulated by sensitive flow and temperature controls.

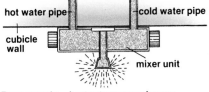

Rear supply – instantaneous shower
The mains (cold-water only) supply comes through or along the wall, and enters the unit for rapid heating and distribution through the rose.

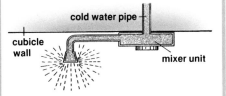

TIP: TEST YOUR SEALS

However much purpose-built shower surround you buy – or however much you build – it must all have a waterproof seal with the tray and any solid cubicle walls. Test all joints for leaks with a hand spray, and if they do leak, make sure they are filled with a flexible non-setting mastic.

BUILDING A SHOWER CUBICLE

The simplest way to add showering facilities to your bathroom is to install the shower over the bath. However, building a separate cubicle is a better solution.

When you come to install a shower in your home, the most obvious place for it is over the bath because you can make use of the bath's water supply and waste facilities. But this isn't the most advantageous site: putting a shower there does not increase your bathing facilities, it merely improves the existing ones. It's far better to have your shower as a separate cubicle, even if the cubicle is in the bathroom itself. If you can put the cubicle in another part of the home, you have as good as provided an extra bathroom.

You may think that you have no room in your home for a shower outside the bathroom, but that is not necessarily true. A shower does not require all that much space and you can make do with an area about 900mm (3ft) square. But you've got to think about how much space you need to get into and out of the shower. It isn't usually that easy or efficient to dry off inside, so you need some space to dry off at the point of exit. You will also have to take into consideration the relationship of the drying area with bathroom fittings.

You can buy a ready-made shower cubicle, or build your own from scratch. The latter course will save a lot of money, and is easier than you might think, but you've got to take care to ensure that it is properly waterproofed.

Putting in the tray

To build a shower cubicle you start with the shower tray. Many people attempt to make one of these themselves by building a box that they cover with some impervious material – usually tiles. However, the construction is not easy because making the box absolutely waterproof can present problems, and then it is difficult to get the right gradient from every part of the tray to carry water to the waste outlet. On the whole, you would do better to buy a tray.

Normally, trays are made in acrylic plastic or glazed ceramics. The latter are dearer, but much longer-lasting, as acrylics can crack. Both types are available in standard sanitary-ware colours, so if you have a modern coloured bathroom suite, you should be able to match it. Trays come in a range of sizes, so be sure to choose one to fit

the space you have, since obviously the size of tray governs the area your installation will take up. Ceramic trays can also be very heavy so it's likely you'll need help to get one into position.

The tray will have a waste outlet, and this may be in one corner, or in the middle of one side. It must be sited so that its waste pipe can discharge conveniently into a hopper of a two-pipe system, or be connected up to an existing waste pipe, or to the main stack of a single-pipe system. The waste pipe must slope downwards all the way, and it is important to get the fall right in order to drain water away efficiently. In general, the fall should be between 6 and 50mm per 300mm run of pipe (¼ to 2in per ft) depending on the length of the run (measured from the actual waste outlet). Too steep a run can produce a siphonage effect that will drain the water out of the trap, thus depriving your home of its protection from drain smells (see pages 14 to 18). It's a good idea to set a fall of 25mm (1in) per 300mm for a short run of say 600 to 900mm (2 to 3ft), but only a 12mm (½in) fall where the run will be 3 to 4.5m (10 to 15ft).

Most shower trays are square, and obviously these can be turned round to place the outlet in the most convenient position. However, for installation in a corner, triangular shaped trays, or quadrants – with two straight

sides at right angles and a curved front – are on sale, but they're quite expensive.

The outlet does not have a plug, because it is never the intention that the tray should be filled up. Since there is no plug, no overflow is required. However, like all your bathroom fittings, it must have a trap. This should be 38mm (1½in) in diameter but, like a bath, does not have to be of the deep-seal variety.

Some trays are designed to have enough depth to enable the trap to be installed above floor level. Others are quite shallow, and the trap must go under the floor, a point to bear in mind if you have a concrete floor. Yet another possibility is to mount the tray on supports, to raise its height, and some manufacturers sell special supports to raise the tray off the ground. Otherwise you can use bricks or timber, suitably disguised by a plinth. It's a good idea to provide an inspection panel should you ever want to get access to the plumbing. Whatever the case, you will never have good access to the outlet plumbing after it's been installed – so be sure to make a good job of it.

Providing a cubicle

A shower tray is best positioned in a corner, so that two sides of the shower enclosure are already provided by the shower tray itself; you can bridge the gap with timber covered with tiles set flush with the top of the tray.

INSTALLING THE SHOWER TRAY

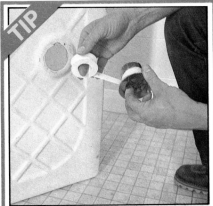

1 Press a sausage of plumber's putty around the underside of the outlet flange, then wind PTFE tape along the length of the thread.

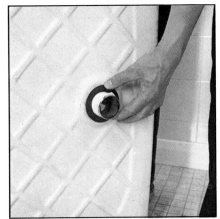

2 Push the flange into the waste hole in the tray, press it home until the putty squeezes out round the edge, and put on the metal washer.

3 Screw on the back-nut by hand and tighten it with an adjustable wrench. This will squeeze more putty out; remove the excess neatly.

4 Take the special low-seal shower trap and screw it onto the outlet flange, after first making sure that the O ring is in place.

5 Measure up the position needed for the waste run, and install the plastic waste pipe in position ready to be connected up to the trap.

6 Lower the tray into place and connect up the trap to the waste pipe. Check that it is level on your prepared base.

Ready Reference

WASTE OUTLET RUNS
You must provide sufficient depth underneath the shower tray to accommodate the waste trap and the outlet pipe. You can:
● support the tray on timber or bricks and face the elevation with panels

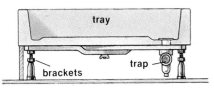

● support the tray with special supporting brackets which are usually available from shower tray manufacturers, and face the elevation with panels

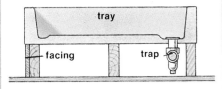

● cut a hole in the floor – if it's made of wood – and run the trap and waste above the ceiling of the room underneath. You can do this only if the joists run in the same direction as the waste pipe.

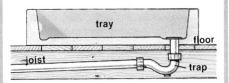

HOW MUCH SPACE?
It's very easy to think of a shower as only occupying the same space as the tray itself. But don't forget that you will usually step out of it soaking wet and so will need sufficient area in which to dry off. If the shower is enclosed on three sides you will need more space than if it's enclosed on one side and curtained on the others.

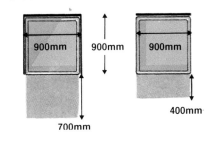

PUTTING UP A SURROUND KIT

1 Mark the position of the wall uprights; use a spirit level to make sure that they will be truly vertical when fixed in position.

2 Drill holes for the upright fixings, then plug them with plastic wall plugs and screw on the uprights with the screws supplied.

3 Slide the first panel into position on the wall upright and fix it; again check that the structure is in a properly vertical position.

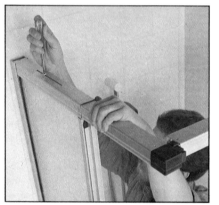

4 Adjust the length of the panel to fit the size of the shower tray and tighten up the screws carefully. Attach the corner bracket.

5 Fix the other panel in position and adjust its length so that it mates up accurately and squarely with the corner bracket.

6 Adjust the bottom runners to the correct size so that they match up with the bottom corner bracket; check they are square to the tray.

7 Screw up the bottom corner bracket, then check that the whole structure is firm and square and that the door opens and closes smoothly.

8 Loosen the wall upright fixings and wedge up each side in turn. Squeeze sealant between the frame and the tray and refix the frame.

9 Check again for alignment, then finish off the base by firmly fixing the supports in position and finally boarding in the sides of the shower.

Existing walls forming part of the cubicle will also need tiling or covering with some laminated material – commonly waterproofed decorative wallboard, or even glass or sheet plastic over paint or wallpaper. It is obviously very important to make sure that all gaps are sealed, otherwise gradual water seepage will occur which will damage the fabric of your house.

The sides of the cubicle you have to install can be home-made or bought as kits. The simplest way to fill one or two sides is with a curtain rail and shower curtain. This works quite well with a shower in the bath, but the sides of a shower tray are much shallower than those of a bath and water is therefore quite likely to splash onto the floor. This means that curtains are really only at all suitable for the entry side of the cubicle where you might protect the floor with a bath mat, or where the floor of your bathroom is tiled and fully sealed.

You can construct any solid sides of the cubicle using a timber framework, but you will have to buy a suitable proprietary door unless you use a curtain. These doors are usually made of aluminium frames with opaque safety glass or plastic panels. They come in a wide variety of designs and colours. You can have, for example, a plain aluminium frame with clear glass, or a gold satin frame with dark smoked glass. If you plan to buy a door, check that you have calculated the size of your cubicle to fit it, and that the door comes with suitable rust-proof fittings to hang it.

The easiest (though most expensive) solution is to buy the complete surround, including a sliding or ordinary door, which will be supplied in kit form. These surrounds are made by the same manufacturers as shower doors and usually come complete with fixing instructions. They are usually adjustable to fit different shower tray sizes, and are simply fitted to the wall at each end to provide a rigid frame. Before finishing they have to be sealed where they meet the tray using a proprietary sealant, to ensure a waterproof joint. If this isn't done perfectly, water will gradually seep in and cause damp on the floor and walls of your bathroom.

Home-made surrounds

Making your own surround will save money, and it has the advantage that you can tailor it exactly to your needs. You might, for example, want a surround which is larger than the tray itself; in which case you can install a shelf or seat next to the tray.

Begin by making a framework of 50mm (2in) square timber. You need a length on every edge, plus extra horizontal ones at 450mm (18in) centres. All should be joined with halving joints. In addition, fit any extra length needed to provide a fixing point (for

the shower rose, for instance). The inside face of the partition should then be clad with 6mm (¼in) plywood. Use an exterior-grade board if the cubicle is to be tiled.

Another possibility is to use 10mm (⅜in) thick plasterboard. The framework for this should consist of a 50mm (2in) square batten on every edge, plus one extra vertical and horizontal in the middle, and any additional member needed to provide a fixing point. Fix the board with galvanised plasterboard nails driven in until the head slightly dimples the surface of the board, but without fracturing the paper liner. You can use 3mm (⅛in) hardboard to cover the outside of the cubicle framework.

Do not fix the exterior cladding for the time being. You should first clad the inside face, then fix the half-completed partition in place by driving screws through the frame members into the floor below, the wall behind and the ceiling too if it is to be a room height job.

The interior of this partition is a good place in which to conceal the supply pipes to the shower. You would then need an inspection panel, held by screws (not glued and nailed) to allow easy access to the pipework should maintenance ever be needed.

If the cubicle is not a floor-to-ceiling one, you will also need extra support at the top as you cannot leave the front top edge flapping free. This can take the form of a 75x25mm (3x1in) batten, decoratively moulded if you wish, spanning the two sides of the cubicle or fixed at one end to a block screwed to the wall, should there be only one side.

The whole interior of the shower cubicle needs to be clad with an impervious material to make sure it is waterproof. The most obvious choice is tiles, and these can be fixed to both the plywood or plasterboard cladding and the plaster of a wall. Make sure that the latter is clean and sound before tiling. Do not, however, fix the tiles direct to the timber part of the framing.

As an alternative to tiles you could use a special plastic-faced hardboard, with a tile pattern and a backing of plain hardboard. Fix the plastic-faced board by glueing and pinning with rustproof nails (if these can be lost somewhere in the pattern). Otherwise use a contact adhesive. This does not need to be spread all over the meeting surfaces. Apply it in a pattern similar to that detailed for the framework of the partitions. Adhesives applied by gun are available for this sort of work. The board on the back wall should be fixed in a similar manner.

Whatever material you use, all joins – where partitions meet the wall, or the tray – should be sealed with a silicone bath sealant. Any parts not clad with impervious material should be well painted with a three-coat system of primer, undercoat and one or two top coats.

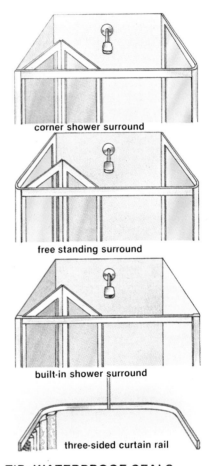
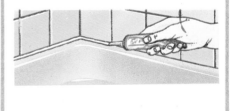

OUTSIDE TAPS AND PIPES

It's vital to know where your main water supply pipes are buried, so you don't damage them by accident and can trace a leak if one occurs. And it's useful to be able to install an outside tap.

Apart from any outside pipes you have, say, supplying a garden tap, the pipe you have to worry about is the service pipe which runs as a branch from the authority's main to supply your house's plumbing system. Usually it will run in a straight line from the authority's stop-valve to the point at which it enters the house and rises through the floor (usually in the kitchen) to become the rising main (see pages 9 to 13).

Because the service pipe is probably the most important water pipe in the home, it's vital that you know where the authority's stop-valve – which controls the flow of water in the pipe – is located. Often you'll find it under a small square or round hinged metal cover set in the pavement just outside the front gate, or in the concrete of your front garden path. It's quite likely that the valve will be protected in a guard pipe beyond the reach of a groping hand. It may have an ordinary crutch handle (the type found on old-fashioned taps) or a specially-shaped square head that can be turned only with one of the water authority's turnkeys.

Provided that you have another 'householder's stop-valve' where the service pipe enters your home, you will rarely have occasion to turn off the authority's stop-valve, but it's nice to be able to feel that you can do so should the need arise. Long-handled keys are available for turning crutch handles, or you may be able to improvise one by cutting a notch in the end of a piece of 75mm x 25mm (3in x 1in) timber and nailing another piece of wood across the other end to serve as a handle. You may have difficulty getting hold of a turnkey for the square-headed type of valve, as the water authority likes to feel that it can turn it off in the event of non-payment of the water rate, without the prospect of it being promptly turned on again, but they are usually entrusted to plumbers in whom the authority has confidence. It's really worth checking out what sort of tap you have, and if you find you haven't got a stop-valve on the rising main inside, you should definitely consider installing one. At the same time you can also make sure the guard pipe is clear of debris; having raised its cover, make sure you replace it securely. You could be liable

to heavy damages if a pedestrian were injured as a result of tripping over a cover that you had left open.

The service pipe stop-valve

The service pipe will run underground directly to your home. It should rise slightly as it does so to prevent any air bubbles being trapped, but it should be at least 800mm (2ft 8in) below the surface of the ground throughout its length. This is an important frost precaution. Even in the most severe winters experienced in this country, frost is very unlikely to penetrate as deeply as this into the soil. Make sure that you don't reduce this protection by, for instance, digging a drainage channel or creating a sunken garden above the service pipe.

Where the service pipe passes under the foundations or 'footings' of the house wall, it should be threaded through a length of drainpipe to protect it against any settlement which could fracture it. Generally it will rise into the home through the solid floor of a kitchen. Where, however, it rises through the gap between the oversite concrete and a hollow boarded floor, it must be protected against the icy draughts that may whistle through the sub-floor space. This is best done by threading the pipe, when it is first installed, through the centre of a 150mm (6in) stoneware drainpipe placed vertically on the oversite concrete and filling the space between the service pipe and the inner walls of the drainpipe with vermiculite chips or other similar insulating material.

It isn't, of course, practical to do this with an existing installation. In such a case the length of pipe in the sub-floor area should be bound with a 100mm (4in) thickness of glass fibre tank wrap or glass fibre roof insulating blanket, which should then be covered with a polythene sheet to prevent it from becoming damp and so useless as insulation.

A leaking service pipe

An underground leak may go undetected for a long period, but there are some tell-tale signs which should raise your suspicions. The main ones include the sound of trickling water when no tap has been in use in the house for a long period, a persistent noise from the main pipework, a loss of pressure in the flow of water from the cold tap over the kitchen sink, or a persistently damp patch on the garden path or on the wall of a basement. If you suspect a leak, contact the water authority. They have listening apparatus with which they are supposed to be able to fix the position of a leak. At least they can advise you on how best to track down the leak.

It is generally best to get professional help to deal with a leak in the underground service pipe. In an older house – where a leak is most likely to occur – this pipe will be of lead or iron which is difficult to repair. If the pipe is a modern copper one it will probably be leaking at a joint. To reduce the risk of this happening, water authorities normally insist upon the use of special manipulative (Type B) compression joints in underground locations. With these the pipe ends have to be widened

INSTALLING AN OUTSIDE TAP

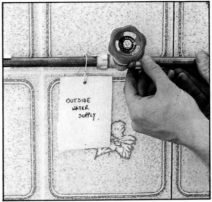

1 After turning off the main stop-valve, cut out a small section of pipe and insert a compression tee in the rising main.

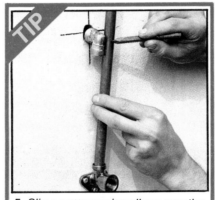

2 Insert a stop-valve in the branch supply as close to the tee as possible. Make sure that the arrow on the tap points in the direction of the flow.

3 Work out where you want the branch pipe to emerge from the inside. Then working from the outside (or the inside) drill a hole through the wall.

4 Feed the branch pipe through the wall, then screw a backplate elbow in place just below it; this will act as the fixing for a new bib-tap.

5 Slip a compression elbow over the branch pipe and measure the length of pipe needed to reach the backplate. Cut and fit it in place.

6 Wind PTFE tape several times round the thread of the bib-tap. Screw the tap into place, making sure it is upright when you finish.

– 'manipulated' – with a special tool as the joint is assembled. You may consider it better to replace the existing pipe with a single length of soft-temper copper tubing. This is obtainable on reels in long lengths that eliminate the need for underground joints.

Many water authorities nowadays also permit the use of black polythene piping. This too is obtainable in long lengths and has the added advantage that its thick walls help to insulate the pipe against frost. And in the unlikely event of the water within the pipe freezing, polythene pipe is sufficiently resilient to accommodate the expansion of the freezing water without bursting.

Putting in an outside tap

The only occasion when you are likely to need a permanent supply of water out of doors is when you put in an outside garden or garage tap. Before doing this you should always seek the permission of the water authority. This is likely to be granted readily enough, but it will involve an additional charge on the water rate, particularly if you are going to use the tap for a hose pipe or sprinkler system. If you already have an outside tap you'll agree that the convenience of not having the garden hose snaking through the kitchen window, and putting the domestic water supply out of action while it is in use, makes this extra payment well worthwhile. Provided that your home has modern copper plumbing, fitting an outside tap is a straightforward job.

If the outside tap is to be fixed to the wall outside the kitchen, you will need a bib-tap with a horizontal inlet for outside water supply, with a threaded nozzle for a hose connector and an angled handle that you can turn without grazing your knuckles on the wall. You'll also need a 15mm wall-plate elbow with a compression elbow bend, one 15mm equal-ended compression tee joint, a screw-down stop-valve with 15mm compression inlet and outlet and a length of 15mm copper tubing – how much will depend on the distance between the rising main and the new outside tap.

As far as tools are concerned, you'll require a couple of wrenches, a hacksaw, a tin of jointing compound, a roll of PTFE thread-sealing tape and some means of cutting through the wall to take the pipe-run outside. It's best to hire a heavy duty electric drill with hole-cutting attachments; the job can be done with a hammer and cold chisel, but this takes longer and is not as neat.

Turn off the main stop-valve and drain the rising main from the cold tap above the kitchen sink and, if there is one, from the drain-cock above the stop-valve. Cut the rising main at a convenient point to take off a

ADDING A SECOND TAP

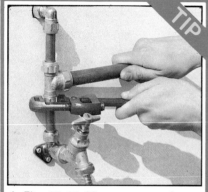

1 Fit a 15x15x22mm compression tee into the existing branch. Use a piece of copper pipe to hold the fitting secure while it's tightened.

2 Fit the polythene pipe to the tee. Then clip it to the wall and take it down to a prepared trench at least 750mm (30in) deep.

3 At the other end of the trench, attach the second tap and a short length of pipe. Then run the polythene pipe up the foot of the post.

4 Link the polythene pipe to the copper using a 22x15mm compression coupling. Finally turn on the supply, check for leaks and back-fill the trench.

length through the hole in the wall. Connect the other end of the other length to the outlet of the new stop-valve.

Next you can go outside and cut the projecting pipe so that 25mm (1in) projects through the wall. Connect the other elbow to this so that its outlet points downward to the position of the new tap. Cut another short piece of pipe to reach the position of the new tap. Fit the wall-plate elbow to one end of this and connect the other end to the projecting elbow bend. Drill and plug the wall, and screw the wall-plate elbow into place. You'll then have to bind PTFE tape round the threaded tail of the tap and screw it into the outlet of the wall-plate elbow. If the tap doesn't point downwards when screwed fully home, you'll have to remove it and add washers to its tail until it does.

The job is now complete, apart from making good the hole through the wall with some mastic filler. With the onset of winter, turn off the new stop-valve and open the outside tap to drain the short branch to protect it from the risk of frost damage. There is no need to insulate the section of pipe on the outside wall.

Installing a garden standpipe

If you have a large garden, or a garage at some distance from the house, one tap fitted against the outside wall of the house may be insufficient, and you may need another standpipe to provide an adequate outside supply. This is an excellent opportunity to use polythene pipe for the water supply because of the long lengths in which it can be obtained. In fact, when new houses are built today this piping is usually chosen for all underground runs.

In order to install a second outside tap you have to carry out the preliminary work described above, but instead of fitting the tap into a backplate elbow, you can use a backplate tee. It is from the lower outlet of this tee that the additional garden supply is taken. You may not be able to get a tee of this kind to which polythene pipe can be directly connected. In this case fit a short length of 15mm copper pipe into the tee outlet and connect the end of the polythene pipe to it by means of a 15mm copper to ½in polythene compression coupling. However, probably the easiest method is to tee off the short section of supply pipe feeding the outside tap already installed.

Although polythene pipe will not be damaged by frost, it should still be laid in a trench about 750mm (30in) deep to avoid the risk of accidental damage from gardening operations. The pipe can be taken underground to any point required, and then connected to a tap fixed to a post or to the wall of an outbuilding by means of the usual backplate elbow.

feed branch pipe. If there isn't a drain-cock above the main stop-valve a little water will flow out as you do this, so be prepared for it. Make another cut 18mm (¾in) away from the first one and remove the 18mm segment of pipe.

Insert the 15mm compression tee into the cut pipe (described on pages 20 to 24) so that the branch outlet of the tee points along the kitchen wall in the direction of the position of the new tap. Cut a short length of copper pipe, say 150mm (6in), and fit it into the outlet of the tee. To the other end of this fit the screw-down stop-valve by means of its compression joint inlet.

There are two points to watch as you do this. Make sure that the arrow engraved on the body of the stop-valve points away from the rising main and towards the position of the new tap. Make sure, too, that the stop-valve handle is angled away from the wall so

you have enough room to turn it with ease.

The first phase of the job is now complete. You can turn off the new stop-valve and turn on the main stop-valve to check for leaks. Because this will restore water to the rest of the house you can carry out the rest of the job in your own time.

Drill a hole – sufficiently large to take a 15mm copper pipe – through the wall above the position of the new tap. When deciding exactly where on the outside wall you want your tap to be positioned, remember that you'll want enough room to be able to put buckets and watering cans beneath it. Then cut two more lengths of copper pipe, one long enough to pass through the house wall and to protrude by 25mm (1in) at each end, and the other long enough to reach from the new stop-valve to the hole that you have made in the wall. Join these two lengths with a compression elbow and push the correct